# An American Journey

## History of the Bunner Family 1736 – 2025

Michael Bunner
Gregory Bunner

**An American Journey**
**History of the Bunner Family 1736 - 2025**

Published through IngramSpark

All rights reserved
Copyright © 2025 by Michael Bunner
Cover art licensed from Alamy stock photos

ISBN: 979-8-218-67707-7

No part of this publication may be reproduced, stored in a retrieval system, or transmitted in any form or by any means electronic, mechanical, photocopying, recording, or otherwise, without the written permission of the author or publisher.

# Table of Contents

*Prologue: The Origins and Evolution of the Bunner Surname*...........v
*Introduction and Background* ............................................................. vii
1. Ulrich Böner ........................................................................................1
2. Palatine German Immigration to Pennsylvania ....................4
3. Reuben Adam Böner ................................................................... 13
4. Johan Wendell Brown (Braun) ................................................. 46
5. Casper Böner (Bunner) ............................................................... 90
6. John Amos Bonner (Boner/Bunner) ..................................... 132
7. The Siblings of John Amos Bonner (Böner/Bunner) ........... 195
8. Reuben Adam Bunner – Oldest Son of John Amos Bunner .... 251
9. Alexander Bunner .................................................................... 281
10. Lafayette Bunner ..................................................................... 306
11. Alexander Bruce Bunner ........................................................ 337
12. John Andrew Bunner .............................................................. 368
13. Robert Lee Bunner ................................................................... 416

*Prologue*

# The Origins and Evolution of the Bunner Surname

The Bunners in this family history immigrated from Germany, and spelled their last name with a letter from the German alphabet that does not exist in the English alphabet. The first twenty-six letters in the German alphabet are identical to the English alphabet, but the German alphabet also includes the four additional letters ä, ö, ü, and ß.

The letters ä, ö, and ü are known as vowels with umlauts, which are the two dots sitting on top of them. The umlaut means that each vowel has a different pronunciation from vowels without the two dots. The German spelling of Bunner is Böner. The German letter 'ö' is pronounced by pursing your lips in an 'o' shape as if you were about to whistle. It is pronounced like the double 'o' in the word 'book'.

Adam and Casper Böner were the original immigrants from Germany, and neither could read or write as ascertained by the fact that they signed all legal documents by affixing an "X" on the signature lines. This required the English-speaking clerks assigned the responsibility for completing their legal documents to spell their name the best they could using the English alphabet. With no English equivalent to the German 'ö', many spelling variations emerged through the first few generations of the Böner/Bunner families in America. Variations in the spelling of Bunner found in legal documents for the first eight generations of the Bunner family include:

- Böner
- Boner
- Bohner
- Buhner
- Bohn
- Boon
- Bonner
- Bönner
- Bonier
- Booner
- Brunner
- Bunner

By the late 1800's, "Bunner" had become the near universal spelling of the family last name in America.

The earliest discovered historical instance (to date) where the modern anglicized spelling of Bunner was used was in the deed for the sale of 365 acres in Berkeley County, Virginia by John Amos 'Bunner' and his mother Mary 'Bunner' to George Braggoona on October 19, 1780.

The convention used in this book is to use the spelling most frequently used in legal documents during each generation of the Bunner family. If the spelling is other than 'Bunner,' this will be noted at the beginning of each chapter in this book.

# Introduction and Background

The Bunner (Böner) family history in America began in the 1730's, the same decade in which George Washington was born. Four different Böners – Rudoph, Adam, Jacob and Casper – all from the Rhineland Palatine region of Germany, immigrated to Pennsylvania between 1732 and 1740 and were among the approximately 40,000 Germans to immigrate to America prior to 1745. They, along with whatever family members they brought with them, entered America through the Port of Philadelphia. Their arrivals were well documented, and those records have been well preserved.

Rudolph settled near Philadelphia in 1732 and became a successful bar owner. It is unknown what, if any, blood relationship Rudolph had with either Adam or Jacob. Adam settled in what is now Berks County, Pennsylvania (Lancaster County at the time) in 1736. Jacob, believed to be the brother of Adam, settled near Adam in 1738.

Adam's oldest son, Casper, emigrated from the Palatine region of Germany through the Port of Philadelphia in November 1740 at the age of twenty, and most likely reunited with his family in what is today Berks County, Pennsylvania. Just a few months after Casper's arrival to America, his father Adam purchased 127 acres of frontier land along the Tulpehocken Creek approximately five miles upstream of the Schuylkill River (near present day Reading) and approximately six miles downstream of the early Palatine German settlement of Bern, Pennsylvania.

It is likely that Casper spent several years helping his father clear enough of the virgin forest covering the land to create sufficient farmland for the family to survive and eventually thrive. Casper probably lived with his father at this location for 5-8 years before marrying and embarking on a life of his own on the Virginia frontier sometime between 1746 and 1749.

Just a few miles up the Tulpehocken Creek from the Adam Böner family lived the Johann Wendell Braun (Brown) family. Wendell and his family had emigrated from the Palatine region of Germany in 1738, two years after Adam Böner had emigrated. Unfortunately, Wendell's wife Margaret became ill either during or immediately after the ocean voyage to America and died in 1739, leaving several children, including eleven-year-old Mary Christiana, motherless. Wendell married Elizabeth Knopf later in 1739, and the Braun (Brown) family was able to carve out a frontier existence over the next several years by clearing and renting farmland from earlier German settlers who had already acquired large tracts of land in the area.

Sometime around 1745-1746, Casper Böner (who was then 25-26 years old) and Mary Christiana Brown (who was then 17-18 years old) met, perhaps at the local Little Tulpehocken Lutheran Church, and began courting. During this same time, Johann Wendell Braun had adopted the anglicized version of his German name and most documents mentioning his name after this date record him as John Wendell Brown, John Brown, or most commonly Wendell Brown. He may have applied for a land warrant to purchase 250 acres in Berks County (Lancaster County at the time) with the Pennsylvania Land Office in 1743. However, if he did, he quickly developed a strong interest in the cheaper and more abundant land that was being offered to settlers on the Virginia frontier.

Historical records reveal that in 1748, Wendell Brown, his oldest son Thomas, and his son-in-law Michael Catt, Jr., were listed on the Augusta County, Virginia 'tithable' tax rolls. [1] (The 'tithable' tax was equivalent to the modern-day capitation tax, or 'head' tax, and every "free" male over the age of sixteen was required to pay this

---

1 Chalkley, Lyman (1980), "Chronicles of the Scotch-Irish Settlement in Virginia, Extracted from the Original Court Documents of Augusta County, 1745-1800", Genealogical Publishing Company, Inc., Volume 1, p. 413

## INTRODUCTION AND BACKGROUND

nominal annual tax.) The most likely date for the Brown family to have made the 240-mile trek from the Pennsylvania frontier to the Virginia frontier was late 1746 or early 1747.

There are at least four possible scenarios to explain how and when Casper Böner resettled to Augusta County, Virginia and was married to Mary Christiana Brown, Wendell's daughter:

1. Casper and Mary were married in Pennsylvania in 1746 and the two of them accompanied the rest of the Brown family when they moved from Pennsylvania to Virginia shortly thereafter.
2. Casper and Mary were married in Pennsylvania in 1746 or 1747 and remained in Pennsylvania for up to two years after the Brown family had moved to Virginia in 1746. Then, in 1748-1749, Casper and Mary moved to the Virginia frontier to join the rest of the Brown family.
3. Casper accompanied the Browns on their move to Virginia in 1746 where he and Mary were married sometime after their arrival (but prior to 1749).
4. Wendell moved his family (including daughter Mary) to Virginia in 1746. Casper followed sometime between 1747 and 1748. Casper and Mary were subsequently married in Virginia prior to 1749.

What is clear is that the entire Braun (Brown) family, including son-in-law Michael Catt, moved from Pennsylvania to the western Virginia frontier prior to the spring of 1747. What is less clear, because no historical records have been discovered to date, is when and where Casper Böner and Mary Brown were married, and when and where they settled on the western Virginia frontier with the Brown family.

However, strong circumstantial evidence, supported by oral family tradition, has Casper and Mary being married and living in Augusta County on the western Virginia frontier no later than 1749. The most likely scenario of the four mentioned above is that Casper and Mary were married in early 1746 and then accompanied the rest of the Brown family when they moved to Virginia later that year.

It is the history of the present-day Bunner family, which descended from Adam through Casper and his wife Mary Christiana, that is the focus of this book. Much of the information in this book is built upon the foundations of two significant family research documents compiled and edited between 1988 and 2012. The most comprehensive document was "*The Bunner Family in America*" by Alan N. Bunner of Alexandria, Virginia who wrote an exhaustive 7,300+ page document which was last revised on June 25, 2012. The second noteworthy document was "*Descendants of Casper (Böner) Bunner and Mary Christiana Brown – Revised Edition*" compiled and edited by Gale Joseph Bunner of Randolph, Massachusetts in 1988.

Both documents succeeded in accurately recording much of the ten-generation genealogy of the Bunner family in America. They also succeeded in consolidating many anecdotal family stories passed down by each succeeding generation through the nearly three hundred years since Adam Böner arrived in America. However, these two accounts left many significant gaps in the historical accounts waiting to be filled, along with several conflicting accounts that needed to be resolved.

Beginning in 2010, my nephew, Greg Bunner of Parkersburg, West Virginia began doing independent research on the Bunner family with a special focus on the descendants of John Amos Bunner, the firstborn and oldest son of Casper and Mary Bunner. Greg was especially interested in this line of Bunner family genealogy because, after ten generations, it led to him. Over the subsequent ten years, Greg completed the most comprehensive genealogical history of the John Amos Bunner branch of the Bunner family tree that has ever been performed. In 2018 Greg started sharing his research with me, which sparked my interest in the Bunner family history. After I retired in 2022, I began collaborating with Greg to fill in some of the gaps in the histories of Adam Bunner and his son Casper, the first two generations of Bunner immigrants from Germany in America.

I was in a geographically ideal location to perform research on both Adam and Casper Böner. Though I grew up in West Virginia and most of my extended family still lives there, my career path took me on a serpentine route that ultimately landed me in Berks County, Pennsylvania, where I have lived since 2002. After my retirement, I had time to begin digging into the archives of the County Clerk offices of Lancaster and Berks counties in Pennsylvania, Frederick County in Virginia, Berkeley, Monongalia, Harrison, and Marion counties in West Virginia, and the historical records of the colonial Land Offices in Pennsylvania and Virginia.

Starting with the many puzzle pieces Greg had accumulated over his decade of research, we were gradually able to find enough additional interlocking pieces to create a more comprehensive picture of the lives of Adam and Casper Böner, and of Casper's ten children. In addition to uncovering much new information that had been long buried by the weight of time, we were able to confirm several of the oral traditions of the Bunner family, and to refute a few others.

One of our efforts was to complete a critical and objective analysis of a document known as *"The Reuben Bunner Revelation, an Orphan's Diary."* The question we wanted to answer was this: Is *"The Reuben Bunner Revelation, an Orphan's Diary"* a legitimate historical document, a forgery, or part historical and part fiction?

One of the conclusions I have reached after much research is that, although I do not reject the document known to Bunner family historians as *"The Reuben Bunner Revelation, an Orphan's Diary,"* I have developed deep concerns about the legitimacy of some of its content.

*"The Reuben Bunner Revelation"* is a document that first came to light in 1976 purporting to be a history of the Bunner family beginning with Ulrich Böner in Germany in the 14$^{th}$ century through the death of Nancy Ann Prickett Bunner in the 1840's. Nancy Ann was the wife of Reuben Bunner, who was the third son of Casper and Mary Böner and a grandson of Adam Böner. Reuben was born circa 1757 and died in 1809.

Both Alan Bunner and Gale Bunner included several passages from *"The Reuben Bunner Revelation"* in their documentations of the Bunner family history. Information from *"The Reuben Bunner Revelation"* is also included in many of the web-based genealogy platforms such as ancestry.com, genealogy.com, geni.com, myheritage.com, and familysearch.com.

Everything that is known about *"The Reuben Bunner Revelation"* was provided by Marion County, West Virginia historian Glenn D. Lough. In July 1976, as a gift for the attendees of a large Bunner family reunion held in Fairmont, West Virginia, he published the following in a special edition of his quarterly newspaper *"Awhile Ago Times:"*

### *"THE REUBEN BUNNER REVELATION"* or *"AN ORPHAN'S DIARY"*
By Glenn D. Lough
July 1976

"About a month ago there was submitted it to this newspaper *("Awhile Ago Times")* for publication ("in whatever manner the editor sees fit") a typewritten manuscript (76 pages, single space typing), entitled, *"The Reuben Bunner Revelation,"* or *"An Orphans Diary."* This manuscript has now been read many times over, and a small part of the content has been wholly or partially verified (historically authenticated in some degree by research). To complete this work of authentication, in so far as may be possible, will require, this writer believes, a year or more of research, reading, checking, compiling. Hundreds of suggested sources would have to be found and "worked out."

A tremendous amount of work stands in the way of such an accomplishment, but then, this is a tremendous manuscript. If true, and it may well be, it is the most important (historically and genealogically) material involving persons, incidents, and events, throughout the Monongahela Valley, in the years 1768-1840, ever to come to this writer's attention.

If, in part, it is fiction, and in part it may well be, then the factual part remaining, if separated by research from the fictional, will certainly prove to be "history" of considerable importance.

More than 50 families, residents in the Monongahela Valley before 1800, are discussed in this manuscript. The work abounds in stories of love, mystery, and adventure, in frontier settings.

Here following is a quote from page one: "Father Bunner told many times that his family was of the family of Ulrich Böner, of a village in Germany named Böner, for the family, and that, the same Ulrich Böner lived and died before Columbus discovered America. Father Bunner told that his father and his grandfather told this many times, saying that Ulrich Böner was a greatly renowned author and was a friend of Kings and Queens."

To say the least this is truly "a wow" of a statement. This writer did not believe that.... until he found this in the 1902 or Werner edition of the' Britannica Encyclopedia" (index volume, page 569): "Böner, Ulrich, German fabulist, 14$^{th}$ Century."

It will be realized, of course, that Ulrich Böner, living in Böner, Germany, in the 1300's (more than 600 or so years ago?) wrote his fables, poems, and stories, before the invention of printing, which, according to "The Standard Dictionaries of Facts", occurred in 1434 at Mayence...

Somewhere in the ancient works in the libraries of Europe there still exists, no doubt, the writings of Ulrich Böner, friend of Kings and Queens, in scrolls and "rolled books," printed by hand....

Certainly, this writer believes that the Bunners of today, of the family of Böner, of German lineage, do, indeed, descend from "the family of Ulrich Böner, in the 14$^{th}$ century. Certain research has been done to cause this writer to so believe.

The "Orphan", compiling the *"The Reuben Bunner Revelation,"* did not say that the Böner descent was directly from Ulrich Böner, but was from the family of Ulrich Böner. (The item should be kept in mind.)

# AN AMERICAN JOURNEY

## "THE ORPHAN"

The chronicle of the *"The Reuben Bunner Revelation,"* throughout the manuscript, signs herself, "The Orphan," or "An Orphan." She does not, so far as the writer has discovered, give her proper name. However, a Bunner descendant writes from Kansas is that the Orphan's name was Jane Finch, that Jane as a small child was captured by Indians and tortured by a group of Indian children, who partially scalped her, and left her alive, hanging head down from a tree by one leg.

In this condition, some two days and a night later, Captain Jacob Prickett, his daughter, Nancy Ann Bunner, and her husband, Reuben Bunner, and others traveling by the Ohio River to the Northwest Territory, to seek out lands and settle found her.

Jane was then eight years old and remembered the Indian attack on her family in Bourbon County, Kentucky, how her father and uncle were thrown to the ground on their backs and spread flat by having their wrists and ankles tied to stakes, and tortured for hours, until they died.

The Indians believed the men had hidden out a keg of gunpowder and were determined to force them to reveal its whereabouts. This they could not do, because there was no hidden gunpower.

Our Kansas correspondent informs that Jane Finch (Bunner) and her brother are mentioned (not by name) in McKnight's *"Our Western Border,"* page 576, as follows: "In a few minutes, six squaws, most of them very old, together with two white children, a girl and a boy, came down to the fire, and seated themselves. The children had lately been taken from Kentucky."

This quote is from the story, *"Adventures of May, Johnston, Flinn, and Skyles,"* pages 571-597, "Our Western Border."

(Note: this information is not from *"The Reuben Bunner Revelation,"* but came by letter, from a subscriber to this newspaper *("Awhile Ago Times")*, living in Kansas.)

INTRODUCTION AND BACKGROUND

This writer does not positively know if the little girl found hanging from a tree by the Ohio River by Captain Jacob Prickett and party was or was not the little girl partly reared by Reuben and Nancy Bunner, who for more than 50 years kept a journal which she titled *"The Reuben Bunner Revelation,"* or *"An Orphans Diary,"*. She may have been Jane Finch (Bunner).... She relates in *"The Revelation"* that she made her home with the Reuben Bunner family for about twenty-five years, "off and on" in Kentucky and after they moved over the river into Ohio.

## TWO REUBEN BUNNERS

After many hours study of the manuscript, it is this writer's belief that the Reuben Bunner of *"The Revelation"* was actually two Reuben Bunners, father and son: Reuben Sr., born in 1760, and Reuben Jr., born in 1789. Also, it seems that Mrs. Reuben Bunner Sr., who was before marriage Nancy Ann Prickett (called Ann), was responsible for much of the information, stories, etc., recorded by the Orphan.

Ann Prickett Bunner was born in 1762 and died eighty years later, in Brown County Ohio in 1842. This information is from her tombstone and is given in *"The Revelation."*

The final item in *"The Revelation"* (page 76 of the manuscript) is the story of Ann Prickett Bunner's death - "we promise to join you in heaven, dear Mother Bunner."

In Thompson's *"History of Brown County,"* Ohio, it is stated (page 846), that "Nancy Ann, child of Jacob and Dorothy [Springer] Prickett, was born in 1762 and died in 1842. She and her husband, Reuben Bunner (1760-1807), came to Brown County and settled in Franklin Township. Both are buried in the Baptist cemetery east of Arnheim in Franklin Township. The names of their children, if any, are not known."

Elsewhere in this newspaper *("Awhile Ago Times")*, the will of Reuben Bunner Jr., appears; in it are the names of a sister, Jane, and a brother, Joseph. There were others, according to *"The Revelation."* This will was recorded in Brown County, Ohio, where it may be found, in the courthouse at Georgetown. Thompson didn't do much research on the Bunners of Brown County.

This writer's intention [1976] is to publish the complete *Revelation* in this newspaper *("Awhile Ago Times")* and elsewhere, when all sources mentioned in it have been researched (checked out), and copies of other material pertaining to it had been given this writer, as promised. @@ Glenn D. Lough"

There are many statements in these and other excerpts from *"The Reuben Bunner Revelation"* provided by Glenn Lough that independent research has proved to be true or "nearly" true. For example, several of the events recorded in the *"Revelation"* proved to be accurate but the dates of their occurrence were off by 1-5 years. However, one claim made in the *"Revelation"* that has proven to be erroneous seems to have been the result of "mistaken identity" by the person who inserted this narrative into the 76-page manuscript submitted to Glenn Lough.

That claim is that Casper and Mary Böner settled in a log cabin on Tom's Creek in Augusta County, Virginia circa 1749. However, this oft-repeated claim is not true, and evidence will be presented in the chapter on Casper Böner that provides irrefutable proof that Casper and Mary settled on the South Fork of the South Branch of the Potomac River in Augusta County, Virginia (present-day Hardy County, West Virginia about seven miles south of the town of Moorefield).

This claim that the Böners settled on Tom's Creek, over 200 miles south of where they really settled, is provably incorrect. It would never have been included in an accurate and legitimate history of the early Bunner family in America. The extent of this error casts significant doubt on the credibility of the rest of *"The Reuben Bunner Revelation."*

INTRODUCTION AND BACKGROUND

A second narrative in the *"Revelation"* is somewhat jaw-dropping and must therefore be balanced with the historical data which is available regarding the events described. This narrative reads:

"Father Bunner *[i.e., Reuben Böner]* often said that his father *[i.e., Casper Böner]* told that he and family moved from here *[i.e., Tom's Creek, Augusta County]* with his father-in-law *[i.e., Wendell Brown]* and family and his brother-in-law, Michael Catt, and family, to near the Monongahela River, a few miles westward of where Colonel Washington (George Washington) fought and was defeated by the French and Indians *[i.e., Fort Necessity]* in 1754, and that after this defeat, he and his family and the Wendell Brown and Michael Catt families, returned south, with Washington's army and all were living on their old farms again, in old Augusta County before Christmas, in the year of Braddock's defeat (1755)." *[clarifying parentheses mine]*

There are several historical truths to this claim, but when compared with multiple published historical accounts, the greater narrative of an extended family move to the western slopes of the Allegheny Mountains near the Monongahela River in 1751 or 1752 lacks corroboration from a second source. This does not mean that this narrative in *"The Reuben Bunner Revelation"* is untrue. It simply means that it has not been validated.

There are several historians who record that Wendell Brown settled on land in the Monongahela River Valley near present Uniontown, Pennsylvania in 1751 or 1752. However, these historical accounts only state that Wendell Brown was accompanied by two of his sons (Maunus and Adam) and possibly by a third son (Thomas).[2][3] There are no published historical accounts specifically stating that Wendell and his immediate family were also accompanied by the families of Wendell's two married daughters, Mary

---

2  Veech, James (1892), "Monongahela of Old", Pittsburgh, P. 109

3  Ellis, Franklin, History of Fayette County, Pennsylvania, L.H. Everts and Co., 1882, p.54

Böner and Catherine Catt, during the two years they were carving out a homestead on the western slopes of the Alleghenies.

There is a document posted on ancestry.com which purports to be a typewritten reproduction of meeting minutes detailing multiple petitions to a Virginia Militia Regiment in 1758. These petitions were made by Virginia residents (mostly soldiers) seeking restitution for injuries and property damage incurred during the previous three years of the French and Indian War. An excerpt from these minutes regarding a petition made by Wendell Brown reads:

> "Petition of John Windell Brown, formerly an inhabitant on the River Monongalia. With his wife and five children he fled on the approach of the enemy in the engagement at Great Meadows between Col. Washington and the enemy. He lost all of his estate. He petitioned for relief, but it was refused at a previous session. He settled his family on the South Branch. In April 1756 he and his eldest daughter (now a prisoner in Canada) were taken by Indians to Fort Duquesne. He suffered cruelties from the Indians and was sent to Quebec from whence he was taken to England with other prisoners. He has lately returned and is incapable of procuring a livelihood. Rejected 23 Sept. 1758." [4]

Every event described about Wendell Brown in this petition did happen. There are independent sources that corroborate them. As a result, it is almost a certainty that Wendell's wife and daughters accompanied him to the Monongahela Valley, as leaving a wife and daughters to fend for themselves in a hostile frontier environment for two years would have been untenable.

However, this petition posted on ancestry.com lends no additional support for the claim made in *"The Reuben Bunner Revelation"* that the extended family of Wendell Brown accompanied him and his sons to the Monongahela Valley in 1752. This extended family

---

[4] Ancestry.com, Johan Wendell Braun, https://www.ancestry.com/mediauiviewer/tree/62370820/person/402207020362/media/697f2dab-59b8-40af-a66b-0f2efaeaf436?destTreeId=196408406&destPersonId=382561276727&hid=1010262120113&_phsrc=bbY2693&_phstart=default&usePUBJs=true&currentPageIsStart=&hintStatus=pending

would include the families of Wendell Brown's son-in-laws Casper Böner and Michael Catt.

History books record that between twelve and fifteen families fled from their homes near the Monongahela River to join Wahington's forces at Fort Necessity at the outbreak of the French and Indian War.[5] Two of those fifteen families could have been the Böners and the Catts.

The Browns, the Böners, and the Catts comprised a tight-knit extended family that had already made the difficult and risky move from Pennsylvania to the Virginia frontier a few years earlier. Thus, a precedent existed for the entire family to make a bold and dangerous move to a new location. It is not a stretch to believe that the entire extended family moved across the Allegheny Mountains as a unit in 1752. The circumstantial evidence supports the account in the *"Revelation."* The account simply lacks a second source to confirm it.

The account about Wendell and one of his daughters being captured by Indians on the South Branch of the Potomac River in 1756, two years after his retreat with George Washington from Fort Necessity, has been independently corroborated by records from the Virginia House of Burgesses and documented in the book *"Setting all the Captives Free"* by Ian K. Steele.[6] This incident will be discussed in greater detail in this book.

Another problem with the excerpts from *"The Reuben Bunner Revelation"* made available by Glenn Lough is that the author ("The Orphan") makes frequent reference to "Father Bunner" and "Mother Bunner." The family last name being spelled "Bunner" did not become common until the late 1800's. The last entry in the "Revelation" is the death of Reuben Bunner's wife, Nancy Ann Prickett Bunner in 1842. The family's last name was still commonly spelled "Böner" or "Bonner" at that time.

---

5  Ellis, Franklin, History of Fayette County, Pennsylvania, L.H. Everts and Co., 1882, p.54

6  Steele, Ian K. (2013), "Setting All the Captives Free", McGill-Queens University Press, p. 452

If the *"Revelation"* presents a legitimate history of the early Böner/Bunner family in America written in the early 1800's, one would think that the author would write of "Father Boner" or "Father Bonner", not "Father Bunner." Of course, it is possible that the name "Boner" or "Bonner" was used in the original version of the *"Revelation"* and the person typing the document submitted to Glenn Lough in 1976 changed all the "Boner" and "Bonner" references to the "Bunner" which is in use today, but this would suggest that the 1976 typist did not place a high value on maintaining the purity and integrity of the original document.

The ultimate verdict on the legitimacy of *"The Reuben Bunner Revelation"* may have been silently handed down by Glenn Lough. He announced at the Bunner family reunion in Fairmont, West Virginia in July 1976 that he had received this seventy-six-page, typewritten, single-spaced document from an anonymous source. He also stated that much research would be required to confirm the accuracy of the many narratives in the document, and that, if his research confirmed that the *"Revelation"* was true, he would publish the entire document in his quarterly newspaper, the *"Awhile Ago Times."*

Two years later, in the July 1978 edition of *"Awhile Ago Times"*, Lough did publish a few more tidbits about the Böner/Bunner family without ever mentioning *"The Reuben Bunner Revelation."* In fact, several of the short narratives he published were prefaced with the phrase "unproven traditions." Lough died in March 1991, fifteen years after first revealing the existence of the *"The Reuben Bunner Revelation,"* without ever mentioning it again.

All of Glen Lough's archives were donated by his daughter to the West Virginia and Regional History Center at West Virginia University. I personally visited this facility in April 2024 to review the Glenn D. Lough archives but found nothing about *"The Reuben Bunner Revelation,"* nothing about the July 1976 special edition of the *"Awhile Ago Times"* in which excerpts of *"The Reuben Bunner Revelation"* were first published, and nothing about the Böner/Bunner family history. I was advised that, due to manpower shortages, there were many documents and files in the Lough collection that had not yet been properly indexed and catalogued and that these archives would not be made available to the public until that work was completed. When I asked how long that might take, I was laughingly told "at least twenty years."

Glenn D. Lough had a passion for the history of the Monongahela Valley and, specifically, Marion County, West Virginia. He was exhilarated to be the recipient of the seventy-six-page document entitled *"The Reuben Bunner Revelation"* in 1976. He believed that if he could confirm the legitimacy of this document, he could publish it as the crowning achievement of his life as a respected regional historian. However, within two years of receiving the *"Revelation"* manuscript he seemed to have lost his passion for completing the project. The most logical conclusion that one can reach is that, after doing extensive research on the many narratives included in the *"Revelation,"* Lough concluded that it was not a historical document.

*"The Reuben Bunner Revelation"* is not necessary to compile the history of the Bunner family in America. Independent research efforts – with confirmed sources - have done that. We know that the first generation of American Bunners left Germany in hopes of a better life in America. The second generation chose the hard life of the American frontier and survived the French and Indian War.

The third generation fought for American independence during the Revolutionary War and then moved to the cutting edge of the American frontier in present day West Virginia. The fourth generation continued moving westward with the leading edge of the American frontier to present day Indiana.

The fifth generation led a quieter and more stable life on farms in present day West Virginia. That generation also witnessed the construction of hundreds of miles of railroad tracks crisscrossing the region that significantly reduced the time to transport people and goods and greatly expanded the economy in western Virginia.

The sixth generation lived through the political and social turmoil of Civil War that saw many families in western Virginia torn apart by their choice of loyalties. They saw President Lincoln assist western Virginia citizens to break away from Virginia, secede from the Confederate States, and rejoin the Union as the thirty-fifth state. It was also the sixth generation that adopted "Bunner" as the proper English spelling of the family name.

# AN AMERICAN JOURNEY

The seventh generation moved from eastern West Virginia to the Parkersburg, West Virginia area on the Ohio River. This generation never owned the land they lived and worked on.

The eighth generation moved from Parkersburg, West Virginia to Zanesville, Ohio, and became the first generation to earn a living as a factory worker and not as a farmer. Unfortunately, the Great Depression caused that factory to close, forcing a return to West Virginia where subsistence farming allowed the family to survive until America's entry into World War II brought the Great Depression to an end.

The ninth generation grew up during the Great Depression, lived through World War II and the Korean War, and saw the emergence of America as a superpower.

The tenth, eleventh, twelfth, and thirteenth generations of Bunners are still alive at the time of this writing. Their stories are currently being written but are unfinished.

These stories of the Bunners in America reveal a deep love of personal freedom and independence across the generations. Unbroken hereditary traits of courage, stamina and inner fortitude gave each generation not only the ability, but the willingness, to take big risks. Every generation has also possessed the ability and the willingness to perform hard physical labor over the course of their lifetimes. In addition, they also possessed an extraordinary ability to persevere through hardships. They were endowed with an inner spirit from which remarkable levels of grit, determination, optimism, hope, and faith have flowed.

I believe the research that Greg Bunner and I have completed over the past several years creates a more complete – and more accurate – history of the early Bunner family in America than previous efforts have been able to achieve. While there are still gaps to be filled, it is our hope that this book will serve as a solid platform from which future generations can appreciate, and even marvel at, the accomplishments of our ancestors. Perhaps our efforts will even inspire a few members of future generations of the Bunner family to do the research necessary to close the gaps that remain in our family history.

Michael Bunner, May 2025

## 1.

## Ulrich Böner

Ulrich Böner has long been regarded as the most influential and famous member of the extended Böner family which lived in northern Switzerland and the Rhineland Palatine region of southwest Germany from the fourteenth century to the seventeenth century. This German family was the progenitor of Adam Böner, who was among the first Böners to emigrate to America in 1736. There is no current evidence that Ulrich Böner was a direct ancestor of Adam Böner, but there is also no evidence that he was not. However, there is a near certainty that Adam Böner and Ulrich Böner shared a common ancestor. If Ulrich Böner was not in the direct lineage of Adam Böner, he would have been a distant great-uncle, which would also make him a distant great-uncle to all the American descendants of Adam and Casper Böner.

Ulrich Böner, (or Ulrich Bönerius, in Latin) wrote the classic fourteenth century book *Der Edelstein* (*The Gemstone*). Böner was a Swiss writer and Dominican monk (who seems to have subsequently married) whose collection of fables in verse was the first book ever to be printed in the German language. It was also the first book in the world ever to be printed with woodcut illustrations (Bamberg edition, printed 1461). Böner lived in Bern, Switzerland, a city in the northern half of the country where the residents spoke German and embraced the German culture. He is mentioned in available records between 1324 and 1349 but is not mentioned in any known records before or after these dates.[1] His dates of birth and death are unknown.

His highly popular book consisted of a hundred animal fables and moral anecdotes dedicated to the Baron Johann 1st von Ringgenberg, a Bernese patrician and poet who provided the funds for Böner to collect, translate, and put to rhyme and verse the fables he included in his book.

Böner translated from original Greek and Latin sources into High Middle German, the common German language used during his lifetime. What he had to say about people's stupidity, ignorance, failures, and evil character still applies today, and his advice on how to correct and improve oneself still carries considerable weight for the modern world. [2]

Böner drew his material from multiple sources. He relied mostly on the fifth century Latin fable collection by Avianus and the twelfth century collection by Gualterus Anglicus. He also borrowed from a variety of other sources of fables, including Aesop (circa 580 B.C.). His contribution consisted of consolidating and translating these ancient fables into rhymes and German verse and bringing them together under a common title.

Böner also invented his own fables. There are numerous differences in the plot development, imagery, and moral and ethical commentaries when compared to the originals. All this makes *Der Edelstein* an independent piece of high quality medieval German literature which exerted a tremendous influence on Swiss and German society well into the sixteenth century.

Böner was deeply convinced of the moral, ethical, and religious value of his fables for people from all walks of life. The lesson he was attempting to teach was that a rational, intelligent, pragmatic approach in life was the only advisable path for people to follow. His stories underscored the importance and value of individual

---

1 Encyclopaedia Britannica. Vol. 4 (11th ed.). Cambridge University Press. p. 203

2 "The Fables of Ulrich Bönerius (CA. 1350)", translated by Albrecht Classen, Cambridge Scholars Publishing, 2020, page ix

freedom. These stories resonated among those living in fourteenth-century Switzerland and the adjoining Palatine region of Germany.[3]

Until recently, this classic Böner masterpiece was all but forgotten. In 2018, Forgotten Books reproduced *Der Edelstein* in the original High Middle German language and made it available to the mass market. Then, in 2020, the government mandated Covid-19 mobility restrictions imposed on global societies motivated Albrecht Classen to use this enforced solitude to translate *Der Edelstein* into English. This English translation is entitled "*The Fables of Ulrich Bönerius (CA. 1350)*", published by Cambridge Scholars Publishing.

This translation resulted in the loss of the rhyming structure and iambic pentameter (the "beat") that existed in the original German, but the verse structure and the morals to the fables remain. This English translation also includes some of the woodcut illustrations from the original 1461 printed version of the book.

---

[3] "The Fables of Ulrich Bönerius (CA. 1350)", translated by Albrecht Classen, Cambridge Scholars Publishing, 2020, pages x-xxiii

## 2.

# Palatine German Immigration to Pennsylvania
## *1680-1775*

The extended Böner family had lived in Northern Switzerland and the Rhineland Palatinate in what is now southwestern Germany for over three hundred years before their lives started becoming unbearable during the mid-seventeenth century. The Thirty Years War in Europe (1618-1648) had left the Palatine region totally devastated. An economic recovery was underway when, in 1674, the armies of French King Louis XIV invaded the region. These attacks turned the Palatine cities such as Heidelburg and Worms into rubble and reduced the recovering Palatine farmlands to chaff. This was followed by protracted disputes among the many neighboring principalities which engaged in localized military skirmishes for many years.

Map showing location of Rhineland Palatinate circa 1700. The first Böners (Bunners) in America emigrated from this region between 1730 and 1740.

William Penn, founder of the Pennsylvania colony, had toured the Rhineland Palatinate in 1677 and in 1682 amid all this warfare and destruction. He had encouraged the German people to settle in Pennsylvania. He had also spread the word about a new kind of religious freedom in the American colonies. He found a receptive audience. Members of several smaller Protestant sects, who were being persecuted in Europe, were especially eager to escape both the religious harassment and the continuous warfare. Substantial numbers of German Mennonites, Quakers, and Amish decided to emigrate to Pennsylvania. Germantown, Pennsylvania, a few miles north of Philadelphia, was established in 1683 by thirteen Mennonite families. Over the next thirty years, thousands of additional religious dissenters followed.

In 1688, partly to vent his hatred against Protestants, the Catholic King of France, Louis XIV, invaded and laid waste to the

German Palatinate and neighboring principalities once again. The region had only partially recovered from that invasion when the War of the Spanish Succession broke out across Europe. The forces of Louis XIV again crossed the Rhine River in May 1707, terrorizing southwestern Germany while plundering and requisitioning supplies freely from the local population, leaving them virtually bankrupt and starving.

To add insult to injury, the rulers of the local principalities imposed onerous taxes on their peasant subjects to pay for the wars they were fighting with each other. They also conscripted many of the young men from the local peasantry to fight those wars.

The final straw for many of the German peasants was the extraordinarily harsh winter of 1708. Historical records from that time report that birds froze in midair, wine froze in its barrels, fruit trees died, grapevines were destroyed, and livestock froze to death. As a result, many Palatine families reached the limits of what they could endure.

To those impoverished families came the enticing advertisements distributed by the English proprietors of the American colonies. Pamphlets extolling life in the New World were disseminated throughout the Rhine Valley. Pennsylvania was, by far, the best advertised of the American colonies. Various books and pamphlets had been published for German consumption over the twenty-five years since William Penn had last visited Palatine. Pennsylvania's significant investment in paper and ink to proclaim the virtues of life in the colony was slowly beginning to pay off. Agents for William Penn entered negotiations and exchanged much preliminary correspondence with interested Palatine families and groups.

Queen Anne of England saw the economic problems in the Palatinate as an opportunity for England and the colonies to solidify their Protestant base and to expand their economies. She began taking steps to capitalize on that opportunity. She invited William Penn to work with the British Parliament to draft a new immigration and naturalization law for England. The law was passed on March 23, 1709. It provided that newly naturalized citizens had to take an oath of allegiance to the British crown. In addition, all the children of naturalized parents were to be considered natural born subjects.

The greatest benefit secured by the act was the right for naturalized citizens to purchase and hold land, which could eventually be transmitted to one's children. Those naturalized were also permitted to take part in trade and commerce, usually forbidden to foreigners.[1]

After the law was passed, Queen Anne allocated considerable sums of money to assist Protestant refugees in making their way from Germany to England and then onward to the English colonies. Word quickly spread among the residents of Palatine and the neighboring principalities about this English largesse. Additionally, a rumor started in Palatine that Queen Anne was going to grant free land in the American colonies to any Palatine refugee that wanted to emigrate and take advantage of the opportunity. As a result, during the spring and summer of 1709, as many as thirty thousand Germans from Palatine and neighboring principalities left their homes seeking refuge in England and passage to the American colonies.

The reasons these Palatines left their homelands included:

- Devastation from multiple wars
- Debilitating taxation
- Significant levels of conscription into the military
- An extremely severe winter
- Memorable, enticing (and effective) advertising by the American colonies
- Desire to escape the feudal system they lived under as peasants and serfs
- Desire for land ownership and adventure
- Benevolent cooperation of the British government
- Religious disagreements (and some religious persecution)

Many erroneously believe the primary reason for the massive emigration from the Palatine region during the first half of the eighteenth century was due to religious persecution. This was not the case. Most of those who had suffered from religious persecution in Palatine (i.e., Quakers, Mennonites, Amish) had already immigrated

---

[1] Archdale, L. C., MSS., 1694-1706, p. 70.

during the latter part of the seventeenth century and the first decade of the eighteenth century. The immigrants who arrived after 1709 were mostly Protestant Lutherans and Calvinists. In November 1705, Catholic Elector Palatine John William (the political leader of the Rhineland Palatinate) had issued a declaration promising liberty of conscience to all Palatinate residents.[2] There is no known recorded instance that either the Lutherans or the Calvinists were being persecuted for their religious beliefs in Palatine during the first half of the eighteenth century.

In the spring of 1709, the first Palatines began arriving in the British American colonies following the harsh winter of 1708-09. One group of about six hundred settled in North Carolina and founded the town of New Bern. Another group established the first Palatine settlement along the Hudson River in New York near present Newburgh. However, most of these Palatine immigrants remained in London during the summer waiting for England to make the final arrangements for them to sail to America.

Most of these immigrants spent all they had just to get to London. They now needed British charity for subsistence while they waited to go to America. Although initially sympathetic to the plight of "the poor Palatines," the English populace quickly turned against them once they began living in London because they were consuming most of the social services intended for needy British citizens. They were no longer seen as refugees but instead were viewed as peasant opportunists bent on acquiring free land.

Within a few months, Parliament passed laws severely restricting the funds Queen Anne could expropriate to subsidize the German immigration effort. As a result, the large group of nearly thirty thousand German immigrants waiting in London to depart for America were stuck. A few decided to return to the homes they had left in Palatine and other neighboring principalities. Some were resettled in Ireland, an experiment that ultimately failed because of language, culture, and religious differences. However, most decided

---

2  Knittle, Walter Allen, "Early Eighteenth Century Palatine Emigration - A British Government Redemptioner Project to Manufacture Naval Stores," Department of History, College of the City of New York, Published Philadelphia, 1937

to stay in London in hopes that – with some luck - they still may make it to America.

After much consternation, a scheme was concocted whereby the colony of New York would pay for the voyage to get many of the Palatines stuck in London to America. In return, the Palatine men would agree to work in a manufacturing facility to be built in the pine forests along the Hudson River in upstate New York. The agreement was these men would work for the colony until they had repaid all the expenses New York had incurred to transport them and their families from England to New York.

The scheme's goal was to manufacture pine pitch and pine tar for the British Navy, but ultimately, the naval stores project cost far too much and could not achieve sufficient yields. In addition, the Palatines viewed this plan as a ploy to make them serfs in their new country, and many of them simply refused to work. The project was eventually abandoned under the leadership of New York Governor Hunter.

The demise of the naval stores project meant the end of British subsidies to support the Palatines, and the immigrants had to find ways to fend for themselves. Some remained settled along the Hudson River, living a desperate existence in the sparse naval stores camps. A few moved to New York City, and some managed to obtain land in New Jersey. Some resettled further north along the Mohawk River, while others still held out a hope that they would be able to acquire lands for farms of their own in the Schoharie Valley near Albany, New York.

In the early 1720's, five of these Palatine Germans living in New York traveled to Pennsylvania. They shared their plight with Pennsylvania governor William Keith, who gave them permission to settle on land about sixty miles northwest of Philadelphia on the Tulpehocken Creek just northwest of present day Reading. In 1723, thirty-three families from New York, led by Conrad Weiser, arrived to begin a new settlement. Weiser and others continued bringing new groups of Germans from the Palatine into Lancaster County (now Berks County), Pennsylvania. Weiser established the Tulpehocken Township in 1729, and its offshoot, the Heidelberg Township in 1734.

When three shiploads of Palatine Germans arrived in Pennsylvania in 1717, Governor William Keith began supporting the adoption of an entry procedure for registering aliens. That entry process became law in 1727 and remained in force for the duration of the colonial period. The statute required that every white male over 15 years of age entering the province sign an oath of allegiance to the British crown as well as an oath of abjuration renouncing the authority of the Catholic Pope. It also required that they all partake of the sacrament of holy communion according to the Anglican (Church of England) ritual before witnesses, who were required to sign a certificate to that effect. To document all of these requirements, four separate 'ship lists' had to be completed by the crew of each ship that carried immigrants from 1727 until the beginning of the American Revolution. All these lists with the names of the immigrants, with a few exceptions, still survive.

The law that mandated these "ship lists" originated due to the concern of Pennsylvania's Englishmen that so many German immigrants, ignorant of the English language and the law of the land, were being admitted to the colony. The qualification for alien immigrants that the leaders of Pennsylvania imposed, however, served two purposes simultaneously. The first was to appease the Englishmen's traditional xenophobia to keep track of "different" peoples coming to live alongside them. The second was to establish a genuinely constructive, regulated first step towards eventual full citizenship for non-British immigrants by permitting settlers from places not under British rule to acquire, hold, and sell property.

To pay for their voyage, many impoverished Palatine immigrants resorted to selling themselves (and sometimes other family members) into indentured servitude - agreeing to be legally bound to an employer in America for several years, until their debt was paid. The conditions of indentured servitude could be very harsh but, unlike slavery, it was entered into voluntarily.

By 1728, the number of immigrants seeking to pay back the cost of their journey through indentured servanthood had increased to the extent that a new international business had to be developed to streamline this process. Between 1728 and 1750, these servitude contracts between Palatine immigrants and their American employers quickly became the core of a business network that connected the German Palatinate, the Port of Rotterdam in the Netherlands, and the Port of Philadelphia in Pennsylvania. Virtually all of the servitude contracts were finalized before the immigrants left Germany, and the employers agreed to pay the owner of the ship at the time their immigrant under contract disembarked from the ship in America.

By the late 1730s, the system of getting German migrants into the Netherlands and then across the Atlantic was standardized and streamlined. The availability of credit guaranteed by the American employers encouraged both increased supply of, and demand for, indentured servants. On the European side, this indentured servitude system removed the single largest cost to emigration – ocean passage fares and initial settlement costs – significantly increasing the opportunities for Palatine Germans to emigrate. By 1750 approximately half of these immigrants traveled to America under contract as indentured servants. They had agreed to work for employers in America for four to seven years in exchange for free passage across the Atlantic and coverage of initial settlement and living expenses.

In addition to the lengthy period before these indentured servants could complete their contracts and regain their independence, there were other downsides to this system of servitude. Sometimes, entire families, including children, often entered servitude agreements before leaving their homes in Germany. During their journey, they found the conditions on the ships to be abysmal. The food was terrible. They were overcrowded and unsanitary, full of illness, disease, and danger. Many died along the way. The expected six-to-eight-week crossing was completely dependent on the weather, with some voyages taking up to sixteen weeks to complete. When the immigrants finally arrived, the passengers were met by their employers upon docking. If an indentured parent had died enroute, their families were generally broken up and placed under servitude to far-flung employers, often never to meet again. There was no guarantee that young men aged sixteen and older, whose parent(s) were under servitude contract, could remain with their families. Often, these young men were forced to sign a separate servitude contract at a distant location, making it difficult, or even impossible, to reunite with their families after their period of servitude was completed.

Looking back on this colonial period, German immigration to Pennsylvania can be divided into three distinct periods. The first lasted from 1683 until 1725. During this time ships brought relatively few German immigrants, and most who did make the voyage were the religiously persecuted Quakers, Mennonites, and Amish.

The second immigration period stretched from the beginning of the "ship lists" in 1727 to the extended peak years of 1749-1754, an era during which the numbers of both ships and immigrants grew rapidly. It was during this period that Adam Böner immigrated in 1736 at the age of thirty-eight, and his son Casper Böner immigrated four years later in 1740 at the age of twenty.

The third immigration period ran from the mid-1750s to the beginning of the American Revolution. German migration generally declined during this period.

Throughout the colonial period, German immigration to America was overwhelmingly through the Port of Philadelphia. By 1745, more than 40,000 Germans lived in Pennsylvania. By the beginning of the Revolutionary War in 1775, it is estimated that 100,000 residents of German descent lived in Pennsylvania.

*3.*

# Reuben Adam Böner
## *1697-1784*

Adam Böner was born in 1697 near Mannheim, a city in southwest Germany along the Rhine River in the region known at that time as Palatine. His parents were Hans Ulrich Böner and Juditha Böner (their last name was also spelled Bühner in some historical German documents). Following the German naming tradition, the name given at birth was the one commonly used, even though it became the middle name at the time of baptism when an additional Biblical first name was given. So Adam Bunner became Reuben Adam Bunner after his baptism. However, his family and friends would have called him Adam, not Reuben.

It is believed that Adam's father Ulrich (he also went by his middle name) died in 1700 at the age of 54 when Adam was only 2-3 years old. It is unknown whether Adam's mother remarried, and if Adam had a stepfather as he grew up. While family tradition holds that Jacob Böner, who immigrated to Pennsylvania from Palatine in 1738 was the brother of Adam, this has never been confirmed. It is unknown how many brothers and sisters Adam had.

However, it is certain that he lived among an extended family, as, in Palatine, grandfathers, fathers, and sons, along with their families, lived together and worked on the same land from generation to generation. Living in extended families was necessary to raise sufficient food for survival in Palatine during the early eighteenth century. As his father was fifty-one years old when Adam was born, it would seem likely that if he had brothers and sisters, he would be one of the youngest in the family, giving him the lowest claim among any brothers on any inheritance. This lowly position would make him more dependent on his extended family members and increase his obligations to them after his father died.

**Old painting of a seventeenth century peasant village** (public domain)

The system of feudalism that developed across the European continent during the Middle Ages still existed in Palatine during the lives of Ulrich Böner and his son Adam. It is a near certainty that Ulrich was not a landowner, meaning that he would have been classified as a peasant. Only a small portion of the population, primarily the wealthy aristocracy, owned land. The peasants were contractually obligated to provide labor for, and pay rent and taxes to, their landlords (who were commonly called their "lords"). Peasants had a double tax burden, one payment to the landlord, and the other to the state. Both were tax payments on the land the peasants cultivated but never owned.

These landlords managed their vast estates and added to their wealth by directing the work of their peasant tenants. Peasants were generally obligated to work two to three days per week on their landlord's land for the landlord's profit. They could then use the balance of their time and labor to grow food and livestock for their own benefit. In some instances, if they were extremely industrious and could afford it, the peasants could pay additional rent in lieu of working on their lord's land. Peasants generally could not leave to work for another landowner without the permission of their 'lord'. As a result, few Palatines were able to "cash out" and move elsewhere.

Peasant houses in Palatine were usually of a single story made of hewn wood or logs. The house that Adam lived in probably had floors made of compacted soil with mats or rushes to walk on. It would have included a hearth, a raised space for beds, and an attic for grain storage. Furnishings included a table and some benches. Cooking required an iron pot and skillet. Meals were eaten off plates made by a village potter. Fuel for cooking and heating their houses was generally wood. To stay warm and to provide security for their animals, the peasant families often slept close to them under the same roof.

Peasant leaders supervised the fields along with administering irrigation and grazing rights. They also maintained public order and operated a village court which handled minor offenses. Within the extended family unit, the patriarch made all the decisions and tried to arrange advantageous marriages for his children and grandchildren. Life in the local village centered around a market for the bartering and selling of goods as well as around church services and the celebration of holy days.

While peasants did not own land, they could buy the right to cultivate it and could also sell that right. The right to live on the land was also inheritable. When a parent was ready to retire, they would either give their sons the right to cultivate the farm or sell that right to them (daughters usually were paid off). Such sales always contained stipulations as to how the conditions of the retirement of the outgoing farmer should be fulfilled.

Adam grew up amidst the devastation and poverty that had befallen the Palatine region during the early eighteenth century. He was born while the Palatines were still trying to recover from nearly a century of wars that had reduced both the cities and countryside to rubble. The decade of Adam's birth also marked the low point of the "Little Ice Age," a period of cold and wet weather that drastically reduced crop yields and caused famines across Europe.[1]

In 1707, when Adam was ten years old, the War of the Spanish Succession was raging across much of Europe. During that year, the military forces of French King Louis XIV crossed the Rhine River and invaded Adam's Palatine homeland. They terrorized his family and neighbors, plundering and requisitioning supplies from them without payment. Many in Palatine that survived this invasion were left bankrupt and starving. To survive, many Palatine peasants relinquished what few freedoms they possessed, contractually agreeing to become lowlier serfs to their landlords in return for food.

When Adam was twelve years old, he lived through the coldest winter experienced in the Palatine region for over a century. Historical records from the winter of 1708-1709 indicate that birds froze in midair, wine froze in its barrels, fruit trees died, grapevines were destroyed, and livestock froze to death. It is unknown what extraordinary measures Adam and his family had to take to survive these desperate times, but we know that he did survive.

As a teenager, Adam likely had little hope for a better life because he had never experienced anything but war, famine and poverty. He probably never allowed himself to dream about living a prosperous life because he knew that such a possibility was out of the reach of a peasant like him living under the Palatine feudal system.

Adam never learned to read or write. Because surviving each day required his full-time commitment, the only education that he received was from the school of hard knocks.

---

1  White, Ian (2011). "Rural Settlement 1500–1770", The Oxford Companion to Scottish History. Oxford University Press. ISBN 978-0-19-211696-3.

After the harsh winter of 1708-1709, many of Adam's neighbors finally gave up on trying to eke out a survival existence on the land they were renting. With some benevolent financial assistance from the Queen of England and an unfortunate rumor that the Queen was going to grant free land in the American colonies to Palatine immigrants, an estimated 30,000 Palatines emigrated to England during the summer of 1709, hoping to ultimately build a new life in the American colonies.

There were many issues and obstacles that caused the dreams and aspirations of this initial group of 30,000 emigrants to flounder. Perhaps the greatest was the after-the-fact realization that Queen Anne of England had never promised free land in the American colonies. There had never been a basis for this rumor that had feverishly circulated among the Palatines.

Another obstacle was the shift in political power in England during this time. In early 1709, Queen Anne had allocated significant funds to assist the Palatines in paying for their costs to immigrate to the American colonies. Later that year, due to changing attitudes of the English populace toward the Palatines, Parliament passed laws severely restricting the Queen's largesse.

As a result, several of Adam's Palatine neighbors who had emigrated as far as London dejectedly returned to the homes they had left. However, most of his former neighbors continued living in London in clusters that became Palatine ghettos. Many of those Palatines who did make it to the American colonies ended up living out nightmares rather than the dreams that had driven them to leave Palatine in the first place.

This sudden exodus of nearly 30,000 residents in 1709 caused several of the German principalities along the Rhine River to implement steps to try to curb emigration to America. They imposed travel restrictions and higher taxes on emigration. They also offered incentives for people to stay put, such as land grants to peasants who met certain qualification criteria. Some principalities reduced taxes on the peasant population and began providing better social services. This was done to try to maintain their workforce and population levels, as they understood that a declining population led to a declining economy.

While the number of emigrants from Palatine to America declined substantially after this initial bubble in 1709-1710, it never stopped. Several hundred emigrated each year with more and more of them going to Pennsylvania. Letters from those who had previously emigrated from Palatine to Pennsylvania repeatedly extolled the better lives they had found in America. This positive feedback about life in Pennsylvania from family members and former neighbors caused other Palatines to decide to pull up stakes and follow in their footsteps.

Adam Böner would have been aware of all these developments, and by his late teenage years a seed had probably already been planted in his mind about the possibility of a better life awaiting him in Pennsylvania. However, he did not act on these thoughts at that time but let them slowly germinate and grow over the next twenty years.

Adam grew into adulthood and by 1719, when he was twenty-two years old, he was married. In 1720, his first son, Casper Böner, was born. Soon afterward, Casper was baptized and his parents decided that his Biblical first name would be Reuben, the same ceremonial first name as his father. However, as was the custom, his family and friends would have called him Casper.

A huge gap exists in the timeline between the birth of Reuben Casper Böner in 1720 and the time that Adam emigrated from Palatine to Pennsylvania in 1736. By jumping to 1774, when Adam sold his Pennsylvania farm to his youngest son William, we learn from that deed of sale that he had a wife named Christina.[2] We also learn from his final estate settlement deed in 1787 that he had five living children. His living sons were named Philip, Frederick, and William. His living daughters were named Mariah Rosina and Hannah Martha.[3] Casper was not named in this document because he had died in 1779, seven to eight years before his father.

---

2   Berks County Pennsylvania Recorder of Deeds, Online Search, Index Books, Deed Grantor 01/01/1751 – 12/31/1926, "Boner, Adam", Book B1, Page 504

3   Berks County Pennsylvania Recorder of Deeds, Online Search, Index Books, Deed Grantor 01/01/1751 – 12/31/1926, "Boner, Adam", Book 10, Page 157

Other gaps and unanswered questions remain in Adam's story. They include:

- Was Christina Adam's first wife or a second wife?
- Was Christina the mother of Casper, or his stepmother?
- Were the five known children of Adam and Christina Böner born in Palatine, in Pennsylvania, or some in Palatine and some in Pennsylvania?
- How many years between the birth of Casper in 1720 and Philip, the next oldest child?
- If the entire family immigrated with Adam in 1736, why did sixteen-year-old Casper remain in Palatine for an additional four years?
- What was Adam's source of funds to pay the family's immigration and initial settlement costs in Pennsylvania?
- Did Adam and his family serve as indentured servants for five years after arriving in Pennsylvania to pay for their immigration costs?

Undisputed facts known about Adam Böner's immigration to Pennsylvania include:

- He arrived at the Port of Philadelphia on the ship Harle on September 1, 1736.
- On the ship lists, he leaves only his "mark" for his signature, indicating that he could not read or write.
- The clerks assigned the task of completing the required ship lists spelled his name on two of the lists as Adam Bohner, and on one list as Adam Bohn. (Some printed documents today also record the last name as Boher.)
- The Harle ship manifest states that in addition to the 165 men on board, there were also 65 women and 167 children under the age of sixteen. [4]

---

4  Rupp, Daniel (1856), "A collection of Thirty Thousand Names of Immigrants in Pennsylvania", Harrisburg, p. 45

It is unknown whether one of the sixty-five women on board was Adam's wife Christina. It is also unknown whether five of the one hundred sixty-seven boys and girls on board were his children Philip, Mariah Rosina, Frederick, Hannah Martha, and William. We do know that Adam's oldest son, Casper, who was sixteen years old at the time, did not accompany his father on this ship. Instead, Casper immigrated to Pennsylvania by himself four years later.

Adam settled in Lancaster County, Pennsylvania (now Berks County) along Tulpehocken Creek. This had become a prime destination for Palatine emigrants since their initial settlement there in 1722. If Adam had signed contracts for his family to serve as indentured servants to reimburse their sponsor for paying their immigration costs, that contract would likely have ended in 1740 or 1741. If Adam and his family did not serve as indentured servants, he would have rented sufficient land for his family to survive on until he could save enough money for a down payment to purchase property of his own.

In either case, Adam and his family would have spent their first 4-5 years in Pennsylvania clearing, building out, and cultivating land owned by others. They were no longer called peasants, but during their first five years in Pennsylvania their lives were reflective of their former lives as peasants in Palatine. The big difference was that in Palatine, Adam had no hope of ever owning the land he cultivated, but in Pennsylvania he had both the hope and the expectation of eventually becoming a landowner.

In November 1740, Adam's twenty-year-old son Casper immigrated to Pennsylvania. It appears that he joined his father in Lancaster County (now Berks County). In May 1741, just a few months after Casper's arrival, Adam obtained a warrant from the Pennsylvania Land Office to purchase 51.5 acres of land near Tulpehocken Creek. On the same day, he also obtained a warrant to purchase 76 acres of land fronting nearly two miles along Tulpehocken Creek that adjoined the 51.5-acre parcel. This second parcel was purchased from William Hetrig, who had initially acquired this land from the Pennsylvania Land Office in 1738.

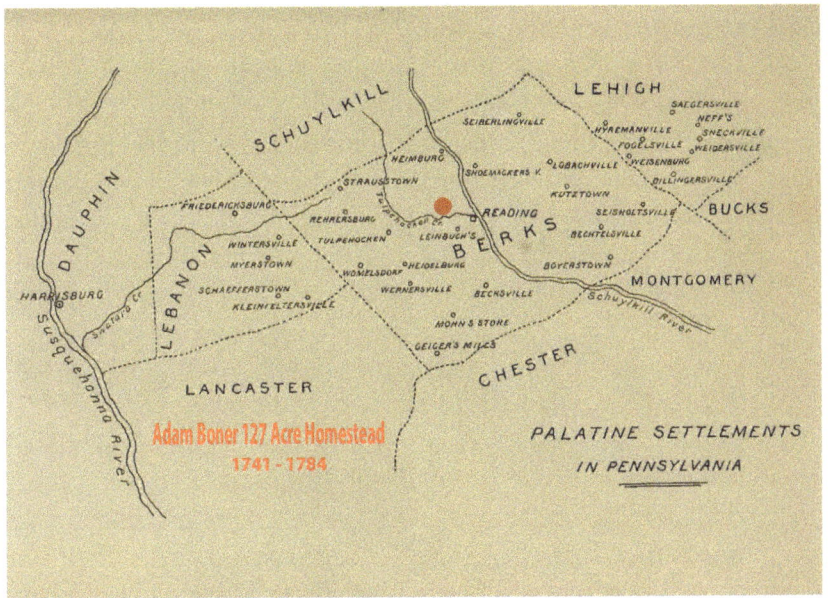

**Red circle shows location of Adam Boner homestead on Tulpehocken Creek**

The legal process that Adam followed to buy his 51.5-acre parcel from the Pennsylvania Land Office was:

1. After selecting the land he wanted to buy, he applied for a warrant to complete a survey. This application was accompanied by half of the purchase price. In 1741, the price for all land purchased from the Pennsylvania Land Office was £15 per 100 acres. As Adam's parcel was 51.5 acres, the purchase price was approximately £7.75. Adam would have paid half of this amount (approximately £3.9) at the time he applied for the warrant. (Adjusting for inflation from 1741 to 2025 and converting from British £ to U.S. $, the purchase price for the 51.5 acres - in 2025 $ - would have been approximately $3,000, with the 50% down payment being $1,500).
2. On May 12, 1741, a warrant to survey the land was issued to the surveyor general's office and a deputy surveyor was charged with making a survey and a plat of the land. Adam

paid the surveyor's fee prior to the survey being completed. Once the warrant was issued, and even before the survey was completed, Adam was legally permitted to move onto the land to begin clearing it, building his house, and growing crops. (Receiving a land warrant in 1741 was roughly equivalent to purchasing land under a long-term mortgage today. Though the purchaser did not yet have a clear title because the property was not fully paid for, they had rights of ownership that allowed them to improve the land, or even sell it, without a clear title in hand.)
3. The survey was completed on September 16, 1743. The surveyor general of Pennsylvania then waited for Adam to remit the remaining 50% of the land purchase price. Rather than paying all at once, Adam probably applied for and received a loan from the Pennsylvania Land Office Bank using the equity in his land as collateral. The interest rate on these loans was generally 5%, and the term was negotiable. According to records, Adam completed the final payment on this loan on April 12, 1760.
4. After Adam made the final payment, the surveyor general prepared a "Return of Survey" which was used to create a patent granting Adam the absolute title to his land.
5. Sometime after April 12, 1760, Adam received the original "Certificate of Patent" and a copy was made for the books of the Pennsylvania Land Office. (The Certificate of Patent would be equivalent to a clear title today.)

After receiving the original patent in 1741, Adam, Casper, and Adam's younger sons spent the next few years clearing a farm out of the virgin forest covering the 51.5-acre parcel. The 76-acre parcel fronting Tulpehocken Creek was never cleared and probably served as a private hunting and fishing preserve for Adam and his family. On the 51.5 acre parcel they built a log house large enough to accommodate the family, a barn, and other outbuildings necessary to sustain a working farm.

Adam's wife and younger children would have been instrumental in planting and tending the crops and then harvesting and preserving the food from their gardens. They also would have assisted in caring for the livestock which would have included cattle, sheep, pigs, chickens and 1-2 horses.

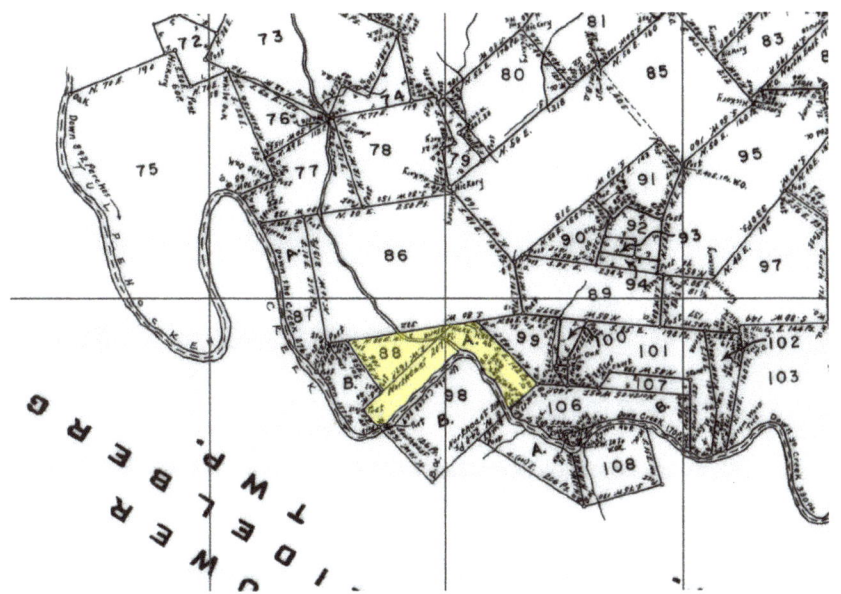

(Southwestern) Bern Township – Berks County, PA –
Early Landowner Plats
Adam Böner Plats - #88 and #98A – Warrant Received 1741[5]

---

5   MacInnis, Sharon, (2019), "Early Landowners of Pennsylvania: Atlas of Township Warrantee Maps of Berks County", Clossen Press, Apollo, PA, p. 18

| WARRANTEE NAME | TRACT NAME | SIZE | WARRANT DATE | SURVEY DATE | PATENT DATE | PATENT BOOK | SURVEY BOOK | # | Coordinates |
|---|---|---|---|---|---|---|---|---|---|
| BONER, Adam | [no name on tract] | 51 ½ acres & allowance | 12 May 1741 | 16 Sep 1743 | 12 Apr 1760 to Adam BONER | A19-493 | A82-73 | #88 | B-5 |
| BROWN, Peter | Abraham's Portion | 47 acres 70 perches & allowance | 6 Aug 1753 | 27 Oct 1758 | 27 May 1774 to Abraham REESER | AA14-375 | C122-245 | #102 | D-5 |
| CARNANT, George | Carnburg; #23 on map | 51 acres 106 perches & allowance | 19 Oct 1752 | 16 Apr 1754 | 26 Jul 1770 to George CARNANT | AA11-372 | C36-46 | #23 | B-3, C-3 |
| CLAY, Nicholas | [no name on tract; #4 on map] | 110 acres & allowance | 13 May 1747 | 26 May 1747 | This tract appears to have been divided into three tracts: Tract A: 46 acres 102 perches & allowance were surveyed 26 May 1747 and patented 29 May 1810 to Elizabeth KLEA as "Widow's Charge". Tract B: 31 acres & allowance were resurveyed 2 Nov 1809 and patented 29 May 1810 to Jeremiah BLATT as "Bloomfield". Tract C: 27 acres 120 perches & allowance were resurveyed 21 Dec 1809 and patented 29 May 1810 to Jeremiah BLATT as "Bloomfield". | Tract A: H4-109 Tract B: H4-110 Tract C: H4-110 | Tract A: H-207 Tract A: C103-200 Tract B: C40-92 Tract C: C40-112 | #4 | C-1, C-2, D-1, D-2 |
| COOKSON, Thomas | [no name on tract] | 154 acres 130 perches & allowance | 10 Jan 1744 | 10 Nov 1763 | This tract appears to have been divided into two pieces: Tract A: 107 acres & allowance were surveyed 10 Nov 1763 and patented 18 Nov 1763 to John REBER. Tract B: 47 acres & allowance were surveyed 10 Nov 1763 and patented 18 Nov 1763 to John REBER. | AA4-447 (both tracts) | Tract A: A8-228 Tract B: A8-227 | #87 | B-4, B-5 |
| DESTER, Jacob | [no name on tract] | 19 acres 10 perches & allowance | 30 Apr 1765 | 27 Jul 1765 | 21 Sep 1765 to Jacob DERSTER | AA6-404 | A89-204 | #30 | D-2 |

## Adam Böner Plat #88 Description – 51.5 Acres – Warranted 12 May 1741[6]

| WARRANTEE NAME | TRACT NAME | SIZE | WARRANT DATE | SURVEY DATE | PATENT DATE | PATENT BOOK | SURVEY BOOK | # | Coordinates |
|---|---|---|---|---|---|---|---|---|---|
| HETRIG, William | [no name on tract] | 231 acres & allowance | 28 Nov 1737 | 21 Apr 1738 | This tract appears to have been divided into two pieces: Tract A: 76 acres & allowance were warranted 12 May 1741, surveyed 21 Apr 1738, and patented 12 Apr 1760 to Adam BONER. Tract B: 155 acres & allowance were warranted 4 Apr 1764, surveyed 21 Apr 1738, and patented 20 Apr 1764 to Hans Peter HAAS. | Tract A: A19-493 Tract B: AA4-175 | Tract A: A46-73 Tract B: A49-31 | #98 | B-5, C-5 |
| KERNAN, Christian | [no name on tract; #26 on map] | 226 acres & allowance | 18 Mar 1750 | 15 Oct 1751 | 28 Jan 1755 to Christian KERNAN | A20-6 | C107-47 | #26 | C-2, C-3 |
| KERNAN, George | [no name on tract; #24 on map] | 201 acres & allowance | 18 Feb 1744 | 23 Jan 1752 | 29 Jan 1755 to George KERNAN | A20-7 | C107-8 | #24 | B-3, C-3 |
| KICKER, Henry | Berwick | 22 acres & allowance | 28 Jun 1769 | 9 Nov 1744 [sic] | 4 Jul 1769 to Henry KICKER | AA11-107 | C102-71 | #107 | C-5 |
| LIGHTFOOT, Thomas | Dryland | 233 acres 67 perches & allowance | 4 Jan 1752 | 19 Jun 1752 | 5 Apr 1771 to Thomas LIGHTFOOT | AA11-529 | L-400 | #97 | C-4, C-5, D-4, D-5 |
| LOSS, Jacob | Contentent [sic]; #22 on map | 8 acres 110 perches & allowance | "Appl. No. 947" Dated Sept. 25, 1765" | 17 Mar 1808 | 21 Nov 1809 to John SHEIDY on a warrant to accept dated 20 Nov 1809 | H2-58 | M-517 | #22 | B-2, B-3 |
| MACHEMER, George | Rockland | 14 acres 61 perches & allowance | 21 Jun 1791 | 19 Jul 1791 | 3 Jun 1796 to George MACHEMER | P29-93 | C130-109 | #100 | C-5 |
| MARSTELLER, Ludwig | [no name on tract; #17 on map] | 71 acres 68 perches & allowance | "Appl. 897" Dated Sept. 25, 1765 ...On Warrant dated Sept. 25, 1765" | Resurveyed 17 Aug 1795 | "Unpatented" | [no patent book reference] | A9-263 | #17 | D-2 |

## Adam Böner Plat #98A Description – 76 Acres – Warranted 12 May 1741[7]

---

6 MacInnis, Sharon, (2019), "Early Landowners of Pennsylvania: Atlas of Township Warrantee Maps of Berks County", Clossen Press, Apollo, PA, p. 22

7 MacInnis, Sharon, (2019), "Early Landowners of Pennsylvania: Atlas of Township Warrantee Maps of Berks County", Clossen Press, Apollo, PA, p. 27

**Adam Böner Homestead, 1741-1784 – Berks County, Pennsylvania**
(map created by Michael Bunner overlaid on 2025 Google Earth image)

Within five years of obtaining the warrant on this property, much of the heavy labor necessary to create a farm out of the wilderness would have been completed. Adam's focus turned from building his farm to making it profitable

Most of the good land in Lancaster County, Pennsylvania had been claimed by 1745, so Adam was one of the last to purchase a desirable parcel directly from the Pennsylvania Land Office. The demand for Pennsylvania land exceeded the supply, so many of the more recent Palatine settlers in Pennsylvania began looking southward toward Virginia and the Carolinas. Virginia had begun opening its frontier for settlement and was especially targeting recent Palatine settlers in Pennsylvania who were finding it ever more difficult to obtain land on which to settle.

Other Palatine settlers decided to move further west in Pennsylvania toward – and even beyond - the Susquehanna River on lands still owned by the Lenape (Delaware) Indians. This created significant rifts in the historically good relationship between the Delawares and the colonial Pennsylvania government. The colonial government, which had been controlled by the pacifist Quakers since the founding of the colony, prided itself in always agreeing to a fair price for the lands they purchased from the Indians before those lands were opened for settlement. These white settlers squatting on Delaware lands without paying for it created an undertow of anger which violently erupted with the outbreak of the French and Indian War in 1754.

Sometime around 1745, twenty-five-year-old Casper met and began courting seventeen-year-old Mary Christiana Brown (Braun), whose family lived on a farm in a nearby township. Mary and her family had immigrated to Pennsylvania from Palatine (or a nearby region) in 1738. Mary's mother had died in 1739 less than one year after arriving in America, and her father, Johann Wendell Brown (Braun) had married Elizabeth Knopf later that year. For whatever reason Wendell had become disenchanted with life in Pennsylvania and was seriously considering relocating to the Virginia frontier along the Shenandoah and Potomac rivers, where abundant land was being advertised at much lower prices than in Pennsylvania.

In 1746, Wendell Brown made the decision to move his family to Virginia, settling on the South Fork of the South Branch of the Potomac River in Augusta County (present-day Hardy County, West Virginia). Casper followed. He and Mary were married sometime between 1746 and 1749. In 1750 they welcomed their first child, John Amos Böner into their family.

Due to the 250 miles that now separated them, Adam and Casper likely had only limited contact with each other after Casper's move to Virginia. Adam remained focused on working on his farm. German immigrants from Palatine were still arriving in ever growing numbers, and by 1745 the German population living along the Pennsylvania frontier had reached approximately 40,000.

To provide more localized services to this growing population, the Pennsylvania Assembly carved several new counties out of Lancaster County. York County was created in 1749, followed by Cumberland County in 1750, and then Berks County, where Adam and his family lived, in 1752.

Reading, a non-existent town consisting of only a few houses in 1752, was designated as the county seat of the new county. Adam's property was only five miles upstream from where Tulpehocken Creek entered the Schuylkill River near the site of the new town.

This proximity afforded Adam a close-up view of the real estate boom that occurred as the town of Reading quickly grew out of the wilderness over the next few years.

Most travel within Berks County was still on foot or by horseback along what had become well-worn paths. In 1752, there were still few roads in the county suitable for horse drawn wagons, and those that existed were dirt roads that became impassable when it rained.

Baptismal records in churches in the Palatine during the late 1600's and early 1700's indicate that the members of the extended Böner family were mostly Lutherans. If Adam and his family maintained this affiliation after immigrating to Pennsylvania, they would have most likely been members of the Christ Little Tulpehocken Church, which had been established by Palatine immigrants in 1729. During the first thirty years of Adam's life in Pennsylvania, this would have been the closest Lutheran Church to where he and his family lived. This log church was approximately seven miles north of the Böner homestead. The original log church building was replaced by a stone building in 1809. This stone building still stands, and the church remains active to this day.

In 1754, with the outbreak of the French and Indian War, Adam and other settlers in Berks County had to wrestle with the threat of deadly Indian attacks on their farms. Because the white settlers were continuing to push westward onto land owned (and occupied) by the Delawares, anger and desire for retribution was already seething among the Indians. This anger quickly exploded into deadly attacks on settlements in lands they had previously sold to the Pennsylvania colonial government, which, in turn, had been settled by immigrants from Palatine.

Early in October 1755, just three months after the French and their Indian allies had defeated British General Braddock's forces on the Monongahela River, Delaware and Shawnee warriors from the Ohio River attacked east of the Susquehanna River. This brought the war to Lancaster and Berks Counties. These surprise raids resulted in the murder of twenty-four settlers, with two additional settlers taken as captives.[8]

Soon afterward, the North Branch Delaware Indians engaged in a deadly attack on several farms just south of the Blue Mountain Ridge in northern Berks County.[9] Six men, one woman, and four children were killed, as was one of the Delaware raiders. A nine-year-old girl was found alive, but scalped, as were all the dead.[10]

Late in 1755, Conrad Weiser, who had become the acknowledged local leader of the Palatine settlers, lamented that "back inhabitants" were terrorizing friendly Indians, who feared "being killed by a mob." When the people of Paxton, a small settlement in northern Berks County, captured an Indian near their farms, Weiser hurried out to interrogate him, but was too late: "shocking to me they shott (sic) him in the midst of them, scalped him and threw his Body into the River." [11]

After this 1755 outbreak of hostilities, the Quaker pacifists lost their long-held majority in the Pennsylvania General Assembly. Lead by Assemblyman Benjamin Franklin, the colony declared war on the Delaware Indians in April 1756. The governor proclaimed a bounty of 150 pieces of eight on Indian male captives over twelve years of age, pledging 130 pieces of eight for their scalps.[12]

Conrad Weiser argued in vain that the small difference in bounties between a captive and a scalp was insufficient to encourage the taking of Indian captives, given the risks and troubles. The difference in the bounties offered for a woman Indian prisoner (130 pieces of eight) and for her scalp (50 pieces of eight) was more substantial,

---

8  Steele, Ian K. (2013), "Setting All the Captives Free", McGill-Queens University Press, Montreal, p. 94

9  Merrit, "At the Crossroads", p. 42, 155, 182, 190

10  Deposition of Captain Jacob Morgan, in PG, 20 November 1755

11  Weiser, Clement (1876), "The Life of (John) Conrad Weiser, the German Pioneer, Patriot, and Patron of Two Races", D. Miller, Reading, PA

12  Young, Henry, "A Note on Scalp Bounties in Pennsylvania", Pennsylvania History: A Journal of Mid-Atlantic Studies, Vol. 24, No. 3 (July, 1957), pp. 207-218, Penn State University Press

but no Indian women were reported captured during the war. [13] (A piece of eight was a Spanish peso, a common coin in the English colonies. It was sometimes called a dollar but was not the same as today's U.S. dollar. In British currency, a piece of eight was worth a little less than one-quarter of a pound, or four shillings and six pence. Adjusted for inflation since 1755, 130 pieces of eight would be equivalent to approximately $90 USD in 2025, and 50 pieces of eight would be equivalent to approximately $35 USD today.)

The Pennsylvania Assembly, having been controlled by Quaker pacifists since its inception, had no militia when the French and Indian War came east of the Appalachian Mountains in 1755. However, after war had been declared in April 1756, a militia was established and its volunteer regiment had three undermanned battalions expected to patrol the frontier. The Assembly called for a string of publicly funded forts to be constructed across the northern and western edges of the Pennsylvania frontier. Four of these forts were to be in Berks County along the southern base of the endless Blue Mountain Ridge (from which most of the Indian attacks had originated). By the end of 1756, only twelve of twenty-five planned forts had been constructed. One had already surrendered and six had been abandoned as indefensible.

Conrad Weiser was appointed Lt. Colonel in charge of the newly established Berks County Militia which recruited several hundred untrained and poorly armed local farmers to protect the residents of the county. It is unknown if Adam Böner (who would have been fifty-eight years old at the time) or any of his three sons (William was likely a teenager, but Philip and Frederick were probably in their late twenties or early thirties) served in this militia. Weiser set up militia headquarters in Reading but often directed the militia from his homestead in Heidelberg Township, approximately ten miles west of Adam Böner's homestead on Tulpehocken Creek and fifteen miles west of Reading.

On November 19, 1755, Weiser sent a letter to Governor Morris of Pennsylvania stating the dire need for arms, ammunition, and

---

13  Shirai, Yoko (1985), "The Indian Trade in Colonial Pennsylvania, 1730-1768: Traders and Land Speculation", pp. 91-92. (Proclamations in PG, 15, 22, 29 April 1756)

supplies for the militia. At the end of his letter, he made the following statement:

> "The people of Tulpehocken have all fled; till about six or seven miles from me some few remain. Another such attack will lay all the country waste on the west side of the Schuylkill.
>
> I am, sir,
>
> Your most obedient,
> Conrad Weiser.
> Heidelberg, Berks County, Nov. 19, 1755." [14]

The situation was dire for the residents of Berks County, especially those west of the Schuylkill River where Adam Böner and his family lived. Numerous small Indian war parties attacked Berks County homesteads south of Blue Mountain and along northern Tulpehocken Creek in 1756 and 1757. Many residents were massacred and many children were taken captive. A letter from a Tulpehocken resident, published in Benjamin Franklin's Pennsylvania Gazette newspaper on July 4, 1757, stated:

> "If we get no assistance from the county all the inhabitants of Tulpehocken will move away. The county should rise and send a large body to drive the Indians off and keep a strong guard in the houses on the frontiers besides the soldiers, or all will be lost." [15]

On July 5, 1757, the following entry was made in the Tulpehocken Church records: "Seven persons (three men and four children), who had been murdered and scalped all in one house, were brought

---

[14] Montgomery, Morton (1886), "History of Berks County in Pennsylvania", Everts, Peck & Richards, p. 123

[15] Montgomery, Morton (1886), "History of Berks County in Pennsylvania", Everts, Peck & Richards, p. 129

to our burying ground for burial. They were killed by the Indians yesterday, about sun-down, five miles from here." [16]

During these two years of atrocities, many residents of Berks County sought refuge in Philadelphia, sixty miles to the southeast. Adam Böner and his family lived on the south end of Tulpehocken Creek, five miles northwest of Reading and twenty miles south of the Blue Mountain Ridge where most of the attacks originated. It is not known if he and his family were among those who took refuge in Philadelphia. Adam and Christina may have concluded that they lived far enough south of Blue Mountain to be beyond the range of a surprise attack. If they did remain on their homestead during these two years, they lived and worked every day with the knowledge that they could come under attack at any time.

The hostilities of the French and Indian War in Pennsylvania started winding down in 1758 after the French abandoned Fort Duquesne (at present day Pittsburgh) and started retreating toward Canada. However, this period of calm was short lived, replaced by the Indian uprising over broken promises that the British would permanently withdraw from the Ohio Valley after the French retreated into Canada. This uprising is often referred to as "Pontiac's War," which lasted from 1761 until 1764. As a result of these new hostilities, the Pennsylvania Assembly reinstituted bounties on Indian prisoners and scalps in July 1763, and again in 1764.

On September 8, 1763, on a Quaker farm in Berks County, heavily armed Ohio Delaware Indian warriors were welcomed and offered food in friendship. In spite of this offer of friendship, the warriors killed the man, his wife, and two sons. They took one daughter captive. These warriors then went on to another nearby farm, where they found six children in the house while the parents were harvesting crops in a nearby field. Presented with another opportunity to take prisoners with little risk, the attackers killed four of the young children and took two as prisoners.

This war party was pursued and exchanged gunfire with provincial troops, and the fleeing Indians left the two children, still tied together but unharmed, as well as loot, including a saddle. This

---

16 Montgomery, Morton (1886), "History of Berks County in Pennsylvania", Everts, Peck & Richards, p. 129

was likely the same war party that regrouped to capture a mother and three of her children the following day, after leaving her three other children scalped alive. During these three attacks, Indians had killed ten and had taken seven children captive, two of whom were released while the raiding party was being hotly pursued. An eight-year-old boy who had hidden during the first attack on the Quaker farm escaped harm and was able to tell the story of what happened.[17]

These massacres unfortunately caused the massacre of peaceful Christian Indians by a group of white settlers known as "The Paxton Boys." In December 1763, this group congregated as a vigilante mob and murdered twenty Indians in Conestoga jail (near Lancaster) where the Indians had sought refuge. The vigilantes justified their actions by claiming that the Indians in Conestoga were colluding with the Delaware and Shawnee tribes who had made multiple attacks on Pennsylvania's frontier settlements during both the French and Indian and the Pontiac Wars.[18] There was no truth to this claim by "The Paxton Boys."

These were the last atrocities to occur in Berks and Lancaster counties during Pontiac's War. A year later, in the fall of 1764, militia forces in Ohio under the command of Colonel Henry Bouquet and Colonel John Bradstreet compelled the warring tribes under Pontiac's leadership to accept terms of peace, which ultimately ended the fighting.

Despite the existential dangers imposed by the French and Indian War, Adam succeeded at building a successful farming enterprise. He was able to completely pay for both of his land purchases and receive the Certificates of Patent (full titles) in 1760, during the short lull in hostilities between the end of the French and Indian War and the beginning of "Pontiac's War."

By the end of Indian hostilities in 1764, Adam's remaining five children had grown to adulthood and started building their own

---

17   Montgomery, Morton (1886), "History of Berks County in Pennsylvania", Everts, Peck & Richards, p. 132

18   Vaughan, Alden (1984), "Frontier Banditti and the Indians: The Paxton Boys' Legacy, 1763-1775", pp. 1-29.

lives as farmers in Lancaster and Berks counties in Pennsylvania. They, like virtually all the other residents of Lancaster and Berks counties, continued to speak German almost exclusively throughout their lives. They also retained much of the culture of their native land. While the original Palatine immigrants to the Pennsylvania frontier never fully acclimated to English life, language, and culture, they did quickly acclimate to freedom, capitalism, and the right to own property. Adam and his family took advantage of these opportunities by enjoying and profiting from the fruits of their own labor.

Adam's children all grew to adulthood and, one-by-one, married, moved away, and pursued their own lives by purchasing farms in Berks and Lancaster counties. By 1774, when Adam was seventy-seven years old, it appears he concluded he could no longer perform the strenuous physical labor necessary to sustain his farm. He and his wife Christina made the decision to sell 104 acres of their 127-acre homestead to their youngest son, William.

In the deed recording this transaction, the clerk, writing in English, was uncertain how to spell the family last name. It was spelled "Boon" throughout the body of the deed, then "Bohn" in the signature section. However, when the clerk referred to the name recorded in the original land patent book in 1760, the entry states "Adam Boon (alias Boner)." That alias linkage and the description of the land in the deed confirms that this was the land originally warranted in 1741 and patented in 1760 by Adam Böner.

What is not known is if Adam and his family had intentionally changed the spelling of their last name to Boon or Bohn by the time this deed was recorded in 1774. The other possibility is the clerk simply made a best effort to enter the name as it sounded coming from the lips of the Böners, who would have spoken only in German. Also of note is that Philip Bohn (Boner) signed this deed as the oldest son of Adam. Casper, the true oldest son of Adam, was living along the Monongahela River in Virginia (present day Rivesville, West Virginia) and not available to witness and sign this transaction.

The following transaction is recorded in the Berks County courthouse archives:

## Deed of Land Sale
## Adam and Christina Boon to son William Boon
### Approximately 104 acres in two adjoining tracts on Tulpehocken Creek – Berks County, PA
### May 9, 1774
('?' entries indicate the cursive words or letters in the original deed are uncertain)

This Indenture made the ninth day of May in the year of our Lord one thousand seven hundred and seventy-four made between Adam Boon on the Township of Bern in the County of Berks in the province of Pennsylvania yeoman and Christina his wife of the one part and William Boon of the same place yeoman of the other part. Witnesseth that the said Adam Boon and Christina his wife for and in consideration of the sum of three hundred pounds lawful money of Pennsylvania to them in hand paid by the said William Boon and before the Ensealing and Delivery hereof the receipt whereof they do hereby acknowledge and thereof do acquit and forever discharge the said William Boon, his heirs, executors, and administrators by these presents have granted, bargained, sold, alined (?), ensossed (?), released, and confirmed and by these presents do grant, bargain, sell, aline(?), ensoss (?), release, and confirm unto the said William Boon and to his heirs and assigns two certain tracts of land situate in the Township of Bern aforesaid bounded and limited as follows:

Viz, one of them beginning at a red cedar standing on the bank of the Tulpehocken Creek, thence by other land of said Adam Boon North ten degrees east nineteen perches to a white oak South eighty degrees east fifteen perches and a quarter to a post standing on Plum Creek and North fifty degrees east forty two perches and a half, thence by land of Frederick From Northwest five perches to a small hickory marked, thence by land belonging to the heirs of John Hiister South eighty degrees west forty perches to a stone and continuing the same course one hundred and eighty one perches and a half to a post, thence by Rees Thomas's land the three following courses and distances, viz, South thirty five degrees east one hundred six perches to a post [west on line?] forty perches to a white oak and South east thirty one perches to another post on said Tulpehocken Creek, thence up the same on several courses thereof to the place of beginning, containing ninety seven acres and a quarter and allowance proportionable to six acres plent (?) for roads and highways. And the other of them beginning at a marked black oak standing on the bank of said Tulpehocken Creek, thence of lands of Peter Haas South seventy degrees east twenty two perches to a stone and South fifty four degrees east sixty eight perches to a marked Spanish oak, thence by land of Henry Gicker North east thirty perches to a marked black oak, thence by land of the aforesaid Frederick From North west forty three perches and a half to a post, and thence of other land of said Adam Boon West seventy two perches to the place of beginning containing seven acres and a half and allowances as aforesaid (the said first above described tract including the whole of a tract of fifty one acres and a quarter of an acre and allowances, and part of a tract of seventy six acres and allowance whereof the said last above described). Tract is also a part which two tracts of seventy six acres and fifty one acres of land and allowances respectively were granted by the Honorable the Proprietaries of the Province aforesaid by patent of the twelfth day of April Anno Domino 1760 (recorded in the Office for Recording of Deeds for the City and County of Philadelphia in Pat[ent] Book A , Volume 19, page 493) unto the said **Adam Boon (alias Boner)** in fee together with all and singular other the houses, outhouses, buildings, barns, stables, gardens, orchards, meadows, pastures, fields, fences, ways, woods, waters, water courses, rights, liberties, privileges, hereditaments, and appurtenances whatsoever thereunto belonging or in any wise appertaining and the reversions property, remainders, rents, issues, and profits thereof and also all the estate, right, title, interest, property, claim, and demand whatsoever of them and the said Adam Boon and Christina his wife of into and out of the same and every part and parcel thereof. To have and to hold the said two above described tracts of ninety seven acres and a quarter and seven acres and a half of land and allowance aforesaid respectively, hereditaments and premises hereby granted as mentioned or intended so to be with the appurtenances unto the said William Boon, his heirs and assigns to the only proper use and behoof of the said William Boon, his heirs and assigns forever, subject nevertheless to the yearly quit rent, to wit of one halfpenny sterling per acre now due and hereafter to become due and payable to the Chief Lord or Lords of the fee thereof. And the said Adam Boon for himself and his heirs doth hereby covenant, promise, and grant to the said William Boon, his heirs and assigns that the said Adam Boon, and his heirs the said two above described tracts of ninety seven acres and a quarter and seven acres and a half of land and allowances aforesaid respectively hereditaments and premises hereby granted or mentioned or intended so to be with the appurtenances unto the said William Boon, his heirs and assigns against him the said Adam Boon against all and every other person and persons lawfully claiming or to claim by from or under him them or any of them shall and will warrant and forever defend by these presents. And further that the said Adam Boon and his heirs and all and every other person and persons and his or their heirs having or lawfully proclaiming any estate, right, title, or interest of in or to the premises hereby granted or any part thereof by from or under him them or any of them shall and will from time to time and at all times hereafter upon the reasonable request and at the proper costs and charges in the law of the said William Boon, his heirs and assigns make, execute, and acknowledge or cause or procure so to be all and every such further and other lawful and reasonable act and acts, thing and things, deeds and devices in the law whatsoever for the further and better assurance and confirmation of the said two above described tracts of land, hereditaments and premises hereby granted or mentioned or intended to be with the appurtenances and every part and parcel thereof unto the said William Boon, his heirs and assigns forever as by the said William Boon and his heirs and assigns or his or their counsel learned in the laws shall be reasonably advised, devised, and requested. In witness whereof, the said parties to these presents have hereunto interchangeably set their hands and seals dated the day and year first above written.

- Adam Bohn / his mark and seal
- Christina Bohn / her mark and seal

**Sealed and Delivered in the presence of us:**

- Phillip Bohn / his mark and seal – in German characters
- William Reesen

Received the day of the date above written Indenture of the above-named William Boon the sum of three hundred pounds lawful money of Pennsylvania. It being the consideration money above mentioned.

- Adam Bohn / his mark and seal

Witnesses present at the signing:

- Phillip Bohn / his mark and seal – in German characters
- William Reesen / his mark and seal

Berks County. Be it remembered that on the ninth day of May Anno Domino 1774 before me William Reesen, Esquire, one of his Majesty's of the Peace of the County of Berks came the within named Adam Boon and Christina his wife and acknowledged the within written indenture to be their act and deed and devised the same might be recorded as such according to law, she the said Christina being of full age secretly and apart examined and the contents thereof first made known to her voluntarily consenting. Witness my hand and seal the day and year above said William Reesen recorded unto this record and the original diligently compared and found to agree exactly word for word and figure for figure the second day of June Anno Domino 1774.[19]

A year after Adam and Christina sold the bulk of their farm to their youngest son William, the Revolutionary War broke out in Lexington and Concord, Massachusetts. The following year, in 1776, America declared its independence from Great Britain in nearby Philadelphia. In 1777, Adam's grandsons, John and Joseph, soldiers in America's Continental Army, spent the winter at Valley Forge, just forty miles from Adam and Christina's homestead. John and Joseph may have visited their grandparents during those months.

Two years later, in March 1779, Adam received word that Casper, his oldest son, had died at his home near Hedgesville in Berkeley County, Virginia (now West Virginia) at the age of fifty-nine. In 1781, when Adam was eighty-four years old, he learned that the American Continental Army, under the leadership of George Washington, had defeated the British forces at Yorktown, Virginia, winning America's independence.

It is unknown if Adam and Christina continued living with their son William and his family on the original homestead, or if they moved to live with one of their older children in Berks or Lancaster County. Based upon the dates of Adam's final estate settlement deed, it would seem he died in in late 1786 or early 1787 at the age of eighty-eight or eighty-nine. There is also a death recorded for an "Adam Bunner" in Lancaster County in 1784. If this death record was for Adam Böner (which is debatable because the cursive handwriting could also be interpreted as Adam Brunner or Adam Brenner), it is the first known instance where the family last name was spelled Bunner, which ultimately became the common spelling eighty years later after the American Civil War.

In June 1787, to complete final settlement of Adam's estate, the remaining 22 acres of the original homestead that he still owned

---

19  Berks County Pennsylvania Recorder of Deeds, Online Search, Index Books, Deed Grantor 01/01/1751 – 12/31/1926, "Boner, Adam", Book B1, Page 504

was bequeathed to his youngest daughter Maria Rosina (Böner) Follmer. The deed calls for Maria Rosina and her husband, Adam Follmer, to pay five shillings to each of Maria Rosina's four siblings in return for Maria Rosina's clear title to the land. The deed recording this transaction in the Berks County courthouse archives reads as follows:

### Adam Bohn – Final Estate Settlement Deed
### Grant of 22 Acres in Berks County, PA to youngest daughter Maria Rosina (Bohn) Follmer
(? Entries indicate the cursive words or letters in the original deed are uncertain)

This Indenture made the 8th day of June in the year of our Lord 1787 between Philip Bohn of the Township of Bern in the County of Berks in the State of Pennsylvania yeoman, eldest son and heir at law of Adam Bohn late of the same place yeoman deceased. William Bohn of the same place yeoman another of the sons of the said deceased, Frederick Bohn of the same place yeoman another of the sons of the said deceased, and Peter Diehm of the Borough of Reading in the said County cordwainer (?) and Hannah Martha his wife understands what that means (late Hannah Martha Bohn) one of the daughters of the said deceased of the one part, and Adam Follmer of the same place yeoman and Maria Rosina his wife (late Maria Rosina Bohn) another of the daughters of the said deceased of the other part. Whereas the honorable Thomas Penn and Richard Penn Esquires, Proprietaries of Pennsylvania by their patent or grant bearing the date of the 12th day of April Anno Domini 1760 for the considerations therein mentioned did grant and confirm unto the said **Adam Bohn (alias Boner)** amongst other lands therein mentioned a certain tract of land situate in the said Township of Bern by metes and bounds in the same patent particularly described containing seventy six acres and the usual allowance for roads and with the appurtenances. To hold the same to him, his heirs, and assigns forever under the yearly quit rent of one-half penny sterling per acre as in and by the said recited patent records in the Office for Recording of Deeds for the City and County of Philadelphia in Patent Book A, Volume 19, page 493, relation being thereunto had more at large appears. By force and virtue of which said recited Patent or of some other good conveyances or assurances in the law duly had and executed the said Adam Bohn became in his life the lawfully seised (?) in his demesne (?) as of fee of and in the said tract of seventy six acres of land and allowance aforesaid with the appurtenances and being so thereof seised (?) did divide and lay out the same between his son the said William Bohn and his daughter the said Maria Rosina the wife of the said Adam Follmer by which division the tract, piece, or parcel of land hereinafter described and intended to be hereby granted was allotted as the part and share of his daughter the said Maria Rosina. But before any legal conveyance was executed by the said Adam Bohn for the part aforesaid, he the said Adam Bohn died so seised (?) thereof, int(?) estate leaving issue five children to wit, the said Philip, William, Frederick, Hannah Martha, and Maria Rosina all of whom except the said Maria Rosina were advanced by their said father in his lifetime. Now this Indenture witnesses that the said Philip Bohn, William Bohn, Frederick Bohn, and Peter Diehm and Hannah Martha his wife, in consideration of their said advancement and for the completion of the intentions of the said Adam Bohn in his life time and respect to the said Maria Rosina and for and in consideration of the sum of five shillings each to them in hand paid by the said Adam Follmer and Maria Rosina his wife at and before the ensealing and delivery hereof of the receipt whereof they do hereby severally acknowledge have and each and every of them hath granted, bargained, sold, and confirmed and by these presents due and each and every of them doth grant bargain, sell, release, and confirm unto the said Adam Follmer and Maria Rosina his wife and to their heirs and assigns all that tract, piece, or parcel of land (part of the tract of seventy six acres and allowance aforesaid).

Beginning at a marked black oak standing on the bank of Tulpehocken Creek, thence by other part of the said tract allotted to the said William Bohn, East twenty two perches to a post in a line of land of Frederick From, thence by the same northwest ninety three perches and a half to a post, thence by other part of the said tract allotted to the said William Bohn the three courses and distances next following. Viz, South fifty degrees west forty-two perches and a half to a post, North eighty degrees west fifteen perches and one quarter to a white oak, and south ten degrees west nineteen perches to a red cedar tree standing on the bank of the said creek, thence down the same on the several courses thereof fifty four perches to the place of beginning containing twenty two acres and one half of an acre. Together with all and singular the houses, outhouses, buildings, improvements, ways, woods, waters, water courses, right, liberties, privileges, hereditaments, and whatever thereunto belonging or in any wise appertaining and the reversions and remainders, rents, issues and profits thereof and also all the estate and estates shares, purparts (?) dividends, right, title, interest, property claim, and demand whatsoever of them the said Philip Bohn, William Bohn, Frederick Bohn, and Peter Diemer and Hannah Martha his wife, or either of them in law or equity or otherwise of, into, or out of the same. To have and to hold the said above mentioned and described piece or parcel of land containing twenty-two acres and a half. Hereditaments and premises hereby granted or mentioned or intended so to be with the appurtenances unto the said Adam Follmer and Maria Rosina his wife, their heirs, and assigns. To the only proper use and behoof of the said Maria Rosina for her heirs and assigns forever, subject to the dower (?) or funds of Christina the widow and relict (?) of the said Adam Bohn therein. And the said Philip Bohn for himself and his heirs, the said William Bohn for himself and his heirs, the said Frederick Bohn for himself and his heirs, and the said Peter Diehm for himself and the said Hannah Martha his wife and their heirs, do severally but not jointly covenant, promise, and grant to and with the said Adam Follmer and Maria Rosina his wife, their heirs, and assigns by the presence that the said Philip Bohn, William Bohn, Frederick Bonn, and Peter Diehm and Hannah Martha his wife, have not nor hath neither of them heretofore done, committed, or wittingly or willingly suffered to be done or committed any act, matter, or thing whatever whereby the premises hereby granted or any part thereof is, are or shall or may be impeached (?), changed, or encumbered in title, charge, estate, or otherwise howsoever. In witness whereof the said parties of these presents have hereunto interchangeably set their hands and seals dated the day and year first above written.

- William Bohn/ mark and seal
- Frederick Bohn/ mark and seal
- Philip Bohn/ mark and seal
- Peter Diehm/ mark and seal
- Hannah Martha Diehm/ mark and seal

Sealed and delivered in the presence of us:

- Collinson Reed
- George Eckert

Berks County the 8th day of June Anno Domini 1787 before me the subscriber one of the justices of the County Court of Common Pleas of the County of Berks came the above named. Philip Bohn, William Baum, Frederick Baum, Peter Diehm and Hannah Martha his wife, and severally acknowledged the above written Indenture to be their act and deed and desired the same might be recorded as such according to law. The said Hannah Martha Diehm being of full age secretly and apart from her said husband by me examined and the contents whereof first made known unto her declaring that she did voluntarily and of her own free will and accord, sign, seal and, as her act or deed, deliver the said Indenture without any compulsion of her said husband.

Witness my hand and seal the day and the year aforementioned.

- John Otto Seal

Recorded and this record and the original diligently compared and found to agree exactly word for word and figure for figure. June 25th Anno Domini 1787.[20]

Christina is not mentioned in this final document so it can be reasonably assumed that she died somewhere between 1774 when she signed the deed selling the property to her son William, and 1787 when this estate settlement deed granting the remaining land in the original homestead to her daughter Maria Rosina. Also in this final document, the family last name is consistently spelled "Bohn." The phrase "Adam Bohn (alias Boner)" along with the included original Land Patent Book number, volume, and page number, are the essential clues to link the transaction described in this document back to Adam Boner's original purchase of this land. It is unknown if Bohn or Boon (or Boone) became the new spelling of the family last name for Adam's five surviving children after his death. This could be easily discovered by anyone interested in the family history of these five children of Adam and Christina.

Adam's death ended the story of the first generation of the Böner/Bunner family in America. Adam was born into peasantry in Germany, and with grit, perseverance, determination, hard work, and a willingness to risk it all, he and his family immigrated to America. There he gained his freedom from the yoke of feudalism, acquired his own land, worked industriously to create a working farm, and ultimately got to enjoy, and profit from, the fruits of his

---

20  Berks County Pennsylvania Recorder of Deeds, Online Search, Index Books, Deed Grantor 01/01/1751 – 12/31/1926, "Boner, Adam", Book 10, Page 157

own labor. His version of the American dream came true for him and his family.

A quick history of Adam Böner's original homestead from the time of his death until today follows:

Adam's son William owned the property until he died in 1823 or 1824. In June 1825, the executor of William's estate (William's last name was spelled "Boone" in this deed) sold the larger part of the property situated on the banks of Tulpehocken Creek to the Union Canal Company of Pennsylvania. This section of Tulpehocken Creek was essential to complete construction of a canal connecting the Schuylkill River in Reading with the Susquehanna River in Middletown approximately eighty miles to the west. This canal was completed in 1828 and operated profitably until 1857 when the completion of the Lebanon Valley Railroad from Reading to Harrisburg started a slow, steady decline in revenues and profits. The Union Canal Company closed operations completely in 1881, no longer able to compete with railroads.

A restored portion of the canal along Tulpehocken Creek is maintained by the Berks County Parks System at the Union Canal Towpath Park in Wyomissing west of Reading. This portion contains one previously restored lock along a towpath now used as a recreational hiking trail.

**Hiking and biking trails along Tulpehocken Creek on land once owned by Adam Böner**
(photographs by Michael Bunner)

In the late 1970's, the U.S. Army Corps of Engineers purchased land along Tulpehocken Creek, including parcels originally purchased by Adam Böner in 1741. This was preparatory for the construction of a flood control dam three miles upstream. The dam, which was completed in 1979, created Blue Marsh Lake which has become a popular recreation area for boaters and fishermen. The Corps of Engineers has also developed hiking and biking trails along Tulpehocken Creek downstream of the lake, approximately two miles of which traverse the land once owned by Adam Böner. The Corps of Engineers has also set aside the Tulpehocken Creek in this area exclusively for fly fishing. It is now possible to drive to this property, park for free in a public lot, and walk down paths along Tulpehocken Creek just as Adam and Casper Bunner did nearly three hundred years ago.

**Tulpehocken Creek along land once owned by Adam Böner**
(photographs by Michael Bunner)

The original 51.5-acre farm site, located on a plateau along Palisades Drive above Tulpehocken Creek, has been subdivided multiple times over the past two hundred years, and now is a mosaic of small homesteads from one to five acres. Along Swiftwater Lane, which today marks what was once the western boundary of the Adam Böner homestead, are several large modern houses, each valued at more than $1 million. The area around the original homestead still has a rural feel and has many recreational opportunities within a short walk or drive.

# 4.

# Johan Wendell Brown (Braun)
## (Circa 1700 – 1769)

Johan Wendell Braun was born near Mannheim, Germany in the region known as Palatine sometime between 1696 and 1701 (this is the range of birth dates stated in multiple sources). Like all other Christians in the German culture, his first name, Johan (John), would have been the ceremonial first name given at the time of his baptism. Wendell, the name given at birth, would be the name used by his family and friends. His wife was named Margaretha and she and Wendell were likely married in 1722. They had several children including Thomas, Maunus, Catherine (or Catrina), Mary Christiana (who became the wife of Casper Böner in the late 1740's), and possibly Philip, and Susanna.

Wendell and his family immigrated to Pennsylvania on the ship 'Nancy and Friendship' on September 20, 1738. When it was time for Wendell to sign the ship list at the Port of Philadelphia, he affixed his mark, an indication that he could not read or write. The cursive signature – the first name on the left side of the mark, the last name on the right side - was recorded by the clerk tasked with completing this list.

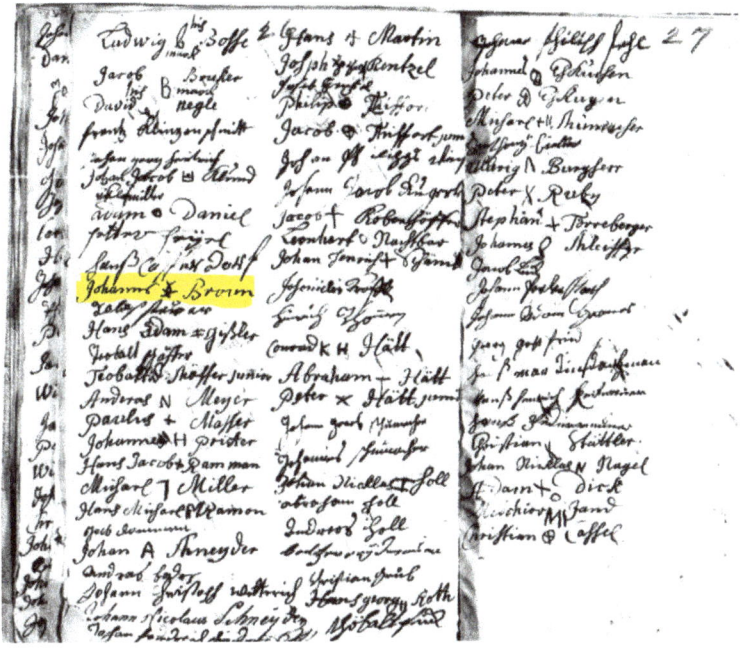

**Johann Wendell Braun mark with signature
written by clerk - September 1738**

It is unknown how Wendell paid for his family's voyage from Europe to America. He may have signed a contract with an American employer while still living in Germany for himself and his family to be indentured servants for four to five years. Or he may have saved enough before leaving Germany to pay for the trip. If he paid for the trip out of his own pocket, he would have still needed to rent up to thirty acres of land from an existing Pennsylvania landowner. This was the minimum amount of land necessary to build a log house and clear sufficient land for garden space the family would need to grow the food necessary to survive. Renting and improving land owned by others was a necessary step for most new Palatine immigrants until they could save enough money for a down payment and survey fee on their own land.

Upon arrival in Pennsylvania, Wendell and his family spent a few weeks in Germantown, an immigrant community several miles north of Philadelphia. This community was used by many Palatine immigrants as a stopping-off point while they finalized preparations for moving to their permanent location. The family moved to Lancaster County (now Berks County), Pennsylvania in late 1738 or early 1739. They most likely settled in either the Heidelberg or Tulpehocken township, near where Adam Boner and his family would buy land and build a homestead two years later.

Wendell's wife, Margaretha, took ill either during the voyage or during their time living in Germantown. She never recovered and died during the summer of 1739 while still in her thirties. Her death left Wendell a widower and several young children motherless in an environment where a wife and mother was a necessity for a family to survive.

Just weeks later on August 27, 1739, Wendell married Maria Elisabetha Knopf at the Christ Little Tulpehocken Church, near where he lived.[1] Over the next few years, it is believed Wendell and Elisabetha had at least two children – Adam and Margaretha.

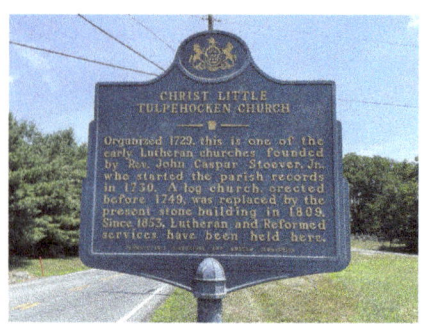 

**Christ Little Tulpehocken Church – near Bernville, Berks County, Pennsylvania. Wendell Brown married Elisabetha Knopf here in 1739 after the death of his first wife** (Photographs by Michael Bunner)

Wendell began using the last name "Brown," the anglicized version of the German "Braun," within a few years after settling in Pennsylvania. In virtually all instances where his name is recorded

---

1 "Berks County Pennsylvania Marriages 1730-1800, Volume I", HP Publishing, pp. 2-3

in history books it is given as Wendell Brown. However, there are a few instances where the name John Brown is used.

A man named John Brown received a warrant to purchase a 250-acre parcel of land in Lancaster County on July 22, 1743. This was five years after John Wendell Brown's arrival in Pennsylvania, the likely amount of time necessary to either fulfill an indentured servant contract or, if he rented land, to save enough money to make the necessary down payment and pay the survey fee on the land.

Combing the Palatine immigration records from 1725 through 1750 revealed that four men with the name Johan Braun (John Brown) immigrated during this 25-year period. John Wendell Brown immigrated in 1738, followed by John Adam Brown in 1744, John Burkhart Brown in 1748, and John Peter Brown in 1750.

John Brown is also a common English name, and since there were several Scotch – Irish immigrants who had settled in southern and western Lancaster County by 1743, it is possible that one of them could have been named John Brown.

Through the process of elimination, only John Wendell Brown or an English/Scotch-Irish John Brown could have received this land warrant. If John Wendell Brown was the recipient of this land warrant, it would have given him the right to begin the work necessary to clear the land, build a log house, and establish gardens. His older sons, Thomas and Maunus, would have assisted him in these heavy labor efforts.

If this warrant was granted to another John Brown, it would mean that Wendell would have found it necessary to rent a parcel of land from an existing landowner that would be of sufficient acreage to sustain his family. If he had to rent, he would have likely still found it necessary to clear the land, build a log house, and clear garden spaces.

For unknown reasons, Wendell was not satisfied with his life in Pennsylvania. By 1745, it appears he was giving serious thought to moving his family to the Virginia frontier. Perhaps he encountered legal, financial, or logistical problems with clearing his land – regardless of whether he purchased or rented - that were too big for him to overcome. Perhaps the low land prices and annual quit rents (taxes) being advertised by the colony of Virginia for desirable frontier land along the Shenandoah and Potomac rivers proved too enticing. [The price to purchase land from the Pennsylvania Land Office in 1745 was £15 per 100 acres. The price to purchase frontier land from the Virginia Land Office in 1745 was only £0.5 per 100 acres, or 3% of what Pennsylvania was charging.] Perhaps Pennsylvania held a sad memory due to the death of his first wife that he felt the need to escape. Perhaps he had an unquenchable desire for adventure and new experiences that caused him to pull up stakes and move on. Whatever the reason, the siren call of the Virginia frontier grew stronger for Wendell during 1745 and 1746.

Wendell Brown and Adam Böner had similar life stories. Both were born and raised into adulthood in the Mannheim area along the Rhine River in Palatine. They were roughly the same age, and both were married circa 1720. Both decided to emigrate from Palatine to Pennsylvania in the late 1730's. Both settled in Lancaster County (now Berks County), Pennsylvania just a few miles from each other. They may have known each other all their lives, or perhaps their paths never crossed until they had each settled in what is now Berks County, Pennsylvania.

What is known is that Wendell Brown and Adam Böner lived near each other during the 1739 – 1745 period. There is one confirmed data point that widower Wendell Brown married Elisabetha Knopf at Christ Little Tulpehocken Church near Tulpehocken Creek on August 27, 1739. The assumption is Wendell was married in this church because he lived near it.

The second confirmed data point is that Adam Böner received warrants for two parcels of land totaling 127 acres along Tulpehocken Creek on May 12, 1741. Adam's land was approximately seven miles downstream of the Christ Little Tulpehocken Church.

The third confirmed data point is that Adam Böner's oldest son, Casper, married Wendell's daughter Mary Christiana sometime between 1746 and 1749. These three data points can be triangulated to reach a conclusion, based on the circumstantial evidence that Casper and Mary met and began courting in 1745 or 1746. In 1746, Casper would have been twenty-six, and Mary would have been eighteen.

Sixteen-year-old Casper had remained in Palatine after his father and the rest of his family had immigrated to Pennsylvania in 1736.

## JOHAN WENDELL BROWN (BRAUN)

He immigrated to Pennsylvania four years later, in 1740, at the age of twenty. It appears he joined his parents after his arrival at the Port of Philadelphia. Five months after his arrival, his father Adam received warrants for 127 acres of land on Tulpehocken Creek. It is likely that Casper assisted his father and his younger brothers to clear this land, build a log house, and establish significant garden areas over the next few years.

As Mary Braun would have been only twelve years old when twenty-year-old Casper first arrived in Pennsylvania, it is doubtful that, even if their paths crossed, they would have paid attention to each other. However, it is reasonable to believe that would have changed over the next four years as Mary grew into womanhood. The way young men and women of marriageable age met in colonial America was at community social events such as weddings, house raisings, church services, and holiday celebrations. By living relatively close to each other, there would have been ample opportunity for Casper and Mary to meet during one of these events. Probably by the time Mary was sixteen and Casper was twenty-four, a connection developed between the two that ultimately led to marriage a few years later.

By late 1746 or early 1747, Wendell had made the decision to leave Pennsylvania, and the family moved to Augusta County, Virginia. They were accompanied by son-in-law Michael Catt, Jr., who had emigrated from Palatine in 1738 at the age of seventeen and who had subsequently married Wendell's daughter Catherine. It seems likely that Wendell's daughter Mary, who had been courting Casper Böner while living in Pennsylvania, moved to Virginia with her family. It is uncertain whether Casper and Mary were married in Pennsylvania after which they accompanied Wendell and the rest of the family on the move, if Casper accompanied the Browns on their move to Virginia to continue his courtship of Mary, or if Casper remained in Pennsylvania for 1-2 years after the Browns moved to Virginia and then followed them to Virginia. The most likely scenario was that Casper and Mary were married in 1746 and accompanied the extended family on their move from Pennsylvania to Virginia. Whatever the case, by 1749 it is certain that Casper Böner and Mary Brown were married and living in Augusta County,

Virginia alongside the Wendell Brown and Michael Catt families. In 1750, their first child, John Amos Böner was born there.

When Wendell moved his family to Virginia, Augusta County was comprised of virtually all the mountainous areas of what is now western Virginia, the state of West Virginia, and the state of Kentucky. Virginia also considered what is now Pennsylvania west of the Allegheny Mountains (present-day Pittsburgh region) as part of Augusta County. The Augusta County seat was Staunton, Virginia, which was not easily accessible to the new residents of this mammoth county but was the only town of sufficient size in the vast Virginia frontier to support a courthouse.

In 1738 when the counties of Augusta and Frederick were established by the Virginia Assembly, the dividing line between the two was designated as running from the headwaters of the Hedgeman River (northernmost branch of the Rappahannock River) to the headwaters of the North Branch of the Potomac River. This was regarded at that time as the southern boundary of the Fairfax Estate, a massive 5.2-million-acre parcel of land that had been granted by King Charles II to political allies in 1649. All of Frederick County, Virginia was within the Fairfax Estate, and Augusta County, lying to the south, was (supposedly) outside of Fairfax lands.

The group of political allies who were awarded this land grant which ultimately became known as the Fairfax Estate had helped King Charles II regain the British throne after his father, King Charles I, was overthrown and executed at the beginning of the English Civil War. Through marriage and other maneuvers, this vast territory was eventually consolidated under the control of Thomas Culpeper, the Fifth Lord Fairfax. His son, Thomas, the Sixth Lord Fairfax, inherited the land as sole owner in 1719.

Lord Fairfax moved to Winchester, Virginia to manage his lands in 1732. His first order of business was to settle a dispute with the Virginia Assembly regarding the location of the southern boundary of his lands. He returned to London, where he filed a lawsuit against the colony of Virginia for selling lands on the Virginia frontier that belonged to him. He ultimately received a favorable verdict from the Privy Council which significantly expanded his Virginia land holdings and precisely defined the boundaries of his estate.

A final survey of the Fairfax land was completed in 1746. The northern border of the Fairfax Estate (also known as the "Northern Neck Proprietary") was established as the Potomac River, running all the way from its mouth at the Chesapeake Bay to the headwaters of the Northern Branch of the Potomac River where present-day Maryland and West Virginia join (near Thomas, West Virginia). The southern border commenced at the same point as the termination of the northern border, that being the headwaters of the North Branch of the Potomac. From there a straight line was drawn to the headwaters of the South Branch of Rappahannock River (also called the Rappidan River). This became known as the "Fairfax Line." From the headwaters of the Rappidan, the border ran along the northern bank of the Rappidan and the Rappahannock Rivers until reaching the Chesapeake Bay.

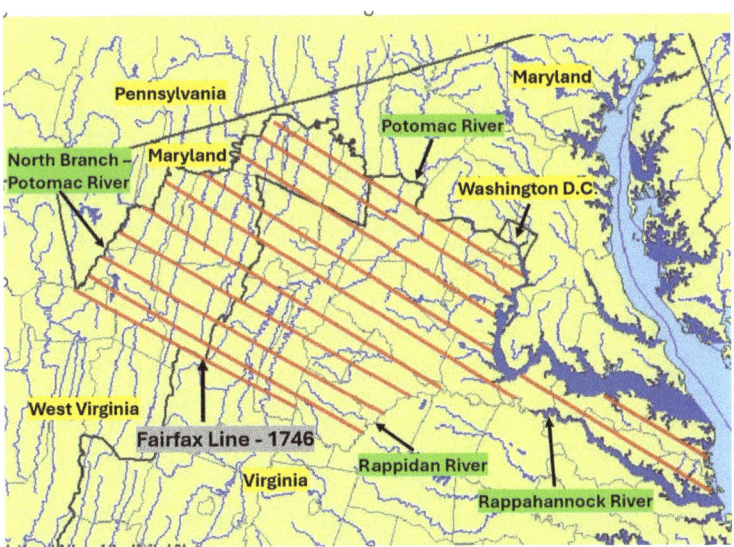

**Fairfax Estate (red stripes) – 1746 - Modern Political Boundaries shown**[2]

Although the Fairfax Line was established and agreed to by the Virginia General Assembly in 1746, it was not until 1753 that

---

2 "The Fairfax Grant", http://www.virginiaplaces.org/settleland/fairfaxgrant.html

Virginia changed the boundary of Augusta County to coincide with the Fairfax Line. These geopolitical changes, and the slowness of the Virginia Assembly to implement them, created much concern and confusion among the wave of settlers moving to the Virginia frontier at that time. It ultimately caused the land settlement and acquisition plans of Wendell Brown, Michael Catt, and Casper Böner, to be quashed.

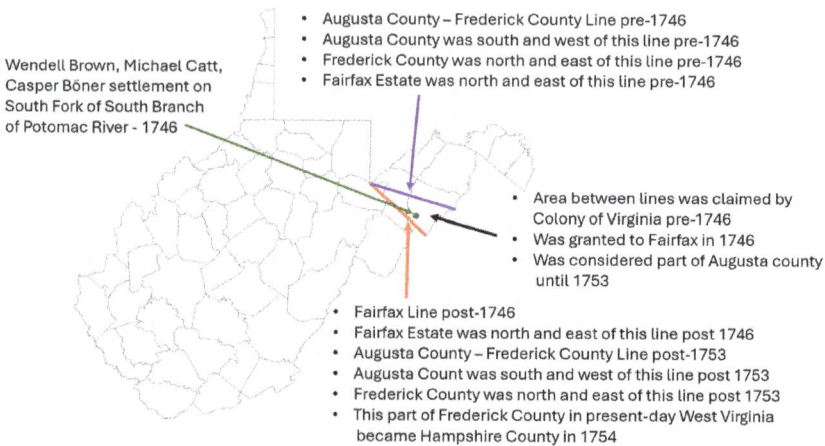

**Fairfax Line shifted southward in 1746, Augusta County boundary shifted to align with Fairfax Line in 1753. Wendell Brown was caught in the 1746 land shift from Virginia to Fairfax**

Settlers in Frederick County had to deal with Lord Fairfax and his agents if they were interested in purchasing any of the land in the county. The Virginia Land Office had no jurisdiction in Frederick County. On the other hand, settlers in Augusta County had to deal with the Virginia Land Office to purchase new land (or so it was thought prior to the extensive surveys done by Lord Fairfax in 1746).

While Fairfax did sell a lot of his land, his long-term intent was to create a feudal system in Virginia much like the one that had existed for several centuries in Europe. Under this system, Fairfax would be the landlord, and he would rent parcels of his land to a lower working class of peasants. These peasants would purchase the right to live on the land and cultivate it, as well as the ability to pass on this right as an inheritance. In addition to collecting rent from his tenants, Fairfax would also charge them an annual quit rent (property tax). This arrangement would allow him to permanently maintain ownership of all the land in his feudal estate while simultaneously extracting lucrative rents and taxes from his under-class tenants.

Before Fairfax could realize his dream of a feudal empire he had to settle many issues with the colony of Virginia. Much of the land sold or granted by the Virginia Land Office prior to 1745 had been land that British courts had ruled belonged to Fairfax. Fairfax filed many lawsuits against Virginia for these unlawful sales of his land. Those lawsuits remained unsettled for nearly fifty years, and were resolved only after America won the Revolutionary War and the newly independent Virginia government no longer recognized the validity of the original royal Fairfax grant made in 1649.

Those who had purchased land or received land grants from Virginia in areas later determined to have been legally owned by Fairfax now possessed deeds that were in limbo, with no legal clarification as to who legally owned the land. Did they own it, or did it belong to Fairfax? If those who thought they owned the land sold it, would the buyers have a clear title, or would they have purchased only a legal document of questionable validity? These confusing complexities about landownership along the Virginia frontier began emerging in 1746, about the same time that Wendell Brown and his family moved from Pennsylvania to Augusta County.

The word was out from other recent immigrants to avoid Frederick County as this was where most of these legal land ownership messes had arisen. Compared to Frederick County, Augusta County was thought to be a much lower risk county in which to settle to avoid land ownership entanglements. The prevailing thought among new settlers at that time was that Lord Fairfax would not be contesting land ownership in Augusta County because his estate in this part of Virginia was confined to Frederick County.

In 1746, just a few months before Wendell Brown and his extended family settled in Augusta County, new surveys had established that the southern border of the Fairfax estate now extended 15-20 miles south of the Frederick-Augusta County line that had previously been established in 1738. The Fairfax Estate suddenly expanded by this distance into Augusta County, formerly believed to contain no Fairfax lands. This new reality was neither well publicized nor communicated to those settlers who had moved into the South Branch of the Potomac River valley. Most of these settlers believed they had settled on land owned by the colony of Virginia. They would not learn they were living on land owned by Fairfax until the extensive surveys ordered by Fairfax were completed in the valley during 1748.

This turn of events ultimately derailed the strategy Wendell was following to obtain land ownership in Augusta County. He planned to go deep into the wilderness of western Virginia, one step beyond civilization, and find a desirable parcel of land on which to settle. There he would carve out a homestead for himself and his extended family, including the Michael Catt and the Casper Böner families.

His thinking was to take the time necessary to get his family and finances stabilized. When he had enough money to make the down payment and to pay the surveyors fee, he would apply for a land warrant from the Virginia Land Office, get the property surveyed, and follow the established legal procedure to gain ownership of the land. But he was not planning to approach the Virginia Land Office for a while. His strategy was to start the process of gaining ownership of this land by being a "squatter."

Few Palatine's who immigrated to America had wealth. Most had been peasants in Palatine and many of those had served for several years as indentured servants to pay for their immigration expenses. Though frontier land in America was inexpensive, it wasn't free, and ownership came with the ongoing obligation of paying annual quit rents to the colonial government. Though America was the new land of opportunity, those opportunities related to land ownership were noticeably unequal.

In colonial America, the sale and purchase of frontier land from the various state Land Offices was a rich man's game. Wealthy men used their money and political influence to purchase large tracts of desirable land along the frontier at nominal costs. Often these were awarded as land grants, deeded at no cost from the colony to the grantee with the stipulation that the grantee had to permanently move a specified number of families onto the land within a specified time. The new owners of these large parcels of land would then sell or rent smaller parcels to settlers to satisfy the terms and conditions of the land purchase or grant.

Using this process, the colonies achieved their objectives of moving the frontier westward while simultaneously creating a buffer between the Indians and the more genteel colonists who lived east of the mountains. However, this process also created a lot of unsettled land. The original owners of these large grants and purchases, having fulfilled their legal obligation of settling a minimum number of families on their land, maintained ownership of the rest of the land in the initial purchase or grant. Being men of wealth, they preferred civilized life over frontier life and most never relocated to the large frontier parcels they still owned. They were absentee landowners.

Absentee ownership gradually became a financial and a strategic problem for the colonies. They wanted annual quit rent payments from as many landowners as possible to pay for the ever-increasing demand for government-provided services, such as roads and bridges. They also wanted the land settled with as many people as possible to create an impenetrable barrier to prevent Indian attacks on settlements east of the mountains.

It also became a social problem, as poor immigrants, and there were many of them, needed land to eke out a subsistence living for their families. These poor immigrants believed it was unethical for absentee landowners to leave so much land idle when there was such a strong need for land ownership from those with minimal wealth. As one poor immigrant, who had been caught by government authorities "squatting" on state lands stated, "It is against the law of God and nature that so much land should be idle while so many Christians wanted it to labor on and to raise their bread." [3]

During the 1740's squatters in significant numbers pressed into the wilderness of western Virginia, always moving beyond the

---

3  Logan Correspondence with John Penn, Pennsylvania Historical Society Memoirs, p. 272

settlements of other immigrants. They had learned by watching others that land could often be acquired even if it was initially settled on without the formality of securing a title. Squatters had both a disregard of existing land laws, which they felt unjustly favored men of wealth, and a spirit of reckless adventure, knowing from the experiences of others that it was improbable, but not impossible, that they would be found out before they decided it was time to start the process of obtaining legal ownership.

The illegal "squatting" strategy utilized by Wendell and his family to lay claim to the land they settled on became legal and institutionalized over the next generation by those colonies which had a western frontier. By 1765, the Virginia Assembly began accepting a frontier land claiming process known as "tomahawk rights" or "settlement rights." This new land claiming process created more opportunities for settlers with little wealth by providing a more level playing field for those who sought land ownership along the frontier. It also eliminated the problem of absentee landowners. In addition, it eliminated the problem of squatting by effectively making it legal.

Although "tomahawk rights" by themselves were not legally binding, they were generally honored among frontiersmen. Tomahawk rights were exercised by hunters or explorers who would find a desirable property and mark it by deadening a few trees by girding them around the perimeter with a tomahawk. They could then claim that land at the Virginia Land Office several years later. The Virginia Land Office would then issue a "settlement certificate" to the person claiming the land.

This settlement certificate did not grant legal ownership to the land but served as an interim document until a patent granting legal ownership of the land was issued by the Virginian Land Office. As the Virginia Land Office did not start issuing patents to those holding settlement certificates until after 1779, these settlement certificates sufficed for legal documents and were bought and sold among those living on the frontier as if they were documents granting legal ownership.

A settlement certificate was obtained by tomahawking trees marking the property boundaries, building a cabin on the property (formerly called "squatting"), and raising a crop of corn. By doing this and then paying forty shillings per one hundred acres to the land office, those claiming the land were granted a settlement certificate (with the promise of eventual ownership) for 400 acres surrounding their cabin. In addition, these new settlers were given the "preemption right" to purchase another 1000 acres of land adjoining their 400-acre parcel within ten years after settling on their initial 400-acre parcel.

Wendell's strategy of "squatting" to eventually gain ownership of the land he settled on, though illegal in 1747, was a common practice among frontier settlers. This method of establishing a land claim became fully legalized as "tomahawk rights," or "settlement rights," by 1765.

Even though "squatting" was illegal in 1747, Wendell's strategy would have likely succeeded had he settled, as he believed, on land owned by the colony of Virginia. There was just one problem. The land he settled on was not owned by the colony of Virginia, but instead by Lord Fairfax. Wendell would not learn this until he and his extended family had invested a year of heavy physical labor to clear enough land and carve a homestead out of the wilderness.

Historical archives confirm that Wendell Brown, his son Thomas, and his son-in-law Michael Catt were living in Augusta County, Virginia in 1747. (The fact that all three were listed together in the county records provides strong circumstantial evidence that they were living on the same homestead). The Augusta County Clerk recorded in 1748 that these three were delinquent in paying their annual "tithable," which was a nominal capitation tax (or "head tax").[4] All "free men" sixteen years and older were classified as "tithables," and the head of each family unit was required to pay this annual tax. All slaves sixteen years and older, both men and women, also had to pay this annual tithable tax. Children under sixteen and white women were exempt.

Wendell was listed as delinquent in payment because he was double taxed in 1747 and apparently refused to pay until the error

---

4 Chalkley, Lyman (1980), "Chronicles of the Scotch-Irish Settlement in Virginia, Extracted from the Original Court Documents of Augusta County, 1745-1800", Genealogical Publishing Company, Inc., Volume 1, p. 413

had been resolved. Thomas Brown and Michael Catt were delinquent because they "had not been found."[5] To be delinquent on paying the 1748 tithable, these three men had to be living in Augusta County in 1747. Casper Böner was not listed as having a delinquent tithable in 1748. This would mean that he had either settled there and paid the tax by the due date, had settled there but was still unknown and unregistered by the county authorities, or had not yet settled in Augusta County.

Other historical documents confirm that Wendell and his extended family settled along the South Fork of the South Branch of the Potomac River approximately seven miles south of present Moorefield, West Virginia.[6] This was a beautiful valley that ranged from half a mile to two miles wide with the South Fork River flowing northward until it flowed into the South Branch of the Potomac River a few miles upstream. Steep mountain ridges covered with virgin forests rose on both sides of the valley.

At the time when Wendell Brown and his family first arrived in Augusta County, the total population of this massive county was estimated to be 4,000. Virtually all settlements in the county were along the South Branch of the Potomac River. A rough and barely passable wagon road leading into the settlements along the South Branch Valley had already been established.

By following a tributary of the South Branch River several miles upstream, Wendell and his family would create a homestead well outside the settled area and beyond the edge of civilization. This tributary became known as the South Fork of the South Branch of the Potomac River, or simply South Fork. Wendell and his family were likely the first family to clear, live on, and cultivate any of the fertile land in this valley. All early settlements in this region were to the north along the South Branch. To the south, east and west there was nothing but mountains, rivers, and forests.

---

5  Chalkley, Lyman (1980), "Chronicles of the Scotch-Irish Settlement in Virginia, Extracted from the Original Court Documents of Augusta County, 1745-1800", Genealogical Publishing Company, Inc., Volume 1, p. 413

6  Patton, Sara Stevens, Men and Manors in the South Branch Valley, Hardy County West Virginia Genealogy Page, https://www.wvgw.net/hardy/index.htm

Within a few months, however, civilization started encroaching on Wendell. Michael Stump settled on land approximately two miles downstream (to the north) of where Wendell and his family had settled. A year later, in April 1748, Stump would forever gain a footnote mention in history books by allowing the Fairfax survey crew, which included sixteen-year-old George Washington, to camp on his site for several days while they surveyed and laid out lots for a planned Fairfax manor along the South Fork.[7]

After the land boundary decision in his favor by a court in London, Fairfax wasted no time in laying out feudal-style manors near the South Branch. During 1747 and 1748 he opened four manors for settlement to renters he envisioned would become tenant peasants for life. He hired a survey team, which included young George Washington, to lay out lots for these manors.

Washington records in his journal that in late March 1748 he and his crew traveled over seventy miles up the South Branch to complete surveys and lay out lots for these Fairfax manors. He specifically mentioned doing surveys on the South Fork of the South Branch where Wendell Brown and his family had settled two years earlier. He records in his journal that on March 29, 1748, they surveyed five hundred acres and then traveled down the South Fork of the South Branch "to one Michael Stump's. On our way, we shot two wild turkies (sic)"[8]

This was Washington's first time living on the frontier, recording in his journal that, except for one night sleeping in a bed in a house, he and his crew slept in a tent with a campfire every night. This wilderness living experience would serve him well many times in the future.[9]

Within each of his four planned manors, Fairfax laid out tracts of land between 9 and 650 acres. Settlers on these tracts generally

---

[7] Washington, George (1997), "George Washington – Writings", Library Classics of the United States, Inc., New York, pp 13-14

[8] Washington, George (1997), "George Washington – Writings", Library Classics of the United States, Inc., New York, pp 13-15

[9] Washington, George (1997), "George Washington – Writings", Library Classics of the United States, Inc., New York, pp 14

signed a lease paying Fairfax an up-front fee for the right to live on and cultivate the land along with the obligation to pay an annual quit rent. Most of Fairfax's standard leases were written for the length of the lives of the leaseholder, his wife, and a son or daughter. However, this was negotiable, and some of these rental agreements covered as little as a single growing season. Long-term rental periods were rare across the South Branch Valley during this time. Rental periods of one or two years were the most common.[10]

Tenants of the Fairfax manors were required to build a house that measured at least 16 x 20 feet with a brick or stone chimney. They were also required to plant a fenced orchard of at least 100 fruit trees, and to maintain the fences around those trees. Crops they would have planted include wheat, rye, corn, flax, and, to a lesser extent, barley, oats, and tobacco. [11]

The first manor Fairfax developed was called the "Wappacomo" (Indian for "Great South Branch of the Potomac"). It consisted of approximately 55,000 acres and lay on both sides of the South Fork from its mouth to the southern end of "The Trough" (a steep seven-mile canyon through which the South Branch River flowed) near Old Fields.[12]

The second tract was "South Branch Manor," which extended from the southern tip of "The Trough" along the South Branch to the south and west, past the present locations of Moorefield and Petersburg, West Virginia to the Royal Glen Gorge.[13]

The third manor was located on 10,000 acres along Patterson Creek in a parallel valley and stream a few miles west of the South Branch. It was divided into thirty-one lots.[14]

---

10   McCleskey, Nathaniel Turk (1990), "Across the First Divide: Frontiers of settlement and culture in Augusta County, Virginia, 1738—1770", William and Mary Scholar Works, p.60

11   Morrison, Charles (1979) "Early Land Grants and Settlers Along Patterson Creek", West Virginia Archives and History, Volume 40, Number 2, pp. 164-99,

12   Patton, Sara Stevens, Men and Manors in the South Branch Valley, Hardy County West Virginia Genealogy Page, https://www.wvgw.net/hardy/index.htm

13   Patton, Sara Stevens, Men and Manors in the South Branch Valley, Hardy County West Virginia Genealogy Page, https://www.wvgw.net/hardy/index.htm

14   Patton, Sara Stevens, Men and Manors in the South Branch Valley, Hardy County West Virginia Genealogy Page, https://www.wvgw.net/hardy/index.htm

## JOHAN WENDELL BROWN (BRAUN)

The fourth manor lay on the South Fork of the South Branch of the Potomac River from its mouth near present Moorefield to a point approximately fourteen miles south, (to the new southern border of the Fairfax lands known as the Fairfax Line). The small unincorporated town of Brake, West Virginia is now located at what was once the southernmost point of the South Fork Manor. This South Fork Valley is where Wendell Brown and his family settled in late 1746 or early 1747 and were living at the time the Fairfax surveys were being performed in 1748. When completed, South Fork Manor would include twenty lots of approximately 400-600 acres each running up the fourteen-mile length of the valley that was on Fairfax land.[15]

Fairfax records reveal that in April 1748, his survey crew laid out these twenty lots in the South Fork Manor. George Washington was a part of that survey crew, and in notes that he allegedly wrote, it is recorded that what became known as Lots #10 and #11 were being lived on by Michael Catt, meaning Michael Catt and family were squatters on Fairfax land. As there is ample circumstantial evidence that Michael Catt, Wendell Brown, Wendell's adult son Thomas and their families were all living on the same land, this evidence confirms the location where they settled in late 1746 or early 1747.[16] It is unclear if Casper Böner had joined the family through marriage to Mary Brown before this time. However, there is a high likelihood that Casper and Mary were already married and were living with Mary's extended family at the time the Fairfax surveying crews were laying out lots for the South Fork Manor.

---

15  Patton, Sara Stevens, Men and Manors in the South Branch Valley, Hardy County West Virginia Genealogy Page, https://www.wvgw.net/hardy/index.htm

16  Patton, Sara Stevens, Men and Manors in the South Branch Valley, Hardy County West Virginia Genealogy Page, https://www.wvgw.net/hardy/index.htm

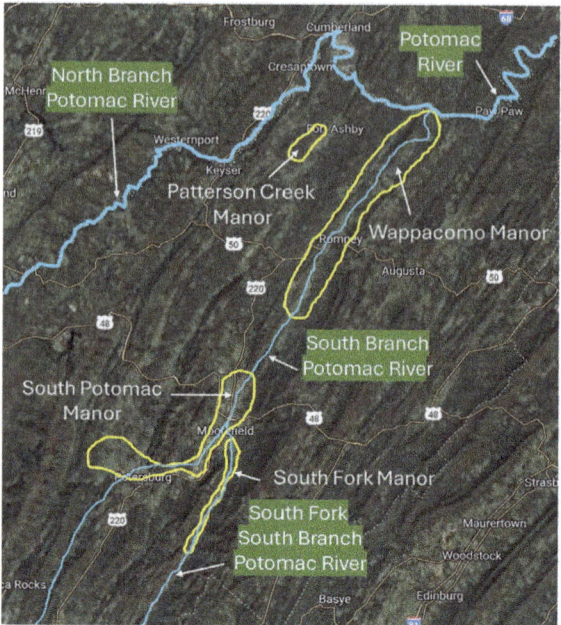

Approximate Original Sites of the four Fairfax Manors in Augusta and Frederick County, VA (circa 1747 – 1780)

Washington records another incident in his journal that, unbeknownst to him or anyone who has read it since, is almost certainly describing the antics of the entire Wendell Brown extended family after they learned they had settled on Fairfax land. Fairfax records and Washington's journal indicate that on Saturday, April 2, 1748, four lots were surveyed and laid out, including the lot where Michael Stump was living (Fairfax Lot # 12). These records also indicate that on this same day, Michael Catt and his family were found living on what is recorded in Fairfax records as Lots #10 and #11. [17] [18]

This would have been the first time that Wendell and his extended family, including Michael Catt and most likely Casper Böner,

---

17   Patton, Sara Stevens, Men and Manors in the South Branch Valley, Hardy County West Virginia Genealogy Page, https://www.wvgw.net/hardy/index.htm

18   Washington, George (1997), "George Washington – Writings", Library Classics of the United States, Inc., New York, pp 14

would have learned they had settled on Fairfax land, not, as they had thought, on land owned by the Colony of Virginia. This likely not only shocked and deflated them but also angered them. However, they probably did not show their emotions to Washington and the other surveyors on that Saturday when they were first made aware of this devastating news.

Sunday, April 3, was a day of rest, and Washington records that his survey crew did no work that day. On Monday, April 4, 1748, Washington records the following in his journal:

> "We did two Lots & was attended by a great Company of People Men Women & Children that attended us through the Woods as we went shewing there Antick tricks. I really think they seem to be as Ignorant a Set of People as the Indians. They would never speak English but when spoken to they speak all Dutch."[19]

The next day, Tuesday, April 5, 1748, Washington wrote:

> "We went out & did 4 Lots. We were attended by the same Company of People that we had the day before."[20]

As the Michael Stump family (where Washington and his crew were camping each night) and the extended Wendell Brown family were the only two families living along this fourteen mile stretch of South Fork at this time, and since the Wendell Brown family had learned just two days earlier that they were living on Fairfax land, the only conclusion that can be reached is that the "men, women, and children" following and taunting the survey crew from the safety of the woods were the members of the Wendell Brown extended family.

This extended family that harassed George Washington and the rest of the Fairfax surveying crew included: Wendell Brown and his wife Elisabetha; their sons Thomas, Maunus, and Adam; their

---

19 Washington, George (1997), "George Washington – Writings", Library Classics of the United States, Inc., New York, pp 14

20 Washington, George (1997), "George Washington – Writings", Library Classics of the United States, Inc., New York, pp 14

daughter Margaretha; Michael Catt and his wife Catherine; and most likely Casper Böner and his wife Mary.

Washington recorded they would not speak to him in English, but only in "Dutch." ("Dutch" is the anglicized version of "Deutsch," which means German). It appears that Wendell and his family believed that their collective two-year investment in hard labor to build a homestead was wasted, and they were venting their anger and frustration by taunting and yelling at George Washington and his survey crew in their native German language.

Though Fairfax had a great desire to be a feudal landlord, he was slowly becoming aware that many who were settling on his land were immigrants who had fled feudalism in Europe. He was also realizing these settlers were repulsed by his attempt to create a new feudal system with him as their "lord" and them as his "peasants." The newly emerging American "melting pot" culture was rejecting feudalism outright.

Fairfax had sold parcels of land on the east side of the Appalachian Mountains for a price of only 5 shillings per 100 acres. This compared favorably to 10 shillings per 100 acres for land purchased from the Virginia Land Office, or the £15 per 100 acres charged by the Pennsylvania Land Office. However, when Fairfax sold land through his agents, he was notorious for taking a long time – often several years – from the time the land survey was completed until he proffered a clear title to the land. During those interim years, he would charge a nominal rental fee for use of the land. In this way, he still operated, at least for a time, as a feudal lord.

However, Fairfax's dream of becoming a feudal lord had its greatest likelihood of success in the four manors that he was developing along the South Branch and South Fork Rivers. He was adamant about renting the farm lots his surveying crew was laying out. None of the land in these four manors was for sale.

There are no known records of what happened after Wendell Brown, Michael Catt, Casper Böner, and their families were found to be living on Fairfax land by George Washington and his survey crew. Archive records indicate Fairfax ultimately leased Lot #10 (462 acres) in the South Fork Manor to Abram Vanderpool, and

Lot #11 (432 acres) to Leonard Neff.[21] These were the lots where Wendell and his extended family had settled two years earlier and had cleared enough land to build 2-3 log houses and create enough garden space to feed the extended family.

Wendell's family had already grown crops on this land during 1747 and were likely preparing the gardens to plant seeds as soon as the risk of frost had passed when they suddenly learned they were living on Fairfax land. It is believed that, after the emotional turmoil of learning they had settled on Fairfax lands had subsided, Wendell and his extended family continued living in their houses and cultivating their gardens.

Fairfax records show his company successfully leased all twenty lots in the South Fork Manor, with Michael Stump leasing two of those lots.[22] However, the names of Brown, Catt, or Böner do not appear on any of these leases. An event that occurred seven years later (in 1756) seems to confirm that, after the Neffs had leased and settled on Lot #11 by early 1749, they subleased a portion of their 432 acres to Wendell Brown. By subleasing from the Neff's, Wendell and his family were able to continue living in their original houses and cultivating their original gardens. This is where Michael and Catherine Catt's son, Michael, was born in 1750.[23] It is where Casper and Mary Böner's first child, John Amos, was also born 1750.

It is known that Wendell and his family remained in the South Fork River Valley after the Fairfax surveys. A thorough check of the online, searchable archives of the Virginia Land Office (which includes sales of Fairfax lands) found no records of any land warrants issued to Wendell Brown, Michael Catt, or Casper Böner during the 1747-1760 period. Also, no records have been found in Fairfax archives to confirm that they rented land directly from Fairfax during this time. Eliminating these possibilities lends credence to the

---

21  Patton, Sara Stevens, Men and Manors in the South Branch Valley, Hardy County West Virginia Genealogy Page, https://www.wvgw.net/hardy/index.htm

22  Patton, Sara Stevens, Men and Manors in the South Branch Valley, Hardy County West Virginia Genealogy Page, https://www.wvgw.net/hardy/index.htm

23  Lough, Glenn D. "Now and Long Ago," Morgantown Printing and Binding Company, Morgantown, WV, 1969, p. 360

belief that Wendell subleased a part of his original homestead from the Neff's from 1749 until 1752, and again from 1754 until 1756.

As a result of this turn of events, Wendell joined the ranks of those settlers who moved to the South Branch Valley seeking land ownership but who failed in their efforts. Fully two thirds of all Augusta County's taxable white male inhabitants - who were initially drawn to the Augusta County frontier by a desire for land ownership - still did not own land after twenty-five years.[24]

Wendell and his family hunkered down in a survival mode for the next three years, during which Wendell likely provided for his family by farming, hunting and trapping. Being a trapper meant that Wendell would have periodically traveled to the trading post at Old Town, Maryland, seventy miles downstream to sell his fur. It is likely that during one of his trips to Old Town he learned of new possibilities that caused him to start developing his next plan to obtain land ownership.

In 1748, the King of England had provided a land grant of 200,000 acres to the Ohio Company for settlement and development of lands in western Virginia south of the Ohio River, West of the Allegheny Mountains, and north of the Kanawha River. This was a bold move on the part of the English Crown to fortify its claim of Ohio Valley lands after they had also been claimed by the French. In the competition between these two international powers for empire, little thought was given to the Indians, who had inhabited the Ohio Valley for hundreds of years and thus had a stronger claim than either of these two European powers.

The royal grant stipulated that the Ohio Company had to settle a minimum of two hundred families in the territory within seven years. The owners of the Ohio Company were several prominent Virginians, including Thomas Lee, Lawrence and Augustine Washington (half-brothers of George Washington), Robert Dinwiddie (Colonial Governor of Virginia), George Mercer, Nathaniel Chapman, and Christopher Gist (the frontiersman who surveyed the Ohio Company's land grant in 1750). The Ohio

---

24 McCleskey, Nathaniel Turk (1990), "Across the First Divide: Frontiers of settlement and culture in Augusta County, Virginia, 1738—1770", William and Mary Scholar Works, p.57

Company was required to construct a fort and provide troops to man the fort and protect the settlement at the company's expense. Also, perhaps of highest importance to prospective settlers, the land was to be rent and tax free for ten years. This was to facilitate rapid settlement.

During the 1748-1751 period, it is both likely and possible that Wendell learned a lot more about land ownership opportunities on the western side of the Allegheny Mountains from Thomas Cresap, the sales agent for the Ohio Company. Cresap had traveled throughout much of the Ohio River Valley as a trader. When he wasn't traveling, he lived in Old Town, Maryland, located directly across the Potomac River where the North Branch and the South Branch of the Potomac Rivers merged. He owned a trading post and would buy furs from hunters and trappers throughout the Pennsylvania, Maryland, and Virginia frontier regions. George Washington records several times in his journal that he stayed overnight with Thomas Cresap on his frequent travels to Wills Creek, Maryland (now Cumberland) and other points west.

Wendell would have periodically traveled to Old Town to sell furs, after which he would use the money to purchase supplies not available in the small settlements upstream on the South Branch. On at least one of those trips, it is probable that he met Thomas Cresap. Cresap's job was to recruit settlers for a new settlement to be laid out on the west side of the Allegheny Mountains on lands that drained into the Monongahela and Ohio Rivers.

Cresap would have listened to Wendell vent his anger toward Lord Fairfax and learned of Wendell's frustration over his failure to become a landowner. He would have recognized that Wendell was the ideal recruit for the new Ohio Company settlement. He was a hardworking, persevering, fearless, rugged frontiersman who harbored dreams of being a landowner. The only thing he lacked was capital, and the Ohio Company had solved that problem for cash-poor immigrants by offering them land they could live on rent and tax free for ten years. After ten years, they could purchase their land for a nominal cost.

As Cresap would be generously paid for each family he recruited for the Ohio Company, he would have worked diligently to entice

Wendell to move his family west of the Alleghenies. He would have told Wendell about how he and famed Indian scout Nemacolin had just completed improvements on an old Indian trail across the Allegheny Mountains to the Monongahela River, making it passable on horseback or by walking with packhorses. He would have explained how the Ohio Company was building a fort and would man that fort with troops to protect residents of the settlement. He would have talked about the rich, rolling farmland that existed on the western side of the mountains. And he would have reiterated many times that settlers could select their land and live there rent and tax free for a period of ten years before they would have to pay the Virginia Land Company two shillings per hundred acres to gain clear title to their land.

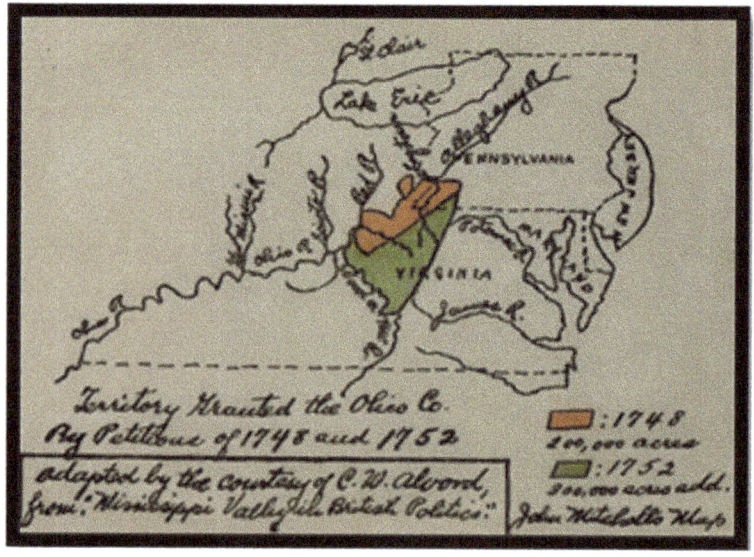

**Map of Ohio Company Land Grants,
1748 and 1752 – Library of Congress**
(public domain)

Cresap ultimately made the sale, and in early 1752, Wendell Brown made the move from the South Branch of the Potomac Valley to the rich farmland on the west side of the Alleghenies. The journey was one hundred sixty miles, of which the most difficult would have been on the Nemacolin Trail from Wills Creek, Maryland across the rugged Alleghenies to Laurel Ridge, the last high ridge of the Alleghenies (near present Uniontown, Pennsylvania).

History books say Wendell was accompanied by two sons, Maunus and Adam, and possibly by a third son Thomas.[25][26] Wendell would have been in his early fifties when he made this move west of the Appalachian Mountains. Thomas and Maunus were likely in their twenties, and Adam would have been a young teenager.

An unconfirmed copy of a petition to a Virginia regiment in 1758 states that Wendell was accompanied on this trip by his wife Elisabetha and all his children (except for two married daughters). A Bunner family history of unconfirmed legitimacy entitled *"The Reuben Bunner Revelation"* says Wendell Brown was accompanied by his wife and children as well as sons-in law Michael Catt and Casper Böner along with their wives and young children. Regardless of who may have accompanied him, Wendell Brown is in the history books as the first white European settler (some say "one of the first") west of the Appalachian Mountains (which include the Allegheny Mountains.)[27] The area he settled in was four miles west of present-day Uniontown, Pennsylvania.

James Veech, an early historian of the region, writes about the Wendell Brown settlement in his history book "The Monongahela of Old – Historical Sketches of South-western Pennsylvania to the Year 1800."

> "We believe the first actual white settlers within our present county limits were the Browns—Wendell Brown and his two sons, Maunus and Adam, if not a third one, Thomas. They came in 1751 or '52. Their first location was on Provance's bottom, a short distance below the mouth of little Jacob's creek. But soon

---

25  Veech, James (1892), "Monongahela of Old", Pittsburgh, P. 109

26  Ellis, Franklin, History of Fayette County, Pennsylvania, L.H. Everts and Co., 1882, p.54

27  Ellis, Franklin, History of Fayette County, Pennsylvania, L.H. Everts and Co., 1882, p.54

after, some Indians enticed them away from that choice alluvial reach, by promises to show them better land, and where they would enjoy greater security. They were led to the lands on which, in part, the descendants of Maunus now reside, and erected their cabin upon the tract now the home of his grandson, Emanuel Brown, really among the best in the county." [28]

Wendell Brown and those family members who accompanied him were the first recruits to arrive at the new Ohio Company settlement. They arrived before Ohio Company surveyor Christopher Gist had laid out the first settlement and before the promised fort had been built. A year later, in 1753, Gist arrived with eleven families who proceeded to clear the land and build their cabins near the Gist house. The settlement became known as the Gist Plantation. The settlement included a fortified storehouse for the Indian trade.

That settlement was located approximately four miles northeast of where Wendell Brown had established his homestead. Rather than give up his heavy labor investment in clearing the land, building a log house, and creating garden spaces, Wendell remained at his original settlement where he established good relations with the Delaware Indians living in the area. He likely learned enough of the Indian language to effectively communicate with them.

Unforeseen by Wendell Brown and the other early settlers living on the Gist Plantation, this region was about to erupt, in large part due to the existence of the Ohio Company settlement they were living on. The French saw the Ohio Company land grant as a direct affront to their claims of all lands in the Ohio Valley. Several Indian tribes were alarmed that white settlers, who previously had remained on the eastern side of the Appalachian Mountains, had now breached those mountains and were living in the Ohio Valley.

The conflict among England, France, and the various Indian tribes was rapidly escalating due to posturing and chest-thumping by all parties. In December 1753, Virginia Governor Dinwiddie of Virginia dispatched twenty-one-year-old George Washington to deliver an ultimatum to the leaders of the French military stationed

---

28  Veech, James (1892), "Monongahela of Old", Pittsburgh, P. 109

## JOHAN WENDELL BROWN (BRAUN)

at Fort Le Boeuf (near present day Erie, Pennsylvania). That ultimatum was for the French to stay out of this region, as England was the legitimate and rightful owner of the Ohio River Valley as well as all the lands west of the Appalachian Mountains.

Wendell Brown and his sons (and likely his extended family which included the Böners and the Catts) were living on this land in the fall of 1753 when Washington, accompanied by their neighbor Christopher Gist, passed nearby on their way to Fort Le Beouf. Washington delivered the ultimatum, which was subsequently ignored by the French.

Washington credited Gist with saving his life twice during this trip. In one instance, Gist prevented an Indian from killing Washington with his tomahawk. In the second instance, Gist pulled Washington from the freezing Allegheny River after he fell off their makeshift raft.

In 1754, Washington was again dispatched to this area to build a fort at the point where the Allegheny and Monongahela merged to form the Ohio River. They were also tasked with widening and improving Nemacolin Trail over the Allegheny Mountains. This was being done to move troops more quickly across the mountains if that became necessary.

During the early morning hours of May 28,1754, while Wendell and his family members were still sleeping in their beds just a few miles down the mountainside, the initial skirmish of the French and Indian War, known as the Battle of Jumonville Glen, took place. During that fifteen-minute battle, several French soldiers were killed, and all other French soldiers were captured by the small military force led by George Washington. That battle took place on top of Laurel Ridge, which overlooked the Wendell Brown homestead below.

A few days after this initial skirmish, when Washington's scouts learned that a significant French force had started pursuing Washington's much smaller forces, the scouts located the fifteen or so families living on the western side of the mountains and told them to flee for their lives. These families dropped everything, leaving buildings, livestock and crops behind. They quickly caught up with Washington's forces in what was called the Great Meadow, a natural clearing located approximately twelve miles east of where Wendell had established his homestead.

This is where uncertainty exists in the history of the Bunner family in America. According to the unconfirmed *"Reuben Bunner Revelation,"* Casper Böner and family, Michael Catt and family, as well as Wendell Brown and family had all been living on this new homestead they had carved out of the wilderness over the previous two years. When they were told to run for their lives, all three families would have fled. The only names recorded in history books to have fled are Wendell, Maunus, Adam, and (possibly) Thomas Brown. The history books also record that approximately fifteen families fled the area at the same time. It is possible that the Casper Böner and Michael Catt families could have been included in this number. It is even probable. Unfortunately, without independent corroborating evidence, there is no way to confirm, so this possibility remains open to debate.

Washington had hastily built a crude fort (which he named Fort Necessity) in this clearing to defend against the French and their Indian allies that were preparing to attack. It is unknown whether Wendell and his family members remained with Washington's forces until he surrendered at the Battle of Fort Necessity on July 4, 1754. It seems more likely that, for the safety of all the families, which would have included many small children and infants, forced to flee from their homes, Washington would have sent them ahead before the battle took place.

Washington would have sent them along the Nemacolin Trail to the British fort at Wills Creek, Maryland (present day Cumberland). Wills Creek was about fifty miles to the east of Fort Necessity over some of the more rugged terrain in the Allegheny Mountains.

Whatever the case, Wendell Brown and those family members who accompanied him would have arrived at Wills Creek in late June or early July 1754, and from there traveled back to their old homestead along the South Fork River that they had departed two years earlier.

After the French and their Indian allies defeated Washington at the Battle of Fort Necessity in July 1754 and were returning to Fort Duquesne (current Pittsburgh), French Commander Monsieur

Celeron is reported by French historians to have not only ordered the houses at the Gist Plantation to be burned down but also dispatched an officer "to burn the houses round about." This would have included all the buildings and newly planted crops on the Wendell Brown homestead.

**Historical Marker near Wendell Brown Homestead
(near present Uniontown, PA)**

Wendell, and all the family members who had accompanied him during his two years west of the mountains, returned to the South Fork of the South Branch of the Potomac River Valley. That the original homestead was still there and available after an absence of two years suggests that either the Neff's had found no new tenants to whom they could sublease this property, or that some of Wendell's extended family members had remained there while Wendell and his sons (and possibly his wife Elisabetha and daughter Margaretha) had crossed the mountains to carve out a new homestead.

Whatever the case, Wendell no doubt was bitterly disappointed and discouraged that he again had been thwarted in his efforts to become a landowner. However, he had no time to feel sorry for himself. To survive back on the old homestead, he continued farming, hunting, and trapping, just as he had done virtually every day since first arriving in America eighteen years earlier.

Within a year, the winds of war started blowing over the mountains and down the valleys of western Virginia. This war would soon become an existential threat not only to Wendell and family, but to all settlers in Virginia west of the Blue Ridge Mountains. The skirmish at Fort Necessity had caused a global escalation in the war between England and France known as the Seven Years War. It played out in America in what we call the French and Indian War.

In 1755, a large British force lead by General Braddock was marching to attack French Fort Duquesne (present-day Pittsburgh) when it was ambushed, routed and decisively defeated by French forces along with their Indian allies. This loss left British and colonial forces in disarray, and it took nearly two years for them to regroup and recover. In the meantime, many frontier settlements from New York to Georgia came under attack. The Virginia frontier was left at the mercy of marauding bands of hostile Indians bent on exacting revenge for the loss of their lands to the European settlers over the previous two decades.

During 1755 and 1756, the colonies of Pennsylvania, Maryland, and Virginia authorized the hasty construction of a series of forts at strategic locations where area residents could gain refuge in the event of Indian attacks. These efforts were only moderately successful, as frontier residents were so dispersed that it was not possible for many of them to get to a fort if an attack was imminent. As a result, many frontier settlers made the decision to abandon their homesteads and move back east, many of them moving beyond the Blue Ridge Mountains, which was proving to be beyond the reach of Indian attacks.

In 1755 and 1756, several small private stockade forts were established in the South Branch Valley, where settlers could seek refuge in the event of an attack. Also, several forts authorized by Virginia were rapidly constructed in the South Branch Valley. Fort Pleasant was built at Old Fields, along the South Branch on the southern end of "The Trough". Fort Bingamon was constructed near present day Petersburg, West Virginia. Fort Seybert was built along the South Fork in current Pendleton County, West Virginia. Fort Upper Tract was also built several miles south of Petersburg. Fort Edward was built on the Great Cacapon River near present-day Capon Bridge, West Virginia.

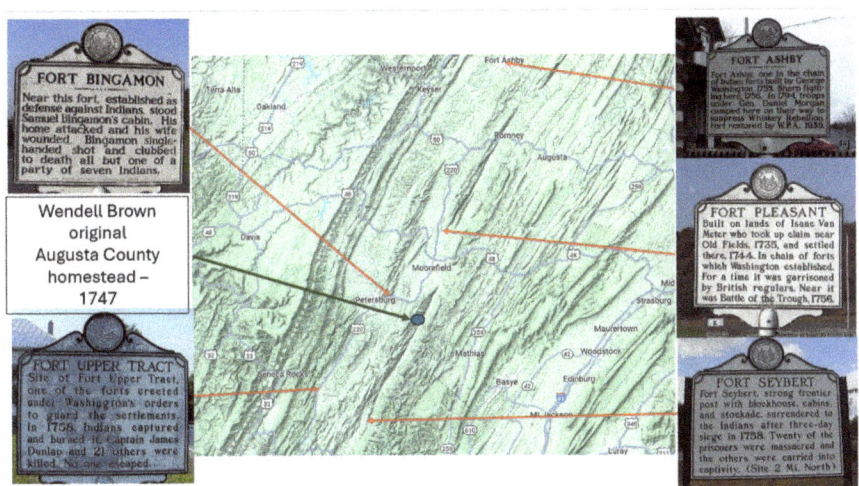

**Forts Constructed by Washington for Frontier Defense during French and Indian War**

For Wendell Brown, Michael Catt, Casper Böner, and their families, the first attacks in their neighborhood came in January 1756, when Fairfax's Patterson's Creek Manor "was entirely destroyed, the smoke of the ruined houses is so great as to hide the adjacent mountains and obscure the day." [29]

---

29 The Gentlemen's Magazine, London, January 1756

**Attack on Patterson Creek Manor – 1756. Painting by Vaningen Snyder**
(Alamy stock photo)

By March of 1756, Virginia had completed the construction of Fort Ashby on Patterson Creek (too late for the residents who lost everything two months earlier) and reorganized its military forces. George Washington was commissioned colonel of the Virginia Regiment and given the seemingly impossible task of halting the Indians victorious surges toward the east and eventually pushing them back across the mountains to the Ohio River.

This first round of Indian attacks in 1756 showed Virginia how unprepared it was to meet the challenges of war. On April 16, 1756, Indian forces under Delaware Chief Killbuck used trickery to get soldiers to leave Fort Pleasant (at Old Fields). They waited until the colonial soldiers were in a disadvantaged position near the canyon called "The Trough" and then ambushed them. The ensuing two-hour fight, known in history as the Battle of the Trough, resulted in seven dead and four wounded colonial soldiers. The victorious Indian forces suffered three dead and several wounded before riding on to their next attack.

**The Battle of the Trough. "Twenty Brave Men"
by Jackson Walker Library of Congress** (public domain)

Two days later, on April 18, 1756, Killbuck ambushed colonial forces under the command of Colonel John Mercer in what history calls the Battle of Fort Edward, or the Battle of Great Cacapon. It was fought near present-day Capon Bridge, West Virginia. Colonel Mercer and at least fifteen of his fifty soldiers were killed. Years later Killbuck declared that all but six of Mercer's soldiers were killed.

On April 20, 1756, just days after the decisive Indian victories at the Battle of the Trough and the Battle of Great Cacapon, a group of Delaware Indians from the Ohio Valley began travelling down the South Fork Valley. Their apparent intent was to capture residents for bounty, ransom, or to replace family members in their tribes who had been killed. They captured Mrs. John Brake at her home on the South Fork. She was pregnant and unable to travel, so she was killed very soon after her capture.[30] (The small town of Brake along the South Fork River is named for her.)

Later that morning, they captured Mrs. Leonard Neff outside of her home along the South Fork. She and her husband were living on the same lot in the Fairfax South Fork Manor that Wendell Brown and family had originally settled on. At about the same time, while Wendell Brown and his teenage daughter Margaretha were walking along the river near their South Fork home, they were surprised by this same group of Indians and taken captive. Had they resisted they would probably have been killed, so it is likely they surrendered peacefully. Perhaps Wendell had developed sufficient Delaware language skills during his two years living alongside them near the Monongahela River to negotiate their survival. Whatever the reason, their lives were spared and they were taken away toward French Fort Duquesne.

---

30   Steele, Ian K. (2013), "Setting All the Captives Free", McGill-Queens University Press, p. 451

# JOHAN WENDELL BROWN (BRAUN)

**Wendell and Margaretha Brown captured by Delaware Indians, April 20, 1756. (Artist – Greg Bunner)**

That Mrs. Neff, Wendell Brown, and his daughter Margaretha were captured on the same day, in the same vicinity, by the same group of Indians provides solid evidence that the Neff's and Browns were neighbors. It also provides strong circumstantial evidence that after the Fairfax surveys in 1748, Wendell Brown had subleased the property containing his original homestead from the Neff family. It also confirms that he returned to this same property after he was forced to leave his Ohio Company settlement on the west side of the Allegheny Mountains in 1754.

After Wendell and Margaretha were captured, they were likely accompanied for a time by fellow captive Mrs. Neff before she suddenly bolted and escaped into the forest thicket.[31]  Upon her arrival back home, she told Wendell and Margaretha's family what happened. That Wendell and Margaretha did not return home after a few days told the family that they did not escape. They had either been taken far away as prisoners, or they had been killed.

**South Fork of the South Branch of the Potomac River in present-day Hardy County, WV. Wendell Brown and daughter Margaretha were captured by Delaware Indians near this spot on April 20, 1756, during the French and Indian War** (photo by Michael Bunner)

The sudden disappearance of Wendell and Margaretha caused the rest of his family to seek refuge in the east almost immediately. The next historical record pinpointing the location of Casper and Mary Böner has them in Frederick, Maryland, east of the Blue Ridge Mountains, on May 10, 1758. This was for the christening of their infant daughter, Susanah Barbel Böner.

It is unknown where Wendell's wife and sons as well as his son-in-law Michael Catt and his family sought refuge, but it is likely the

---

31    Steele, Ian K. (2013), "Setting All the Captives Free", McGill-Queens University Press, p. 515

entire extended family fled as a group. If so, it is probable that they were also in the Frederick, Maryland area from mid-1756 through mid-1757. Casper, Mary and their children never returned to their original home site along the South Fork River.

In November 1756, seven months after Casper Böner and his young family had fled from their South Fork homestead, and eight months after taking command of the Virginia Regiment, George Washington wrote to Governor Dinwiddie:

> "In short, they [the inhabitants] are so affected with approaching ruin that the whole back country is in a general motion toward the other colonies; and I expect that scarce a family will inhabit Frederick, Hampshire or Augusta County in a little time."[32]

It cannot be determined how many frontier settlers in western Virginia fled to the east during the 1756 -1758 period of peak hostilities, but the number was significant. Settlers began to slowly return after the Easton Treaty of 1758, but sporadic Indian raids inhibited a full recovery of the population to its pre-war levels until after 1765.

After Wendell was captured, he was taken by the Indians to Fort Duquesne. A bounty was paid by the French to the Indians for his capture, and he was held prisoner for a time by the French at Fort Duquesne. Within a few months, he was transferred to French Fort Quebec, after which he was shipped directly to France (or possibly to England after payment of a ransom and a prisoner exchange between the English and the French). Wendell returned from England to America in September 1757 where he was eventually reunited with his family.[33]

His daughter Margaretha followed a different path after her capture. It was reported in proceedings of the Virginia House of Burgesses in 1758 that she was "said the be with the Oschachi in

---

32  George Washington Letter to Virginia Colonial Governor Robert Dinwiddie, November 9, 1756 https://founders.archives.gov/documents/Washington/02-04-02-0001-0001

33  Steele, Ian K. (2013), "Setting All the Captives Free", McGill-Queens University Press, p. 452

Prairie West." [34] It is unclear who the Oschachi were or where Prairie West was located. What seems to have happened is that she was taken by the Indians who captured her to their home west of the Ohio River. There she was probably adopted into their tribe and, based upon her age, likely became a young Indian wife. There is no record that she was ever in contact with any member of her original family for the rest of her life.

After Wendell's return to America and reunification with his family, it is doubtful that he returned to the old homestead as significant hostilities were still taking place along the South Branch and the South Fork Rivers. Because of his 18-month imprisonment, Wendell was destitute. Based upon a document that appears to be credible (but has not been confirmed as authentic) on an ancestry.com family tree that includes Wendell Brown, Wendell twice petitioned an unspecified Virginia Regiment for financial relief. This petition reads:

> "Petition of John Windell Brown, formerly an inhabitant on the River Monongahela. With his wife and five children he fled on the approach of the enemy in the engagement at Great Meadows between colonel Washington and the enemy. He lost all of his estate. He petitioned for relief, but it was refused at a former session. He settled his family on the South Branch. In April 1756, he and his eldest daughter (now a prisoner in Canada) were taken by the Indians to Fort Duquesne. He suffered cruelties from the Indians and was sent to Quebec from whence he was taken to England with other prisoners. He was lately returned and is incapable of procuring a livelihood. Rejected 21 September 1758."

By the end of 1758, the French had abandoned Fort Duquesne and were retreating toward Canada. The hostilities being perpetrated on the western frontier began subsiding and British and colonial forces destroyed Fort Duquesne and replaced it with Fort Pitt. Additional fortifications were built at Redstone Old Fort (present day Brownsville, Pennsylvania) on the Monongahela River. The

---

34 Steele, Ian K. (2013), "Setting All the Captives Free", McGill-Queens University Press, p. 452

Braddock Road, which followed the old Nemacolin Trail across the mountains, was further improved and supply lines were reestablished to points west of the Allegheny Mountains. Though the risk was high, some settlers followed the military across the mountains and began settling along the Monongahela River as early as 1759.

Sometime between 1760 and 1762, Wendell Brown, his wife, and his three sons returned to the Monongahela River area and settled on the land they had originally settled on in 1752. There was no more Ohio Company to protect their land claim, so they, like the hundreds of other settlers who had moved to this area since 1759, became squatters.

The Peace Treaty of 1763 ended the French and Indian War. The British king promised the Indians that no white settlements would be allowed west of a line defined as the Eastern Continental Divide in the Appalachian Mountains. In effect, all lands that drained into the Ohio and Mississippi Rivers would be reserved for the Indians, and all lands that drained to the Atlantic Ocean would be reserved for colonial settlement. This became known as the Proclamation of 1763.

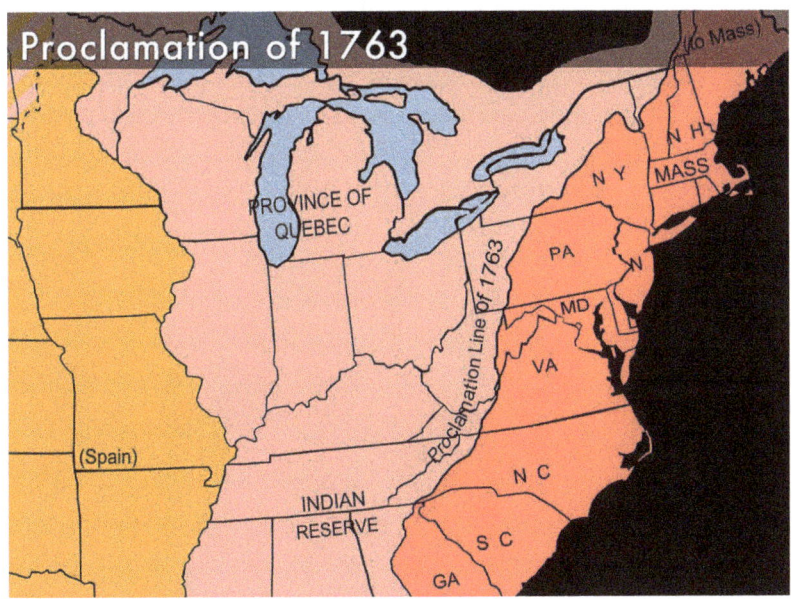

**Proclamation Act Line of 1763**

After making this Proclamation, the king ordered that all white settlers west of this line resettle to the east of this line. These renegade settlers, which included Wendell Brown and his family, ignored the king's edict. The king then sent a military detachment to give notice to the trespassers to leave the country, again to little effect. In the summer of 1767 soldiers from Fort Pitt were again sent out to expel the squatters, but as soon as the soldiers returned to Fort Pitt, the settlers returned from their hiding spots in the woods. The exasperated lieutenant governor of Pennsylvania got a law passed stating that any person not leaving the forbidden territory "shall suffer Death without benefit of clergy."

This act proved impossible to enforce. A commission was appointed by the governor to inform the settlers that they had to leave the country. Some of the settlers promised to leave but didn't. In the end, all efforts by the government to prevent settlement on Indian land failed.

In retrospect, the Proclamation of 1763 created many more problems than solutions. The British government had already assigned land grants to many colonial and British speculators that were now in the forbidden zone. This included the 500,000-acre grant to the Ohio Company prior to the French and Indian War.

Also, in what may have been the most impactful result due to the Proclamation of 1763, George Washington and many of the officers and soldiers who served in the French and Indian War may have felt their first tinge of animosity toward British rule. They had been granted lands west of the Proclamation line as payment for their wartime services. This Proclamation forbade them to settle on those lands.

As a result of near universal disagreement with the king over the Proclamation of 1763, he finally relented. The boundary line established by the Proclamation of 1763 was adjusted in 1768 with the Treaty of Fort Stanwix. Among other things, this treaty ceded Indian lands in Pennsylvania all the way from the northern branch of the Susquehanna River to the Forks of the Ohio at present day Pittsburgh to the British colonists. It also ceded all Indian lands south of the Ohio River to the colonists. Also in 1768, the Treaty of Hard Labor opened much of what is now Kentucky and West Virginia to colonial settlement.

## 1768 Boundary Line Treaty Map

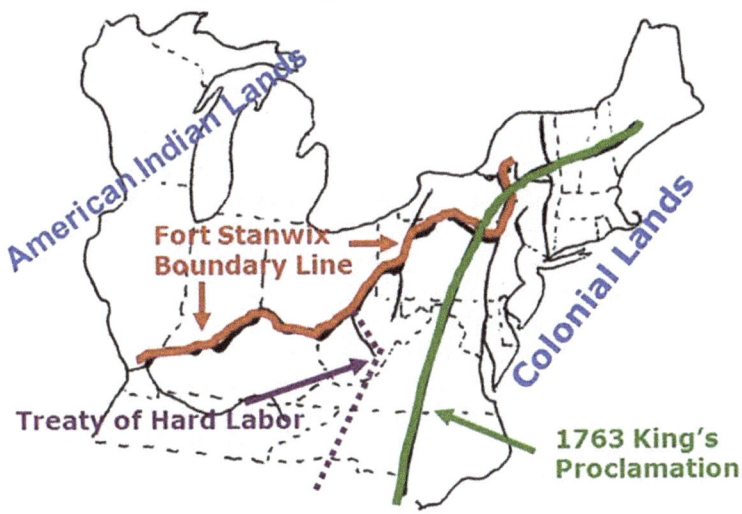

Treaty of Fort Stanwix and Treaty of Hard Labor in 1768 opened western Virginia, Kentucky, and western Pennsylvania for settlement

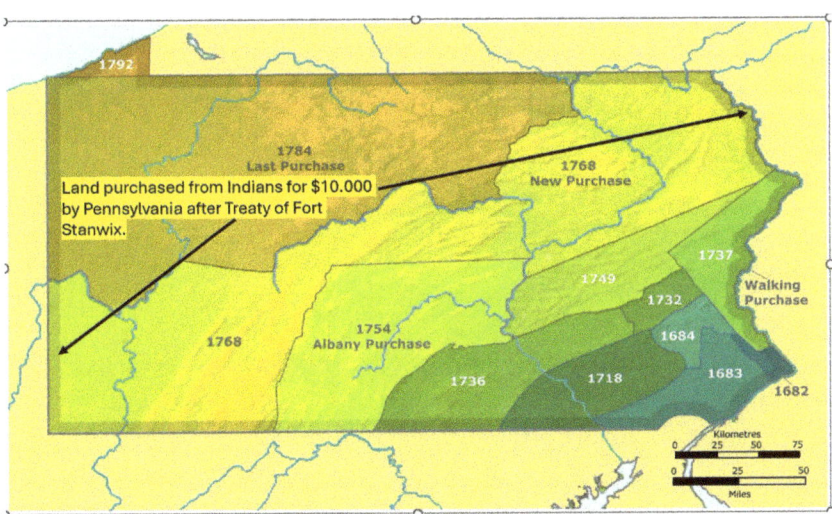

After the Fort Stanwix Treaty of 1768, Pennsylvania paid $10,000 for the ceded land

Virtually all who had illegally settled on land west of the 1763 Proclamation Line had made improvements such as erecting log houses and raising crops. The Land Office in Philadelphia received nearly 3,000 applications for land warrants before they made the land available for purchase in 1769. As it was impossible to process so many applications at one time, the Land Office decided to implement a lottery. These lottery drawings took place every one or two days from April 3 through September 5, 1769. In all, 3,853 New Purchase applications from squatters were recorded in the Land Office register.

Maunus and Adam Brown were among the squatters who submitted their names for this land lottery. There is no record of their oldest brother Thomas submitting his name. Thomas Brown, the son of Wendell Brown, was not the founder of Brownsville, Pennsylvania as many think. The Thomas Brown who founded Brownsville was from Queen Anne Parish, Prince George's County, Maryland. There is no record that Thomas Brown, the oldest son of Wendell, owned land at any time during his life.

Maunus Brown received his land warrant for 306 acres on June 14, 1769.[35] Adam Brown received his land warrant for 327 acres on June 14, 1769.[36] These two parcels adjoined and, according to Land Office records, were the same lands that Wendell, along with sons Maunus and Adam, had originally settled on in 1752.

There is no record of Wendell Brown ever becoming a landowner either in western Virginia or western Pennsylvania. However, for the last 5-10 years of his life he would have the satisfaction of living on the land where he and his sons had initially settled in 1752. He died in 1769 at the probable age of sixty-nine and was buried on the farm owned either by Maunus or Adam. It is possible that he lived to see Maunus and Adam become landowners in America. If so, it must have given him a deep sense of fulfillment to know that his

---

35   MacInnis, Sharon, Early Landowners of Pennsylvania: Atlas of Township Warrantee Maps of Fayette County, PA, Third Edition, Page 131

36   MacInnis, Sharon, Early Landowners of Pennsylvania: Atlas of Township Warrantee Maps of Fayette County, PA, Third Edition, Page 131

lifelong dream of being a landowner in America was at last being fulfilled through his sons.

Wendell Brown was both a tragic and heroic figure who, unbeknownst to him, burst into American history as the first white settler west of the Appalachian Mountains. His lifelong persistence in overcoming seeming insurmountable obstacles, disappointment, and heartbreak is the substance of legends. He possessed determination, grit, perseverance, and the ability to perform heavy physical labor from sunup to sundown every day of his life. He also had the ability and the willingness to take large risks, and the ability to recover when things did not go as planned. He was the epitome of the rugged, independent, fearless frontiersman revered by many in the American culture today.

5.

# Casper Böner (Bunner)
## (1720 – 1779)

Casper Böner was born in 1720 near Mannheim, a city in southwest Germany along the Rhine River in the region known at that time as Palatine. His parents were Reuben Adam and Christiana Böner. At his baptism he was given the first name of Reuben, but in German tradition, this was his ceremonial Christian name and not the name he used. He was called Casper by his family and friends.

Casper grew up in feudal Palatine and would have been considered a peasant in Palatine society. He was the oldest of six children. His younger siblings were Philip, Frederick, Hannah Martha, Mariah Rosina and William.[1] All are believed to have been born in Palatine except possibly for William, the youngest child, who may have been born in Pennsylvania after the family immigrated to America.

His parents and younger siblings immigrated to Pennsylvania in 1736 on the ship Harle. It is unknown why sixteen-year-old Casper did not accompany his family on this voyage. As the oldest, perhaps he needed to stay behind to provide for aging members of his extended family that he would have lived with. It may have been financial in that Casper, as a sixteen-year-old male, would be required to pay the same fare as an adult male and that may have been more than the family could afford. It may have been that his

---

1 Berks County Pennsylvania Recorder of Deeds, Online Search, Index Books, Deed Grantor 01/01/1751 – 12/31/1926, "Boner, Adam", Book 10, Page 157

parents had entered contracts to serve as indentured servants for an employer in Pennsylvania to pay their immigration and initial settlement costs. Since Casper was already sixteen, he would have been required to enter a separate and independent indentured servant contract that could have separated him from his family for up to seven years upon arrival in America.

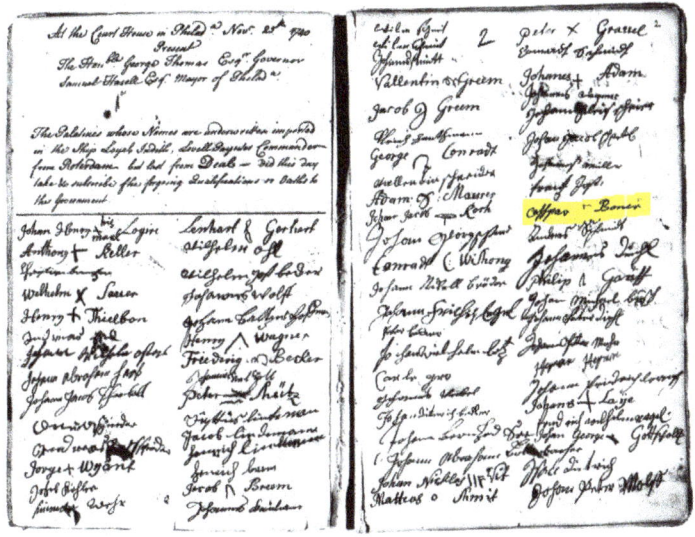

**Casper Böner's "mark" (recorded as Casspar 'Boner') on the ship Loyal Judith**

Whatever the reason, Casper remained in Palatine for an additional four years before he immigrated to Pennsylvania at the age of twenty. He arrived at the Port of Philadelphia on the ship Loyal Judith on November 25, 1740. He placed his "mark" on the signature page of the ships list, which indicated he could neither read nor write. The clerk who wrote his first name on the left side of his mark and his last name on the right side of his mark spelled his name Casspar Boner. The clerk recording his signature for the Oath of Allegiance to the King of England spelled his name Jasper Bonner.

It appears that either his father Adam paid his immigration expenses or Casper scraped together the money necessary to pay for his trip to America. There is no evidence that he worked as an indentured servant. Instead, he likely worked for his father after his arrival.

Just five months after Casper's arrival in Pennsylvania his father purchased 127 acres of land along the Tulpehocken Creek in Lancaster County, Pennsylvania (present-day Berks County). Between 1740 and 1746, it is believed that Casper, along with his father Adam and his younger brothers Philip and Frederick cleared approximately fifty acres of virgin forest to create productive farmland. They would have constructed a barn and other types of outbuildings necessary for an efficiently run and productive farm.

In addition to growing corn and wheat, staple crops for farms in this region, they would have grown the vegetables and fruits they needed for their own sustenance. In addition to cultivating their land, they raised cattle, sheep, pigs, chickens, and probably maintained 1-2 horses. The 75 acres of forest along the steep banks of Tulpehocken Creek were never cleared. They served not only as a source of firewood for cooking and heating, but also as a convenient hunting and fishing preserve to provide food for the family.

Sometime around 1745 or 1746, Casper met Christianna Maria Brown ("Mary"), who lived several miles upstream near Tulpehocken Creek. At that time Casper was twenty-six and Mary was eighteen. Mary was the daughter of Wendell Brown, who had immigrated to Pennsylvania with ten-year-old Mary and the rest of his family in 1738. Wendell and his family had previously lived in the same Palatine region of Germany as Adam and Casper Böner.

Mary's mother became very ill either during or just after the voyage to America and never recovered. She died during the summer of 1739 when Mary was eleven years old. Mary's father Wendell married Elisabetha Knopf on August 27, 1739, at the Christ Little Tulpehocken Church. This church was seven miles upstream from the site where Adam Böner, with help from Casper, would soon be carving his homestead out of the wilderness.

Nothing is known about the courtship and marriage of Casper Böner and Mary Brown. In fact, there are no known sources of any information for the period between 1740 and 1758 beyond the unconfirmed *"Reuben Bunner Revelation"* and oral family history about Casper and Mary. After 1758 significant documentation exists on the whereabouts of Casper, Mary, and their children.

Experience has taught that oral family history not only contains some kernels of truth, but also contains elements of myth, legend, exaggeration, and misidentification. Family tradition and oral history about Casper and Mary Böner during the 1746 - 1758 period that is supported by substantial circumstantial evidence includes:

- They were married sometime between 1746 and 1749.
- They lived alongside Mary's family in Augusta County, Virginia (present-day Hardy County, West Virginia) during the period 1749-1752.
- During 1752-1754, they lived either on the same Augusta County homestead where they lived from 1749 to 1752, or west of the Allegheny Mountains near present-day Uniontown, Pennsylvania. (If they lived alongside Mary's father on the west side of the mountains during 1752-1754, they fled back to their original Augusta County, Virginia with the outbreak of the French and Indian War in 1754).
- They lived alongside Mary's family on the original homestead in Augusta County, Virginia during the period 1754-1756.
- They had four children between 1750 and 1756: John (1750), Joseph (1752), Elizabeth (1754), and Margaret (1755).

Several legal documents generated later in their lives confirm that Casper Böner and Mary Brown were married. However, some questions remain. These include: When and where were they married? Were they married in Pennsylvania or on the frontier in western Virginia?

Regarding the Brown family move to Augusta County, Virginia, it has been confirmed they moved from Pennsylvania to the western Virginia frontier in late1746 or early 1747.[2] Were Casper and Mary

---

2 Chalkley, Lyman (1980), "Chronicles of the Scotch-Irish Settlement in Virginia, Extracted from the Original Court Documents of Augusta County, 1745-1800",

married prior to this and did they accompany the rest of the family to Virginia, or did they stay in Pennsylvania for up to two years before joining the Brown family? If Casper and Mary were not married before this move, it is assumed that Mary made the move to western Virginia with the rest of her family. Did Casper accompany the Brown family to Virginia, or did he wait for up to two years before following?

Extended families often moved as a unit during frontier settlement, as it generally took more than a husband and a wife to build a homestead out of the daunting and unforgiving wilderness. It has been confirmed that when the Brown family moved to the western Virginia frontier no later than early 1747, they were accompanied by Wendell's adult son Thomas as well as Wendell's son-in-law Michael Catt, who had married Wendell's oldest daughter Catherine (or Catrina).[3] There is strength in numbers, and a group the size of the extended Brown family had a better chance of survival and success living on the frontier than a smaller group. This is why the most likely scenario regarding Casper and Mary was that they were married in Pennsylvania in late 1756 and then accompanied the Browns and the Catts on their move to Virginia in late 1756 or early 1757.

Moving as an extended family was even more critical for the Brown family because their ability to speak English would have been very poor. When the Browns, Catts and Böners emigrated from Germany to Pennsylvania, they had all settled in what is now Berks County, where nearly every one of the first-generation residents had emigrated from Germany. They lived and worked in a German enclave and never had to acclimate to the English language or culture. As a result, the Wendell Brown family move to western Virginia would be more like moving to a foreign country than their move from Germany to Pennsylvania had been.

Regarding the children of Casper and Mary Böner born during the period 1749 – 1756, it has long been held that John Amos was

---

Genealogical Publishing Company, Inc., Volume 1, p. 413

3 Chalkley, Lyman (1980), "Chronicles of the Scotch-Irish Settlement in Virginia, Extracted from the Original Court Documents of Augusta County, 1745-1800", Genealogical Publishing Company, Inc., Volume 1, p. 413

their firstborn circa 1750. Legal documents recorded thirty years after his birth confirm John was their oldest son.[4] It is possible that he was born as early as 1748 or as late as 1751. The family holds as fact that he was born in Augusta County, Virgina. Since 1976, when excerpts of the unconfirmed document known as *"The Reuben Bunner Revelation"* were published by Glenn D. Lough for presentation to a Bunner family reunion in Fairmont, West Virginia, it became entrenched in Bunner family lore that the Casper Böner family settled on Tom's Creek in Augusta County, Virginia. It also became an entrenched "fact" that John Amos Böner was born in their Tom's Creek cabin in 1750.

However, this Tom's Creek narrative withers under the weight of research and needs to be excised from the Bunner family history. It is not true and is a simple result of mistaken identity.

In the *"Chronicles of the Scotch-Irish Settlement of Virginia Extracted from the Original Court Records of Augusta County 1745-1780,"* Volume 3, page 321, the editor Lyman Chalkley records that a Casper Bonier was living on Tom's Creek in Augusta County, Virginia in 1754:

"Page 61 – 10th February 1754. Same to James Lingell, 280 acres on Tom's Creek as above. Cor[ner] Casper Bonier, Draper's lines."

It appears that the person who wrote *"The Reuben Bunner Revelation"* concluded that the Casper Bonier mentioned in the Chalkley *"Chronicles"* was Casper Böner, the German immigrant who had married Christianna Mary Brown and who lived in Augusta County, Virginia during the second half of the 1750's.

However, additional research into this Casper Bonier who lived on Tom's Creek in Augusta County, Virginia revealed that Casper Bonier and Casper Böner were two different people. This can be easily discerned from the following:

---

4   Berkeley County Deed Book 12, 1795-1796, p.398, John Bunner to William Mercer, 50 acres,   https://lva-virginia.libguides.com/land-grants

- The settlement on Tom's Creek in Augusta County, Virginia was near where modern-day Blacksburg, Virginia is located.
- The settlement on Tom's Creek began with a large land grant (over 10,000 acres made by the Virginia Land Office) to Colonel James Patton during the period 1749-1751 with the stipulation that he must settle a minimum of ten families on this land within five years. [5]
- The Chalkley *"Chronicles"* document that Patton sold twelve parcels of this land totaling more than 6,000 acres between January 1 and June 30, 1754. One of those parcels was 507 acres sold to Casper Barrier on February 10, 1754. (The spelling of "Barrier" was changed to "Bonier" by a clerk who entered the name of the owner of this 507-acre parcel elsewhere in the *"Chronicles"*) [6]
- Casper Barger (the same person whose last name is spelled "Barrier" and "Bonier" in other Chalkley entries naming the owner of this 507-acre parcel) was severely wounded on his Tom's Creek property by warring Shawnee Indians on July 5, 1755. The warring party also killed three of the Tom's Creek settlers, including the proprietor Colonel James Patton. Casper Barger/Barrier/Bonier died from his wounds on July 31, 1755. This early French and Indian War conflict is known in history as "The Draper Meadow Massacre."[7]

Anyone who has engaged in family history research understands that multiple spellings of first and last names are commonly found in legal documents created during earlier times. Until the late 1800's, most people were illiterate and when their names were

---

[5] Virginia Colonial Land Office, James Patton-Grantee, Multiple Land Office Grants between 1749-1751,

[6] Chalkley, Lyman (1980), "Chronicles of the Scotch-Irish Settlement of Virginia Extracted from the Original Court Records of Augusta County 1745-1780," Genealogical Publishing Company, Inc., Volume 3, page 321,

[7] https://www.werelate.org/wiki/Person:Casper_Barger_%28%29

recorded in official documents the clerks making the entries did their best to spell the name as they heard it enunciated. In addition, the cursive style of handwriting used during earlier times is often difficult to decipher. The "n's" and "r's" are nearly indistinguishable, as are the "m's" and "u's." Also, the "s's" often look like "f's," and the "g's", "y's", and "j's" are often indistinguishable.

To compound the problem, there was no standardized protocol for the spelling of names or words, so multiple spellings of the same names and words was considered acceptable. Having the last name of Barger also spelled as Barrier and Bonier in other legal documents written just days or months apart was common during those times.

Extensive research of geographical and geological records, including old maps, dating back to 1730 has failed to locate any other streams in old Augusta County, Virginia that have ever been named "Tom's Creek." The only Tom's Creek that has ever existed was the stream (which still bears the same name today) that flows into the New River near present day Blacksburg, Virginia.

This historical linkage of Casper Bonier and Tom's Creek in Augusta County Virginia was fulfilled only by the Casper Bonier/Barrier/Barger who purchased 507 acres of land on Tom's Creek in 1754 and was massacred by Indians in 1755 at the beginning of the French and Indian War. As a result, it can be concluded with certainty that Casper Böner, one of the patriarchs of the Bunner family in America, was not Casper Bonier/Barrier/Barger who was massacred by Indians in 1755. It can also be concluded that Casper Böner, the patriarch, never lived alongside a stream called Tom's Creek.

Gale Bunner, in his 1988 compilation of *"Descendants of Casper (Boner) Bunner and Mary Christiana Brown – Revised Edition,"* made the following statement:

> "In 1754, we find a Casper Boner and his family living on Tom's Creek, Augusta County, Virginia. A survey for a neighbor, Jacob Lingell, is mentioned as cornering on Casper Boner's and Draper's lines. (See "Chalkley - Augusta County, Virginia Court Records," (three volumes, check indexes.) the county clerk in this instance wrote the name as "Casper Bonier.""

Gale Bunner made an honest mistake in assuming that the Casper Bonier in the Chalkley *"Chronicles"* was the same person as his ancestor Casper Böner. He changed the name listed in the *"Chronicles"* from Bonier to Boner on the assumption that the clerk who had written this name in the document simply misspelled Boner as Bonier. This made it fit well with Gale's narrative. It is possible that Gale had been led to this conclusion from what he had read in *"The Reuben Bunner Revelation,"* which makes the following claim:

> "Casper Bunner and his wife settled here on Tom's Creek at about the same time as did Wendell Brown and family, in 1749 or 1750, and at this time he was married to Wendell Brown's youngest daughter, Christina (Christiana). Father Bunner *[i.e., Reuben Bunner]* often said that his father *[i.e., Casper Bunner]* told that on Tom's Creek his first child *[i.e., John Amos Bunner]* was born." *[clarifying parentheses mine]*

As previously shown, this claim made in *"The Reuben Bunner Revelation"* is in error and is based upon a mistaken identity and erroneous understanding of the entry in the Chalkley *"Chronicles"*. It is provably incorrect and would never have been included in the accurate and legitimate history of the early Bunner family in America. The extent of this error casts significant doubt on the credibility of the rest of *"The Reuben Bunner Revelation."*

Research has confirmed that Mary Brown Böner's family did move to the Virginia frontier in Augusta County in late 1746 or early 1747. However, they did NOT settle on Toms Creek. Instead they settled on the South Fork of the South Branch of the Potomac River approximately seven miles south of present Moorefield, West Virginia.[8] Unbeknownst to Mary's father, Wendell, the land on which he and his family settled was part of the vast 5.2-million-acre Fairfax Estate.

In 1748, Lord Fairfax hired a surveying crew which included sixteen-year-old George Washington to lay out lots along the South Branch of the Potomac River and its tributary, the South Fork of the

---

8   Patton, Sara Stevens, Men and Manors in the South Branch Valley, Hardy County West Virginia Genealogy Page, https://www.wvgw.net/hardy/index.htm

South Branch River. Fairfax had the dream of using his vast estate to create a feudal manor along the Virginia frontier that mirrored the feudal system of land ownership that had been prevalent across much of Europe for several hundred years. Fairfax would maintain ownership of the land, and he would rent the land to a lower working class of tenants who would pay him rent and annual quit rents (property taxes) for the right to live on and cultivate the land. In effect, Fairfax would be the lord, and his tenants would be his peasants.

In April 1748, while the surveying crew was laying out what would eventually become Lots #10 and #11 in Fairfax's South Fork Manor, they recorded that they found the family of Michael Catt living on the land.[9] This would have not only included the Michael Catt family, but also Michael's father-in-law Wendell, Wendell's wife Elisabetha and their five or six unmarried children. It is unclear if Casper Böner had married Mary Brown and joined the family by April 1748, but there is a high likelihood that they were married and living on the same homestead alongside the Browns and the Catts at that time.

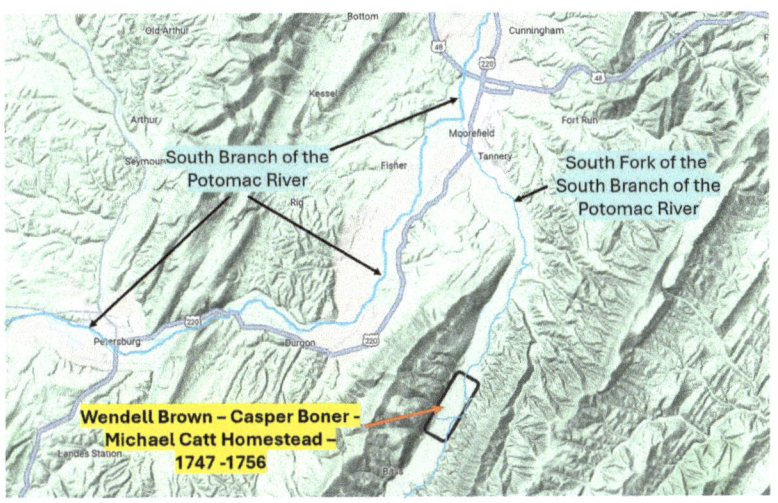

Casper and Mary Böner settled along the South Fork River – present day Hardy County, WV. Their first four children – John, Joseph, Elizabeth, and Margaret - were born here.

---

9  Patton, Sara Stevens, Men and Manors in the South Branch Valley, Hardy County West Virginia Genealogy Page, https://www.wvgw.net/hardy/index.htm

Mary's father Wendell believed he had settled on land owned by the colony of Virginia and had planned to go through the legal process of applying for a land warrant, getting the property surveyed, and obtaining legal ownership from Virginia as soon as he had built a homestead and got his finances stabilized. He was shocked and disheartened to learn he had settled on Fairfax land.

Within a year after the Fairfax surveys were completed, the land on which Wendell Brown and his extended family had settled was leased by Fairfax to the Leonard Neff family.[10] Rather than lose his significant sweat investment in creating his homestead, Wendell negotiated a sub-lease agreement with Leonard Neff, renting that portion of Neff's 432 acres which included his family's houses and gardens. It is likely that the Browns, the Catts, and the Böners each had their own cabin, located close together on the subleased property.

Casper engaged in farming, hunting, and trapping to support his family. Farming and hunting were necessary to provide the food for survival. During the winter and early spring, virtually all meals were meat only from the wild game that was caught. By June of each year, the gardens started yielding vegetables and fruits to supplement the heavy meat diet. By early December, the daily diet reverted to mostly meat until the next summer.

---

10  Patton, Sara Stevens, Men and Manors in the South Branch Valley, Hardy County West Virginia Genealogy Page, https://www.wvgw.net/hardy/index.htm

# CASPER BÖNER (BUNNER)

**1747 - 1756 site of Casper Böner/Wendell Brown/Michael Catt Homestead on South Fork River, Augusta County, Virginia (present-day Hardy County, West Virginia)**
(photograph by Michael Bunner)

Trapping would have been Casper's only means of earning cash. Wendell Brown, Michael Catt, and Casper likely operated as a team in their trapping efforts. They would catch and skin the animals and then hang the fur up for drying. Once they had collected enough fur, one of them would load a pack horse to make the seventy-mile trip down the South Branch Valley and across the Potomac River to Old Town, Maryland, where renowned frontiersman Thomas Cresap owned a trading post. There, the furs would be sold for cash. In most instances, that cash would immediately be spent to purchase necessities that the family could not provide for itself.

Such goods as salt, dishes, gunpowder and iron would be purchased at the trading post. Knives, forks, and spoons were purchased from a local blacksmith. All these purchased items were hauled the seventy miles back to the South Fork Valley via the same packhorse that carried the fur to market.

Items like soap and candles were not purchased but instead were made at home. The same with the clothing the family wore. Mary would have been skilled at using a spinning wheel and spent much of her time converting the fibers from the flax the family grew in their garden into linen cloth from which she made their clothes. Their shoes were made at home, mostly in the form of moccasins from tanned deer hide. Gardening tools such as hoes, rakes, mattocks, and shovels were also made at home from the flat iron sheets purchased at the trading post.

During at least one of these trips to the trading post in Old Town, Casper's father-in-law Wendell would have learned of a new settlement being planned one hundred miles west of Old Town on the far side of the Allegheny Mountain range. Thomas Cresap, owner of the Old Town trading post, had been hired by the Ohio Company to recruit families to move to the other side of the mountains where land was being offered for settlement with no downpayment, no rent, and no taxes for ten years.

This was being done to solidify English claims to the land in the Ohio River Valley. In 1748, the King of England had made a grant of 200,000 acres to the Ohio Company, a group of aristocratic Virginians which included colonial Virginia Governor Robert Dinwiddie and two of George Washington's half-brothers. The grant required the Ohio Company to settle at least two hundred families in the area west of the Allegheny Mountains, south of the Ohio River, and north of the Kanawha River within seven years. The "no cash outlay for ten years" offer was intended to expedite settlement.

Cresap was targeting Palatine German immigrants as Ohio Company recruits because most of them immigrated to America to escape the poverty of peasantry. Over half of them worked as indentured servants from four to seven years after arriving in America to repay their employer for their immigration expenses. Few ever had cash in their pockets for more than a few minutes, and even fewer had any form of savings. Yet all came to America with the dream of becoming a landowner.

In late 1751 or early 1752, Wendell Brown made the decision to move across the mountains and settle on Ohio Company lands. He probably embarked as soon as the snow had melted in the spring of 1752. This gave him time to complete the trip, select his land, and clear enough of it to build a cabin and plant a garden by mid- May when the threat of a late frost no longer existed. History books record that Wendell was the first white settler in America west of the Allegheny Mountains.[11] They also record that he was accompanied by his sons Maunus and Adam, and possibly also by his adult son Thomas.

Other family members may have also accompanied Wendell and his sons to establish a new homestead across the mountains. An unconfirmed petition Wendell made to a Virginia Regiment in 1757 seeking financial relief from loss of his Ohio Company estate due to the outbreak of the French and Indian War in 1754 claims he was also accompanied on this journey by his wife Elisabetha and five children (three of whom were sons Thomas, Maunus, and Adam).[12] In addition, the unconfirmed *"Reuben Bunner Revelation"* claims that Wendell was accompanied not only by his wife and five children, but also by the families of son-in-laws Michael Catt and Casper Böner.

Christopher Gist, hired as the surveyor and overseer of the first settlement to be made on Ohio Company lands, arrived on Ohio Company lands in early 1753 with eleven additional families that had been recruited by Thomas Cresap and the owners of the Ohio Company. They settled in an area that became known as the Gist Planation, which was a few miles northeast of where Wendell Brown had already established his new homestead.

There are no known historical records to corroborate Wendell Brown's unconfirmed 1757 petition to a Virginia Regiment, which states that Wendell's wife and daughters accompanied him to the Ohio Company lands. There are also no known historical records to corroborate the unconfirmed *"Reuben Bunner Revelation,"* which states that the families of Michael Catt and Casper Böner accompanied Wendell and his sons to their new homestead. It is possible these events occurred. It is even probable when considering that this

---

11  Veech, James (1892), "Monongahela of Old", Pittsburgh, P. 109

12  Ancestry.com, Virginia Colonial Soldiers Militia Petitions-Johann Wendel Brown

extended family had taken a similar daring risk just five years earlier when they moved from Pennsylvania into the Virginia wilderness.

Although the probabilities are high that Casper and Mary Böner made this move to Ohio Company lands with Wendell Brown, there are reasons to be skeptical. These reasons include:

- Casper and Mary would have had two-year-old John, and Mary was either several months pregnant with Joseph or had just given birth to Joseph when this trip was completed. This one hundred sixty-mile trek included crossing one hundred miles of rugged mountains, fording at least three major rivers, and then, upon arrival, having to live outdoors until land could be cleared and log houses could be built. At least from a twenty-first century perspective, the timing was not good for Casper, Mary, and their infant children to make such a journey.
- When Wendell and those who accompanied him to Ohio Company land had to flee their homesteads due to the rapid advancement of French forces from Fort Duquesne in June 1754, they returned to their original homestead on the South Fork of the South Branch River. That the house and grounds were immediately available suggests (but does not prove) that a part of Wendell's extended family may have remained behind, perhaps with intentions of joining Wendell and the rest of the family when the new homestead was suitable for small children. Casper and Mary could be the ones who continued living and working on the site of their original settlement in Augusta County, Virginia (which became Hampshire County, Virginia in 1754).

Whether Casper and Mary remained in Augusta County or moved with Wendell to a new homestead west of the Alleghenies during the period 1752-1754, the work Casper and Mary would have to do each day to survive would have been the same. Casper would have been heavily involved with clearing land, cutting firewood, farming, hunting, and trapping. Mary would have been heavily involved with taking care of her babies, raising vegetables, fruits, and flax in the gardens, cooking the meals, drawing water from springs or streams on the property, washing clothes, and making the necessities of clothing, shoes, soap, and candles for the family.

Also, regardless of whether the extended family or only Wendell and his sons were living on the new homestead west of the Alleghenies, the result in June 1754 was the same. Those individuals and families who had settled on Ohio Company lands had to flee their new homesteads with the advance of French troops from Fort Duquesne. They caught up with George Washington's small contingent at Fort Necessity, approximately twelve miles east of where Wendell had established his new settlement.

Since there were approximately fifteen families (three of which could have been the Browns, Böners and Catts) which fled to Fort Necessity, it is doubtful that Washington wanted them to be there when the larger French forces arrived. It is probable that, for their safety, he sent these families on to the British fort at Will's Creek (present-day Cumberland, Maryland). To get there, they would have followed the Nemacolin Trail east across fifty miles of rugged mountain terrain, a trip that would have taken five to six days on foot.

From Wills Creek, the fleeing families split up and returned to their old homes. For Wendell Brown and those family members who had accompanied him, that meant returning to the homestead they had been subleasing on the South Fork of the South Branch of the Potomac River.

On July 3-4, 1754, just a few days after the fleeing families would have departed the fort at Wills Creek, Washington's small army was defeated by the French forces and their Indian allies at the Battle of Fort Necessity. After surrendering, Washington and his soldiers retreated to Wills Creek while the victorious French burned the houses, barns, and gardens of the Ohio Company settlers. The estate Wendell Brown had been building was among those destroyed. The French and Indian War had begun.

By the middle of July 1754, Wendell Brown and his extended family were living together again in the South Fork Valley. They reverted to their survival routine of farming, hunting and trapping, oblivious to the war that was slowly percolating up all around them.

The following summer, British General Braddock's army was ambushed by French and Indian forces near the Monongahela River as they marched toward Fort Duquesne. Within hours, Braddock had been mortally wounded and his forces had been soundly defeated. George Washington, assuming command from the wounded Braddock, began a slow retreat back across the Allegheny Mountains.

This defeat reverberated through both the colonies and Great Britain, causing a lot of handwringing and the recognition that they were not adequately prepared for this war. This show of indecision and weakness emboldened the Indians, who saw an opportunity to gain revenge against Great Britain and the colonists for forcing them from their lands. It also gave many of them the confidence to engage in fierce warfare to regain some of these lands.

During the latter half of 1755, murderous guerrilla attacks by small groups of warring Indians shocked frontier settlers from New York down to the Carolinas and made them fear for their lives. The colonies of Pennsylvania, Maryland, and Virginia quickly authorized the construction of forts along the frontier to provide refuge for settlers who were under immediate threat of Indian attack.

Because the frontier settlers were so widely dispersed, with some living up to twenty miles from the nearest fort, this network of forts was unable to provide the envisioned protection for most settlers. As a result, many settlers made the decision to abandon their wilderness homesteads and retreat to the east of the Blue Ridge Mountains, which seemed to be beyond the reach of Indian attack.

In January 1756, the fragile peace that had existed along the South Branch and the South Fork River Valleys was shattered. Lord Fairfax's Patterson Creek Manor, approximately forty miles north of where Casper and Mary Böner lived on the South Fork, was attacked by Indians led by Delaware Chief Killbuck. Many residents were killed or wounded, and several more were taken captive. Over thirty homesteads were burned to the ground. Nothing was left standing in the settlement.

## CASPER BÖNER (BUNNER)

This incident caused many Hampshire and Augusta County residents to retreat down the Potomac River to safety. For many frontier refugees, the initial stop during their retreat was Frederick, Maryland, the first significant settlement close to the Potomac River on the east side of the Blue Ridge Mountains. Frederick served as a stopping off point for a number of refugees until they could arrange a return to the places they had lived prior to moving to the Virginia frontier. A few refugees stayed in Frederick until frontier hostilities started diminishing in 1758.

On April 16, 1756, Indian forces under Chief Killbuck defeated colonial forces stationed at Fort Pleasant at Old Fields (just north of present-day Moorefield, West Virginia) on the southern end of the seven-mile canyon on the South Branch River known as "The Trough." Two days later, Killbuck's forces ambushed a colonial regiment under the command of Colonel John Mercer at Fort Edward (near present Capon Bridge, West Virginia) in the Battle of Great Cacapon. Killbuck soundly defeated Mercer's forces, killing Mercer and at least fifteen of his soldiers.

Four days later, the war literally came to Casper and Mary Böner's backyard. On April 20, 1756, a group of Delaware Indians from the Muskingum Valley in Ohio began travelling down the South Fork Valley. Their apparent intent was to capture residents for bounty, ransom, or to replace family members in their tribes who had been killed. They captured Mrs. John Brake at her home on the South Fork just a few miles upstream from where Casper and Mary were living. She was pregnant and unable to travel. As a result, she was killed soon after her capture.[13]

During that same day, this group of Indians captured Mrs. Leonard Neff outside of her home on the South Fork.[14] Wendell Brown had been subleasing his homestead from the Neff family, so she was Casper and Mary's next-door neighbor. At about the same time, Mary's father Wendell and her younger sister Margaretha

---

13   Steele, Ian K. (2013), "Setting All the Captives Free", McGill-Queens University Press, p. 451

14   Steele, Ian K. (2013), "Setting All the Captives Free", McGill-Queens University Press, p. 515

were walking along the South Fork River on the property they were leasing. They were suddenly surrounded and captured by this same group of Indians.[15] Had they resisted they would probably have been killed, so it is likely they surrendered peacefully. For whatever the reason, their lives were spared and they were taken away.

After Wendell and Margaretha were captured, they were accompanied for a time by fellow captive Mrs. Leonard Neff. However, at a time that she saw as opportune, Mrs. Neff suddenly bolted and ran, making a successful escape.[16] Upon her arrival back home, she undoubtedly told Wendell and Margaretha's family what happened. That Wendell and Margaretha did not return home after a few days told the family that they did not escape. They had either been taken far away as prisoners, or they had been killed.

This sudden disappearance of Wendell and Margaretha caused the rest of his family to immediately seek refuge in the east. As the river water levels were higher in spring, they probably built makeshift log rafts to hasten their retreat down the rivers. They gathered those important belongings they could easily carry and left the rest behind. After the seventy-mile trip down the South Fork and South Branch Rivers, they continued down the Potomac River to a destination east of the Blue Ridge Mountains. Historical archives suggest they ended their journey in Frederick, Maryland.

Casper and Mary's four young children accompanied them during this retreat. John was six, Joseph four, Elizabeth two, and Margaret was one. Mary may have been newly pregnant with their fifth child Reuben during this retreat, but she probably did not know it at the time. Reuben was most likely born in early 1757. Because the extended Wendell Brown family had always been close knit, it is probable that Wendell's wife and unmarried children, as well as the Michael Catt family, joined in this retreat.

After Wendell was captured, he was taken to Fort Duquesne where a bounty was paid by the French for his capture, and he was

---

15   Steele, Ian K. (2013), "Setting All the Captives Free", McGill-Queens University Press, p. 452

16   Steele, Ian K. (2013), "Setting All the Captives Free", McGill-Queens University Press, p. 515

held prisoner for a time. Within a few months, the French transferred him to Fort Quebec, after which he was shipped directly to France (or possibly to England after payment of a ransom and a prisoner exchange between the English and the French). Wendell returned from England to America in September 1757 where he was eventually reunited with his family, possibly in Frederick, Maryland.[17]

After they were captured, Wendell's daughter Margaretha apparently accompanied him as far as Fort Duquesne. After that, they did not see each other again. Wendell believed she was being held prisoner in Quebec at the time he was released, but a report submitted to the Virginia House of Burgesses in 1758 claimed that she was "said to be with the Oschachi in Prairie West."[18] It is unclear who the Oschachi were or where Prairie West was located. Likely, she was taken to Ohio where she was adopted into the Delaware tribe that kidnapped her. After time spent acclimating to the Indian culture and language, she probably became an Indian wife.

In October 1764, after the peace treaty had been signed to end the French and Indian War, Colonel Henry Bouquet led forces onto Indian lands along the Muskingum River in Ohio to force the release of white captives taken during the war. He gained the release of over three hundred. However, Margaretha was not among those who were returned. After last being seen by Wendell at Fort Duquesne in 1754, her family never saw or heard from her again.

There is only one known historical archive to provide a glimpse of the whereabouts of Casper Böner and his family during the bloody frontier years of 1757 and 1758. On May 10, 1758, there is a record of the christening of Susanah Barbel Böner, Casper and Mary Böner's infant daughter.[19] Susanah was their sixth child. On this document, Casper's name is recorded as Caspar Bonner, and

---

17   Steele, Ian K. (2013), "Setting All the Captives Free", McGill-Queens University Press, p. 452

18   Steele, Ian K. (2013), "Setting All the Captives Free", McGill-Queens University Press, p. 452

19   "Maryland Births and Christenings, 1650-1995", database, FamilySearch, Susanah Barbel Bonner, Frederick, MD, 1758, https://www.familysearch.org/search/collection/1674912

Mary's name is recorded as Anna Maria Bonner. Susanah's name is entered as Susanah Barbel Bonner. The christening took place in Frederick, Maryland. The time and location of this event suggests – but does not prove - that Casper and Mary may have lived in Frederick during these two years.

In early 1757, William Pitt was placed in charge of Great Britain's war effort against France. The decisive strategies he implemented in the American colonies began turning the tide of the French and Indian War in England's favor. In November 1758, the French abandoned Fort Duquesne and burned it to the ground before beginning their retreat toward Quebec.

At the same time, British forces entered the Ohio Valley and built a new fort at the confluence of the Allegheny and Monongahela Rivers where Fort Duquesne had stood. It was named Fort Pitt in honor of William Pitt. Also in 1758, Colonel James Burd built a fort and supply depot at Redstone Old Fort (present-day Brownsville, Pennsylvania) on the Monongahela River. In addition, the original Nemacolin Trail across the Allegheny Mountains from Cumberland, Maryland (formerly Wills Creek) had become known as the Braddock Road. This road was improved in 1758 to make it easier for horse drawn wagons to traverse.

As a result of these events, the Indian forces that had been wreaking havoc along the Virginia and Pennsylvania frontiers between 1756 and 1758 began withdrawing to their lands north of the Ohio River. Some of the settlers that had retreated east of the Blue Ridge Mountains in 1756 began returning to their frontier homes. Emboldened by the presence of British and colonial forces along the Monongahela River, some settlers began moving all the way west to the Monongahela River to establish new homesteads on lands claimed concurrently by the French, the English, and the Indians.

Sometime during their two-year sojourn as refugees, Casper Böner and a large landowner in Frederick County, Virginia made a connection. In 1734, James Davis had originally purchased 1,175 acres just south of the Potomac River (near present-day Hedgesville, West Virginia) from Lord Fairfax. In 1744, James sold 400 acres of this tract to his young son Robert Davis. Most of this land was cleared and became productive farmland.

As wheat had become the cash crop for most farmers with large landholdings in this area, it is reasonable to believe that Robert Davis grew wheat on his farm, had it ground to flour at nearby grist mills, and shipped the flour to burgeoning markets such as Philadelphia and Baltimore.

According to property deeds, both James and Robert Davis were residents of Frederick County, Virginia when Robert purchased the property from his father in 1744. However, in his estate settlement deed in 1760, Robert's residence was listed as Chester County, Pennsylvania (near Philadelphia). Chester County was approximately 180 miles from Robert's Virginia farm.

Records indicate that Robert Davis died at a relatively young age in 1760 and that sometime between 1756 and 1759 he had sold 27 acres of his 400-acre farm to Casper Böner. When Casper Böner and Robert Davis initially met, and under what circumstances, is unknown. Why Robert would be motivated to sell 27 acres of some of his best land to Casper is also unknown.

One possibility is that Casper got a job working for Robert Davis on his farm after fleeing the Virginia frontier in 1756. Robert's farm was approximately forty miles west of Frederick, Maryland where it is believed Casper and his family had lived for a while after fleeing from the war. Frederick County, Virginia was still prone to Indian attacks, but much less frequently than in Hampshire and Augusta counties further to the west. Robert may have lost some of his employees who fled further east to safety with the outbreak of hostilities in 1756. However, it is unlikely that such a scenario would have caused Robert to think it was a good deal for him to part with 27 acres of land to attract and keep one employee.

Another possibility is that Robert became ill and unable to be the hands-on manager of his farm. This could explain his return to Chester County, Pennsylvania. In this scenario, Robert could have conducted a search for someone to manage his farm in his absence, and Casper was selected for the position. To entice Casper to accept such a position in an area still prone to Indian attack, he may have offered him the 27-acre parcel.

Whatever the case, Robert Davis and Casper Böner entered a private contract whereby Casper was the legal owner of the 27-acre property. However, Casper was not permitted to sell it without the approval of Robert Davis. Davis also had the right of first refusal if Casper ever wanted to sell.

As this was a private transaction between Robert Davis and Casper Böner, it was not recorded by the Frederick County Clerk. The most likely year for this transaction was 1757 but could have been as early as mid-1756.

At the time Casper purchased this land, only landowners could vote. It is unknown if this type of land ownership – a private deed not recorded by the County Clerk – would have conferred voting rights to Casper. If so, in 1758 he would have voted for one of the following candidates to be his representative in the Virginia House of Burgesses: George Washington, Hugh West, a Colonel Marin, and a Captain Swearingen.

Based on accounts settled after the election, Washington spent £39.6 to win this seat. His campaign outlays were for 46 gallons of beer, 35 gallons of wine, 2 gallons of cider, 3.5 pints of brandy, and 40 gallons, 1 hogshead, 1 barrel, and 10 bowls of rum punch.[20] These outlays helped Washington eke out a win in a tight race. The results were: George Washington – 307, Colonel Marin – 240, Hugh West – 199, Captain Swearingen – 45.[21] Whether Casper voted for Washington or not, George Washington served as Casper's representative in the House of Burgesses until 1765.

Casper and his family were living on and farming this property when Robert Davis died in 1760. Robert's widow Dinah was the executor of his estate. His will directed that his 400-acre farm was to be sold to George Myles, but that Casper Böner (recorded as Gasper Boner in the deed) would be allowed to maintain legal ownership of

---

[20] Charles Smith to George Washington July 26, 1758, The Papers of George Washington, Colonial Series, https://founders.archives.gov/documents/Washington/02-05-02-0273-0001.

[21] Charles Smith to George Washington, July 24, 1758, The Papers of George Washington, Colonial Series, https://fouman(1980)nders.archives.gov/documents/Washington/02-05-02-0264.

his 27 acres. This deed was recorded on June 8, 1760, in the Frederick County, Virginia County Clerk's Office.[22]

Casper and Mary Böner and their growing family lived on and farmed this property for approximately ten years before they sold it in 1768. This is where their oldest child, John Amos grew from an eight-year-old boy into an eighteen-year-old young man. It is where their sixth child and fourth daughter, Catherine, was born circa 1765, and where their seventh child and youngest son, Casper, Jr. was born circa 1767.

It is unknown if Casper's only responsibility was to help his family survive on this 27-acre property, or if his primary responsibility was to supervise some of the operations on the larger 400-acre farm owned by Robert Davis and, after 1760, by George Myles. If Casper had additional responsibilities, most of the farming chores on the 27-acre parcel would have fallen to Mary and their two oldest sons, John and Joseph.

This 27-acre parcel was located on prime farmland, situated on the south side of Tulissus Branch and the west side of Harlan Run. Both streams converged at the northeastern corner of the property and flowed northward for approximately three miles to the Potomac River. The location is near present-day Spring Mills, West Virginia, approximately two miles northeast of current Hedgesville, West Virginia. It is just a few hundred feet west of the Falling Waters Presbyterian Church, which existed near this same site as a log structure when the Casper Böner family lived here.

---

22 Frederick County, VA County Clerk's Office, Deed Book 12, Page 9-14, Robert Davis Estate to George Myles with 27-acre Gasper 'Boner' exclusion, June 8, 1760

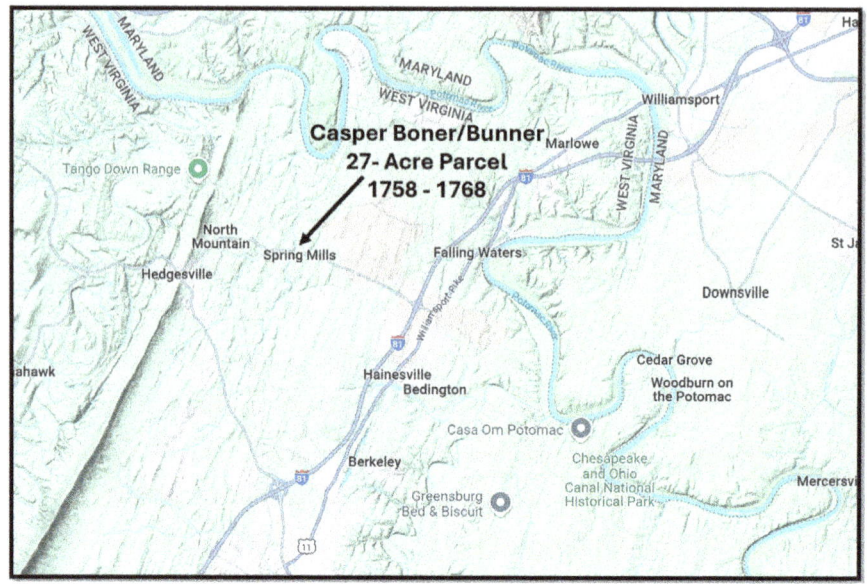

**Location of Casper Böner 27-Acre Property
near present-day Spring Mills, WV**

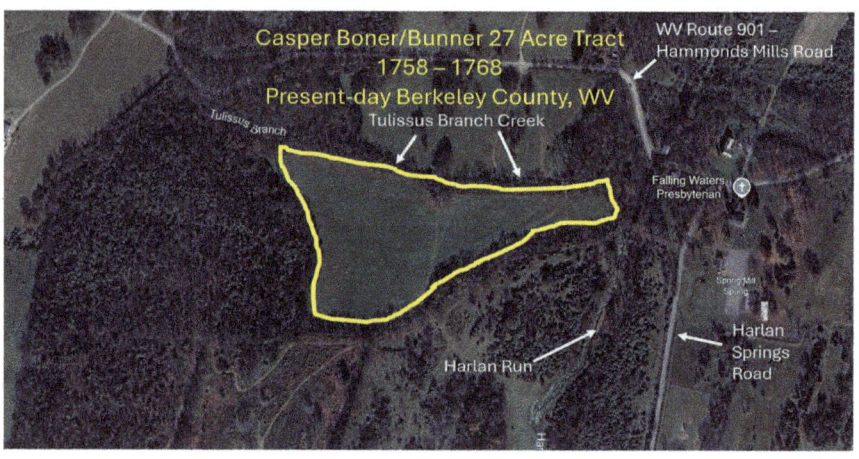

**Present-day Satellite view of Casper Böner
27-Acre Property near Spring Mills, WV**
(Map created by Michael Bunner overlaid on Google Earth 2025 image)

# CASPER BÖNER (BUNNER)

**Casper Böner 27-Acre Property looking west from Harlan Run**
(photograph by Michael Bunner)

**Looking west up Tulissus Branch -
Casper Böner 27-Acre Property on left**
(photograph by Michael Bunner)

**Looking north down Harlan Run –
Casper Böner 27-Acre Property on left**
(photograph by Michael Bunner)

**Falling Waters Presbyterian Church –
Casper Böner 27-Acre Property 1,000 feet to west**
(photograph by Michael Bunner)

## CASPER BÖNER (BUNNER)

The capture of Wendell Brown and his daughter Margaretha by Indians, and the subsequent retreat of the rest of Wendell's family, brought an end to the communal family unit comprised of the Browns, Catts, and Böners. Sometime between 1756 and 1758, Casper and Mary Böner, along with their six children, moved to the 27-acre property in Frederick County, Virginia that Casper had acquired from Robert Davis.

Around 1760 or 1761, Wendell Brown, aware of the rapid settlement along the Monongahela River despite sporadic Indian attacks, decided to return to the land he fled due to the outbreak of the French and Indian War. Wendell, as well as the thousands of other early settlers in this area, dismissed and ignored the King of England's Proclamation of 1763, which made all colonial settlements on land that drained into the Ohio River illegal.

The Michael Catt family did not join the Browns in this move to the Monongahela River Valley, but it is believed they moved to Fayette County, Pennsylvania in the late 1760's. There is no evidence that any of the three families ever returned to their original homestead in Augusta County (which became Hampshire County, Virginia in 1754 and is present-day Hardy County, West Virginia).

By late 1767, it appears that Casper's focus shifted towards acquiring land to bequeath to his sons. On February 3, 1768, he sold his 27-acre parcel of land to George Myles for £25.[23] This large sum for 27 acres suggests Casper's family either had made significant improvements or George Myles paid a substantial premium due to his strong desire to own the property.

In 1768, £25 was sufficient to acquire 10,000 acres of unoccupied and undeveloped land from the Fairfax Land Office. In early 1768, Casper applied to the Fairfax Land Company for warrants to purchase two parcels of vacant land in Frederick County, Virginia. One parcel, located about midway along the road from Hedgesville to Warm Springs (present-day Berkeley Springs, West Virginia), measured 365

---

23  Frederick County, VA County Clerk's Office, Deed Book 12, Page 109-112, John Davis and Casper 'Boner,' 27-acres to George Myles, Feb. 1768

acres.[24] The second parcel, also situated along the same road between North Mountain and Back Creek, measured 334 acres. Surveys on both properties were completed on August 6, 1768. The chain bearers on the survey crew were two of Casper's sons, eighteen-year-old John 'Bonner' and eleven-year-old Reuben 'Bonner'.[25]

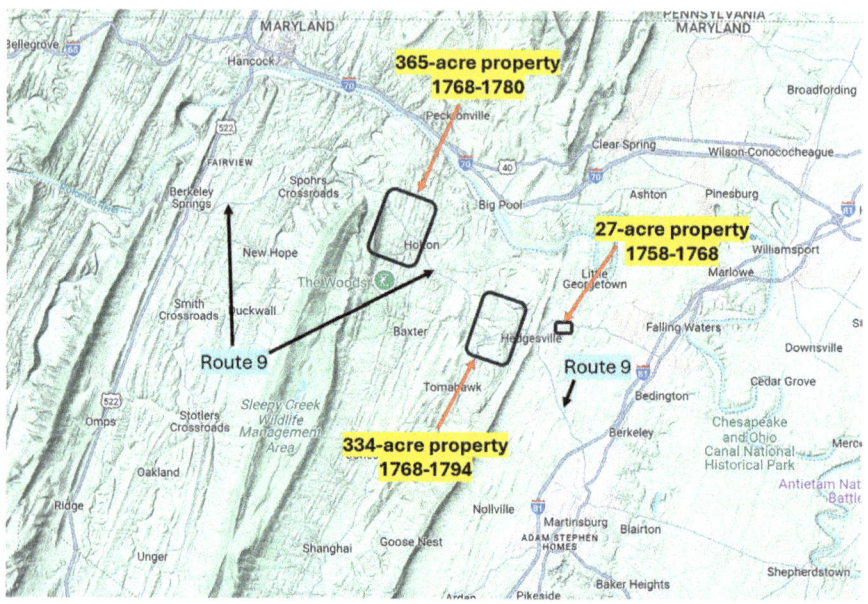

Three properties owned by Casper Böner. 334 and 27-acre properties in present-day Berkeley County, WV. 365-acre property in present-day Morgan County, WV.

---

24  Joyner, Peggy (1987), "Abstract of Virginia's Northern Neck Warrants and Surveys, Volume 4, p. 80

25  Virginia Colonial Land Office, 334 Acre Grant to 'Gasper Banner,' July 24, 1789, https://lva-virginia.libguides.com/land-grants

## CASPER BÖNER (BUNNER)

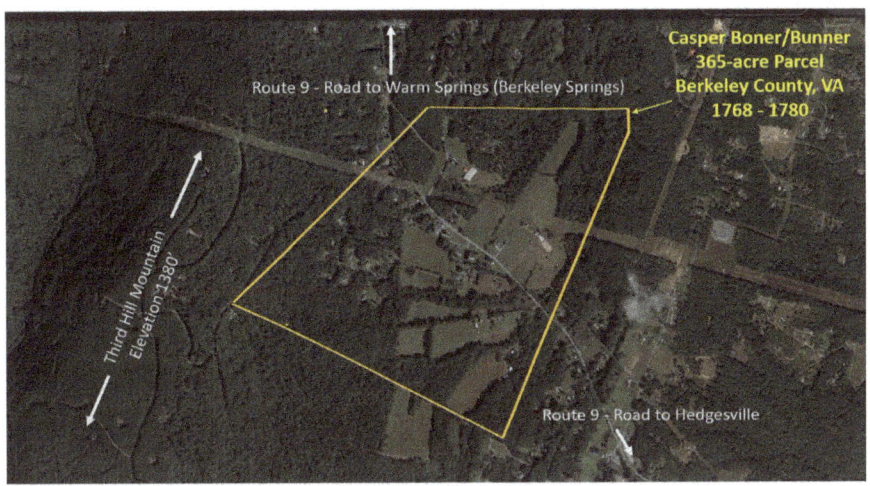

**365-acre Parcel of Fairfax land
for which Casper received a warrant to buy in 1768**
(Map created by Michael Bunner overlaid on Google Earth 2025 image)

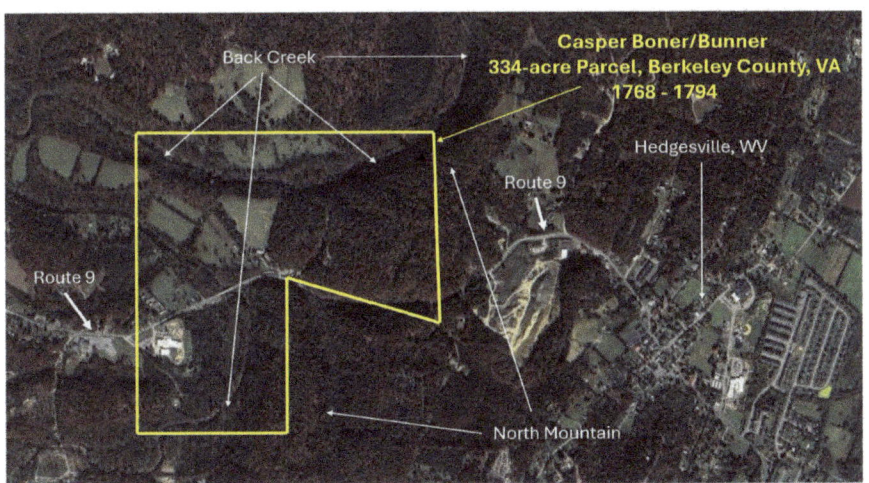

**334-acre Parcel of Fairfax land
for which Casper received warrant to buy in 1768**
(Map created by Michael Bunner overlaid on Google Earth 2025 image)

Casper completed the necessary steps to purchase the land from Fairfax and then waited for Fairfax to provide the land patents (deeds). Upon receiving the patents, Casper would pay the remaining balance to complete the purchase and obtain clear title to the land. Buying these two parcels from Fairfax, including surveyor fees, would have cost about £2, less than 10% of what Casper was paid for his 27-acre property.

Fairfax delayed delivering the patents to Casper without explanation, despite accepting down payments and issuing purchase warrants to him. Casper paid the surveyor fees upon completion of the surveys. At this point in the land purchase process, he was legally allowed to begin improvements to both parcels.

For a short time, it is likely that Casper rented the 27-acre property he had previously sold to George Myles. Casper and his elder sons John and Joseph expended significant labor clearing the land and constructing a log house on the 334-acre parcel. This property was located approximately three miles west of the 27-acre parcel that Casper had owned for at least ten years. The family made the move from the 27-acre property to the 334-acre property in late 1768 or early 1769.

While waiting for Fairfax to finalize the land patents, Casper and his family learned of Mary's father Wendell's death in 1769. Wendell had lived his final years on the Monongahela River Valley land he originally settled in 1752 before fleeing due to the outbreak of the French and Indian War.

Casper also learned that in 1769, Mary's brothers, Maunus and Adam, had acquired the parcels of land from the Pennsylvania Land Office on which they and their father had initially settled in 1752. Each of their adjoining lots measured over 300 acres. These events, along with Casper's growing frustration with the Fairfax Land Office, gradually caused him to begin considering land ownership in the Monongahela Valley for himself and his sons.

The family continued farming and improving the land on the 334-acre tract, still hoping for patents but becoming more disillusioned with time. Months turned into years, and by 1771, three years after the surveys had been submitted, Fairfax still had not delivered the patents. Casper decided it was time to look for land ownership opportunities in the Monongahela Valley

Between 1768 and 1771, Mary had two more daughters, Mary Christina and Charlotte. This completed Casper and Mary's family with ten children.

By late 1771, most prime land along the Monongahela River from the forks (now Pittsburgh) up to Redstone Settlement (now Brownsville, Pennsylvania) had already been claimed. As a result, Casper looked further upstream and southward. He learned about a property along the Monongahela (present-day Rivesville, West Virginia, north of present-day Fairmont, West Virginia), fifty miles south of Redstone Settlement, and decided to investigate it.

In 1766, Zackwell Morgan, a son of Morgan Morgan – the traditionally acclaimed first settler in what is now West Virginia - initially settled on this property. He acquired a "settlement certificate" under the "Settlement Rights" law recently enacted by the Virginia General Assembly.

"Settlement Rights" allowed anyone to claim unoccupied land on the Virginia frontier by building a cabin and growing one crop of corn. After completing these tasks and paying 40 shillings per hundred acres, the settler could apply for a patent and become the legal owner. This law also allowed settlers to claim an extra 1,000 acres next to their 400-acre property within ten years for 40 shillings per hundred acres. This option to purchase 1,000 adjacent acres was commonly known as "Preemptive Rights." The colony of Virginia issued "settlement certificates" as an interim document while they worked out the details of surveys, payments, and finalizing the land patents (deeds).[26]

In 1770, Zackwell Morgan possessed "settlement certificates" for a 400-acre parcel and an adjacent 1,000- acre parcel. He transferred ownership of his 400-acre "settlement certificate" to Thomas Douthet. Shortly after acquiring this property, Mr. Douthet chose to establish a settlement on land that is now part of Uniontown, Pennsylvania. As a result, Douthet was looking to sell his "settlement certificate" at the same time Casper Böner was seeking to

---

26  Lough, Glenn D. (1969), "Now and Long Ago – A History of the Marion County Area", Morgantown Printing and Binding Co., Morgantown, WV, p. 245

purchase land in the area. Douthet sold the 400-acre tract to Casper in late 1771 or early 1772. [27]

At the age of fifty-two, Casper relocated his family from the property in Berkeley County, where he had been attempting to obtain a free and clear deed since 1768, to this new property in the upper Monongahela River Valley in western Virginia. Mary was forty-four. Their children were John (22), Joseph (20), Elizabeth (18), Reuben (16), Susanah (14), Catherine (7) Casper, Jr. (5), Mary Christina (2), and Charlotte (1). Their daughter Margaret had married in Berkeley County just a few weeks before the move and stayed behind with her new husband.

Much vacant land along this section of the Monongahela River was quickly being claimed using the "Settlement Rights" law. Casper advised his sons to find suitable parcels of land to claim for themselves using "Settlement Rights". In late 1772, John found land on the east side of the river, built a cabin and created a clearing to grow corn. In 1773, he grew the crop and applied for a patent for 400 acres.[28] He received a "settlement certificate" for this property. Although this certificate did not confer legal ownership rights, frontiersmen respected and honored "Settlement Rights" even without legal documents. Nobody attempted to claim John's 400 acres, even though he did not permanently settle on the land until after his service in the Revolutionary War. John ultimately received the patent on this 400-acre tract from the Virginia Land Office in 1785, several years after he settled on it and started raising a family.

In 1773, Casper's son Reuben followed the same procedure as his brother John to claim a 400-acre parcel with drains to White Day Creek. This tract was about two miles from his brother John's property. It is unknown why Joseph Böner did not go through the same procedure as his brothers John and Reuben to lay claim to a 400-acre parcel of vacant land for himself. Perhaps he planned

---

27  Lough, Glenn D. (1969), "Now and Long Ago – A History of the Marion County Area", Morgantown Printing and Binding Co., Morgantown, WV, p. 245

28  Virginia Colonial Land Office, 400 Acre Grant to John 'Boner,' July 24, 1789, October 10, 1786, https://lva-virginia.libguides.com/land-grants

to do it, but those plans were interrupted by the outbreak of the Revolutionary War.

Zackwell Morgan lived on his 1,000-acre tract adjacent to Casper Boner's 400-acre property until 1779, when he sold this parcel to his older brother David. He then purchased land fifteen miles downstream on the Monongahela River to establish Morgantown, named after him.[29]

In 1772, shortly after the Böner family had moved to their new Monongahela Valley homestead, Berkeley County, Virginia, was formed from Frederick County, Virginia. The properties Casper was in the process of purchasing from Fairfax were now in Berkeley County. Casper 'Boner' was listed as a renter on the initial Berkeley County renter roll in 1772 even though he had moved his family to the Monongahela Valley. This listing was likely for the 334-acre property Casper had partially paid for and was "renting" from Fairfax while he was waiting for Fairfax to issue his patents.

In 1774, Casper's eldest daughter Elizabeth, who was approximately twenty years old, married John Miller, a recent settler in the Monongahela Valley. Also in 1774, the newly formed Berkeley County, Virginia published it's "Tithables" (head tax) list, which included Casper, John, Joseph, and Reuben 'Boner'.[30] None were living in Berkeley County at the time, so this list was a carryover from the original 1772 Berkeley County "Tithables" before the family moved to the Monongahela Valley. The primary revelation gained from this list is the inclusion of Reuben 'Boner'. As those males on the "Tithables" list had to be age sixteen or older, it confirmed that Reuben 'Boner' was born prior to or during 1757, not in 1760 as is commonly recorded.

In 1774, an event occurred along the northern Ohio River where a group of troublemaking white frontiersmen killed a group of Indians, including several members of the family of Logan, chief of the Mingo Indians. Logan had been a strong advocate for peace

---

29 Lough, Glenn D. (1969), "Now and Long Ago – A History of the Marion County Area", Morgantown Printing and Binding Co., Morgantown, WV, p. 245

30 Berkeley County Virginia Tithables, Chapter 7, Robert Carter Willis' List, 1774, page 32-33

between the Indians and the white settlers since the end of the French and Indian War and Pontiac's War.

Following the death of his family, Logan sought revenge. He led raids across the upper Ohio Valley and into the Monongahela Valley. The summer of 1774 saw significant violence along the Ohio River and the western Virginia frontier.

Due to increased Indian attacks along the Monongahela River in 1774, the local militia and most able-bodied adults joined forces to hastily build a fort on property owned by Jacob Prickett that became known as Prickett's Fort. It was located across the river from Casper Böner's property and was intended to serve as a place of refuge for area residents.

Chief Logan and his warriors were responsible for four deadly ambushes near Prickett's fort between June and October 1774. An incident in July, during which one settler was killed and two were captured, caused most residents within fifteen miles of the fort to seek refuge there for over ten weeks. Casper and Mary Böner and their children were likely among them. John, Joseph, and Reuben, along with others, likely assisted the local militia to maintain round-the-clock watch over the fort during this sixteen-week period.

On October 2, 1774, a tragedy occurred that traumatized the entire Prickett's Fort community. As nightfall approached, Isaiah Prickett, the fourteen-year-old son of Jacob Prickett, accompanied Susan Oxx, the pregnant young wife of Michael Oxx, outside the fort to drive their cows back toward the fort for the night. When they did not return, a search party left to look for them. They soon found Isaiah murdered and scalped. The search party gave chase to the Indians, catching up and killing two of them. However, Logan and his other warriors got away, taking their captive, Susan Oxx, with them. Susan was never seen again.

Fourteen-year-old Isaiah Prickett and sixteen-year-old Reuben Böner had become good friends soon after the Böner's moved to the area in 1772. During the summer of 1772 both had worked as chain-bearers for the local crew that was surveying the lands owned by Isaiah's father, Jacob[31]. As a result of the closeness in the com-

---

31  Lough, Glenn D. (1969), "Now and Long Ago – A History of the Marion County Area", Morgantown Printing and Binding Co., Morgantown, WV, p. 258

munity, the Böner's, the Prickett's, and all their neighbors were devastated by this event.

The Virginia government response to this 1774 Indian uprising is commonly known as Dunmore's War, which culminated at the Battle of Point Pleasant at the confluence of the Ohio and Kanawha Rivers. That battle was fought on October 10, 1774, between forces under Shawnee chief Cornstalk and Virginia militiamen under Colonel Andrew Lewis. After a furious fight with many dead and wounded on both sides, Cornstalk retreated across the Ohio River where he was pursued by Colonel Lewis and another force led by Lord Dunmore, the colonial governor of Virginia.

They eventually caught up with Cornstalk and compelled him to agree to a treaty ceding all Shawnee claims on land south of the Ohio River (present-day West Virginia and Kentucky). This treaty brought an end to this frontier uprising. Those settlers who had been living at Prickett's Fort since mid-July finally felt safe enough to return to their homes.

In 1775, the American Revolution commenced with the battles at Lexington and Concord in Massachusetts. The outbreak of the war in 1775 barely affected frontier settlements, but the 1776 Declaration of Independence compelled many frontiersmen to join George Washington's Continental Army to fight for American independence. Casper's sons, John and Joseph, went to war. Eighteen-year-old Reuben volunteered to help defend Prickett's Fort as part of the local militia. While serving at Prickett's Fort, he met Nancy Ann Prickett, Jacob's daughter. They later married.

In 1776, Casper and Mary moved back to Berkeley County, possibly due to ongoing concerns about Indian attacks, the absence of help from their two oldest sons, the western frontier threats of "back door" British invasion due to the Revolutionary War, or Casper's health issues. Casper sold his 400-acre property on the Monongahela River to his new son-in-law, John Miller.[32] This property remained the residence of John and Elizabeth Miller for many years. Children returning to Berkeley County with Casper

---

32  Lough, Glenn D. (1969), "Now and Long Ago – A History of the Marion County Area", Morgantown Printing and Binding Co., Morgantown, WV, p. 245

and Mary were Susanah (18), Catherine (11) Casper, Jr. (9), Mary Christina (6), and Charlotte (5).

Casper and Mary returned to the same Berkeley County property they had been living on in early 1772. This was the 334-acre parcel located approximately one mile west of Hedgesville along Back Creek. Casper continued to pay a nominal rent, estimated to be 3-4 shillings per year, for each of the two properties while waiting to receive the patents from Fairfax. There were no apparent legal issues with Fairfax when they returned to this property in 1776, but eight years had transpired since Casper had made the initial down payments and completed the surveys.

With the outbreak of the Revolutionary War, Lord Fairfax found himself in a precarious position. His landownership was based upon a long-standing grant from the King of England. If the American colonists won their independence, his vast estate was likely to be confiscated. To add to his dilemma, his good friend and former protege, George Washington, was now leading the Continental Army against the British. This undoubtedly introduced many complications and uncertainties in all Fairfax land transactions. This included the two parcels that Casper had been trying to purchase since 1768.

There must be an explanation for the Fairfax stalling tactics on issuing the land patents to Casper Böner that has been buried by the sediments of time. Most of the Fairfax land offices had a reputation for being notoriously slow at scheduling closings and issuing land patents (deeds). Some of this stall was intentional because Fairfax could charge monthly rentals on the property being sold until the closing date. The longer the stall, the more the incoming rental revenues. The standard operating procedure for most Fairfax land offices was to stall for a year or two from the date the surveys were submitted until they issued the patents. However, stalling for eight years was virtually unheard of.

Some of the Fairfax sales agents were known to be corrupt, and most had strong prejudices against anyone who was not English. The time required to have patents issued by the Fairfax land offices could often be significantly shortened with payment of an "expediting fee" directly to the sales agent. Perhaps Casper never paid an "expediting fee" and the sales agent was holding out until he received one.

Perhaps prejudice was the explanation. The English colonists generally viewed the German Palatine immigrants as ignorant peasants. Most, if not all, of the sales agents working for Lord Fairfax were of English descent and harbored such prejudices. They would have found it not only distasteful, but unacceptable for lowly German peasants to be landowners of the same social class as the English gentry. If this were the case, these sales agents would have seen it as their patriotic and civic responsibility to keep the English aristocracy from being sullied by placing German peasantry in the same social class.

Whether it was greed, corruption, or prejudice, the patents for the two properties being purchased by Casper were not forthcoming. However, since Casper had long ago made the required down payment on the properties and had submitted the required property surveys, he was legally allowed to live on and continue making improvements to the properties while he waited for the patents to be issued.

Casper continued to live on and farm the 334-acre parcel, with his only available help now being his nine-year-old son, Casper Jr. and his young daughters. Casper may have been suffering from a debilitating disease that was slowly sapping his life energy, making it difficult to complete all the necessary work to operate and maintain the farm.

Casper's son Joseph served in the American Continental Army from 1776 until 1780, participating in campaigns in Quebec, Ticonderoga, Brandywine, Paoli, Germantown, Monmouth, and spending a winter at Valley Forge. It is unlikely that Joseph was able to visit, let alone help, his family during this period.

John served in the Continental Army from late 1776 to early 1778 and then in the militia at Redstone Settlement until the end of the war. He married Martha Evans after resigning from the Continental Army in the spring of 1778. It is doubtful that Casper and Mary attended his wedding as it was held in Morgantown, a hundred- and thirty-mile trip each way over the mountains.

Sometime in early February 1779, Casper Böner died on his farm in Berkeley County at the age of fifty-nine. On February 25, 1779, Mary signed an affidavit at the Berkeley County Clerk's office testifying that "Casper 'Bonner' is deceased, and I empower my son John Bonner to act in his father's behalf in having a deed issued in the name of George Braggoona."[33]

On March 2, 1779, less than a month after Casper died and nearly eleven years after he had applied for warrants to purchase two parcels of land from Fairfax, he received one of the deeds. The deed was not for the 334-acre property where he and his family had resided, but rather for the 365-acre property located approximately six miles to the west that was to be sold to George Braggoona.[34] Casper's name was spelled 'Gasper Bonner' in this deed.

John and his mother Mary (their last name is recorded as 'Bunner' in the legal documents) sold the 365-acre property to George Braggoona on October 19, 1780, for £45. John's residence at that time is recorded as Redstone Settlement (present-day Brownsville, Pennsylvania).[35]

This sudden turn of events so soon after Casper's death seems to indict the prejudice of the Fairfax sales agent as the cause of the "unending stall." As soon as the sales agent became aware that the property was to be sold to someone who was not German, the patent was immediately forthcoming. However, the patent for the 334-acre property was not forthcoming at the same time. The apparent reason is that this is where the "ignorant German peasants" were currently living, and where they would continue to live after they had free and clear ownership of their land. English culture and society had to be protected. Preventing ignorant German peasants from becoming full-fledged landowners was one way to do it.

Casper's burial location is unknown, but it is likely on his 334-acre farm. On May 19, 1779, Casper Böner's (recorded as Casper

---

33 Joyner, Peggy (1987), "Abstract of Virginia's Northern Neck Warrants and Surveys, Volume 4, p. 80

34 Fairfax Land Office to Gasper Bonner, 365 acres, March 2, 1779

35 Berkeley County, West Virginia County Clerks Office, John and Mary Bunner to George Broggona, October 10, 1780

## CASPER BÖNER (BUNNER)

Bunner) administrative bond listed his wife, Mary Bunner, as administrator. On August 17, 1779, an inventory and appraisement bill for the estate of Casper Bunner was recorded. The articles on which Casper's family paid an "estate tax" included: 1 mare, 1 cow, 2 heifers, 7 sheep , 1 sow and pigs, 9 hogs, 2 pots and hooks, 1 hatchet, 1 handsaw, 1 augur, 1 hammer and anvil, 1 hammer to shape a scythe, 1 box dross, 1 pair steelyards, 1 old ax, 1 mattock, 1 old lamp, 1 bell, 1 iron wedge, 1 put rack, 1 coulter, 2 dishes, 3 basins, 1 pint, 1 sugar bowl, 6 plates, 6 spoons, 1 frying pan, 1 piggin, 1 sifter, old iron clevises, 1 dough trough, 1 old chest, old bedsteads, 3 brought chains, 1 harness with staples and hooks, 2 tubs, 2 powdering tubs, 1 churn, and 2 kegs.[36]

Mary remained in the same Berkeley County home for several years. At the time of Casper's death, their children at home were Catherine (14), Casper Jr. (12), Mary Christina (9), and Charlotte (8). After Joseph left the Continental Army in 1780, he returned to Berkeley County to live with his mother and younger siblings, taking on the main responsibility for the crops and animals on the 334-acre property.

Family tradition holds that Mary lived in Berkeley County with her younger children until about 1785, after which she moved to Brownsville, Pennsylvania to be closer to her brothers Thomas, Maunus, and Adam Brown. A 1790 census of Fayette County, Pennsylvania, Luzerne Township records a Christianna Boner living there. She was recorded as the head of a family that included two white males over sixteen, and two white females over sixteen. [37]

It is believed the two white females over sixteen were the two daughters, Mary Christina and Charlotte, who accompanied Mary when she moved to Brownsville. In 1790, Mary Christina would have been twenty, and Charlotte would have been nineteen. The two men over age sixteen may have been the husbands of Mary Christina and Charlotte.

---

36 Berkeley County, West Virginia County Clerks Office, Death Appraisement Book, "Gasper Bunner," August 17, 1779, page 167

37 "Heads of Families at the First Census of the United States in the Year 1790 – Pennsylvania," Fayette County, Luzerne Township, https://www.census.gov/library/publications/1907/dec/heads-of-families.html

From the collection of interviews archived by Mr. Adam O. Heck (*"The Heck Interviews"*), a schoolteacher and Marion County, West Virginia historian who lived from 1851 to 1926, comes a story of a lady named Christianna 'Boner'. She was living near New Salem, Pennsylvania. Once, when she was very old, she walked alone from New Salem to what is now Rivesville, West Virginia to visit relatives.[38] This was a fifty-mile trek. This story has some credibility because Mary lived near New Salem, and her son John and daughter Elizabeth (Miller) lived near Rivesville in the early 1790's.

In another interview, Rev. Jesse Nixon (1816-1906) told Adam O. Heck (*"The Heck Interviews"*) that "his father and Mr. Bunner [one of the sons of John Amos Bunner] went to [Brownsville] Pennsylvania in 1825, when he, Rev. Jesse, was nine years old, to see General Lafayette, when he visited there, in the fine mansion of Mr. Gallatin, and he (Rev. Jesse) was permitted to go with them. The log house where Mr. Bunner's grandmother Bunner had lived for so many years still stood upright and was being used as a hay barn. He said that Mr. Bunner said that his grandmother Bunner "was way up" in years when she died, in that house."[39]

Mary is believed to have died in Brownsville, Pennsylvania circa 1795.

After America won the Revolutionary War, the new Commonwealth of Virginia eventually assumed legal responsibility for all land formerly owned by Lord Fairfax. On July 24, 1789, twenty-one years after making a down-payment and paying for the property survey, ten years after he died, and six years after the end of the Revolutionary War, Casper Böner (recorded as Gasper Banner) received the deed for the 334-acre parcel of land in Berkeley

---

38  Bunner, Gale J., "Genealogy Descendents of Casper (Boner) Bunner And Mary Christianna Brown, Revised Edition, 1988, p. 13, excerpt from the "Adam O. Heck" interviews published by Glen D. Lough, Fairmont, WV

39  Bunner, Gale J., "Genealogy Descendents of Casper (Boner) Bunner And Mary Christianna Brown, Revised Edition, 1988, p. 13, excerpt from the "Adam O. Heck" interviews published by Glen D. Lough, Fairmont, WV

## CASPER BÖNER (BUNNER)

County.[40] Casper's son Joseph lived on and farmed this land until he moved to the Monongahela River Valley circa 1815. John Böner (recorded as John 'Bonner' and John 'Bunner' on the deeds), as executor of the Casper Böner estate, subdivided and sold parcels of this property between 1795 and 1815.[41][42]

---

40  https://lva-virginia.libguides.com/land-grants Banner, Gasper. grantee.; Northern Neck Land Office.; Library of Virginia. Archives.1789 – 0724, 334 acres, Land Grant 24 July 1789

41  Berkeley County, West Virginia County Clerks Office, John Bunner to William Mercer, 50 acres, 1795, Deed Book 12, Page 398

42  Berkeley County, West Virginia County Clerk's Office, John Bunner to Jeremiah Evans, 217 acres, 1815, Deed Book 27, Page 542

# 6.

# John Amos Bonner (Boner/Bunner)

[Author's Note: John's last name was spelled three different ways during his life – Boner, Bonner, and Bunner. As Bonner was predominantly used in historical and legal documents, I have used this as the default spelling in this chapter. I specifically note where historical and legal documents use one of the other spellings. I continue to use Böner as the default spelling for the last name of John's parents, Casper and Mary.]

John Amos Bonner was the oldest child of Casper and Mary Böner. He could have been born as early as 1748 or as late as 1751, but his generally accepted birth date is 1750. There is an erroneous family tradition that he was born in the family's log cabin on Tom's Creek in Augusta County, but research has revealed that he was born in an extended family settlement along the South Fork of the South Branch of the Potomac River in Augusta County, Virginia (approximately seven miles south of present-day Moorefield in Hardy County, West Virginia).[1]

---

1  Patton, Sara Stevens, Men and Manors in the South Branch Valley, Hardy County West Virginia Genealogy Page, Michael Catt entry, https://www.wvgw.net/hardy/index.htm

## JOHN AMOS BONNER (BONER/BUNNER)

**John Bonner birthplace on the South Fork River in present-day Hardy County, West Virginia is now a cattle farm. Virgin forests covered this land in 1750.**
(Photograph by Michael Bunner)

In addition to his parents, the extended family sharing that homestead where John was born included his mother's father Wendell Brown; her stepmother Elisabetha; her brothers Thomas, Maunus, and Adam; her younger sister Margaretha; her older sister Catherine who was married to Michael Catt; and likely two or three young children of Catherine and Michael Catt who would have been John's cousins. One of Michael and Catherine's children was a son named Michael who was born here in 1750.[2] Being the same age as John, the two would have been playmates during their early years.

John's parents broke with the German tradition of giving their children a ceremonial biblical first name at the time of their christening. John was his first name (and it was biblical), and that was the name he was called by his family. However, archives exist from his later life suggesting that many of his friends called him Jack.

---

2  Lough, Glenn D., "Now and Long Ago – A History of the Marion County Area," Morgantown Printing and Binding Co., 1969, p. 360

There is no record of his christening as an infant, but such events were rarely documented by the pastors of the simple log churches dotting the early Virginia frontier. Christening of their infant newborns was an important occasion for Casper and Mary Böner, but the only christening of their ten children that was recorded was that of their sixth child, Susanah Barbel Bonner in 1758 when John was eight years old.[3] This christening was likely recorded because it took place in a more established and stable church in Frederick, Maryland after Casper and Mary retreated there for a time, seeking refuge during the bloodiest years of the French and Indian War.

John's first six years were lived on the leading edge of the Virginia frontier. He watched his father, grandfather, and uncle clear land, plow gardens, raise livestock, hunt for food, and trap animals for their fur. He watched his mother, grandmother, and aunt working in the gardens, cooking meals, washing clothes, and taking care of the children. He also watched them making soap, candles, and shoes. He observed all the women in his extended family as they spent endless hours operating spinning wheels to convert the flax grown in their gardens into linen cloth used for making the clothing worn by the family.

By the time John was three years old he was helping his parents with garden chores and helping his father skin squirrels, rabbits, and wild turkeys for their meals. His diet consisted mostly of meat from December through June of each year. This was supplemented with vegetables and fruits grown in their gardens from June through early December.

John never attended a school and never learned to read or write. He learned from his parents and grandparents what was essential for survival – hunting; farming; killing bears, mountain lions, rattlesnakes, and copperheads before they killed him; and assuming an unfriendly Indian was lurking behind every tree eager to take his scalp.

John was too young to understand, but the land his family had settled on three years before he was born was part of the vast Lord

---

3 "Maryland Births and Christenings, 1650-1995", database, FamilySearch, Susanah Barbel Bonner, Frederick, MD, 1758, https://www.familysearch.org/search/collection/1674912

Fairfax estate and not land owned, as the family had believed, by the colony of Virginia. As a result, all the improvements the family had made to the land did not belong to them, but to Lord Fairfax. Learning this was a crushing blow, especially to John's grandfather Wendell Brown who had led the family to this wilderness paradise harboring the dream that they would someday own it.

Rather than lose the family's investment in time and labor to improve the property, Wendell Brown subleased the parcel on which their houses and gardens were located from the family that ultimately leased the land directly from Lord Fairfax. However, Wendell Brown still yearned to own his own land and when John was two years old he moved with his sons (Maunus, Adam, and possibly Thomas) all the way across the rugged Allegheny Mountains to the Monongahela River Valley in pursuit of his dream.

Wendell was drawn there by an offer from the Ohio Company that would allow settlers to select the land for their homestead and live on it rent and tax free for a period of ten years. After ten years, the settlers could purchase the land they had lived on and improved for a nominal cost.

In 1748 the King of England granted the Ohio Company 200,000 acres of land west of the Allegheny Mountains, south of the Ohio River and north of the Kanawha River with the stipulation that they had to settle a minimum of two hundred families on the land within seven years. This was being done to strengthen England's claim on the Ohio River Valley which was also being claimed by France. In 1752, the grant was increased to 500,000 acres.

This move forever placed John's grandfather, Wendell Brown, in history books as the first white European settler on the western side of the Allegheny Mountains[4] (some history books say, "one of the first").[5] What is less clear is who, besides his sons, accompanied Wendell to this new settlement one hundred and sixty miles from their homestead on the South Fork River.

---

4  Veech, James (1892), "Monongahela of Old", Pittsburgh, P. 109

5  Ellis, Franklin, "History of Fayette County, Pennsylvania," L.H. Everts and Company, Philadelphia, p 54

One unconfirmed account, a petition for financial relief filed by Wendell Brown with an unspecified Virginia Regiment in 1757, claimed that Wendell was accompanied on this expedition by his wife Elisabetha, his sons Thomas, Maunus, and Adam, and his youngest daughter Margaretha.[6] Another unconfirmed account, *"The Reuben Bunner Revelation,"* claims that Wendell was accompanied by his wife and children as well as the families of his two married daughters Catherine (or Catrina) Catt and Mary Böner. This would include Catrina's husband, Michael, and Mary's husband, Casper, as well as the small children of each family.[7]

It is possible, and even likely, that John accompanied his parents and the rest of the extended family on this move, but there is also reason to doubt. To date, no other archives have been discovered to corroborate the move of the larger family. Also, in the spring of 1752, when this move took place, Mary was several months pregnant with her second child Joseph. This would have made an already treacherous trip even more difficult, and they were moving to a wilderness with no clear ground, no house to live in, and no garden to provide a ready food supply.

If Casper and Mary Böner did make this move, it would make more sense that they moved in late 1752 or early 1753 after Wendell and his sons had cleared land, built a log house, and created garden spaces. The one-hundred-and-sixty-mile trip over the mountains would have still been difficult with a three-year-old and a one-year-old, but there would have been a house to live in when they arrived.

It is also possible that, due to their personal situations, Casper and Mary decided to remain at their home on the South Fork River with the intent to join the rest of the family at some future time. This scenario fits well with the fact that Wendell and his sons (and probably his wife and unmarried daughter) were able to easily move

---

6 Ancestry.com, Johan Wendell Braun, https://www.ancestry.com/mediaui-viewer/tree/62370820/person/402207020362/media/697f2dab-59b8-40af-a66b-0f2efaeaf436?destTreeId=196408406&destPersonId=382561276727&hid=1010262120113&_phsrc=bbY2693&_phstart=default&usePUBJs=true&currentPageIsStart=&hintStatus=pending

7 Bunner, Gale, "Descendants of Casper (Boner) Bunner and Mary Christiana Brown – Revised Edition," 1988

back to the South Fork homestead when they were forced to flee the Monongahela River Valley in June 1754 with the outbreak of the French and Indian War.

Whether young John lived with his family in the Monongahela Valley for two years, one year, or not at all, the result was the same. Hostilities between England and France over ownership of the Ohio River Valley culminated in a deadly skirmish between forces led by George Washington and the French commander Joseph Jumonville, known as the Battle of Jumonville Glen, in May 1754. This battle took place just a few miles from Wendell Brown's new homestead.

Three weeks after this battle, scouts from George Washingtons small army at nearby Fort Necessity hurriedly rode by the homesteads of the fifteen families that had settled on Ohio Company lands telling them to flee for their lives. A large French army from nearby Fort Duquesne, along with their Indian allies, was moving down the Monongahela River in pursuit of the forces led by George Washington. The settlers would likely be killed if they got in the way.

Wendell and his sons (and possibly his entire extended family) did not have time to plan an orderly retreat. They, like all the other families that had recently established homes on Ohio Company land, dropped everything and immediately headed in the direction of Fort Necessity, approximately twelve miles to the east. It is possible that three of those fleeing families were the Browns, the Böners, and the Catts.

Some history books suggest that Wendell and his sons stayed at the fort and participated in the battle that took place on July 3-4, 1754. One historical account even claims that Wendell and his sons supplied food to Washington's soldiers.[8]

Both claims seem dubious, as these same history books also record there were approximately fifteen families that fled for their lives to Fort Necessity, which would have included wives and many small children. It is doubtful that Washington wanted such a contingent in the small fort as he prepared for the upcoming battle. Also, regarding food, it was early June and none of the gardens would be

---

8   Veech, James (1892), "Monongahela of Old", Pittsburgh, P. 109

producing food that early in the season. Even if the fleeing families brought a milk cow or two, that would not even make one meal for Washington's three hundred soldiers.

It is more likely that Washington sent these families ahead to the British fort at Will's Creek (present-day Cumberland, Maryland), fifty miles to the east and a five-to-six-day trip by foot. From Wills Creek, the fleeing families would have split up and returned to their old homes. For Wendell Brown and those family members who had accompanied him, that meant returning to their homestead on the South Fork of the South Branch of the Potomac River.

On July 3-4, 1754, Washington's small army was defeated by the larger French forces and their Indian allies at the Battle of Fort Necessity. After surrendering, Washington and his soldiers retreated to Wills Creek while the victorious French burned the houses, barns, and gardens of the Ohio Company settlers. The estate Wendell Brown had been building was among those destroyed. His two-year investment in time and sweat to build his new homestead went up in smoke. So did his latest dream of land ownership.

By the middle of July 1754, Wendell Brown and his extended family were living together again in the South Fork Valley. John was four years old and his younger brother Joseph was two. Within weeks, John's first sister, Elizabeth, was born.

Within a few months, the daily routine of life fell into a pattern that seemed 'normal' for John. He was too young to be aware of, or to understand, that a war was brewing across the wilderness of the American colonies.

A year later, in 1755, John's mother presented him with his second sister, Margaret. He was now the big brother of three siblings and learning what it meant to assume responsibilities. He was assigned chores around the house and in the garden and knew that if he didn't successfully complete those chores it would make life more difficult for other family members who were counting on him.

Also in 1755, John may have overheard family members discussing the defeat of General Braddock's army by French and Indian forces along the Monongahela River but would not understand its significance. He likewise may have heard his father and grandfather talk about the many new forts being constructed along the Virginia frontier in 1755 but would have only a vague understanding of why they were being built.

By early 1756, alarming events were occurring near where John and his extended family lived that he would understand as existential threats, even though these words were not in his vocabulary. Delaware Indian forces led by Chief Killbuck were destroying settlements, attacking forts, and killing settlers and soldiers along the South Branch and Cacapon Rivers in Hampshire and Augusta Counties. John could sense the worry, anxiety, and fear in the voices of his parents and grandparents when they talked about these events. He would have absorbed some of their anxiety and fear.

The concerns of the family became a reality on April 20, 1756. John's grandfather Wendell and his teenaged aunt Margaretha were walking along the banks of the South Fork River near their house when a group of Delaware Indians on horseback surrounded them and took them captive.[9] Knowing that if they resisted they would likely be killed, they surrendered peacefully. As Wendell had lived near a group of Delaware Indians during the two years he lived in the Monongahela Valley, he may have learned enough of their language to negotiate their survival. For whatever reason, their lives were spared.

After traveling a short distance with their captors, Wendell and Margaretha were joined by another group of Indians who had captured Mrs. Leonard Neff, the wife of Wendell's landlord and neighbor. A short time later, Mrs. Neff suddenly bolted and ran, making a successful escape into the thickets.[10] Upon her arrival back home that evening, she told Wendell and Margaretha's family what happened. The entire family, including six-year-old John, became distraught.

That Wendell and Margaretha did not return home after a few days told the family that they did not escape. They had either been taken far away as prisoners, or they had been killed.

---

9  Steele, Ian K. (2013), "Setting All the Captives Free", McGill-Queens University Press, p. 452

10  Steele, Ian K. (2013), "Setting All the Captives Free", McGill-Queens University Press, p. 515

This sudden disappearance of Wendell and Margaretha caused the rest of his family to immediately seek refuge in the east. As the river water levels were always high in the spring due to the melting snow and the spring rains, it is likely that they built log rafts to hasten their retreat down the rivers and then to the east. Taking only those important belongings they could easily carry they started the seventy-mile trip down the South Fork and South Branch Rivers. Once they reached the mouth of the South Branch they continued down the Potomac River to a destination east of the Blue Ridge Mountains. Historical archives suggest they ended their journey in Frederick, Maryland.[11]

At age six, it is certain that the trauma of believing that his grandfather and aunt may have been murdered by Indians, followed by the panic filled one hundred thirty-mile retreat down the Potomac River, are memories that John lived with for the rest of his life. Today it would be called "post-traumatic stress syndrome." During John's time it was called "growing up."

Within a few months after fleeing from the frontier, Mary Böner gave birth to her third son, Reuben. He was Casper and Mary's fifth child.

Also within a few months after fleeing, Casper Böner made a connection with Robert Davis, a large landowner near Hedgesville in Frederick County, Virginia. The circumstances under which they met are presently unknown, but for some reason Robert Davis became motivated to sell 27 prime acres of his 400-acre farm to Casper. The two entered a private deed contract making Casper the legal owner of the 27-acre parcel, with the stipulations that Casper had to get permission from Robert Davis if he ever wanted to sell the property, and Davis maintained a right of first refusal if Casper did sell the property.

It seems likely that Robert Davis sold this property in return for Casper agreeing to assume some supervisory position for managing day-to-day operations of the Davis farm. As this was a private deed

---

11 "Maryland Births and Christenings, 1650-1995", database, FamilySearch, Susanah Barbel Bonner, Frederick, MD, 1758, https://www.familysearch.org/search/collection/1674912

## JOHN AMOS BONNER (BONER/BUNNER)

contract, it was never recorded at the Frederick, Virginia County Clerk's office.

The timing for this transaction is unknown, but the earliest date would have been mid-1756 and the latest would have been late 1758. Sometime between 1756 and 1758, Casper and Mary Böner, along with their children, moved to this 27-acre property in Frederick County, Virginia.

In the meantime, John's grandfather, Wendell Brown, suddenly reappeared in September 1757. After his capture he had been held prisoner at Fort Duquesne, then Fort Quebec, and then shipped to France as a prisoner of war. England and France had a prisoner of war exchange in mid-1757, and Wendell was shipped back to America where he eventually reunited with his family.

However, Wendell's return was bittersweet because his daughter, Margaretha did not return with him. The last time Wendell saw her was when the Indians who had captured the two of them turned Wendell in at Fort Duquesne for a bounty. The Indians likely took Margaretha to their settlement in Ohio, where she was adopted into their tribe. Afterward, she would have been acclimated to their culture and language, and then likely became an Indian wife. Her family never heard from her again.

In May 1758, Casper and Mary welcomed Susanah Barbel Bonner to the family as their sixth child. She was christened in a church in Frederick Maryland on May 10, 1758.[12] It is unclear whether Casper and Mary were living in Frederick at the time, Mary temporarily moved from Hedgesville, Virginia to Frederick Maryland (forty miles) to have the baby, or the family took a short break from their Hedgesville responsibilities to travel to Frederick to celebrate the christening.

By mid-1758, the tide of the French and Indian War had changed with the English advancing toward the west and the French retreating toward Canada. The Indian forces that had been terrorizing the Virginia, Maryland and Pennsylvania frontiers between 1756 and

---

12 "Maryland Births and Christenings, 1650-1995", database, FamilySearch, Susanah Barbel Bonner, Frederick, MD, 1758, https://www.familysearch.org/search/collection/1674912

1758 slowly began withdrawing to their lands north of the Ohio River.

As a result, some of the settlers that had retreated east of the Blue Ridge Mountains in 1756 began returning to their frontier homes. Emboldened by the growing presence of British and colonial forces west of the Allegheny Mountains, some settlers began moving all the way across the Allegheny Mountains to the Monongahela River Valley to establish new homesteads on lands claimed concurrently by the French, the English, and the Indians.

John's grandfather and grandmother, Wendell and Elisabetha Brown, along with uncles Thomas, Maunus, and Adam Brown were among these early returnees to the Monongahela Valley. They arrived early enough to be able to resettle on the land from which they were forced to flee during the outbreak of the French and Indian War in 1754. The most likely date for this move was 1760 or 1761.

In early 1760, Robert Davis died and his widow, Dinah, sold his 400-acre farm to George Myles. However, Robert had made one stipulation in his will – that Casper Böner would continue to own the 27-acre property that Davis had previously sold to him. This parcel owned by Casper was completely contained within the larger 400-acre property. Dinah Davis and George Myles honored the Robert Davis will, and the 27-acre "carve out" for Casper Böner (spelled Boner in the legal documents) was noted in the deed which transferred the 400-acre property to George Myles.[13]

Casper and Mary Böner and their growing family lived on and farmed this 27-acre property for approximately ten years before they sold it in 1768. This is where John grew from an eight-year-old boy into an eighteen-year-old young man. It is also where Casper and Mary's seventh child Catherine was born circa 1765 and their youngest son, Casper, Jr. was born circa 1767.

As the oldest son, John would have been responsible for many of the farm chores that had to be completed to provide for the family. He would have fed and taken care of the cows, sheep, pigs, and chickens. He would have assisted his father in butchering one or

---

13 Frederick County, Virginia County Clerk's Office, Deed Book 6, Robert Davis Estate to George Myles, pages 9-14

two pigs each autumn and salting the meat to prevent it from spoiling during the winter.

He would have plowed the gardens each spring, done much of the work to take care of the growing crops during the summer, and provided much of the heavy labor for harvesting the crops in the fall. He would frequently hunt and fish to provide some of the meals for the family. He would engage in trapping activities to harvest fur that could be sold to raise cash for necessities that could not be grown or made at home. He also shared responsibility with his parents for training his younger siblings to do the farm work.

He learned to ride a horse and how to hitch it to a wagon, and would have made runs to Hedgesville, Martinsburg, Warm Springs (present-day Berkeley Springs, West Virginia), and Hagerstown, Maryland to sell furs and purchase necessities. These outings helped him to develop and refine his social skills outside his home. It also allowed him to begin taking notice of the young girls his age that he would pass along the way.

Casper and Mary Böner were Christians who maintained a Lutheran affiliation both in Germany and after they immigrated to Pennsylvania. However, when they lived on their 27-acre property there were only two churches within easy travel distance. One was the Presbyterian church at Falling Waters, about two miles to the east. The other was the Episcopal Church in Hedgesville, about two miles to the south.

Most families attended church worship services in the mid-1700's and it is reasonable to believe that Casper, Mary, and their children attended Sunday services at one of these two churches. The Mount Zion Episcopal Church in Hedgesville, West Virginia and the Falling Waters Presbyterian Church in Spring Mill, West Virginia still exist today, but their original log buildings were replaced with brick buildings during the 1800's. George Washington attended several worship services at the Mount Zion Episcopal Church during the 1750's and 1760's while he was Frederick County's representative in the House of Burgesses. It is possible that Casper, Mary, and their children may have attended one – or more - of those same services.

In 1768, when John was eighteen years old, George Myles, who had purchased the Robert Davis farm from Robert's widow in 1760, approached Casper Böner with a lucrative proposal. He was willing to pay Casper £25 for his 27-acre property. This compared to a price of £.07 for a 27-acre property from Lord Fairfax. In other words, Casper could take the £25 received for selling his 27-acre property and purchase 10,000 acres of undeveloped land from Fairfax. It is unknown why George Myles was willing to pay such a premium price for this property, but Casper accepted the Myles offer and sold his property in February 1768.

As part of the deal, it seems that Casper and his family continued living on the 27-acre farm for several months while he completed the purchase of a larger parcel of land nearby. As Casper was forty-eight years old, he had in mind to purchase a property of sufficient size to bequeath to his four sons. During the spring of 1768, he identified two nearby parcels of vacant and available land owned by Lord Fairfax.

One was a 334-acre parcel approximately one mile west of Hedgesville and approximately three miles west of the 27-acre farm Casper had just sold. It included the western slope of North Mountain and approximately 200 acres of flat bottom land along Back Creek. It also included "the gap" through the North Mountain ridge through which the road (present-day Route 9) from Hedgesville to Warm Springs (present-day Berkeley Springs) ran.

The second parcel was a 365-acre tract located approximately six miles west of the 334-acre property. This parcel had the road from Hedgesville to Warm Springs running through the middle. The terrain was mostly rolling and once cleared, would be very suitable for farmland and livestock grazing.

Casper applied for warrants to purchase both parcels of land from the local Fairfax land sales office. The applications were accompanied by the standard down payment of 50% of the purchase price, which would have been approximately £1 for each of the two properties. Casper soon received both warrants, which were necessary for him to schedule surveys on each property. Both surveys were completed on August 6, 1768. Eighteen-year-old John and his eleven-year-old brother Reuben are recorded as working for the surveying crew as "chain bearers."[14]

---

14  Virginia Colonial Land Office, 334 Acre Grant to 'Gasper Banner,' July 24, 1789, https://lva-virginia.libguides.com/land-grants

## JOHN AMOS BONNER (BONER/BUNNER)

Casper paid for the surveys, and the surveyors submitted the surveys to the Fairfax land sales office. The next step was for Fairfax to issue the land patents (deeds) and schedule a closing at which Casper would pay Fairfax the remaining 50% he owed on the properties and Fairfax would provide Casper with free and clear deeds giving him legal ownership to both parcels.

Casper, John, Joseph, and Reuben began clearing some of the 334-acre property and building a log house. They also constructed barns, outbuildings and fences for their livestock. It is possible that by the onset of winter in 1768 that the family had completed the move from the 27-acre property to their new log house on the 334-acre property. They began paying Fairfax a nominal rent (probably in the range of 3-4 shillings per year) while waiting for the land patents to be issued.

In late 1769, John learned of the death of his grandfather, Wendell Brown. Wendell never realized his American dream of land ownership. However, he did live to see his sons Maunus and Adam acquire the Monongahela River Valley land on which they had originally settled in 1752 before fleeing due to the outbreak of the French and Indian War. Maunus and Adam had acquired adjacent properties, each of which measured over 300 acres, in June 1769.

John and his younger brothers Joseph and Reuben gradually took over the jobs requiring heavy labor from their aging father as they settled in and continued making improvements to their 334-acre tract. At the beginning of each month, they had hopes that it would be the month when Fairfax would finally issue the land patents. However, months turned into years, and by 1771, three years after the surveys had been submitted, Fairfax still had not delivered the patents.

During this three-year period, Mary had two more daughters, Mary Christina, and Charlotte. This completed Casper and Mary's family with ten children. John was a full generation older than his two new sisters.

Also in 1771, Casper's growing frustration with the Fairfax land sales office, and likely some cajoling from his brothers-in-law

Maunus and Adam Brown, drove him to the Monongahela Valley seeking land for himself and his sons.

By this time, most of the desirable land along the Monongahela River from present-day Pittsburgh to present-day Brownsville, Pennsylvania had already been claimed, so Casper focused his search further upstream near present-day Fairmont, West Virginia. He found a unique 400-acre parcel of flat land on a plateau on the western bank of the Monongahela River (present-day Rivesville, West Virginia) that was for sale. He purchased the "settlement certificate" for this land and began planning to move his family from their Hedgesville property to this newly acquired property along the Monongahela River.

John, Joseph, and Reuben were likely dispatched by their father in early 1772 to clear enough of the Monongahela River land to plant a garden and to build a large enough log house for their family. They probably completed this work by late spring and returned to the Hedgesville property to help the family prepare for the move. During this time, their sister Margaret was married to a Mr. Harmison who was already a Berkeley County landowner. By early summer, the entire family – less Margaret - set out for the move to their new home along the Monongahela. Casper was age fifty-two and Mary was age forty-four. The nine children who accompanied them ranged in age from one to twenty-two.

They crossed the Potomac River and followed the road along the river to Cumberland, Maryland. From their they followed the Braddock Road across the Allegheny Mountains until they reached the Monongahela River at Redstone Settlement (present-day Brownsville, Pennsylvania). They likely stopped just east of Redstone Settlement to visit Mary's brothers Maunus, Adam, and Thomas and her stepmother Elisabetha.

From Redstone Settlement, the family traveled southward on a wide path that was suitable for foot or horse travel, but not for a horse drawn wagon. The distance from Redstone Settlement to their new home was approximately fifty miles. They arrived at their new wilderness home overlooking the Monongahela River by mid-July 1772.

## JOHN AMOS BONNER (BONER/BUNNER)

Soon after arriving, John began exploring the area and introducing himself to his new neighbors. He first met Zackwell Morgan. Zackwell was the son of Morgan Morgan, a Welsh immigrant who is traditionally considered the first colonial settler in what is now West Virginia. Zackwell had served as an officer in the French and Indian War, after which he decided to take advantage of the new "Settlement Rights" provisions enacted by the Virginia General Assembly to promote settlement along the mountainous Virginia frontier.

He had originally settled on the land now owned by Casper Böner in 1766. He then exercised his "preemption right," which allowed him to purchase an additional 1,000 acres adjacent to his original 400 acre claim. He now lived on this adjacent 1,000-acre parcel, where he had built a very nice log house with a commanding view of the valley, the river, and the mountains beyond.

Zackwell introduced John to his brother David. David was fifty years old and had long-ago established a reputation as a fierce Indian fighter. He was over six feet tall, with chiseled features, piercing black eyes, good teeth, and black hair without a streak of gray. He was intense, blunt, and to the point in his communications, but he was also known as an honest and kind man who was always helping others.[15]

David also had gained much experience as a surveyor and had been hired along with George Washington to survey the lands of Lord Fairfax in 1746. He helped identify the western boundaries of the 5.2-million-acre Fairfax estate and worked with the crew that placed the original Fairfax Stone, which today defines the boundary between Maryland and West Virginia.

David had also worked for Christopher Gist doing survey work for the Ohio Company. He then became one of the original settlers along with John's grandfather Wendell Brown (and perhaps Casper and John) on the Ohio Company land. In 1753 he had established a new homestead on the "Gist Plantation" (near present-day Uniontown, Pennsylvania) only to have to flee the following year with the outbreak of the French and Indian War.

Afterward, David served as an officer in the French and Indian War and served under General Edward Braddock in the disastrous

---

15 Lough, Glenn D., "Now and Long Ago – A History of the Marion County Area," Morgantown Printing and Binding Co., 1969, p. 118-119

march on Fort Duquesne in 1755, during which he had been struck by a sword, leaving a large scar on his left cheek. He was one of the few survivors at the Battle of Great Cacapon in 1756, where Delaware Indian Chief Killbuck soundly defeated the colonial forces led by Colonel John Mercer

David told John about being hired just two years earlier by George Washington to survey properties Washington had been granted along the Ohio River (present-day Washington Bottom, south of Parkersburg, West Virginia). This land had been granted to Washington as payment for his service during the French and Indian War. Although David was nearly thirty years older than John, the two bonded and quickly became good friends. They would share many experiences over the next thirty years.

John also introduced himself to Jacob Prickett, who lived about a mile downstream and on the opposite side of the Monongahela River. Jacob and his family had previously lived along Back Creek in Frederick County, Virginia, approximately fifteen miles upstream from where John had grown up. Jacob had moved with his family to this previously unsettled area in 1759 or 1760 when the hostilities of the French and Indian War had begun subsiding.

Jacob lived here with his wife, six sons, and five daughters. He operated a trading post and a grist mill on his property. The King of England's Proclamation of 1763 had made Jacob's settlement "illegal" but he had disregarded the Proclamation and remained on his land. By the time John met Jacob in 1772, Jacob held a "settlement certificate" for the 1,400 acres of land he was living on (but he did not gain final legal ownership from the Virginia Land Office until 1786).[16]

On advice from his father, Casper, as well as from Zackwell Morgan and Jacob Prickett, John spent much time exploring the area to identify desirable land that was still vacant that he could claim under the "Settlement Rights" law. He found a parcel on the east side of the river that sloped steeply up from the river but plateaued on top with approximately 300 acres of rolling land. This parcel was approximately three miles downstream of his father's property, and two miles downstream of the Jacob Prickett property.

---

16  Lough, Glenn D., "Now and Long Ago – A History of the Marion County Area," Morgantown Printing and Binding Co., 1969, p. 234, 246

## JOHN AMOS BONNER (BONER/BUNNER)

In 1772, John built a cabin on this tract, cleared enough land for a garden, grew and harvested a small crop of corn, and submitted a settlement claim on this 400-acre tract to the colonial Virginia Land Office. He received a "settlement certificate" acknowledging he had completed the prerequisite steps for claiming the land, but this certificate was not a legal document conferring ownership. However, an unofficial code of conduct had developed among frontiersmen that honored "Settlement Rights" and "settlement certificates" even without legal documents. John's claim was safe among pioneers, explorers, trappers, and other frontiersmen.

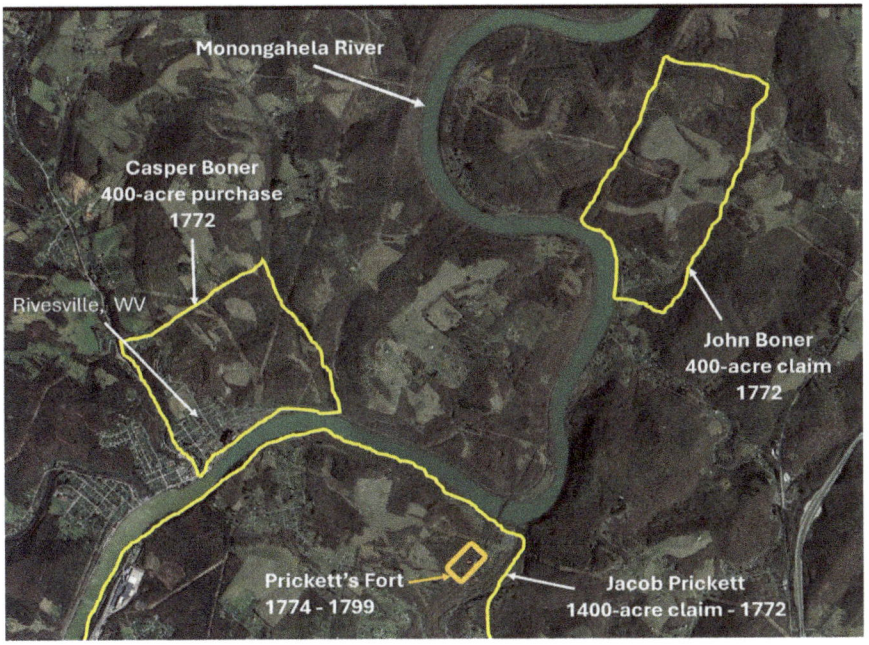

**Casper Böner, John Bonner (Boner) and
Jacob Prickett Monongahela properties - 1772**
(Map created by Michael Bunner overlaid on Google Earth 2025 image)

John Bonner's name (spelled Bunner in the document) is included in a James Morgan (son of Zackwell Morgan) land entry which provides independent confirmation that he had made a land claim in the area in 1772:

> "James Morgan assignee of Moses Templin, who was assignee to William Anderson, is entitled to 400 acres of land in Monongalia County on the Monongahela River, adjoining land claimed by John Bunner to include his settlement made here in the year 1772".[17]

In 1774, John's oldest sister Elizabeth, who was four years younger than him, married John Miller. They built a log house adjacent to the Casper Böner house on Casper's 400-acre plot. They lived in this house until after John Miller's death in 1820.

During this time, John Bonner gained some notoriety in the local community. From the collection of Adam O. Heck interviews published in *Now and Long Ago* by Glenn D. Lough, Mrs. Keziah Batten Shearer, who knew both John Bonner (spelled Bunner in the reference document) and David Morgan, made the following statement:

> "Nobody whipped David Morgan, and the only time he was ever "out shot with rifles" was at a shooting – match at Pettyjohn's, and then young John Bunner did it."[18]

(Pettyjohn's was the site of a Monongahela River ferry crossing south of Prickett's Fort.)

1774 also saw bloody skirmishes rekindled between the Indians and the settlers on the Virginia and Pennsylvania frontiers. An inexcusable event occurred along the Ohio River that would have tragic reverberations for John, his family, and all their Monongahela

---

17  Bunner, Gale, "Descendants of Casper (Boner) Bunner and Mary Christiana Brown – Revised Edition," 1988, p. 15

18  Lough, Glenn D., "Now and Long Ago – A History of the Marion County Area," Morgantown Printing and Binding Co., 1969, p. 302-303

Valley neighbors. A small contingent of white frontiersmen massacred a group of Indians, including several members of the family of Logan, chief of the Mingo's. Logan had been a very vocal advocate for peace between the Indians and the white settlers since the end of the French and Indian War. After his family was murdered, Logan's voice for peace became silent. He sought revenge. He led raids across the upper Ohio Valley and the Monongahela Valley, vowing to take one white scalp for every Indian killed in the Ohio River massacre. The summer of 1774 erupted with significant violence along the Virginia frontier.

Historical marker on State Route 2 along the Ohio River, two miles south of Newell, West Virginia

Due to increased Indian attacks along the Monongahela River, Zackwell Morgan and Lt. James Chew, both veterans of the French and Indian War, formed a local militia consisting of forty-five men. Jacob Prickett and his sons, along with the members of the militia, built a fort on land owned by Prickett. Although John, Joseph, and Reuben Bonner are not recorded as being part of this militia, it is almost certain that they and all other able-bodied area residents assisted in the hasty construction of this fort. Construction started in late March 1774 and was completed by early May. When completed, the fort was able to provide a place of refuge for up to ninety area families in the event of Indian attack.[19]

Chief Logan and his band of approximately fifteen warriors struck four times in the Monongahela Valley near Prickett's Fort during 1774. The first was on June 11. Captain Francis McClure and Samuel Kincaid had spent the previous day on a scouting expedition up the Tygart River Valley. They returned and spent the night at Prickett's Fort. The next morning they departed for Redstone Fort fifty miles downstream. Along the way Logan and his warriors ambushed them, killing McClure and gravely wounding Kincaid.

The second incident occurred in early July. Logan and his warriors attacked nine men hoeing corn on Dunkard Creek (approximately five miles north of present-day Morgantown on the west side of the Monongahela River). Three of the men got away; the other six were murdered and scalped.

The third incident was on July 12 along the West Fork River at the mouth of Simpson's Creek twenty miles south of Prickett's Fort (near present-day Bridgeport, West Virginia). Logan and his band surprised William Robinson, Thomas Hellen, and Coleman Brown while they were harvesting flax in a field. The Indians opened fire from the rear, killing Coleman Brown. The other two were not hit and ran for their lives. They were captured and taken to Logan's tribe where they were initially tortured but were later adopted by the tribe.

The fourth incident occurred ten weeks later in early October. After the murder of Coleman Brown and the capture of William Robinson and Thomas Hellen, virtually all the area residents near Prickett's Fort had retreated to the fort for refuge. At Powers Fort, located on Simpson's Creek near where Brown had been murdered, forty-three settlers were turned away because of overcrowding

---

19   Prickett Fort State Park, Fairmont, WV, Visitors video

conditions. They found refuge at Prickett's Fort.[20] The entire community around Prickett's Fort, including the Casper Böner family and the newlyweds John and Elizabeth Miller, moved to the fort. Approximately eighty families ended up living at the fort for nearly fourteen weeks. John and his brothers, Joseph and Reuben, along with all other men who were proficient with a rifle, likely supplemented the volunteer militia as sentries working in shifts to provide round the clock protection of the fort.

As night fell on the evening of October 2, Isaiah Prickett, the fourteen-year-old son of Jacob Prickett and Mrs. Susan Oxx, a young wife pregnant with her first child, left the fort to locate their cows and drive them back toward the fort for the night. As they were returning to the fort with their cows, they were ambushed by Logan and his band, who were drawn to them by the tinkling of the cow bells.

When the two never returned, a search party went out looking for them. Isaiah Prickett was found murdered and scalped, and Mrs. Oxx was nowhere to be seen. Jacob Prickett, David Morgan, and others, perhaps including John Bonner, trailed and overtook the Indians who had murdered Isaiah. There was a fight in the darkness during which two Indians were killed. The others, including Chief Logan, escaped into the darkness with Mrs. Oxx.

After the fight, Isaiah's scalp was found on the belt of one of the dead Indians. Isaiah's father, Jacob, brought it back to the fort and gave it to his daughter-in-law Charity Prickett, saying he would be pleased if she could use it in such a way as to enable his son to be buried whole. The night before Isaiah was buried, Charity and Isaiah's mother stitched his scalp to his head, then fixed his hair so that "it appeared nothing was apart from the unusual..."[21]

The Virginia colonial government response to this series of Indian attacks is known as "Dunmore's War," but it is better understood as "Logan's Revenge." This war lasted a little less than one

---

20  Lough, Glenn D., "Now and Long Ago – A History of the Marion County Area," Morgantown Printing and Binding Co., 1969, p. 307

21  Lough, Glenn D., "Now and Long Ago – A History of the Marion County Area," Morgantown Printing and Binding Co., 1969, p. 119

year and consisted of a series of deadly skirmishes that culminated in one major engagement, the Battle of Point Pleasant. That battle was fought on October 10, 1774, at the confluence of the Ohio and Kanawha Rivers. Indian forces under Shawnee chief Cornstalk and Virginia militia forces under Colonel Andrew Lewis fought a furious day-long battle that left many dead and wounded on both sides. As night fell, Cornstalk retreated across the Ohio River where he was pursued by Colonel Lewis and another force led by Lord Dunmore, the colonial governor of Virginia.

They eventually caught up with Cornstalk and compelled him to agree to a treaty ceding all Shawnee claims on land south of the Ohio River (present-day West Virginia and Kentucky). This treaty brought an end to these frontier uprisings and helped those who had been living at Prickett's Fort for over three months to feel secure enough to return to their homes.

During this same time, a long-standing border dispute between Virginia and Pennsylvania was coming to a head. The southwestern corner of present-day Pennsylvania, which included the lower Monongahela Valley, had long been contested by both colonies. By the early 1770's the relationship between the two colonies had deteriorated to the point that both were electing officeholders and appointing judges who spent considerable time threatening and arresting each other. Settlers made land claims and followed the laws of the colony they believed – or hoped – they were living in.

Pennsylvania claimed ownership primarily due to the original 1681 land grant from the King of England and the commonwealth's 1768 purchase of the land from the Indians after concluding the Treaty of Fort Stanwix. To strengthen their claim, Pennsylvania established Westmoreland County in 1773, which included the lower Monongahela Valley.

Virginia claimed the land by virtue of winning Dunmore's War in 1774, which forced the Shawnees to cede all lands east and south of the Ohio River to Virginia. At the conclusion of the war, Governor Dunmore went as far as to travel to the abandoned Fort Pitt (present-day Pittsburgh) and renamed it Fort Dunmore. This was simply chest-thumping on Dunmore's part to stake out a stronger Virginia claim to this territory.

Also in 1774, to counter Pennsylvania's establishment of Westmoreland County, Virginia established the District of West Augusta which included the entire Monongahela Valley and overlapped all of Pennsylvania's Westmoreland County. In 1776, Virginia divided this West Augusta District into Monongalia, Ohio, and Yohogania County. Yohogania County included the greater part of the present-day Allegheny and Washington Counties in Pennsylvania.

On August 28, 1780, in the middle of the Revolutionary War, this boundary dispute was finally settled by both Pennsylvania and Virginia agreeing to extend the Mason Dixon line westward to a point five degrees west of the Delaware River. From that point, a straight-line running due north defined the western boundary of Pennsylvania. Virginia would maintain the small strip of land between the western boundary of Pennsylvania and the Ohio River.

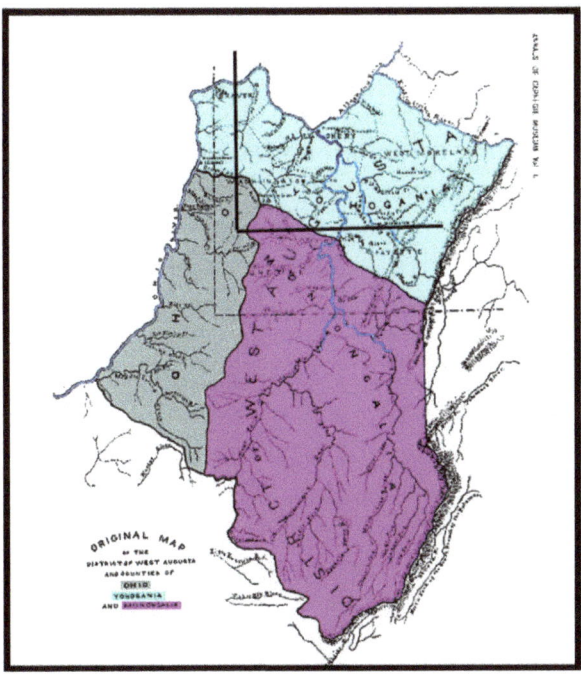

**Map of the District of West Augusta, Virginia and the three counties formed from it in 1776 - Library of Congress** (public domain)

There were two underlying, unheralded reasons why Pennsylvania ultimately won this dispute. First, the large population of Pennsylvania Germans who had settled this area were lovers of religious liberty, one of the reasons so many German immigrants had originally settled in Pennsylvania. Virginia had established Anglicism (Church of England) as the official religion of the colony and imposed financial penalties for those who adhered to the beliefs of any other religious denomination. Second, the Pennsylvania Germans who had settled in Westmoreland County were bitterly opposed to slavery, an institution that was flourishing in Virginia and would continue to do so for another eighty-five years.[22]

Thomas Jefferson was governor of Virginia when this agreement was finalized. He realized that the will of the majority of those living in the disputed territory was not on the side of Virginia. His only stipulation in the final agreement was that Pennsylvania honor the settlement claims issued by Virginia for land that was now in Pennsylvania.

In 1776, Zackwell and David Morgan surveyed the site of the town of Pleasantville (present-day Rivesville, West Virginia). At this time according to Monongalia County land records there were at least seven dwellings at this location: James Jolliffe (who died before 1772), Adonijah Little, Henry Batten, Matthew Hoult, Casper Böner, Sr. (spelled Bunner in the reference document), John Miller (Casper Böner's son-in-law) and Zackwell Morgan. This small town was the first one west of the Allegheny Mountains to be legally incorporated, properly surveyed, and parceled into lots with reasonable trustees appointed.[23]

While all this was going on along the frontier, events in London, Boston and Philadelphia were driving the American colonies inexorably toward war with Great Britian. A rapid progression of decisions in London that negatively impacted the colonies had created chasms that could not be bridged.

---

22   https://www.baltzermeyer.com/post/virginia-s-1774-border-dispute-with-pennsylvania

23   Lough, Glenn D., "Now and Long Ago – A History of the Marion County Area," Morgantown Printing and Binding Co., 1969, p. 402

## JOHN AMOS BONNER (BONER/BUNNER)

The colonists refusal to accept these English edicts had culminated in the Boston Massacre in 1770, the Boston Tea Party in 1773, the meeting of the First Continental Congress in September 1774, and Patrick Henry's fiery "Give me liberty, or give me death" speech in March 1775. On April 18-19, 1775, the British responded by sending armed troops to Lexington and Concord, Massachusetts to quash the rebellion. The American Revolution had begun.

In late 1775 and early 1776, the war with England was the talk among all the colonists. Along the frontier a staunch patriotism arose among most pioneers, and many of the young frontiersmen showed a willingness to fight for the cause of American independence.

Volunteer militia units started forming in the newly formed and overlapping Monongalia County, Virginia and Westmoreland County, Pennsylvania. The purpose of these militias was to protect local communities from "back door" attacks by British forces stationed to the west in forts at Detroit and Vincennes. There was also great concern that the British would establish alliances with the Indians that could precipitate another bloody frontier war.

In late 1775 George Wilson, who had been appointed Justice of the Peace in recently formed Westmoreland County, Pennsylvania, began recruiting soldiers to serve full-time to protect the western frontier along the Lower Monongahela Valley. Wilson had previously lived near Jacob Prickett and still owned a large parcel of land along White Day Creek near John Bonner's 400-acre tract.[24] Wilson recruited several volunteers in the Prickett's Fort area, including twenty-five-year-old John Bonner and his twenty-three-year-old brother Joseph.[25]

Joseph, like John, was an excellent marksman. He was selected to join Captain John Nelson's Independent Company of Riflemen and given the rank of Corporal. He joined on February 21, 1776, and his unit was immediately dispatched to Canada. The mission of his company was to fight the British forces in Canada and to

---

24   Lough, Glenn D., "Now and Long Ago – A History of the Marion County Area," Morgantown Printing and Binding Co., 1969, p. 246

25   Lough, Glenn D., "Now and Long Ago – A History of the Marion County Area," Morgantown Printing and Binding Co., 1969, p. 334

entice the Canadians to join the American colonies in their fight for independence.[26]

Soon after Joseph departed for Canada, Casper and Mary Böner decided to move back to the 334-acre farm in Berkeley County they had moved from four years earlier. The reason for this move is unknown, but it may have been due to ongoing concerns about Indian attacks, the departure and loss of help from their two oldest sons, the western frontier threats of "back door" British invasions, or possibly health issues that Casper was experiencing.

Before departing for Berkeley County, Casper sold his 400-acre property to his son-in-law, John Miller. This property remained the residence of John and Elizabeth Miller until after John's death in 1820.[27] Nineteen-year-old Reuben decided to stay behind to protect Prickett's Fort (and to continue his courtship of Nancy Ann Prickett, Jacob's daughter). Joseph had already departed,[28] and John would soon depart, to do his part to win American independence.

Sometime in 1775 or early 1776, John met Martha Evans, and a romance developed. Martha was the daughter of John Evans, who was one of the earliest settlers in what soon became known as Morgantown, Virginia. This new settlement was located on the Monongahela River fifteen miles downstream of John's property and was named for Zackwell Morgan, who had purchased land and moved there one year before Evans arrived.

Evans was born in 1738 in the part of Prince William County, Virginia that became Fairfax County in 1742. While he was still young, his father, John Evans, Sr. (an immigrant from Wales) died of a rattlesnake bite. His mother, Margaret, remarried and sent her son to school in Alexandria where he became the first ancestor in

---

26 Montgomery, Thomas Lynch, "Pennsylvania Archives, Fifth Series, Volume 2," Harrisburg Publishing Company, State Printer, 1906, p. 75

27 Lough, Glenn D., "Now and Long Ago – A History of the Marion County Area," Morgantown Printing and Binding Co., 1969, p. 401

28 Montgomery, Thomas Lynch, "Pennsylvania Archives, Fifth Series, Volume 2," Harrisburg Publishing Company, State Printer, 1906, p. 75

the Bunner family line in America to be able to read and write. John Evans married Ann Martin circa 1758.[29]

Early in the 1760s Evans traveled west to the Monongahela River and marked trees on the land he planned to claim with tomahawk slashes. He returned to build a cabin and grow a crop of corn, and in the mid-1760s he, his family, and their servants prepared to move there. Fear of Indian hostilities interrupted their plans, however, and they lived for a time at Fort Cumberland, in Maryland. In late 1769 or early 1770 they moved to the land previously claimed near the new settlement of Morgantown.[30]

Evans built a log house near Morgantown on land that is now occupied by the Evansdale Campus of West Virginia University. (That house remained standing until the early 1900's when it was demolished to make way for new construction.)[31]

**John Evans house built circa 1769 on land now occupied by WVU's Evansdale Campus in Morgantown. (This picture of the original house was taken circa 1910 before the house was razed. Notice the openings on the second floor from which to shoot rifles.)**
(photo courtesy of West Virginia and Regional History Center)

---

29  https://www.wikitree.com/wiki/Evans-6330

30  MacKay, Iain. "John Evans (1737-1834)." Clio: Your Guide to History. October 1, 2020. Accessed February 13, 2025. https://theclio.com/entry/115653

31  https://www.wikitree.com/wiki/Evans-6330

**Marker in Morgantown, WV commemorating
Zackwell Morgan and John Evans**
(photo courtesy of West Virginia and Regional History Center)

In preparation for possible British invasion from Detroit, John Evans had received a commission as a major in the Monongalia County militia and was promoted to colonel within a few weeks. He recruited and maintained a volunteer force of warriors who could respond quickly to any British or Indian attack around the Morgantown area. Back east, these militia forces were called "Minutemen."[32]

By mid-summer 1776, there were over six hundred volunteers for the regiment formed by George Wilson. Private John Bonner

---

32  Library of Virginia, Dictionary of Virginia Biography, Colonel John Evans, www.lva.virginia.gov

was one of them. This unit was designated the 8th Pennsylvania Battalion (and shortly thereafter the 8th Pennsylvania Regiment) with the field officers being Aneas McKay, Colonel; George Wilson, Lieutenant Colonel; and Richard Butler, Major. The names of these leaders were submitted to the Continental Congress for approval and confirmed on July 20, 1776.[33] The 8th Pennsylvania Regiment became part of the Continental Army. The soldiers served full time. As a private, John would be paid $6.25/month.

The 8th Pennsylvania was originally raised for the defense of the western frontier, which is why George Wilson was so successful in his recruiting efforts. The recruits believed they would be protecting their homes and their families, and did not envision they would have to experience extended periods of family separation on distant battlefields. Unfortunately, the misfortunes that befell George Washington's army in New York and New Jersey during the summer and fall of 1776 caused a crisis that required a sudden change in plans. All available forces were ordered to fall under Washington's command and all troops raised by Pennsylvania and New Jersey were ordered to "fall in on the communication leading from New York to Philadelphia, at Brunswick, or between that and Princeton."[34]

The leadership as well as the soldiers of the 8th Pennsylvania were dismayed and distressed by these orders. They had volunteered to defend the western frontier where they lived, and now they had been ordered to undertake a march of nearly four hundred miles across the mountain wilderness of Pennsylvania all the way to New Jersey during the dead of winter. Lieutenant Colonel Wilson sent a letter to Colonel James Wilson (no relation), a member of the Continental Congress expressing his concerns. His letter, with original spelling and grammar, follows:

---

33 Lough, Glenn D., "Now and Long Ago – A History of the Marion County Area," Morgantown Printing and Binding Co., 1969, p. 334

34 The St. Clair Papers, I, pp. 379-379.

"Ketaning, Decr. 5th, 1776.

Dr. Colonall:

Last Evening we Recd Marching orders, Which I must say is not Disagreeable to me under ye Sircumstances of ye times, for when I enterd into ye Service I Judged that if a necessity appeared to call us Below, it would be Don, therefore it Dont come on me By Surprise; But as Both ye officers and men understood they Were Raised for ye Defence of ye Western frontiers, and their familys and substance to be left in so Defenceless a situation in their absence, seems to Give Sensable trouble, altho I Hope We Will Get over it, By leaving sum of ower trifling Officers Behind who Pirtend to Have more Witt than seven men that can Rendor a Reason. We are ill Provided for a March at this season, But there is nothing hard under sum Sircumstanccs. We Hope Provision Will be made for us Below, Blankets, Campe Kittles, tents, arms, Regementals, etc., that we may not Cut a Dispisable figure, But may be Enabled to answer ye expectation of ower Countre. " I Have Warmley Recomended to ye officers to lay aside all Personall Resentments at this time, for that it Would be construed By ye Worald that they made use of that Sircumstance to Hide themselves under from ye cause & ye countrie, and I hope it Will have a Good Effect at this time. We have iehned ye Neceserey orders, and appointed ye owt Parties to Randezvous at Hanows Town, ye 15th instant, and to March Emeditly from there. We have Recomended it to ye Militia to Station One Hundred Men at this post until further orders. "I Hope to have ye Pleasure of Seeing ye Soon, as we mean to take Philadelphia in ower Rout. In ye mean time, I am, With Esteem, your harty Wellwisher and Hmble Servt.

G. Wilson."[35]

---

35 Albert, George Dallas, "History of the County of Westmoreland, Pennsylvania," L.H. Everts Company, Philadelphia, PA, 1882, pp. 87-92

## JOHN AMOS BONNER (BONER/BUNNER)

Knowing that he was soon going to be deployed to the east, John Bonner likely visited his sister and brother-in-law near Prickett's Fort during Christmas of 1776. On his way back to Kittanning, he likely stopped in Morgantown to see Martha one last time to say goodbye before his deployment.

The 8th Pennsylvania departed Kittanning (located thirty-six miles north of present-day Pittsburgh on the Allegheny River) on January 6, 1777. The ensuing winter march through the mountain wilderness of Pennsylvania was harsh and debilitating. The snow was deep and the temperatures were below freezing. The men lacked adequate clothing, tents, blankets, and many other necessities. The soldiers had to hunt along the way to supplement their meager food supply. Many suffered from frostbite and most developed bad colds, or perhaps even influenza, which caused them to have fevers, sore throats, and deep coughs. Several men deserted and went home. The soldiers suffered more terribly from this frigid march than from any battle.[36]

In mid-February 1777, the regiment staggered into Quibbletown, New Jersey and set up camp. Within a short time, one-third of the regiment was on the sick list and 50 men died, including both senior officers, Mackay and Wilson.[37] It is unknown if John was among the approximately two hundred soldiers who were placed on the sick list when his unit arrived in New Jersey, but it is known that he ultimately survived this horrendous winter march.

On March 27, Colonel Daniel Brodhead IV transferred from the 4th Pennsylvania Regiment to take command of the 8th Pennsylvania.[38] Richard Butler was promoted to lieutenant colonel to replace George Wilson.

The 8th Pennsylvania fought at the Battle of Bound Brook (New Jersey) on April 13, 1777, under the command of Lieutenant Colonel

---

36 Albert, George Dallas, "History of the County of Westmoreland, Pennsylvania," L.H. Everts Company, Philadelphia, PA, 1882, pp. 87-92

37 Zipfel, Nathan. "Chapter X: The Eighth Pennsylvania". Westmoreland County Genealogy Project. 27 January 2012.

38 Boatner, Mark M. III (1994). Encyclopedia of the American Revolution. Mechanicsburg, Pa.: Stackpole Books. ISBN 0-8117-0578-1.

Butler.[39] Although the British and Hessian forces under General Cornwallis had the element of surprise, they fell short of capturing the garrison. They did take some prisoners, but their victory was not nearly as decisive as they had hoped.

In June, Lieutenant Colonel Butler and 140 men of the 8th Pennsylvania were detached to Colonel Daniel Morgan's elite fighting unit known as "Morgan's Rifles." Due to John Bonner's excellent marksmanship and rifle skills, it is likely he was one of the men selected for this assignment. Morgan's Rifles fought brilliantly at the Battles of Freeman's Farm and Bemis Heights north of Albany, New York in September. They then moved on to what would prove to be a decisive battle near Saratoga in early October.

**Colonel Daniel Morgan and his riflemen played a key role in the actions at Freeman's Farm in September, and Bemis Heights and Saratoga in October 1777. Painting by Hugh Charles McBarron**
(U.S. Army Center of Military History - public domain)

---

39  Boatner, Mark M. III (1994). Encyclopedia of the American Revolution. Mechanicsburg, Pa.: Stackpole Books. ISBN 0-8117-0578-1.

Morgan's Rifles played a crucial role in the American victory at the Battle of Saratoga. They inflicted heavy casualties on General Burgoyne's forces with their precise marksmanship. This victory was the turning point in America's war for independence because it convinced France to enter the war as an American ally.

While a part of their regiment was fighting at Saratoga, the remainder of the 8th Pennsylvania served in the Philadelphia Campaign during the summer and fall of 1777. Serving under Anthony Wayne, they fought in the Battles of Brandywine (September 11), Paoli (September 20-21), and Germantown (October 4). Although the British won all three of these battles, the Americans fought with skill and courage. Through these experiences they had learned that they were as skillful in battle as the British. Rather than these close losses causing discouragement, they served to increase their confidence. This confidence was bolstered considerably when they learned of the huge victory won by their compatriots at Saratoga.

In late November, the sharpshooters who had served with Colonel Morgan returned from Saratoga and rejoined the 8$^{th}$ Pennsylvania.[40] The British troops now occupied Philadelphia where they would remain for the winter. Washington made the decision to encamp his troops for the winter at Valley Forge, located along the Schuylkill River approximately twenty miles northwest of Philadelphia. Valley Forge was a naturally defensible plateau where the army could train and recoup from the year's battles, and the wet and frigid winter weather, muddy and impassable roads, and scant supplies made major battles less likely.[41]

---

40  Zipfel, Nathan. "Chapter X: The Eighth Pennsylvania". Westmoreland County Genealogy Project. 27 January 2012.

41  NPS.gov - Park Home - Learn About the Park - History & Culture - What Happened At Valley Forge

"The March to Valley Forge" – artist William B. Trego, 1883 (public domain)

John weathered the hard winter at Valley Forge along with 12,000 other Continental soldiers. He likely reconnected with his brother Joseph who also spent the winter there. The winter of 1777-78 was not the coldest nor the worst winter experienced during the war, but regular freezing and thawing, plus intermittent snowfall and rain, coupled with shortages of provisions, clothing, and shoes, made living conditions extremely difficult.

Rather than wait for deliverance, the encamped soldiers procured supplies from local farmers, hunted and fished to supplement their food supply, built log cabins to stay warm, constructed makeshift clothing and gear, and cooked subsistence meals of their own concoction.[42] Unfortunately, by early March as the temperatures rose and the men spent more time outdoors, typhoid fever and smallpox began spreading through the encampment, killing over 2,000 soldiers.

---

42  NPS.gov - Park Home - Learn About the Park - History & Culture - What Happened At Valley Forge

**The Valley Forge encampment included more than 1,500 log huts and two miles of fortifications** (National Park Service - public domain)

Washington spent the winter with his troops at Valley Forge. His continual presence and steady leadership were crucial to keeping the army intact. He hired former Prussian military officer Friedrich Wilhelm Baron von Steuben, who used the parade ground in the center of the camp to train the soldiers in Prussian military maneuvers. He ran the troops through a gamut of intense Prussian-style drills. He taught them to efficiently load, fire and reload weapons, charge with bayonets and march in compact columns of four instead of miles-long single-file marches. By the end of the winter, he had transformed the battered Continental Army into a fighting force capable of beating the British.[43]

---

43  https://www.history.com/topics/american-revolution/valley-forge

**Baron von Steuben at Valley Forge, 1778**
(Library of Congress – public domain)

On March 5, 1778, the 8th Pennsylvania was ordered to Pittsburgh for the defense of the western frontiers. This was necessary because of the hostile actions the Indians and the British military garrison in Detroit were beginning to take.[44]

While John had been fighting in the east as part of the Continental Army, the Pennsylvania General Assembly had passed a law establishing a statewide militia. The "Act to Regulate the Militia of the Commonwealth of Pennsylvania" passed on March 17, 1777. It mandated that all white men between the ages of 18-53 capable of bearing arms serve two months of active duty in the militia each year.[45]

The act called for eight militia battalion districts to be created in each Pennsylvania county. The role of the militia was to protect local communities, to provide immediate response in the event of enemy attack, and to supplement Continental Army units on an "as needed" basis.[46]

---

44 Albert, George Dallas, "History of the County of Westmoreland, Pennsylvania," L.H. Everts Company, Philadelphia, PA, 1882, pp. 87-92

45 https://www.pa.gov/agencies/phmc/pa-state-archives/research-online/research-guides/revolutionary-war-militia-overview.html

46 https://www.pa.gov/agencies/phmc/pa-state-archives/research-online/research-guides/revolutionary-war-militia-overview.html

When John arrived back in Westmoreland County after one year of service with the 8th Pennsylvania, he resigned from the regular army and joined the Westmoreland County militia. He was assigned to the 4th Militia Battalion which was based at Redstone Settlement.[47]

However, before moving to Redstone Settlement, he proposed to Martha Evans and during spring 1778 they were married. John was twenty-eight, and Martha was seventeen. They established a residence in Redstone Settlement (present-day Brownsville, Pennsylvania), and soon Martha became pregnant with their first child.

The mission of John's militia unit was to protect the western frontier from a "back door" attack, the same mission John thought he volunteered for when he joined the Pennsylvania 8th Regiment. For the duration of the Revolutionary War (the Treaty of Paris ending the Revolutionary War was signed in 1783), John, Martha, and their small children lived in Redstone Settlement. Their first child, Reuben Adam, was born there in 1779.

At about the time that Reuben Adam was born, John received word from Berkeley County that his father, Casper, had died. On February 25, 1779, John's mother, Mary, had appointed John to be executor of Casper's estate, with the first matter to be settled being the sale of the 365-acre property in Berkeley County.[48] This was the larger of the two parcels Casper had been attempting to purchase from Lord Fairfax since he had made the initial down payment and submitted the completed surveys in 1768.

Most likely due to discrimination by the Fairfax sales agent against German immigrants, the Fairfax land sales office had never issued the final deeds giving Casper the free and clear title to the land. When the Fairfax office learned that George Braggoona wanted to purchase this property from the Casper Böner estate, the patent from Fairfax was immediately issued. After an eleven year

---

47 Bunner, John tombstone inscription, "John Bunner, Pennsylvania, Pvt, Wilson, 4th Bn, Rev. War, 1810"

48 Joyner, Peggy (1987), "Abstract of Virginia's Northern Neck Warrants and Surveys, Volume 4, p. 80

wait, the deed was issued to Casper Böner posthumously on March 2, 1779. (Casper's name was spelled 'Gasper Bonner' in this deed.)

John and his mother Mary (their last name is recorded as 'Bunner' in the legal documents) sold the 365-acre property to George Braggoona on October 19, 1780, for £45. Of significance, John's brother Joseph signed this deed as a witness, confirming that when he completed his four-year tour of duty in the Revolutionary War that he had returned to the 334-acre Berkeley County farm where his mother and younger siblings still resided.

Although the Fairfax land office had finally issued the patent on the larger property, they continued to stall in the issuance of the patent for the property Mary and her children were living on. As a result, Mary continued to pay a nominal rent (estimated at 3-4 shillings per year) to the Fairfax office for the right to live on her own land, for which she had more than enough money to pay the balance owed.

While John was selling property for his mother in Berkeley County, he was adding property to his holdings near his Monongahela Valley tract. In October 1781, while still living in Redstone Settlement, John acquired four hundred acres from Edward Huss. This was the original John Jolliffe "Settlement Rights" property claimed by Jolliffe in 1774. Jolliffe was killed during the American Revolution and the property passed to Dennis Springer, then to Edward Huss. [49] This tract was less than one mile downstream from the 400-acre "Settlement Rights" claim John had made in 1772.

---

49 Bunner, Gale J., "Genealogy Descendents of Casper (Boner) Bunner And Mary Christianna Brown, Revised Edition, 1988, p. 15

## JOHN AMOS BONNER (BONER/BUNNER)

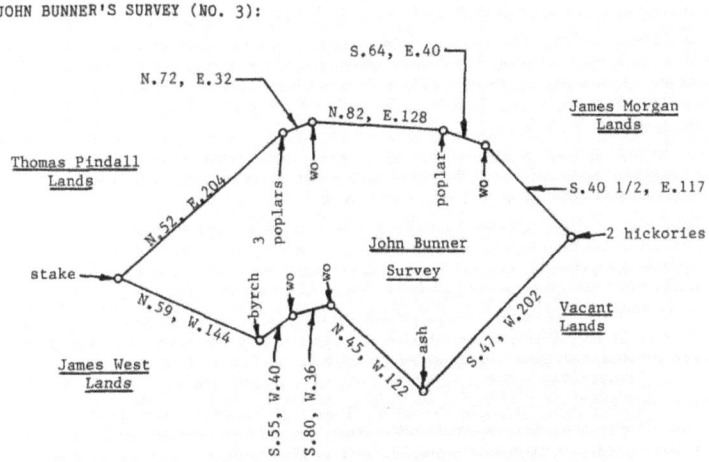

**Survey of 400-acre tract John Bonner purchased from Edward Huss – October 1781[50] Property was located on White Day Creek and was surveyed on August 24, 1785.**

No records have been discovered showing that John ever owned land in or near the Redstone Settlement. He most likely rented quarters for his family in the village and set about developing a skill where he could earn a living for the ten months each year that he was not on active duty with the militia. As it is known that after 1797, John operated a blacksmith shop on land he purchased from his brother-in-law John Miller on the Monongahela River (a portion of the 400-acres originally owned by his father Casper), it is assumed he learned this trade while he lived in Redstone Settlement. In his *"History of Fayette County, Pennsylvania,"* Franklin Ellis states, "There was John Boner, the village blacksmith, and soon afterwards Alexander Campbell who thought the field so promising that he too opened a smithy."[51]

---

50  Bunner, Gale J., "Genealogy Descendents of Casper (Boner) Bunner And Mary Christianna Brown, Revised Edition, 1988, p. 15

51  Ellis, Franklin, "History of Fayette County, Pennsylvania," L.H. Everts and Company, Philadelphia, p. 658

Ellis was describing events in the Menallen Township of Fayette County in the late 1700's. A John Bonner (spelled Boner on the tax list) is listed in the 1783 Menallen Township tax list for Westmoreland County, [52] which is the year the peace treaty was signed to end the Revolutionary War. It was also the year Fayette County, Pennsylvania was created from Westmoreland County, Pennsylvania and the last year John lived in Redstone Settlement before returning to his Monongahela Valley property in Virginia. Circumstantial evidence forces the conclusion that the John Boner who ran a blacksmith shop in Menallen Township, Fayette County in the late 1700's, the John Boner who paid taxes in Menallen Township, Westmoreland County in 1783, and the John Bonner who returned from Redstone Settlement, Menallen Township to his Virginia property at the end of the Revolutionary War in 1783 is the same person.

The above information is corroborated by a story contained in "The Heck Interviews" published by Glen D. Lough.

> "Rev. Jesse Nixon (1816-1906) told Adam O. Heck that his father and Mr. Bunner) [one of the sons of John Amos Bunner] went to [Brownsville] Pennsylvania in 1825, when he, Rev. Jesse, was nine years old, to see General Lafayette, when he visited there, in the fine mansion of Mr. Gallatin, and he (Rev. Jesse) was permitted to go with them. On the second day of their trip they visited Mr. Bunner's relatives, four families named Brown, near New Salem, a few miles west of Uniontown, and were there shown the Smithery owned and operated by Mr. Bunner's father in an early time, where he made very true bells and very fine guns."[53]

Nothing is known of John's militia activities during his five-year enlistment, but there was significant military activity all along the western frontier between 1778 and 1783, so it is certain that John

---

52  Westmoreland County, Pennsylvania 1783 Tax Rolls, Menallen Township, p. 92

53  Bunner, Gale J., "Genealogy Descendents of Casper (Boner) Bunner And Mary Christianna Brown, Revised Edition, 1988, p. 13, excerpt from the "Adam O. Heck" interviews published by Glen D. Lough, Fairmont, WV

saw his share of action. Most military responses were defensive in nature, but some were proactively bold and courageous.

For example, in 1778, the Monongalia County militia led by John's father-in-law, Colonel John Evans, joined an expedition led by General Lachlan McIntosh into the area north of the Ohio River as a show of force to the Indians who were believed to be planning an attack. Also in 1778, the Evans led militia helped build Fort McIntosh on the Beaver River in Pennsylvania and Fort Laurens on the Tuscarawas River in present-day Ohio.[54]

Another militia accomplishment on the western front was the defeat of a Tory plot by the militia forces led by Zackwell Morgan. There were a few hundred residents in the Monongahela Valley who were Tories, or Loyalists, who did not wish to rebel against England. These Tories became such a security concern that Zackwell Morgan raised a militia to put down any "mischief" they may cause. One of the leaders of the Tories was captured, bound, and handed over to Morgan to place under arrest. While Morgan was transporting him across the river in a small boat, the boat capsized and the Tory drowned, but Morgan was able to swim to safety. Morgan was charged with murder but was acquitted by the jury.[55] [56]

After this incident, the Tories grew quieter but remained steadfast in their loyalty to Great Britian. However, their activities continued to be closely monitored by their neighbors, with suspicious activities reported to Zackwell Morgan.

In 1778, the 13th Virginia Militia Regiment, commonly called the West Augusta Regiment, was raised in Monongalia County by Colonel William Crawford. This unit was assigned to Fort Pitt, doing duty along the Ohio and Allegheny Rivers.[57] Colonel Zackwell

---

54 Library of Virginia, Dictionary of Virginia Biography, Colonel John Evans, https://www.lva.virginia.gov/public/dvb/bio.asp?b=Evans_John

55 Lough, Glenn D., "Now and Long Ago – A History of the Marion County Area," Morgantown Printing and Binding Co., 1969, p. 354-358

56 Amber, Charles Henry, "West Virginia Stories and Biographies," Rand McNally and Co., 1927, p.85-86

57 Lough, Glenn D., "Now and Long Ago – A History of the Marion County Area," Morgantown Printing and Binding Co., 1969, p. 333

Morgan warned Crawford that he had received intelligence reports that several Tory operatives had infiltrated his militia. Crawford used trusted members of his militia to infiltrate the Tory group and learn of their plan to blow up Fort Pitt. The traitors were exposed, convicted, and summarily hanged.[58] This Tory plot to open the "back door" to the British was completely quashed by the local militia forces.

Also in 1778, perhaps the most daring and strategically significant military maneuver on the western front was executed by Colonel George Rogers Clark. Clark recruited one hundred and fifty Virginians in the upper Monongahela valley, with musters held at Kerns Fort (present-day Morgantown, West Virginia) and Prickett's Fort (present-day Fairmont, West Virginia). He then marched to Fort Redstone (present-day Brownsville, Pennsylvania) and there prepared for his expedition against the British and Indians west of the Ohio River. His militia left Redstone floating on flatboats down the Monongahela and then the Ohio rivers. On the evening of July 4, 1778, his forces arrived on the Mississippi River at Kaskaskia (in present-day Illinois south of St. Louis) and forced the surrender of the British fort without a single shot being fired. Clark left Kaskaskia on February 6, 1779, and marched to the British fort at Vincennes (in present-day Indiana). After a brief siege, British Lieutenant Governor Henry Hamilton, who had marched with his British forces from Detroit to defend Vincennes, surrendered the fort. Hamilton was known as the "hair buyer" because he paid the Indians a substantial bounty on every American patriot scalp provided to the British.[59]

---

58 Lough, Glenn D., "Now and Long Ago – A History of the Marion County Area," Morgantown Printing and Binding Co., 1969, p. 357-358

59 Lough, Glenn D., "Now and Long Ago – A History of the Marion County Area," Morgantown Printing and Binding Co., 1969, p. 358

**Routes to Vincennes by Henry Hamilton and George Rogers Clark**
(National Park Service Image – public domain)

The impact of these victories on the outcome of the Revolutionary War cannot be overstated. They significantly reduced the risk of a "back door" British invasion from the west and allowed Washington to focus more exclusively on the battles he was fighting in the east. The loyal frontier militia soldiers had proven themselves to be forces to be reckoned with, and Washington trusted them to keep the frontier secure.

While living in Redstone Settlement, it is believed that John and Martha had three additional children. With the signing of the Treaty of Paris in 1783, John and his family moved from Redstone and settled on the land he had claimed in 1772. There he began the difficult task of clearing the virgin forests that covered his land to create a productive farm.

In 1786, John finally received the patent on his original 400-acre "Settlement Rights" claim from the Virginia Land Office (his name is recorded as Boner in this document).[60] He had filed his

---

60 Virginia Land Office, Land grant 10 October 1786. Boner, John. grantee.; Virginia. Land Office. Register. Library of Virginia. Archives. 1786 – 1010, https://

initial claim in 1772 and had made all improvements on the land under the authority of his "settlement certificate" over the ensuing fourteen years. The patent gave him free and clear legal ownership.

Over the ensuing ten years, John lived on his farm with Martha and their growing family, which increased to nine children. The years and the order of their birth are uncertain, but their names were: Reuben, Joseph, Mary, John, Jr., Rachel, Rebecca, James, Amos, and Enoch. It is believed Enoch was their last child and that he was born in 1793.

After the war, Martha's father, Colonel John Evans, turned his focus to politics. He had been elected as the Monongalia County representative to the Virginia House of Delegates for a single year term during the war in 1779. He was also elected to the Virginia House of Delegates for single terms in the years 1791, 1794, and 1800.[61] He was elected as the Monongalia County Clerk in 1782, a position he held until he resigned in 1807. It was during his tenure that many early records of the county were destroyed in 1796 when fire consumed the outbuilding on his farm that he had been using as his office. In 1785 he was appointed as a Trustee for the recently incorporated city of Morgantown, which had become the county seat of Monongalia County, Virginia in 1783.

Although the war was over, there was still a deadly Indian menace along the Monongahela River that prevented the settlers from ever feeling secure. In 1785, Thomas Stone, who was one of John's neighbors, was surprised by Indians while alone in a clearing. They murdered and scalped him. His body was found by Jacob Prickett, Sr. who, along with John Bunner, Nathaniel Springer and David Morgan trailed the Indians for two days and nights to Middle Island Creek where the trail was lost during a rainstorm.[62]

---

lva-virginia.libguides.com/land-grants

61 The New Dominion, Morgantown, WV, October 1,1925, p. 12. Microfilm at the University of West Virginia Library, Colson Hall, Morgantown, WV. 1 Descendants of Evans Hear Family History.doc

62 Lough, Glenn D., "Now and Long Ago – A History of the Marion County Area," Morgantown Printing and Binding Co., 1969, p. 39

## JOHN AMOS BONNER (BONER/BUNNER)

In 1784 or 1785, John's mother Mary and his two youngest sisters moved from their 334-acre Berkeley County, Virginia farm to Redstone Settlement, Pennsylvania, which had just changed its name to Brownsville. This move allowed Mary to be closer to her brothers, who were all living on their nearby farms. John's brothers Joseph and Casper Jr. continued living on the 334-acre Berkeley County farm. Casper Jr. was now eighteen years old.

With the death of Lord Fairfax in 1781 and the victory of America in the Revolutionary War, the Fairfax Estate and the Fairfax Land Company became defunct. After a period of transition, the Commonwealth of Virginia assumed legal responsibility for all land formerly owned by Lord Fairfax. John still hoped to eventually receive a patent for the 334-acre property that Joseph was living on from the Virginia Land Office.

In March 1788, John's father-in-law, Colonel John Evans was one of two Monongalia County delegates elected to the Virginia state convention which had been called to consider the proposed Constitution of the United States. Evans sided with the anti-Federalists led by Patrick Henry and George Mason. Their primary arguments against the proposed Constitution were that a consolidated government would put an end to Virginia's liberties and would overburden Virginians with direct taxes. The proposed Constitution also lacked a Bill of Rights. The Federalists, led by James Madison and Edmund Randolph, promised that a Bill of Rights would be added after ratification and persuaded enough votes to their side to make Virginia the tenth state to ratify the Constitution. The final vote was eighty-nine for ratification, seventy-nine against. Colonel Evans continued living on his 360-acre estate two miles west of Morgantown until his death in 1834 at the age of ninety-six.

On March 4, 1789, the Articles of Confederation, which had governed the thirteen states since the end of the Revolutionary War, were replaced by the United States Constitution. The new Constitution provided for a much stronger national government with a Chief Executive (President), a two-house legislature, courts, and taxing powers. On April 30, 1789, George Washington was sworn in as the first President of the United States.

That same year, John's brother Reuben, who had married Nancy Ann Prickett circa 1780, decided to move west to Kentucky. The Reuben Bunner family, along with several other members of the Prickett family, traveled on flat boats down the Monongahela and Ohio Rivers until they reached Kentucky. After living in Kentucky for a brief time, they moved across the river into the Northwest Territory (Brown County, Ohio near present-day Cincinnati), where they were among the first settlers. They lived there the rest of their lives.

On July 24, 1789, twenty-one years after making a down-payment and submitting the property survey, ten years after he died, and six years after the end of the Revolutionary War, Casper Böner (recorded as Gasper Banner) received the deed for the 334-acre parcel of land in Berkeley County.[63] John, as the executor of Casper's estate, took legal possession of the property. John's brother Joseph continued to live on and farm this tract.

In 1790, John received the shock of his life when his sixty-two-year-old mother Mary showed up at his house for a visit. She had walked the fifty miles from Brownsville to visit John and his family as well as Elizabeth and her family. [64]After staying for a few days, John probably helped her to hitch a ride on a flat boat floating down the river back to Brownsville.

Sometime in the early 1790's most likely after his brother Reuben had settled in Kentucky or Ohio, it appears that John made a trip of his own down the Ohio River. Gale Bunner included the following story in *"Genealogy Descendents of Casper (Boner) Bunner And Mary Christianna Brown, Revised Edition,"* the Bunner family history he documented in 1988. The original source of this story is unknown.

"John Bunner Sr. was looking for land on which to settle, in Indiana Territory when he was met in the woods by several old Indian

---

63  Virginia Colonial Land Office, 334 Acre Grant to 'Gasper Banner,' July 24, 1789, https://lva-virginia.libguides.com/land-grants

64  Bunner, Gale J., "Genealogy Descendents of Casper (Boner) Bunner And Mary Christianna Brown, Revised Edition, 1988, p. 13, excerpt from the "Adam O. Heck" interviews published by Glen D. Lough, Fairmont, WV

friends, friends who had fought with him against the British. The Indians insisted he visit their town, and this he did, and here he... But let us at this point inject a paragraph from the book, "Indiana Miscellany," by W.C. Smith, "After he (John Doddridge) had resided in Indiana ten or fifteen years, he received intelligence (from John Bunner) concerning a sister older than himself but whom he had never seen. She had been captured in Virginia by the Indians when a small girl, before he was born. The Doddridge family had received no tidings of this lost child from the period of when she was carried off till now. They supposed she had been dead many years. When Mr. Doddridge received information of her being still alive he went to the Indian nation and saw his sister. She was now old, and had lived so long among the Indians that she would not leave them and return to her natives." John Bunner had recognized the old woman by a scar he had heard she had on the back of her neck, from being scalped as a baby. This woman was of the family of Joseph Doddridge, the historian, who wrote a story of her capture." [65]

Alan Bunner included a much more abbreviated version of this story as his 7,400-page epochal family history ("*The Bunner Family in America*,"). The original source of this story is also currently unknown:

"John Bunner Sr. may have explored the Indiana Territory more than once as research states, "John Bunner Sr. went early to Indiana Territory, looking for a place to settle himself and his family. Illness (a fever) caused him to return home to what is now Marion County." [66]

On November 17, 1795, John and his wife Martha (with last name recorded as 'Bunner' on the deed) sold a fifty-acre parcel of

---

65   Bunner, Gale J., "Genealogy Descendents of Casper (Boner) Bunner And Mary Christianna Brown, Revised Edition, 1988,

66   Bunner, Alan N., "The Bunner Family in America" Alexandria, Virginia 7,300+ page document on CD, revision dated June 25, 2012.

the 334-acre Berkeley County farm that his brothers Joseph and Casper Jr. and their families had been living on to William Mercer for £32. John, as executor of his parents' estate, maintained ownership of the remaining 284 acres.

By late 1795, wolves were becoming so numerous in the Upper Monongahela Valley that they had become a menace to persons and livestock. A meeting of residents was called to consider a massive hunt to remedy the problem. The meeting was held at the home of Stephen Morgan sometime during February 1796. More than one hundred men attended.

**Wolves became a menace in the upper Monongahela Valley in 1795**
(Sketch by Greg Bunner)

Companies of hunters were formed and captains appointed to each of the twelve companies. Appointed company captains were Paw Paw Company, Stephen and Zackwell Morgan; Prickett's Creek Company, Josiah Prickett and John Bonner (spelled Bunner in the reference document); Buffalo Creek Company, Adam Ice and Azeph Martin; West Fork Company, Daniel Booth Boone and

## JOHN AMOS BONNER (BONER/BUNNER)

Henry Anderson; Tygart Valley Company, Solomon Work and Thomas Ashcraft.

An oversight committee was formed to establish rules and ensure they were enforced. The committee consisted of David Morgan, John Hill, Robert Ferrell and William Jolliffe. The hunt commenced at daybreak on a Monday morning and continued for three days and nights. Beginning at White Day Creek the more than one hundred hunters spread out over a two-mile swathe through the woods as far as Coons Run and then proceeded in the same manner through the woods from Hellens Run to Indian Creek. In addition to the men, there were approximately fifty dogs running with them. All wolves killed were scalped and given to the oversight committee to ensure an accurate count. At the end of the hunt the scalp count was 675. Nathaniel Springer killed the most, shooting and scalping seventy-one wolves.[67]

1795 is also the most accepted date for the death of John's mother, Mary, in Brownsville, Pennsylvania. If this date is correct, she would have lived there for approximately ten years after moving from the Berkeley County farm, and she would have been sixty-seven years old.

On September 27, 1797, John Bonner (spelled Bunner in the legal documents) purchased 123 acres on the Monongahela River above the mouth of Parkers Run from his brother-in-law, John Miller.[68] This was part of the 400-acre tract his father, Casper, had purchased in 1772 and sold to his son-in-law John Miller, in 1776.

John set up a smithery (blacksmith shop) there. John Mahon, who lived in this area in the late 1700's, spoke of this to Adam O. Heck in an interview conducted in the late 1800's when Mahon was nearly one hundred years old. That interview was published by Marion County, West Virginia historian Glenn D. Lough in July 1976.

---

67  Lough, Glenn D., "Now and Long Ago – A History of the Marion County Area," Morgantown Printing and Binding Co., 1969, p. 49

68  Monongalia County Clerk's Office, Land Deed Grantee Index, John Miller to John Bunner, 123 acres, September 1797, p. 153

"He [John Bunner Sr.] purchased land in what is now Rivesville from his brother-in-law John Miller. Shortly after this, he established his smithery there, where he became favorably known in the manufacture of bells and guns. He [John Bunner Sr.] was living here, in a two-story log house built by Calder Haymond when he died." [69]

According to family historian, Scott Randolph Bunner, John Bonner was probably among the first of the early settlers to use coal, which he used as an energy source for a lime kiln as early as 1785.[70] John also likely used coal as an energy source in his smithery.

In 1800, Casper Bunner, Jr. and Joseph Bunner are recorded in Berkeley County, Slaughter District, town of Tuscarora, Virginia. They were both still living on the family farm near Hedgesville.[71]

On December 8, 1800, John Bunner purchased 400 acres from James West. This property was situated on Tygart Valley Waters adjoining William Pettyjohn's settlement made in 1774. West had acquired this land in January 1784. On the same date of December 8, 1800, John Bonner (recorded as Bunner in the legal documents) sold the 123 acres on the Monongahela River that he had purchased in 1797 to James West. [72] As this is the land on which John had established his blacksmith shop, it appears that, after this land trade, John either retained a small parcel where his smithery was located, or he paid James West rent for that portion of the property taken up by the smithery.

---

69  Awhile Ago Times, Bunner Family edition, July 1976. This 10-page edition of a "historical newspaper of the Upper Monongahela Valley", edited and published by Glenn D. Lough of Fairmont, WV

70  West Virginia Hillbilly, 3 June 1978, 10 June 1978, articles on "The Bunner Family in Western Virginia", based on research by Scott Randolph Bunner

71  Bridges, Steven A, "Virginians in 1800: Counties of West Virginia", 1987, p.13

72  Monongalia County Clerk's Office, Land Deed Grantee Index, John Miller to John Bunner, 123 acres, September 1797, pp. 151, 153

## JOHN AMOS BONNER (BONER/BUNNER)

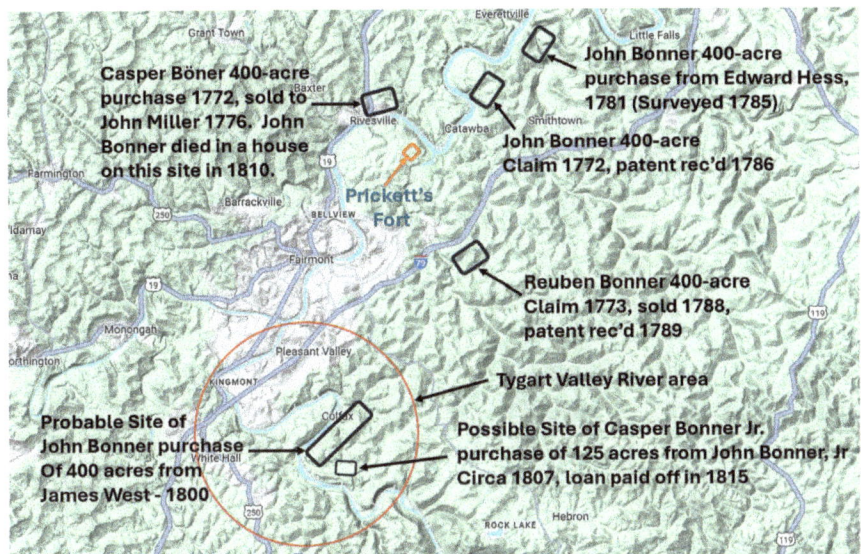

**John Amos Bonner Monongalia County Landholdings - 1800**

In 1806, John Bunner Sr. gave 90½ acres to his son Joseph Bunner.[73]

"This indenture made in the year of our Lord One thousand eight hundred and six between John Bunner and Martha his wife of the county of Monongahela and Commonwealth of Virginia of the one part and Joseph Bunner, their son of the county and state aforesaid of the other part witnesseth that the said John Bunner and Martha his wife in consideration of the natural love and affection which they the said John Bunner and Martha his wife hath… Situate on the Monongahela River and White Day Creek being part of a larger tract of 400 acres by survey bearing date the twenty fourth of August, 1785 and bounded as follows… meeting up with Reuben Bunner's land…"[74]

---

73  Monongalia County Clerk's Office, Land Deed Grantee Index, John Miller to John Bunner, 123 acres, September 1797, pp. 153

74  Bunner, Alan N., "The Bunner Family in America" Alexandria, Virginia 7,300+ page document on CD, revision dated June 25, 2012, Chapter 8, p. 122

AN AMERICAN JOURNEY

This land which John and Martha gifted to their son Joseph was part of the 400-acre tract that John purchased from Edward Huss in October 1781 and had it surveyed in August 1785. This land transaction was mentioned in John's last will and testament.

On August 28, 1806, John and Martha Bunner sold 217 acres of the 284 acres they still owned of the Berkeley County farm to Jeremiah Evans. This parcel was part of the original 334-acre farm in the Casper Böner estate for which John was the executor. The sales price was $1,050. John agreed to accept periodic payments from Jeremiah Evans until the total amount had been paid.[75] This left sixty-seven acres of the original 334 acres unsold and in the possession of John Bonner as of 1806. There are no known records indicating when and to whom this remaining acreage was sold.

It appears that John's health had sufficiently declined in the early months of 1810 that he completed his last will and testament on July 28, 1810. It read as follows:

> "In the name of God Amen: I John Bunner of Monongalia county and State of Virginia being weak and low, but of sound mind and memory do constitute this my last Will and Testament revoking and disannulling all other former wills heretofore by me made and constituting this as my last Will and Testament and first of all I most humbly bequeath my soul to God beseeching his most gracious acceptance of it through the all sufficient merits and mediation of Jesus Christ who is able to serve to the uttermost all that came unto God by him. In this hope and confidence I trust and render up my Soul unto him with comfort. Secondly, I give and bequeath my Body to the earth from whence it was taken to be buried in a decent manner at the discretion of my beloved wife and executor hereafter named. As to my worldly Estate I give and bequeath in manner and form following:
>
> That is to say first - I give and bequeath to my beloved wife Martha Bunner the House and one third of the land I now live on and her choice of one horse, two cows, two sheep, a negro girl by the name

---

[75] Berkeley County Clerk's Office, Martinsburg, WV, Deed Book 27, Page 542

## JOHN AMOS BONNER (BONER/BUNNER)

of Nancy, and all the house hold furniture during her widowhood and no longer and after her decease or in case she should remarry the property bequeathed to her (the Land excepted) shall be sold and an equal distribution made amongst my three Daughters, namely Rebecca Ferrel, Mary Grubb, and Rachel Morgan. But in case Nancy should have any children during my wife's natural life or widowhood the increase I bequeath to my son Enoch.

Item - I give and bequeath to my son Reuben Bunner the Land he now lives on (to him and his heirs) it being laid off to him some time past being about ninety and a half acres more or less, to my son John Bunner to him and his Heirs the plantation he now lives on being about one hundred Acres more or less -

Item - I give and bequeath to my son James Bunner to him and his heirs the plantation he now lives on being about one hundred and fifty acres more or less -

Item - I give and bequeath to my son Amos to him and his heirs the Plantation he now lives on being one hundred fifty acres more or less and the land is to be divided between my sons James and Amos Bunner as I have formerly directed so that an equal dividend takes place -

Item - I give and bequeath to my son Enoch Bunner to him and his heirs the plantation I now live on also a young sorrel mare Colt -

I give and bequeath to my sons James and Amos twenty dollars each to be paid out of my stock - and after my wife takes her choice of the one horse, two cows, and two sheep as before mentioned the residue of my horses, cattle, and sheep to be sold and an equal distribution to be made amongst my three daughters namely Rebekah Ferrel, Mary Grubb, and Rachel Morgan, reserving twenty dollars to each of my two sons James and Amos as before specified.

It is to be observed that I have Bond on Jeremiah Evans of Barkly [Berkeley] County, Virginia for two hundred dollars which became due the first day of September Eighteen hundred and Eight - My will is that the money be collected and equally divided amongst my three sons Reuben Bunner, Joseph Bunner, and John Bunner.

I have also another Bond on the aforesaid Jeremiah Evans which became due the first day of September eighteen hundred and Seven of the same sum - My will is that one hundred and fifty dollars of that money be given to my son John Bunner the residue of the money together with the whole of the interest be delivered when collected, to my brother Gasper [Casper] Bunner the hundred and fifty dollars directed to be paid to my son John Bunner, is to be paid in behalf of Gasper Bunner account of the Land my brother Gasper Bunner bought of my son John Bunner –

I have another Bond will be due on the first day of September next on the aforesaid Jeremiah Evans of the amount of two hundred dollars - my will is that my brother Joseph Bunner have sixty dollars of the money when collected, the balance of the money to be equally divided amongst my six sisters and one nephew namely Catharine Strain, Susanna Baremore, Mary Gibson, Margaret Harmeason, Elizabeth Miller, Charlotte Sterne and Reuben Bunner of Kentucky. I will nominate and appoint James G. Watson and Reuben Bunner my executors to this my last Will and Testament.

In witness whereof I have hereunto set my hand seal this twentieth day of July one thousand eight hundred and ten.

John x Bunner (Seal)

Signed sealed and Delivered, in the presence of,
John Kirbey
Joseph x Benner [Bunner]
Gasper x Benner [Bunner]

His (John x Bunner's) Mark [76]

---

76   Monongalia County Clerk Office, Morgantown, West Virginia, Will Book 1, page 336

In this Will, it appears that John Bunner, Sr. knew of his brother Reuben's passing in 1809 and thus put "nephew Reuben Bunner of Kentucky" in his will to receive what John would have bequeathed to his brother Reuben.

The clerk who wrote John's will misspelled the married names of at least four of his sisters. Catherine Strain and Charlotte Sterne both had the same last name as they married brothers. The brothers spelled their last name as Starn. Margaret Harmeason's married name was more commonly spelled as Harmison. Susanah Laremore's married name was most commonly spelled as Laramore and, less frequently, as Larimore.

The issue of John's wife at the time he wrote his will must also be addressed. There is a strong family tradition that John's first wife, Martha Evans Bunner, died circa 1800 and John married a woman named Martha Jolliffe within a year or two of the death of his first wife.

Exhaustive research has found no evidence that Martha Evans Bunner preceded her husband John in death. Aside from John purchasing 123 acres from his brother-in-law, John Miller, in Pleasantville and setting up a blacksmith shop there circa 1798, there are no obvious disruptions or changes in John's life to suggest that Martha had died and that he was adjusting to life without her.

Searching for records of a person named Martha Jolliffe who lived in western Virginia, Maryland, or Pennsylvania during the late 1700's and early 1800's proved fruitless. The only family of Jolliffe's that could be found living in this region during this time was that of William J. Jolliffe, Sr. He and his family settled in present-day Uniontown, Pennsylvania around 1771. He was the father of eighteen children, including sons James, John, and William J. Jolliffe, Jr., all three of whom settled in the upper Monongahela Valley during the early 1770's.

James Jolliffe settled on the Monongahela near Paw Paw Creek in 1770, but he died in 1771 at the age of eighteen. He had no children. John Jolliffe settled in the area and claimed 400 acres in 1774 or 1775 but was killed in May 1777 during the Revolutionary War. He had no children. Gale Bunner, in his *"Genealogy Descendents of Casper (Boner) Bunner And Mary Christianna Brown, Revised Edition,"* states that "His [John Jolliffe's] sister Martha resided here [on John Jolliffe's land] for a while, then "turned the land over" to Dennis Springer."[77]

William J. Jolliffe, Jr. moved to the upper Monongahela Valley circa 1775 and was a friend and contemporary of John Amos Bunner. William J. Jolliffe, Jr. had twelve children born between 1780 and 1802. None of his daughters were named Martha, and all would have been too young to marry John Bunner had he become a widower during this time.

William J. Jolliffe, Sr. had nine daughters, who would have been sisters of James, John, and William, Jr. According to the William J. Jolliffe family tree posted on Ancestry.com, none of his daughters were named Martha. Five of his daughters died before 1800, and a sixth died before John Bonner's death in 1810. The three daughters who were still alive in 1810, and who could have possibly been called "Martha" and who could have been John's widow, were Ann (1762-1827), Margaret (1770-1823), and Elizabeth (1768–1818).[78]

Ann was a contemporary of John. She was born in 1762, but she married Reverend Samuel Woodbridge in Fayette County, Pennsylvania where she resided until her death in 1827. Margaret and Elizabeth would both have been too young (Elizabeth would have been nine, Margaret would have been seven) to live by themselves on their brother John's property after he was killed during the Revolutionary War in 1777. They would have also been too young to legally "turn John Jolliffe's land over" to Dennis Springer, as recorded by Gale Bunner.

Also, Margaret died in 1823 in Erie, Ohio. This eliminates her from contention as John's widow after 1810, because the Monongalia County Clerk's records indicate that the Martha Bunner estate settlement was held in Morgantown, West Virginia in 1822 after her death in 1818. This leaves only Elizabeth Jolliffe to be the "Martha Jolliffe" that John Bonner could have married during his widowerhood. Her date of death matches up with the Monongalia County

---

77 Bunner, Gale J., "Genealogy Descendents of Casper (Boner) Bunner And Mary Christianna Brown, Revised Edition, 1988, p. 15

78 https://www.ancestry.com/family-tree/person/tree/168022476/person/282183539186/facts?_phsrc=bbY2927&_phstart=successSource

records, but her given name was not Martha, and she would have only been nine years old when her brother John was killed, so it is unlikely that she is the "Martha Jolliffe" named in the Gale Bunner family history.

Reviewing the family tree of Colonel John Evans posted on Ancestry.com, Martha Evans is listed as his daughter. This listing records that she was born in 1761 and died in 1818. This exactly matches the records of the Monongalia County Clerk. (The John Evans family tree erroneously names Martha's spouse as Joseph Bunner, John's younger brother.)

John's wife, Martha, was still living in 1817, when her name appears on a bill of sale. [79] Martha Bunner died in late 1818 or early 1819, as the sale of her estate took place on February 13, 1819. [80] [81]

From this research, the evidence seems conclusive that John Amos Bunner preceded his only wife, Martha Evans Bunner, in death in 1810. It seems that Martha Evans Bunner died in 1818. As a result, it seems that John was never a widower and was never married to a woman named Martha Jolliffe. Aside from the single mention in the Gale Bunner family history, there is currently no other evidence that a person named Martha Jolliffe ever existed.

John died sometime between July 28, 1810, and October 8, 1810. He was sixty years old.

John's estate inventory as of October 8, 1810, along with the inventory appraisals on which his estate paid "death taxes," was signed by the Monongalia County, Virginia County Court on November 4, 1810. Following is a transcription of that document:

---

79 West Virginia History, Volumes 1, 5, 8, 20; West Virginia Historical Magazine

80 Cemetery Records of Marion County, West Virginia, Marion County Genealogy Club, Volume 1: Winfield District, 1983

81 Monongalia County Clerk's Office, Settlement of Estate bequeathed by John Bunner to his widow Martha after Marth's death. Son Reuben Adam Bunner – Executor. Settled on Sept 4, 1820, recorded by the Court during Oct 1822 session.

## John Bonner (spelled Bonner in the document) Estate Appraisal and Inventory October 8, 1810

Agreeable to an order of Monongalia County Court held on this eighth day of October 1810 of us directed. The following is a list or inventory of the estate of John Bonner deceased as appraised by us the undersigned this 4th November 1810.

| One Bay Gelding | $35.00 |
|---|---|
| One Sorrel Gelding | $35.00 |
| One Sorrel Yearling Colt | $70.00 |
| One White Cow | $9.00 |
| One White Faced Brindal Heifer | $10.00 |
| One White Heifer | $8.00 |
| One White Faced Red Steer | $8.50 |
| One White Red Eared Heifer | $8.00 |
| One White Yearling [?] | $5.00 |
| One Red White Faced Steer | $5.50 |
| One White Yearling Heifer (red eared) | $5.00 |
| One White Yearling Heifer (red eared) | $5.00 |
| Two White Spring Calves | $4.50 |
| 4 Wegthers [?] | $7.00 |
| 2 Wheat Stacks (suppose 44 bushels) | 25.00 |
| 2 Rye Stacks Buts [? (suppose 30 bushels) | 11.25 |
| 2 Oat Stacks (suppose 50 dozen each) | 15.00 |
| 1 Small Rye Stack (suppose 7½ bushels) | 2.80 |

## JOHN AMOS BONNER (BONER/BUNNER)

| | | |
|---|---|---|
| 1 Stack of Watered Flax | 6.25 | |
| ¾ Field of Indian Corn Standing | 30.00 | |
| 2 Stacks of Hay (suppose 20 wt.) | 5.00 | |
| 1 Stack of Hay | 5.00 | |
| 3 Stacks of Hay | 10.00 | |
| 2 bar shears, 1 shovel, 1 coulter, 2 clevises | 4.00 | |
| 1 Lot [?] chains, 2 bridles, and log chain | 3.00 | |
| 2 Hoes, Doubletree, 4[?] inch auger | 2.25 | |
| 2 Still Tubs, Keg | 0.75 | |
| Wearing Apparel | 12.00 | |
| 1 Woman Saddle | 3.00 | 371.46 |
| 1 Cutting Saw[?] | 1.33 | |
| 2 Pitch Forks | 1.25 | |
| 1 Mans Saddle | 4.00 | 5.58 |
| | | 377.04 |
| Potatoes, suppose 15 bushels dug | 2.75 | |

Jan 26th, 1811

| One Black Spotted Sow | 2.50 |
|---|---|
| One Red and Black Spotted Sow | 1.75 |
| One Red and Black Spotted Sow | 1.75 |
| Two Red and Black Spotted Barrows | 2.25 |
| One White Barrow, One Sow | 2.00 |

         Thomas Ewall
         Isaac Powel

At a court held for Monongalia County March (?), 1811. This inventory and appraisement of the personal estate of John Bonner deceased was produced in court examined and ordered to be recorded.

         N. Evans

---

John was buried on a knoll on the Monongahela Valley property he had initially claimed in 1772. His tombstone reads:

      John Bunner
      Pennsylvania
      Pvt. *[Private]*
   Wilson's 4 BN *[4th Battalion]*
   Rev War *[Revolutionary War]*
       1810

His brother, Joseph Bunner, who died in 1828, is buried nearby. The small cemetery in which they are buried is now known as the Malone Cemetery and is located just south of the Monongalia – Marion County, West Virginia line approximately six miles north of present-day Fairmont, West Virginia.

## JOHN AMOS BONNER (BONER/BUNNER)

These two soldier-frontiersmen-patriot-heroes of the Monongahela Valley lie buried side-by-side in graves marked by Daughters of the American Revolution (D.A.R.) gravestones of High Honor. Circa 1962, Thomas Orth Bunner, a descendent of Joseph Bunner who resided in Morgantown, West Virginia, coordinated efforts with the D.A.R. to replace the original, barely legible, tombstones that had marked the graves of John and Joseph from the time of their deaths.[82] It is unknown how John and Joseph's last name was spelled on the original tombstones, but it was spelled Bunner on the replacements, which aligns with the present-day spelling of the family name.

It is also possible that the Revolutionary War battalion number on John's new tombstone may have been erroneously transcribed from the barely legible inscription on the old. John served in the Pennsylvania 8th Battalion (later changed to 8th Regiment) under Lieutenant Colonel Wilson (whose name is on his tombstone) during the war.[83] However, his tombstone says, "4 BN," not "8 BN." If this is not a transcription error, then perhaps what was intended was to communicate that John served in the war as a Private under Lieutenant Colonel Wilson and also as a member of the 4th Battalion of the Westmoreland County, Pennsylvania Militia.

Likewise, Joseph's tombstone is inscribed "9 PA RGT," not "8 PA RGT." Joseph did serve as a Private in the 9th Pennsylvania Regiment, but he also served as a Corporal in Captain Nelson's Independent Rifle Company, a Private in the 8th Pennsylvania Regiment, and as a full-time soldier for one year in the Virginia Militia. During the Battle of Paoli, during which he was wounded, he was also attached to the 7th Pennsylvania Regiment. That is obviously too much to fit on one tombstone, so the "9 PA RGT" is a simple, humble reminder to all who see it of the debt we owe to Joseph.

Letters engraved in stone can never do justice to the lives of those being memorialized. John and Joseph were rugged, self-

---

82   Bunner, Alan N., "The Bunner Family in America" Alexandria, Virginia 7,300+ page document on CD, revision dated June 25, 2012.

83   Lough, Glenn D., "Now and Long Ago – A History of the Marion County Area," Morgantown Printing and Binding Co., 1969, p. 334

sufficient pioneers who voluntarily withdrew from their families and their pursuit of personal ambitions for several years to fight for American independence. They left a legacy of freedom, liberty, and independence not only to their families, but to all Americans. Their names, their lives, and their sacrifices will be honored for as long as there is a land called America.

(Photograph by Michael Bunner)

7.

# The Siblings of John Amos Bonner (Böner/Bunner)

[Author's Note: In this chapter I continue to use Bonner as the default spelling of the family last name, as this was the most common spelling during this generation. When Bunner is used, it denotes the actual spelling used in the document being referenced. Bunner was becoming more commonly used by the early 1800's but it was not until the early 1870's that it became the near universal spelling of the family last name. In those instances where I mention Casper and Mary, the parents of John Amos Bonner and his siblings, I will continue using Böner, which was the original German spelling.]

## Joseph Bonner

Joseph was born in 1752, the second son of Casper and Mary Böner. He was most likely born on the family homestead along the South Fork of the South Branch of the Potomac River (near present-day Moorefield, West Virgina) where his older brother John was born in 1750. However, there is the possibility that he was born on land claimed by his grandfather, Wendell Brown, and the rest of his extended family in an Ohio Company settlement near present-day Uniontown, Pennsylvania. If he was born on the Ohio

Company lands, it would make him the first known white settler ever born west of the Allegheny Mountains.

Joseph never attended a school and never learned to read or write. However, his parents and grandparents taught him how to raise a garden, shoot a rifle, and be self-sufficient in the wilderness.

After his birth, Joseph's life mirrored that of his older brother, John, until the outbreak of the Revolutionary War in 1775. By then, John was twenty-five and Joseph was twenty-three, and both were living with their parents and younger siblings in a small settlement along the Monongahela River at present-day Rivesville, West Virginia. Joseph and John both volunteered to join the Continental Army in 1776 as members of the 8th Pennsylvania Battalion, later renamed the 8th Pennsylvania Regiment.[1] Both were skilled marksmen and sharpshooters.

Soon after enlisting, Joseph was selected to join Captain John Nelson's Independent Company of Riflemen and given the rank of Corporal on February 22, 1776.[2] This Westmoreland County, Pennsylvania fighting unit was ordered to Canada for the two-fold purpose of fighting the British forces stationed there and to entice the residents of Canada to join the Americans in their fight for independence.

Once Joseph's fighting unit arrived in Canada, it was attached to Colonel John Philip De Haas' 1st Pennsylvania Battalion. Nelson and his company participated in several skirmishes with British forces in Canada and then participated in the messy retreat from Canada as the invasion fully collapsed in June 1776.[3]

The Canadian Department of the Continental Army served more as a reflection of the aspirations and hopes of the Continental Congress than as a fighting unit intended to execute well-planned strategic maneuvers. Unfortunately for the soldiers on the ground,

---

1   Lough, Glenn D., "Now and Long Ago – A History of the Marion County Area," Morgantown Printing and Binding Co., 1969, p. 334

2   Montgomery, Thomas Lynch, "Pennsylvania Archives, Fifth Series, Volume II," Harrisburg Printing Company – State Printer, Harrisburg, PA, 1906, p. 75

3   Fort Ticonderoga Online Collection, https://fortticonderoga.catalogaccess.com/people/4475

it soon became apparent that the residents of Canada had no interest in gaining their independence from Great Britain.

While his unit was still fighting in Canada, Captain Nelson was involved in a tragic incident. While attempting to fire his gun to clear it after it had gotten wet, it misfired; when he lowered the gun to prime it again after the misfire, it went off unexpectedly. The shot killed Daniel McCullough, one of Joseph's compatriots in his fighting unit. Investigations into the death determined that Nelson had received permission to discharge his rifle and that the death was an accident.[4]

After the failed invasion of Canada, the Canadian Department of the Continental Army ceased to exist. By July 9, 1776, Joseph and the other soldiers in his retreating company had arrived at Fort Ticonderoga in upstate New York. This fort had been captured from the British after a surprise attack by Ethan Allen and his Green Mountain Boys on May 10, 1775. Joseph and his unit remained at Fort Ticonderoga for seven months. While there, they reinforced positions around the fort in preparation for a possible British attack.[5]

On August 23, 1776, while still assigned to Fort Ticonderoga, Captain Nelson had written a letter to the president of Continental Congress requesting that his company be transferred to a regiment defending Westmoreland County, Pennsylvania, where he and his soldiers had believed they would be serving when his company was initially created in January 1776. While he insisted in the letter that "I do not mean by this to insinuate that I am tired of the service to the northward, as I am ready and willing at all times to march wherever ordered", he stated that service in western Pennsylvania would let him "be of service to the publick and my family". His request was disapproved.[6]

---

4   Fort Ticonderoga Online Collection, https://fortticonderoga.catalogaccess.com/people/4475

5   Fort Ticonderoga Online Collection, https://fortticonderoga.catalogaccess.com/people/4475

6   Fort Ticonderoga Online Collection, https://fortticonderoga.catalogaccess.com/people/4475

Near the end of his one-year enlistment in Captain Nelson's Company, Joseph had to make the decision whether to resign and return home, or to re-enlist. Sometime before December 31, 1776, while still assigned to Fort Ticonderoga, Joseph made the decision to re-enlist in Captain Nelson's Rifle Company for three additional years.[7]

On February 20, 1777, Joseph's company was ordered to march south to join forces with Colonel Anthony Wayne's 4th Pennsylvania Battalion which was fighting in New Jersey and eastern Pennsylvania. Captain Nelson was assigned responsibility for recruiting volunteers for the newly created 9th Pennsylvania Regiment, which had not yet met its recruitment quota.[8]

Soon thereafter, a scandal involving Captain Nelson surfaced. Once he joined the 9th Pennsylvania, Nelson did not stay with it long; on May 15, 1777, he was "cashiered from the army". In present-day terms, being "cashiered" meant to be dishonorably discharged from military service due to serious misconduct, with the subsequent loss of rank and reputation. The exact circumstances of Captain Nelson's cashiering are unclear, but he appears to have been charged with and found guilty of selling some of his new recruits, sending them to another regiment in exchange for money or other considerations.[9]

On June 2, 1777, Nelson was still under arrest in Philadelphia and requesting parole so that he could collect attestations and vouchers proving how he had spent sums given to him for recruiting. On August 24, 1778, according to a letter from Alexander Hamilton to newly promoted General Anthony Wayne, Nelson was still imprisoned, possibly now at army headquarters in White Plains, New York, and had not been brought to trial. Nothing is known of Nelson's life outside

---

7   Monongalia County Clerk's Office, Morgantown, WV. Joseph Bunner Application for Revolutionary War Pension, 1818,1820

8   Ticonderoga Online Collections, Captain John Nelson, Westmoreland County, PA https://fortticonderoga.catalogaccess.com/people/4475

9   Ticonderoga Online Collections, Captain John Nelson, Westmoreland County, PA https://fortticonderoga.catalogaccess.com/people/4475

the army (except that he was a resident of Westmoreland County, Pennsylvania) or of what happened to him after his cashiering.[10]

After Nelson's disgraceful ouster, the men assigned to his rifle company, including Joseph Bonner, were temporarily assigned to the 9th Pennsylvania Regiment under the command of General "Mad Anthony" Wayne. Joseph's rank in the Continental Army was Private. The first major battle in which he fought after being attached to the 9th Pennsylvania was Brandywine, fought on September 11, 1777. During this battle, Joseph was under the command of General William Alexander of New Jersey (more commonly referred to as 'Lord Sterling').[11]

**Battle of Brandywine, September 11, 1777 – Painting by F.O. Yohn**
(public domain)

---

10  Ticonderoga Online Collections, Captain John Nelson, Westmoreland County, PA  https://fortticonderoga.catalogaccess.com/people/4475

11  Monongalia County Clerk's Office, Morgantown, WV. Joseph Bunner Application for Revolutionary War Pension, 1818,1820

Joseph also fought in the Battle of Paoli, while attached to the 7th Pennsylvania Regiment under the command of Lieutenant David Grier. This battle took place overnight on Sept. 20-21, 1777. It is remembered as one of the bloodiest battles of the Revolutionary War. [12]

Commonly referred to by Americans as the "Paoli Massacre," at least 53 Continental Army soldiers were killed and roughly 200 were wounded or taken prisoner during this surprise bayonet assault by about 1,200 British troops. Few – if any - shots were fired. It was all British bayonet attacks on sleeping American soldiers between midnight and daybreak. Captain Robert Wilson, Joseph's company commander, was stabbed in the side of the head by a bayonet during the battle, but he recovered and survived. Joseph was also wounded by a bayonet stab,[13] but, refusing to be impeded by his bayonet wound, he still fought in the Battle of Germantown two weeks later on October 4, 1777.[14]

---

12   Paoli Battlefield Preservation Fund, https://pbpfinc.org/background-to-the-battle-of-paoli/

13   Paoli Battlefield Preservation Fund, https://pbpfinc.org/known-casualties-alphabetically/

14   Monongalia County Clerk's Office, Morgantown, WV. Joseph Bunner Application for Revolutionary War Pension, 1818,1820

General George Washington conducting the American Attack
on the Chew House at the Battle of Germantown on
4th October 1777 - painting by Alonzo Chapell
(public domain)

After the Continental Army lost the battles of Brandywine, Paoli, and Germantown, the British gained control of Philadelphia, where they decided to spend the winter of 1777-78. George Washington made the decision to take his 12,000 Continental Army soldiers to Valley Forge, approximately twenty miles northwest of Philadelphia, to spend the winter. Joseph was among those 12,000 soldiers, as was his brother John.[15] Joseph likely connected with John during the three months they spent together at Valley Forge.

---

15  Valley Forge Legacy, http://www.friendsofvalleyforge.org/muster.asp

"Washington at Valley Forge" by Percy Moran (Library of Congress)
(public domain)

In the early spring of 1778, John's unit, the 8th Pennsylvania Regiment, was ordered to Pittsburgh to help prevent "back door" attacks on the Pennsylvania and Virginia frontier by British soldiers from Detroit and by Indians who were being financially incentivized to create frontier skirmishes and to turn in American scalps for bounty.[16] Upon return to Westmoreland County, John resigned from the 8th Pennsylvania and joined the Westmoreland County militia, in which he served until the Treaty of Paris was signed in 1783, ending the Revolutionary War and granting independence to the American colonies.

Due to Joseph's three-year reenlistment, he continued to serve in the Continental Army. During 1779, the third year of his enlistment, Joseph served under Colonel Richard Butler, who

---

[16] https://en.wikipedia.org/wiki/8th_Pennsylvania_Regiment

## THE SIBLINGS OF JOHN AMOS BONNER (BÖNER/BUNNER)

was now Commander of the 9th Pennsylvania.[17] Butler served under General Anthony Wayne, who in turn served under George Washington.

The first battle Joseph's unit was involved in after Valley Forge was the Battle of Monmouth (New Jersey), fought on June 28, 1778. In that battle, all Continental Army forces were under the command of George Washington.

**"Washington Rallying the Troops at Monmouth" by Emanuel Leutze**
(public domain)

The Battle of Monmouth was the largest battle of the American Revolution in terms of number of fighting soldiers. It ended in a tactical draw because the British forces escaped to New York to fight another day. However it proved to be a strategic propaganda victory for the Continental Army because they claimed they had forced the British to retreat.

---

17  Monongalia County Clerk's Office, Morgantown, WV. Joseph Bunner Application for Revolutionary War Pension, 1818,1820

The "victory" solidified Washington's tenuous position as the Commander of the Continental Army. Horatio Gates, the winning commander at the Battle of Saratoga, had been aggressively lobbying members of the Continental Congress to name him as the Commander of the Continental Army. This "win" at Monmouth gave Washington's supporters the ammunition they needed to maintain Washington in his position. The battle also proved to the British officers that the American soldiers were as disciplined and as capable as the British soldiers.

The Battle of Monmouth may have been the last major Revolutionary War battle that Joseph fought in. For some reason, in late 1778 or early 1779, he resigned from the Continental Army and served the fourth year of his enlistment as a full-time Virginia militia soldier. Little is known about the year he served in Virginia. The only account of this final year of Joseph's four year Revolutionary War enlistment comes from information provided by Joseph in his application for a Revolutionary War pension forty years later in 1818. There are no other known records giving additional insights into this year of his life.

According to Joseph, he went through an ordeal trying to get his final pay and his discharge papers in late 1778 or early 1779. In his initial application for a Revolutionary War pension in 1818, Joseph records that when he "went to Philadelphia to get his depreciated pay and his discharge papers, he was so long detained that he sold his pay for three guineas and gave up his discharge."[18]

Also unknown is why Joseph decided to spend the last year of his enlistment with the Virginia militia. It may have been that sometime in late 1778 Joseph received word from his mother that his father's health was failing, and Joseph approached his commanding officer to plead a hardship case that he needed to be closer to his family to take care of his mother and younger siblings. It may have been that after three years in the Continental Army with inadequate shelter, food, clothing, and pay, that Joseph "had enough." (The soldiers were paid in Continental dollars, which by 1779 were worthless, leading to a common euphemism of the time that something of low

---

18  Monongalia County Clerk's Office, Morgantown, WV, Joseph Bunner pension application, dated 27 May 1818

value "is not worth a Continental"). It may have been that Joseph married or became engaged during his annual furlough in 1778 and he wanted to be geographically closer to his wife (or fiancé).

Whatever the reason, Joseph spent 1779, his last year as a Revolutionary War soldier, in Virginia. Where he was stationed is unknown. His father, Casper died in February 1779 at his home in Berkeley County, Virginia. It is unknown if Joseph was able to spend any time at home with his family during the mourning period.

In late 1779 or early 1780, after completing his one-year enlistment in the Virginia militia, Joseph, accompanied by his wife, one year-old son Joseph Jr., and newborn daughter Catherine moved to the 334-acre family farm in Berkeley County. It is believed that Joseph's wife was named Elizabeth and they married circa 1778-1779, but beyond this rudimentary information, nothing else regarding the date, location, and circumstances of their marriage is currently known. Those family members already living on the family farm when Joseph and his family arrived were Joseph's mother Mary (age 52), his youngest brother Casper, Jr. (age 13), and his three youngest sisters (ages 9, 10, and 15).

After Casper's death in 1779, Mary had designated Joseph's older brother, John, as executor of Casper's estate. On October 19, 1780, John and Mary sold the 365-acre Berkeley County, Virginia property that Casper had initially purchased from the Fairfax land office in 1768. This property was approximately six miles west of the 334 acre Berkeley County farm which Mary, Joseph, and their families were living on.

The Fairfax land office had not issued a "free and clear" title to the 365-acre parcel until March 2, 1779, approximately two weeks after Casper's death. The sale of this land was made to George Braggoona.[19] Joseph signed this deed as a witness, confirming that after he had completed his four-year tour of duty in the Revolutionary War he returned to Berkeley County.

Over the next thirty-five years, Joseph and Elizabeth lived on and farmed this 334-acre property near Hedgesville with their growing family. The dates and the order of birth are uncertain, but

---

19   Berkeley County, West Virginia County Clerk's Office, John and Mary Bunner to George Broggona, October 10, 1780

their children's names were Joseph, John, Casper, Henry, Marcy, Catherine, Elizabeth, Margaret (Peggy) and Rutha. It is believed that Rutha was their youngest child and that she was born in 1798.

334-acre Farm where Joseph and Casper Bonner Jr. lived
for many years after Casper's death in 1779.
Jeremiah Evans acquired most of this property in 1815.[20]
(Map created by Michael Bunner overlaid on 2025 Google Earth image)

Circa 1785, Joseph's mother Mary decided to move to Brownsville, Pennsylvania (formerly Redstone Settlement) to be closer to her three brothers, Thomas, Maunus, and Adam. It appears her two youngest children, Mary Christina (15) and Charlotte (14) moved with her. Joseph's sister Catherine, who was twenty, and his brother, Casper Jr., who was eighteen, chose not to move with their mother and sisters, but remained in Berkeley County with Joseph and his family. In 1786, Catherine married John Starn in Berkeley County, after which they moved to Hampshire County, Virginia (present-day West Virginia).

On July 24, 1789, twenty-one years after making a down-payment and submitting the property survey, ten years after he died,

---

20 Berkeley County, West Virginia County Clerk's Office, John Bunner to Jeremiah Evans, 217 acres, 1815, Deed Book 27, Page 542

six years after the end of the Revolutionary War, and three months after George Washington became first President of the United States, Casper Böner (recorded as Gasper Banner by the Virginia Land Office) received the free and clear deed for the 334-acre parcel of land in Berkeley County that Joseph and his family were living on.[21] Casper's widow Mary and oldest son John, as the executor of Casper's estate, took legal possession of the property. Joseph and his family would continue living on this property for approximately twenty-five more years.

**Small portion of Casper Böner 334-acre farm near Hedgesville, West Virginia as it appeared in 2024** (photo by Michael Bunner)

Joseph's mother Mary is believed to have died in Brownsville, Pennsylvania in 1795 at the age of sixty-seven. Soon afterward, John probably talked to Joseph about his interest in purchasing the 334-acre farm he had been living on to settle the estate of Casper and Mary. If Joseph did consider buying the property, he decided against it.

---

21 Virginia Colonial Land Office, 334 Acre Grant to 'Gasper Banner,' July 24, 1789, https://lva-virginia.libguides.com/land-grants

Circa 1795, Casper Jr. married Sarah Morgan (some say her maiden name was Miller). It is believed the marriage took place in Berkeley County, Virginia. He was twenty-eight, and she was twenty-one. It is likely that Casper, Jr. built a separate log house on the Hedgesville property for him and Sarah to live in.

Also in 1795, John subdivided the 334-acre property that Joseph had been living on and sold 50 acres to John Mercer.[22] Joseph and his family continued living on the larger, unsold parcel. In 1800, a Slaughter District, Town of Tuscarora, Berkeley County, Virginia tax list records "Joseph Bunner" and "Casper Bunner" Jr. living there. [23]

In 1806, Jeremiah Evans of Berkeley County made an offer to purchase the land Joseph was living on. John likely discussed this offer with Joseph before agreeing to accept it. On August 28, 1806, John and Martha Bunner sold 217 acres of the 284 acres they still owned as part of the Casper and Mary Böner estate to Jeremiah Evans. The sales price was $1,050.[24]

John agreed to accept installment payments from Jeremiah Evans until the total amount had been paid. There appears to have been an agreement that Joseph and his family could continue living on and farming this property until Evans had paid in full for the land. The initial contract between John and Jeremiah Evans called for the payments to be completed by September 1810.[25]

According to John's will, Evans was significantly in arrears on his payments at the time of John's death in 1810. Berkeley County Deed records indicate that Evans did not make his final payment until 1815.[26] It appears that Joseph and his family continued living on this land until that date.

---

22  Berkeley County, West Virginia County Clerk's Office, John Bunner to William Mercer, 50 acres, 1795, Deed Book 12, Page 398

23  Bridges, Steven A, "Virginians in 1800: Counties of West Virginia", 1987, p.13

24  Berkeley County, West Virginia County Clerk's Office, John Bunner to Jeremiah Evans, 217 acres, 1815, Deed Book 27, Page 542

25  Monongalia County Clerk Office, Morgantown, West Virginia, Will Book 1, page 336

26  Berkeley County, West Virginia County Clerk's Office, John Bunner to Jeremiah Evans, 217 acres, 1815, Deed Book 27, Page 542

Circa 1816, after the land sale was completed, Joseph and his family moved to Monongalia County, Virginia. By then, most of his children had grown, married, and moved away. It appears that only two daughters, Margaret (Peggy) and Rutha, accompanied Joseph and his wife on this move. Peggy's husband must have died or they were divorced, as her two small children also made the move with her.[27] It is believed the family settled near the Tygart Valley River (near present-day Colfax, West Virginia) where Casper Bonner, Jr. had settled with his family circa 1807.

For the next two years, Joseph worked on a small farm that he had rented, growing food in his garden and taking care of his small herds of sheep and pigs. When he was sixty-six years old and losing the physical ability to do the heavy labor required to maintain his farm and provide for his family, Congress passed the Revolutionary War Pension Act of 1818. This law provided pensions to veterans of the Continental Army. It granted lifetime pensions of $8 per month to non-officers who had served for at least nine months on active duty. The terms of the law required that veterans apply in person at their local county courthouse and swear to facts about their military service.

Joseph initially applied for his pension in 1818 and began receiving his payments of $8 per month in 1819.

A copy of Joseph's initial pension application submitted at the Monongalia County Courthouse in Morgantown, Virginia, dated May 27, 1818, stated that he was:

"Aged about 66 years" and a resident of Monongalia County. He swore under oath that he "enlisted as a soldier under Capt. Nelson for one year, and at the end of that year enlisted again under Nelson for 3 years. That after Nelson was disgraced, he served under Capt. Grant, afterward by Capt. Davis in the Virginia State Troops, and in the Regiment commanded by Colonel Butler in the Pennsylvania line under General Wayne. That he was in the battles of Brandywine under the command of Lord Sterling, and that he fought at the Battle of Germantown. That in all he served four years, one of which was in the Virginia State Troops and three

---

27 Monongalia County Clerk's Office, Morgantown, WV. Joseph Bunner Application for Revolutionary War Pension, 1818,1820

in the United States Continental Army. Afterwards, he went to Philadelphia to get his depreciated pay and was detained so long that he sold his pay for 3 guineas and gave up his discharge. That he is much disabled and not well able to support himself by labor....."[28]

In 1820, Congress passed an additional law stipulating that all Revolutionary War pension recipients had to provide a list of their property and other assets to continue receiving their pension.

On July 24, 1820, Joseph submitted his listing of property and assets. He also restated his war service record and his personal circumstances which he had included in his initial 1818 application. A copy of Joseph's 1820 submission follows:

Joseph Bonner
Revolutionary War Pension Application # 40,021

Virginia

"Be it remembered that a county court held in and for the county of Monongalia, at the courthouse of the said county, on Monday the 24th of July in the year 1820, personally appeared in open court [Joseph Bonner mark placed on document] being a court of record, which proceed according to the course of the common law, with a jurisdiction unlimited in point of amount, and keeping a record of its proceedings [Joseph Bonner mark placed on document] Joseph Bonner, aged about 66 years, resident in said county, who being first duly sworn according to law, doth on his oath declare and he served in the Revolutionary War as follows viz. he the said Bonner enlisted as a soldier under Capt. Nelson for one year, and at the expiration of the same year he again enlisted under said Nelson for three years. That after said Nelson was disgraced, he served under Capt. Grant, afterward under Capt. Davis, in the regiment commanded by Col. Butler in the Pennsylvania line and under General Wayne, that he was in the battle of Brandywine under Lord Sterling and at the battle of Germantown. That he served four years, one

---

28 Monongalia County Clerk's Office, Morgantown, WV. Joseph Bunner Application for Revolutionary War Pension, 1818

of which was in the Virginia State troops and three in the United States troops. That the date of his original declaration is the 22nd day of May 1818, that he has received a pension and the number of the certificate is 5218, and I do solemnly swear that I was a resident citizen of the United States on the 18th day of March 1818, and that I have not since that time by gift, sale, or in any other manner disposed of my property or any part thereof, with intent thereby to diminish it as to bring myself within the provision of an act of Congress entitled 'An Act to provide for certain persons engaged in the Land and Naval service of the United States in the Revolutionary War', passed on the 18th day of March 1818, and that I have not, nor has any person for me [earned] interest in the properties or securities, contracts or debts due me, nor have I any income, other than what is hereto annexed by me. Subscribed, one horse, eight head of sheep, a borr [sic] and seven pigs, nine pewter plates and one set of knives and forks, one barshear plow, one hoe."

"And I believe I will require most of this property to discharge the rent due for the land on which I live as that rent amounts to Sixty dollars. That I am much disabled and my eyesight considerably impaired. That formerly I was a farmer but owing to my disabilities I am utterly unable to support myself and family. That my family consists of five persons viz. my wife about 60 years old very infirm, my daughter Peggy and Ruthy, both young women and my grandchildren Nancy and John the children of Peggy - that my family, instead of being a support to me, is rather a burthen [sic] to me."

Signed [mark indicating the signature of] Joseph Bonner

Sworn in declared before the aforesaid court on the day and date first hearing written.[29]

---

29  Monongalia County Clerk's Office, Morgantown, WV. Joseph Bunner Application for Revolutionary War Pension, 1820

```
                                                        Active Duty
                                                           Line

   BUNNER, JOSEPH,                              Rank    PVT.

   Unit   9TH REGT.

   Depreciation computed from

   Amount Settled £  60.13.7            Renewed £

   Date of Certificate                      No.    1192

   Series   PHILADELPHIA (19 APRIL 1792 TO THIS TIME)

                    Authorities:              ⎫  "Public Debt,"
          Accounts of Auditors of Depreciation Accounts,  ⎬  Records of the
                                              ⎭  Comptroller Gen-
          Book   A  , Register of Depreciation Certificates,   eral, at D.P.R.
                 P. 162
          EITHER OF THE BASIC RECORDS PROVES ACTIVE DUTY PERFORMED WITHIN
                         THE PERIOD 1 JA● 77 – 1 AUG. 1780.
   MA-1-14M
```

**Joseph Bunner Revolutionary War Pension Card. Joseph received a Revolutionary War pension of $8/month from 1819 until his death in November or December 1828**

Joseph's wife died sometime between 1820 and 1828. Joseph died in November or December 1828. He is buried near his brother John in the old Bonner graveyard (now known as the Malone Cemetery) near the head of Bunners Run on the property initially claimed by John in 1772. New grave markers of white marble were erected in 1962 by Joseph's descendant, Thomas Orth Bunner of Morgantown, West Virginia. This headstone replacement was done in coordination with the Daughters of the American Revolution.

A copy of Joseph Bunner's will on file with the Monongalia County Clerk's office in Morgantown, West Virginia follows:

> I, Joseph Bunner, of Monongalia County, State of Virginia, make this my last will; after my decease, my property be sold and all gets paid from the proceeds. Anything remaining to go to my nine children: Mary Stacy, Katherine Swisher, Elizabeth Swisher,

## THE SIBLINGS OF JOHN AMOS BONNER (BÖNER/BUNNER)

Joseph Bunner, Rutha Stayrn (Starn), John Bunner, Casper Bunner, Margaret Lea (Lee), and Henry Bunner.[30]

Joseph appointed his son, Joseph, his executor. This will was made the 10th day of November 1828. Witnesses were Joseph Bunner Jr., Thomas Starn, and Stephen Wilson Sr.

### Reuben Bonner

Reuben Bonner was the fifth child, and third son, of Casper and Mary Böner. Virtually all family records list his birth year as 1760, but recent additional research suggests this is incorrect. The 1774 list of "Tithables" in Berkeley County, Virginia indicates that Casper Böner and his three sons John, Joseph, and Reuben were required to pay Tithables that year.[31] The "Tithable" was an annual capitation tax, or "head tax" imposed on all male residents of Virginia who were age sixteen or older.

If Reuben Bonner was required to pay a "Tithable" tax in 1774 he must have been born prior to December 31, 1758. Because it has been confirmed that Reuben's sister, Susanah Barbel Bonner was born in May 1758, it is impossible for Reuben to have been born any time during 1758. For Reuben's mother, Mary, to have given birth to his sister Susanah in May 1758, her pregnancy with Susanah would have likely commenced in August 1757. This means that the latest date for Reuben's birth would be June or July 1757. It was probably a few months earlier than this. For purposes of this book, Reuben's birth in early 1757 is assumed.

Regarding Reuben's inclusion on the 1774 Berkeley County Tithables list, Casper and his family had moved from their home in the newly formed Berkeley County to the Monongahela River Valley in 1772. However, since Casper did not sell his Berkeley County properties, and he probably did not notify the Berkeley County courthouse employees that he and his family had moved,

---

30  Bunner, Gale J., "Genealogy Descendents of Casper (Boner) Bunner And Mary Christianna Brown, Revised Edition, 1988, p. 10

31  Berkeley County, Virginia Tithables List, 1774, p. 33

the courthouse employees would have likely assumed the family was still living in Berkeley County. As their records indicated that Reuben would have been sixteen years old in 1774, and courthouse employees dutifully placed him on the "Tithables" list.

Returning to events near the time of Reuben's birth, by early 1757, Casper and Mary had achieved semi-stability in their lives after their panicked retreat from their frontier homestead in 1756. This retreat was forced by the occurrence of several bloody skirmishes along the South Branch of the Potomac River during the French and Indian War. Settlements had been burned, settlers had been killed, and deadly battles between colonial forces and the Indians had occurred near where Casper and Mary lived with their family. The capture of Mary's father and sister by Delaware Indians on April 20, 1756, had convinced he rest of the extended family to flee to safety east of the Blue Ridge Mountains. There is evidence that they found their refuge, at least for a time, near Frederick, Maryland.

Sometime between late 1756 and mid-1758, Reuben's father Casper purchased 27 acres of farmland near the village of Hedgesville in Frederick County, Virginia (now Berkeley County, West Virginia).[32] This is where Reuben grew from infancy to an eleven-year-old, and where he learned to farm and to hunt. It is where his sister Catherine was born circa 1765, and where his youngest brother, Casper Jr., was born circa 1767. His father sold this 27-acre property in 1768 for £25, enough money to purchase 10,000 acres from the local Fairfax Land Office.[33] Casper didn't need, or want, this much land, but at age forty eight, he probably had in mind to purchase enough acreage to bequeath sustainable farmlands to each of his four sons.

At that time, Lord Fairfax owned all the vacant, undeveloped land in what was called the "Northern Neck" of Virginia. His estate consisted of 5.2 million acres and extended up to eighty miles southward from the Potomac River all the way from the Chesapeake

---

32 Frederick County, VA County Clerk's Office, Deed Book 12, Page 9-14, Robert Davis Estate to George Myles with 27-acre Gasper 'Boner' exclusion, June 8, 1760

33 Frederick County, VA County Clerk's Office, Deed Book 12, Page 109-112, John Davis and Casper 'Boner,' 27-acres to George Myles, Feb. 1768

Bay (east of present-day Washington, D.C.) to the headwaters of the Northern Branch of the Potomac River near present-day Thomas, West Virginia.

During the spring of 1768, Casper and his sons identified two nearby parcels of vacant and available land to purchase from the Fairfax Land Office. One was a 334-acre tract located approximately three miles west of the farm where Reuben grew up. The second was a 365-acre tract located approximately six miles west of the 334-acre property. Both properties were along the Martinsburg to Warm Springs (present-day Berkeley Springs) road.

Casper applied for a warrant on both properties along with making the required 50% down payment, which would have amounted to approximately £1 for each property. Fairfax promptly awarded the warrants to Casper, and Casper arranged to have the properties surveyed. Surveys on both properties were completed on August 6, 1768.[34]

The surveys document that eleven-year-old Reuben and his eighteen-year-old brother John served as chain bearers for the surveying crew.[35] Casper submitted the surveys to the Fairfax Land Office. The next step in the land sale process was for Fairfax to schedule a closing date. At the closing, Casper would pay the remaining 50% he owed on the properties, and Fairfax would issue patents (deeds) providing Casper free and clear legal ownership of both tracts.

In the meantime, since Casper had already made a 50% down payment, he was legally allowed to begin making improvements on the land while he waited for the final patents to be issued. During autumn of 1768, Casper and his three older son Johns, Joseph, and Reuben cleared enough land on the nearby 334-acre tract to build a new log house for the family and outbuildings for their livestock. It is likely they had completed the three mile move from their 27-acre

---

34  Joyner, Peggy (1987), "Abstract of Virginia's Northern Neck Warrants and Surveys, Volume 4, p. 80

35  Joyner, Peggy (1987), "Abstract of Virginia's Northern Neck Warrants and Surveys, Volume 4, p. 80

farm to their new home on the 334-acre property by Christmas of 1768.

The family continued living on and making improvements to their new farm while they awaited the patents from Fairfax. By late 1771, Casper's frustration with Fairfax had grown to the point that he began looking elsewhere for land he could bequeath to his sons. In 1769, his brothers-in-law, Maunus and Adam Brown, had each purchased adjoining 300+ acre tracts on the same land in the Monongahela River Valley they and their father Wendell Brown had settled on in 1752.[36] They had been forced to abandon and flee that land in 1754 during the outbreak of the French and Indian War.

Casper turned his attention to the upper Monongahela River Valley and found a 400-acre parcel for sale on a plateau alongside the river about fifty miles upstream from where Maunus and Adam Brown lived. He purchased this land [37] and moved his entire family, which now included nine children (his tenth child, Margaret, had married earlier in 1772 and remained in Berkeley County). The nine children making the move ranged in age from twenty-two down to one. Reuben was fifteen years old.

Reuben could not have known it at the time, but this is where he would live for the next eighteen years. In addition to helping his family clear the virgin forests from their property along the Monongahela River (present-day Rivesville, West Virginia), he worked as a chain bearer along with neighbor Isaiah Prickett for the William Pettyjohn survey crew. In 1772, just months after arriving to his new home, Reuben and Isaiah served as chain bearers during the survey of Jacob Prickett's 324-acre property across the river from his father's new homestead.[38]

In 1773, sixteen-year-old Reuben located a vacant and unclaimed 400-acre parcel of land about two miles southeast Prickett's Fort. He

---

36 MacInnis, Sharon, Early Landowners of Pennsylvania: Atlas of Township Warrantee Maps of Fayette County, PA, Third Edition, Page 131

37 Lough, Glenn D., "Now and Long Ago – A History of the Marion County Area," Morgantown Printing and Binding Co., 1969, p. 245

38 Lough, Glenn D., "Now and Long Ago – A History of the Marion County Area," Morgantown Printing and Binding Co., 1969, p. 258

built a small cabin on the land and planted and harvested a crop of corn. This was sufficient for him to claim the land. He was granted a "settlement certificate" which protected his claim but did not give him legal ownership of the land.[39]

Many believe that, during this time, those under age twenty-one needed an adult to cosign their legal documents. As Reuben's father, Casper, was living nearby, it is likely he fulfilled this role if it was necessary.

In early 1774, bloody frontier skirmishes led by Mingo Chief Logan began along the Ohio and Monongahela River Valleys. These attacks were vengeful retaliations by Logan for the massacre of his family and other tribal members at his Ohio River village by a small group of dastardly white frontiersmen. As a result, a local militia had been formed by some of Reuben's neighbors and a fort had been hastily built on property owned by Jacob Prickett to serve as a place of refuge for local settlers.

Due to a number of Indian attacks and murders in the area, most local settlers, likely including Reuben's family, had taken up residence inside Prickett's Fort as early as June 1774. By October, approximately eighty families were living there. On the evening of October 2, Isaiah Prickett, friend of Reuben and son of Jacob Prickett, and Mrs. Susan Oxx, a young wife pregnant with her first child, stepped outside the fort to round up their cattle and drive them closer to the fort for the night. They never returned. A search party found Isaiah murdered and scalped, and there was no sign of Mrs. Oxx. The search party quickly caught up with the fleeing Indians and a battle ensued. Two Indians were killed, but Chief Logan, their captive Susan Oxx, and the rest of his warriors escaped into the darkness of the night. Mrs. Oxx was never heard from again.[40]

Reuben, his family, and all their neighbors were traumatized by these events. However, the reverberations from this tragedy were soon overtaken by disquieting news coming from the east. Heavy

---

39  Lough, Glenn D., "Now and Long Ago – A History of the Marion County Area," Morgantown Printing and Binding Co., 1969, p. 264

40  Lough, Glenn D., "Now and Long Ago – A History of the Marion County Area," Morgantown Printing and Binding Co., 1969, p. 302-303

British taxes and restrictions on the colonies, and the subsequent colonial resistance, had escalated to the point that the British army had attacked colonial militia forces at Lexington and Concord, Massachusetts on April 19, 1775. America's war for independence had begun.

The outbreak of the Revolutionary War caused many sudden upheavals in Reuben's family. His older brothers John and Joseph volunteered for full-time duty in the Continental Army. Joseph was deployed in February 1776 and John in December 1776. Reuben's parents Casper and Mary made the decision to return to their 334-acre property in Berkeley County. His oldest sister, Elizabeth, who had married John Miller in 1774, planned to remain in Monongalia County. Casper sold his 400-acre property to his son-in-law John and daughter Elizabeth before moving back to Berkeley County.[41]

Reuben was in a romantic relationship with Nancy Ann Prickett, daughter of Jacob Prickett, and did not want to leave. As a result, he made the decision to remain in Monongalia County, join the local militia that was defending Prickett's Fort, and continue his pursuit of Nancy Ann. He served at Prickett's Fort under Captain William Haymond in 1776-1777.[42]

At this time Reuben was nineteen years old. With his father and his two older brothers leaving the area, he may have needed an adult over age twenty-one to cosign his legal documents. According to family historian Gale Bunner, in the 1800's Adam O. Heck claimed that Reuben Bunner's uncle, Thomas Brown, who lived in Westmoreland County, Pennsylvania fifty miles downstream on the Monongahela River, served this role for Reuben. Adam O. Heck claimed to have once owned a copy of Reuben's "settlement certificate," and that it was co-signed by Thomas Brown.[43]

Reuben's brothers and sisters returning to Berkeley County with Casper and Mary were Susanah (age 18), Catherine (age 11),

---

[41] Lough, Glenn D., "Now and Long Ago – A History of the Marion County Area," Morgantown Printing and Binding Co., 1969, p. 245

[42] Prickett's Fort State Park, Fairmont, WV, visual display in Visitor's Center

[43] Bunner, Alan N., "The Bunner Family in America" Alexandria, Virginia 7,300+ page document on CD, revision dated June 25, 2012. Chapter 41, p. 1143

## THE SIBLINGS OF JOHN AMOS BONNER (BÖNER/BUNNER)

Casper, Jr. (age 9), Mary Christina (age 6), and Charlotte (age 5). A year later, in 1777, Susanah married James Laramore and moved to Hampshire County, Virginia where she and her new husband started their family.[44]

In 1778, Chief Logan and his warriors stole Reuben Bonner's horse from Prickett's Fort.[45] Although this story cannot be proven, it is both possible and probable. Chief Logan fought against the colonists in the American Revolution as an ally of Great Britain. If this horse stealing narrative is true, it occurred near the end of Chief Logan's life, as he was murdered by a nephew near Detroit in 1780.

During February 1779, Reuben's father Casper died at his home in Berkeley County. It is likely that Reuben returned to Berkeley County for a time to be with his mother and younger siblings. After the mourning period, he returned to Monongalia County.

Two years later, in 1781, Reuben and Nancy Ann Prickett were married.[46] They settled on the 400-acre property that Reuben had claimed in 1773 and for which he possessed a "settlement claim." This property was at the western edge of what eventually became known as Bunners Ridge, where generations of Bunners have lived since the Revolutionary War. It is located near present-day Fairmont, West Virginia.

---

44 Bunner, Alan N., "The Bunner Family in America" Alexandria, Virginia 7,300+ page document on CD, revision dated June 25, 2012. Chapter 36, p. 1094

45 Bunner, Gale J., "Genealogy Descendents of Casper (Boner) Bunner And Mary Christianna Brown, Revised Edition, 1988, p. 13, excerpt from the "Adam O. Heck" interviews published by Glen D. Lough, Fairmont, WV

46 Bunner, Alan N., "The Bunner Family in America" Alexandria, Virginia 7,300+ page document on CD, revision dated June 25, 2012. Chapter 41, pp. 1143-46

**Sign for Bunners Ridge Road at I-79 Exit 139 near Prickett's Fork State Park, five miles north of present day Fairmont, West Virginia** (photo by Michael Bunner)

The unconfirmed document known as *"The Reuben Bunner Revelation,"* a purported history of the early Bunner family in America written by an orphan who was adopted by Reuben and Nancy Ann Bonner in Kentucky circa 1792, includes the following story from 1782. "Father Bunner" in this narrative refers to Reuben Bunner.

"In the middle of May 1782, Hugh McGary and John Beasely were ready to travel to Pennsylvania to sell some (Indian) scalps they had got in fights. Father Bunner said that they wanted him and Mod Morgan to go with them to show them the safest way. They (Reuben and his family) were in the corn, and they (McGary and Beasley) stayed at the Bunners' and helped hoe. Uncle Tom Brown was there and said he'd stay behind and scout for Indians so none would be surprised by a bunch coming in on them. Father Bunner said the corn was very thrifty and ankle high and had to be watched day and night to keep the deer and elk from nibbling it off. They had about eight acres in, he said. Uncle Tom Brown said he and the women would watch the corn. So they (Reuben Bunner and Mod Morgan) went to show the way. First they traveled by dugout down the (Monongahela) River to Redstone. There they left the dugout with Father Bunner's Brown cousins and traveled west through the country. Father Bunner said the county there was Westmoreland, but in July the part west of the river was made into Washington County. Some thought the territory was Virginia and some thought Pennsylvania. The place where the Pennsylvania people were buying scalps was called Catfish Camp. Father Bunner said it was later named Washington City and was the capitol (County seat) of Washington County. Father Bunner met some friends who had settled in that part. They were John and Thomas Strain and Hugh Sherer and Samual Leeper. The Strains made him and Mod Morgan acquainted with the great scout Adam Poe, who was there as they were to sell some scalps he and his friends had taken in fights by the Ohio River. The men learned it was against the law to buy scalps, but the authorities took Mr. Poe's scalps and paid him a good price, more than twelve pounds apiece. Our men's scalps were refused because the Indians who had owned them were killed on the upper waters of the Monongahela River and not in Pennsylvania. This was a thin excuse and made Mr. McGary very angry and he threatened to fight over it. But a gentleman there named Swearingen took the scalps and paid top price with his own money because he hated Indians so much. The men returned home in about two weeks. At this time (June 1782), Father Bunner remembers, the people at the Bozarth settlement [near present-day Fairmont, West Virginia] were busy putting in stockades to protect the Jonathon Bozarth blockhouse, on land Thomas Barnes had bought from Mr. Bozarth. Some of the Barnes people were living in the blockhouse, and hearing of terrible murders of Preacher Corbley's wife and children by Indians, on Muddy Creek [now in Greene County, Pennsylvania], the people decided to build a stockade for the house and spring. Father Bunner says this fort was called "old house fort" because of an old rock house that people supposed the

Indians built hundreds of years back, being nearby, and a little ways down the hill toward the river."[47]

Over the next several years, Reuben and Nancy had several children. These included John (1783), Nancy Ann (1784), Isaac (1785), Charlotte (1786), Joshiah (1788), and Reuben, Jr. (1789). All were born at their home in Monongalia County, Virginia.

During this time, the American Continental Army under George Washington won the Revolutionary War and gained America's Independence. The 1783 Treaty of Paris formally ended the war and also ceded the land west of the Appalachian Mountains and north of the Ohio River to the United States. This became known as the Northwest Territory.

The Congress of American Confederation passed the Northwest Ordinance on July 13th, 1787. The ordinance defined the process by which the territory would be divided into no less than five states. It was also decreed that when the adult male population reached 5,000 the residents could elect their own legislature. Also, when the population reached 60,000, the territories would be granted statehood. On July 15th, 1788, the Northwest Territory government was established with the territorial capital at Marietta, Ohio. In 1790, the capital was shifted to Fort Washington near the new settlement of Cincinnati, Ohio.

These events started a new land rush to the Northwest Territory. Many of the pioneers who had settled along the Virginia and Pennsylvania frontiers became motivated to move further west into this new territory. The land was fertile and flatter and could be more easily farmed than the existing homesteads they had carved from mountainous terrain.

In 1788, a survey was recorded of Reuben Bunner land that was located on Reuben's Run, a tributary of Prickett's Creek. According to Alan Bunner in *"The Bunner Family in America,"* this tributary is believed to have actually been called Reuben Bunner's Run.[48] The

---

47  Bunner, Alan N., "The Bunner Family in America" Alexandria, Virginia 7,300+ page document on CD, revision dated June 25, 2012. Chapter 41, pp. 1143-46

48  Bunner, Alan N., "The Bunner Family in America" Alexandria, Virginia 7,300+ page document on CD, revision dated June 25, 2012. Chapter 41, pp.

land that was surveyed is believed to have been the 400-acre parcel that Reuben had claimed in 1773 and on which his family had been living. This survey may have been performed in preparation for selling this land prior to the move to Kentucky which Reuben was contemplating for the following year.

In 1789 the lure of new lands and new adventures caused Reuben and Nancy Ann and their six young children to depart down the Monongahela and Ohio Rivers to Mason County, KY. They were accompanied by many members of the Prickett family along with several other Monongahela Valley families. Their plan was to temporarily settle in Kentucky until it was safe to settle on the other side of the Ohio River in the Northwest Territory, which had long been the home of many Indian tribes.

The Reuben Bonner family likely made this trip in "dugouts" which were almost universally made of yellow poplar. The yellow poplar canoe was hewed from a single trunk and was nearly impossible to sink because of the buoyancy of the wood. A canoe on the river floating downstream with the current could cover 40 or 50 miles per day compared to a packhorse that could travel about twenty miles each day. These poplar dugouts came in all sizes. One large dugout could carry the equivalent of ten packhorses. It is also likely that some of the families made the trip in keel boats, which was also a popular mode of transportation down the Ohio River.

On October 12, 1789, the Virginia Land Office issued the patent to Reuben Bonner for the 400-acre parcel he had claimed under "settlement rights" in 1773.[49] It is probable that Reuben had already sold this land by the time he received this patent, as he had already settled in Kentucky by this date. It is believed that the Monongalia County, Virginia records memorializing Reuben's sale of this land were destroyed by fire in 1796.

The supposed author of the document known as *"The Reuben Bunner Revelation"* entered the Reuben and Nancy Ann Prickett Bonner narrative soon after they arrived in Kentucky. One of the

---

1143-1146

49   Virginia Colonial Land Office, 400 Acre Grant to 'Reuben Boner,' October 12, 1789,   https://lva-virginia.libguides.com/land-grants

children of Reuben and Nancy Ann was named Jane. She was not their biological daughter but was instead an orphan they adopted soon after they settled in Kentucky.

Many of the known stories in *"The Reuben Bunner Revelation"* have been found to be true, but a few have been debunked, so the historical authenticity of the document remains in doubt. This document did not surface until early 1976, when a seventy-six-page, single spaced, typewritten manuscript was submitted to Marion County, West Virginia historian Glenn D. Lough. It is believed this manuscript was provided to Lough by descendants of Reuben and Nancy Ann Prickett Bunner who lived in Kansas. Lough excerpted and published some of the narratives contained in this document but withheld releasing the entire manuscript until he could authenticate it as a credible historical document. By the time of Lough's death in 1991, he still had not released the full manuscript. Several efforts to find this document in Lough's archives, now in a collection owned by West Virginia University, have proven fruitless.

However, the excerpts from *"The Reuben Bunner Revelation"* that have been published are now part of the lore of the Reuben Bunner family story, so a few are included in this narrative. The following may be true, but the reader is advised to remain skeptical until that time in the future that this story can be corroborated and authenticated by other sources.

> "In the *Reuben Bunner Revelation*, the "Orphan" states when she was eight years old, Indians attacked her family in Bourbon County Kentucky, how her uncle and father were thrown to the ground on their backs and spread flat by having their wrists and ankles tied to stakes, and tortured for hours, until they died. The Indians believed the men had a keg of gun-powder and were determined to force them to reveal its whereabouts. This they could not do, because there was no hidden gunpowder.
>
> The Orphan states she was partly reared by Reuben and Nancy Ann Bunner and made her home with the Reuben Bunner family

for about 25 years on and off, in Kentucky and after they moved across the Ohio River into Ohio."[50]

Another story from the unconfirmed *"Reuben Bunner Revelation,"*

"In August 1789 (not long after Reuben and Ann arrived in Kentucky) Shawnee Indians attacked the home of Reuben and Nancy Ann Prickett Bunner. In the house at the time were William Bunner, Ann (Reuben and Ann's infant), two daughters of Jacob and Mary Prickett Lucas, and Elias Washburn, a neighbor. William Bunner shot and killed the first Indian. The second Indian shot Bunner in the head. Washburn killed the second and third Indians with his axe. The fourth Indian escaped. William Bunner recovered from his wound." [51]

Sometime between 1794 and 1798, Reuben and his family moved across the Ohio River to be counted among the earliest settlers in Adams County, Ohio (which became Brown County, Ohio after 1817). Reuben and Nancy Ann settled on the West Fork of Straight Creek near present day Arnheim in Franklin Township. According to the 1850 census, their daughter, Susannah, was born there in 1799.[52] Their youngest child, Hosea, was born there in 1801.

Many other new settlers swarmed into the Northwest Territory along the Ohio River between 1794 and 1803. By 1803, when Thomas Jefferson was president, the population of that part of the territory now called Ohio had crossed the threshold for statehood set by the Northwest Ordinance of 1787. Ohio was admitted to the Union as the 17th state on March 1, 1803, during the second year of the Thomas Jefferson presidency. What was left of the original Northwest Territory

---

50  Bunner, Alan N., "The Bunner Family in America" Alexandria, Virginia 7,300+ page document on CD, revision dated June 25, 2012. Chapter 41, pp. 1143-1146

51  Bunner, Alan N., "The Bunner Family in America" Alexandria, Virginia 7,300+ page document on CD, revision dated June 25, 2012. Chapter 41, pp. 1143-1146

52  "Brown County (Ohio) History"

after Ohio was carved out as a state was redesignated as the Indiana Territory. This territory included the lands that would eventually become the states of Indiana, Illinois, Michigan, and Wisconsin.

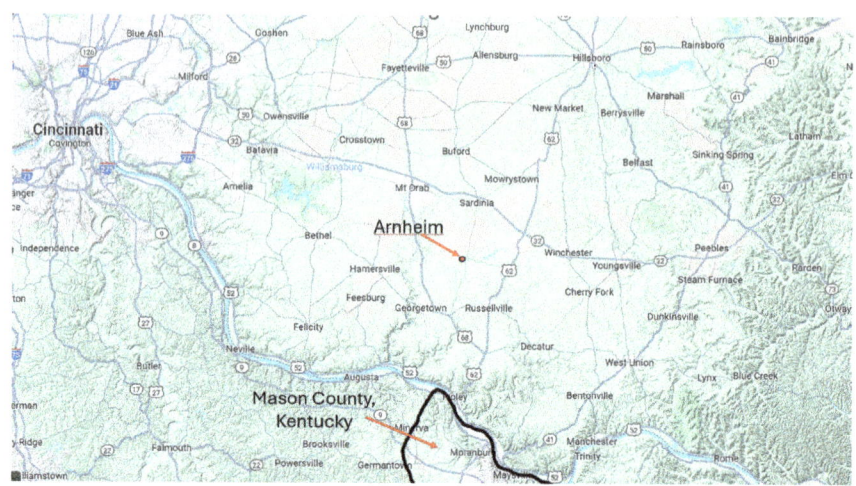

Reuben Bonner and family settled in Mason County, KY circa 1789.
They settled on the West Fork of Straight Creek
near present day Arnheim by 1798

Children of Reuben and Nancy Ann Bonner born while they lived in Kentucky and Ohio were Jacob (1791), Mary (1794), James (1798), Susanah (1799), and Hosea (1801). Jane (whose birth name is thought to have been Jane Finch) is believed to have been born circa 1782 and adopted circa 1792. If *"The Reuben Bunner Revelation"* is an authentic historical document, she is believed to have been the author.[53] However, it is unclear how she learned to read and write as an orphan "living off and on" with Reuben and Nancy Ann Bunner. These skills were almost non-existent among frontier settlers.

Reuben Bonner is believed to have died at his home in what is now Brown County, Ohio in late 1809 or early 1810. According to *The Reuben Bunner Revelation*, he died "sometime before tax time

---

53  Bunner, Alan N., "The Bunner Family in America" Alexandria, Virginia 7,300+ page document on CD, revision dated June 25, 2012. Chapter 41, pp. 1143-1146

in 1810, as his oldest son John was assessed for his Brown County land that year." Interestingly, Reuben's younger son Reuben Jr., was named his executor, not his eldest son John.

Reuben Bonner was buried in the Straight Creek Baptist Churchyard, Franklin Township, Brown County, Ohio. His illegible gravestone is no longer standing.[54]

A deed was recorded on December 4, 1810, to the "Reuben Bunner Heirs." A description of part of the land that passed into the hands of Reuben's children is given in an 1810 quit-claim agreement in which Reuben's children paid Joseph and Nancy Kerr of Ross County $200 for 115 acres, probably adjoining farms already occupied by children Isaac and Reuben Jr. An abstract of this agreement follows:

"This indenture made this 4th day of December, 1810, between Joseph Kerr and Nancy his wife of the County of Ross and State of Ohio, of the one part and the heirs of Reuben Bonner (spelled Boner in this document), deceased, of the County of Adams of the other part, witnesses that... in consideration of $200 current money of the United States paid to them, they forever acquit... and confirm to the said heirs all that tract or parcel of land in the County of Adams, viz: 115 acres on the waters of Straight Creek, beginning at two hickories, south-east corner of the original tract running thence west 115 poles to three beeches, thence north 150 poles to an elm and ash, thence east 115 poles to a small beech in the line of Robert Higgins survey Nr. 4253, thence with said line south 150 poles to the beginning, it being a part of a tract which was surveyed for Robert Price and by him transferred to Joseph Kerr, together with all improvements.....

(signed) Joseph Kerr, Nancy Kerr
(witnesses) Amasiah Davisson, Reuben Knowles
(signed) Wm. Wallace, Justice of the Peace, Ross County

Recorded May 31, 1811 by Samuel Bradford, Recorder."[55]

---

54 Bunner, Alan N., "The Bunner Family in America" Alexandria, Virginia 7,300+ page document on CD, revision dated June 25, 2012. Chapter 41, pp. 1143-1146

55 Bunner, Alan N., "The Bunner Family in America" Alexandria, Virginia 7,300+ page document on CD, revision dated June 25, 2012. Chapter 41, pp. 1143-1146

Reuben evidently willed that his farm be divided into 11 equal shares among his children. In 1846, after daughter Polly (Mary) Johnson had moved to Jennings County, Indiana, she sold her 11½ acre share to her brother Reuben Bunner (Jr.), who remained most of his life in Franklin Township. [56]

Reuben's death was evidently known to his family back in Monongalia County, Virginia, prior to July 1810, as he is the only sibling of John Amos Bunner not mentioned in John's 1810 will, although Reuben's son received a small inheritance from John as "my nephew Reuben Bunner of Kentucky".[57]

The widow Nancy Ann was living with a single son, perhaps the widowed Reuben, Jr. and her unmarried daughter Jane in 1830. Nancy Ann Prickett Bonner (spelled Bunner on her gravestone) died on July 13, 1842, living past the age of 80. Nancy Ann was buried beside Reuben in the Straight Creek Baptist Churchyard, Franklin Township, Brown County, Ohio. Her grave marker reads, "Ann, Wife of Reubin Bunner died 13 July 1842, aged 80 yrs. 4 mo. 5 d's"[58]

The last entry in *"The Reuben Bunner Revelation"* is a farewell to Nancy Ann Prickett Bunner from "the orphan." It reads: "We promise to join you in Heaven, dear Mother Bunner."[59]

## Casper Bonner, Junior

Much less is currently known about Casper Bonner Jr., than is known about his three older brothers. There is also much historical confusion between Casper Böner the father, and Casper Jr., the son

---

56 Bunner, Alan N., "The Bunner Family in America" Alexandria, Virginia 7,300+ page document on CD, revision dated June 25, 2012. Chapter 41, pp. 1143-1146

57 Bunner, Alan N., "The Bunner Family in America" Alexandria, Virginia 7,300+ page document on CD, revision dated June 25, 2012. Chapter 41, pp. 1143-1146

58 Bunner, Alan N., "The Bunner Family in America" Alexandria, Virginia 7,300+ page document on CD, revision dated June 25, 2012. Chapter 41, pp. 1143-1146

59 Bunner, Gale J., "Genealogy Descendents of Casper (Boner) Bunner And Mary Christianna Brown, Revised Edition, 1988, p. 8

which, when sorted out, reveals more about the history of Casper Sr., the father, and leaves us with less knowledge about the history of Casper Jr., the son.

For example, Marion County, West Virginia historian Glenn D. Lough, in his book "*Now and Long Ago*" wrote:

> "In 1772, Zackwell Morgan sold 400 acres of land (now lower Rivesville on the river) to Thomas Douthet. Tradition informs that Douthet failed to pay for the land, and reclaiming it, Morgan sold the property to Casper Bunner, listing it in the records as an assignment from Douthet to Bunner. At this time, Douthet lived at present Uniontown, Pennsylvania, where he and Henry Beeson are credited with being the first settlers. Casper Bunner – the name was first spelled "Boner" – was first to "chop a clearing" and "raise a cabin" on the tract (now occupied by the Rivesville power station), and here, though he soon sold the greater part of the land to John Miller, Sr., he continued to live until 1820 when he died."

In this historical account, Lough made the mistake of merging the lives of Casper Sr., the father, and Casper Jr., the son. Casper Jr. is believed to have been born in 1767, so he would have been five years old in 1772. The original purchaser of this 400-acre tract had to be Casper the father, as it is implausible to believe that a five year old boy would purchase 400 acres of wilderness mountain land in 1772. Land deeds that survived the 1796 fire which destroyed most of the land transaction records in Monongalia County, Virginia between 1776 and 1796, confirm that Casper Böner sold this entire 400 acre parcel to his son-in-law, John Miller, in 1776. Miller had this 400-acre parcel surveyed in 1790. [60]

Casper Jr. never purchased any part of the 400-acre parcel where he had lived as a child from 1772 to 1776. John Miller had married Casper Sr.'s daughter (Casper Jr.'s sister), Elizabeth, in 1774 and had built a cabin adjacent to the cabin of his father-in-law for them to live in. It was John Miller's family which lived on this 400-acre

---

60  Lough, Glenn D., "Now and Long Ago – A History of the Marion County Area," Morgantown Printing and Binding Co., 1969, p. 266

property until John died in 1820. That Casper Jr. also died in 1820 seems to have been the historical datapoint that confused Glenn D. Lough when he attempted to reconstruct the historical chronology of the early settlement of the upper Monongahela River Valley.

By removing these historical inaccuracies from the Casper Bonner Jr. biography, his history becomes much easier to reconstruct. Casper Jr. was born on the family's 27-acre farm located two miles north of Hedgesville in Frederick County, Virginia (present-day Berkeley County, West Virginia). He was the seventh child, and the fourth son, of Casper and Mary Böner. His birth could have been as early as 1760 and as late as 1772. Most sources place the date between 1767 and 1770. A birth date of 1767 is assumed in this book.

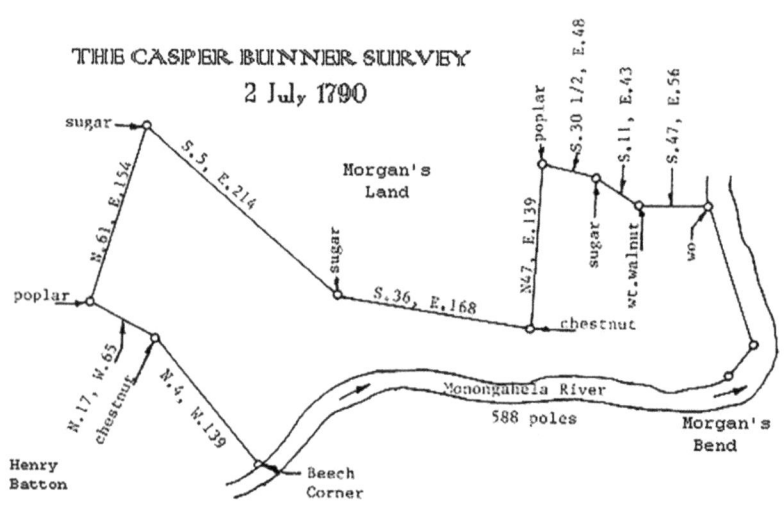

**John Miller 1790 Survey of 400-acre tract purchased from Casper Böner in 1776**

In 1768, when Casper Jr. was one year old, he moved three miles west with his family to their new 334-acre farm located on the west side of North Mountain along Back Creek. Four years later, in 1772, he again moved with his family 140 miles to the west to the 400-acre tract his father had purchased on the upper Monongahela River. Then, four years later, at the outbreak of the American Revolution in

## THE SIBLINGS OF JOHN AMOS BONNER (BÖNER/BUNNER)

1776, Casper Sr. – the father – moved back to his former homestead in Berkeley County.

However, the number of family members that returned to Berkeley County was much smaller than the number that had moved from Berkeley County four years earlier. Casper Jr.'s older brothers John, Joseph, and Reuben did not accompany the family on this return trip as they were all doing their part to win America's independence from Britain. His older sister Elizabeth had married John Miller in 1774 and stayed in Monongalia County with her husband. Those siblings returning to the Hedgesville farm along with nine year old Casper, Jr., were his eighteen-year-old sister Susanah, eleven year old sister Catherine, six-year-old sister Mary Christina, and five- year-old sister Charlotte.

During 1777, Casper Jr.'s oldest brother John had been deployed to New Jersey and then likely to upstate New York as a member of the Continental Army. That same year, his brother Joseph served first in Canada, then was assigned to Fort Ticonderoga for several months. During September and October he fought in the Battles of Brandywine, Paoli, and Germantown in the Philadelphia area. In early December, both John and Joseph were among the 12,000 Colonial Army soldiers who accompanied George Washington to Valley Forge, where they spent the winter. Also in 1777, his other older brother, Reuben, served under Captain William Haymond at Prickett's Fort.

A year after returning to their Berkeley County farm, Casper Jr. and his family attended the wedding of his older sister Susanah. Susanah married James Laramore in 1777, and the two moved to Hampshire County, Virginia (now West Virginia) to start their family.

In February 1779, less than three years after returning to Berkeley County, Casper Sr. died. At the age of twelve, Casper, Jr. had been thrust into the role of man of the house. He continued living on the family farm with his widowed Mother, Mary and his three sisters Catherine, Mary Chistina, and Charlotte. He helped his mother by taking care of the animals, working in the gardens, and performing the multitude of unending chores necessary to keep their farm functioning.

His brother John was helping his mother from afar. Soon after Casper, Sr. died, Mary had named John the executor of his estate. In 1778, John had resigned from the Continental Army after one year of service, and had joined the Westmoreland County, Pennsylvania militia, whose role was to protect the western frontier from British and Indian attacks. He had married Martha Evans and they were living in Redstone Settlement (present-day Brownsville, Pennsylvania). John was required to serve full-time on active duty with his militia unit for two months each year, and to be on immediate standby for the other ten months. During those times John was not needed by the militia, he operated a blacksmith shop in Redstone settlement specializing in making bells and guns.

John's first order of business after his father's death was to sell the 365-acre tract his father had purchased from the Fairfax Land Office in 1768, but for which Fairfax had never issued the patent giving Casper, Sr. the free and clear title to the land. Casper, Sr. and his sons had done little to improve this parcel since 1768, as their focus had always been on improving the 334-acre tract closer to Hedgesville where they lived.

A Berkeley County resident named George Braggoona had expressed an interest in buying the 365-acre tract. As executor, John interceded, telling the Fairfax Land Office that he needed them to issue the patent on this property so he could sell it to Braggoona. After stalling for eleven years, the Fairfax office issued the deed to Casper, Sr. within a few days. On March 2, 1779, two weeks after his death, Casper Böner posthumously received the deed for this property. The Fairfax Land Office spelled his name Gaspar Bonner on the deed.

In retrospect, the only logical explanation for the Fairfax Land Office eleven-year delay in issuing this patent to Casper, Sr., was due to a strong prejudice of the Fairfax English sales agent against German immigrants. The English gentry in colonial Virginia were known to harbor strong prejudices against the immigrants of other countries and ethnicities. They especially looked down their noses at German immigrants, whom they saw as ignorant peasants unworthy of being in the same class as the English aristocracy, of which Lord Fairfax was a prominent member.[61] It is telling that the very day the Fairfax sales agent learned that the land was to be sold to a non-German immigrant, the patent was issued. If no ethnic discrimination existed, the Fairfax office should have simultaneously issued the patents on both 365-acre property and the 334-acre property on which Casper Sr.'s family had been living.

Instead, the issuance of the patent on the 334-acre property continued to be stalled by the Fairfax office. It wasn't until 1789, after the Americans won the Revolutionary War and the Fairfax Estate and all their land sales offices had long become defunct, that the Virginia Land Office issued Casper, Sr., the patent for this land. By that time, he had been dead for twenty years.

In early 1780, older brother Joseph took some of the weight of responsibility off Casper, Jr's shoulders. Joseph had completed his four-year enlistment as a Revolutionary War soldier – three years in the Continental Army and one year of full-time service in the Virginia Militia. Joseph had married in late 1778 or early 1779 at about the time he resigned from the Continental Army and joined the Virginia militia.

After completing his one-year stint with the Virginia troops, Joseph and his wife moved to the family farm in Berkeley County to live with Joseph's mother and younger siblings. Joseph took over management of the farm and Casper, Jr. became his right-hand man.

It is believed that Joseph's wife was named Elizabeth. When she and Joseph first arrived in Hedgesville, they were accompanied by their one-year-old son Joseph, Jr. and infant daughter Catherine.

John visited Berkeley County one or two times during 1780 to prepare for the sale of the 365-acre property to Geroge Braggoona. On October 19, 1780, the sale was completed. The sellers were John and Mary Bunner. Joseph Bunner was listed as the witness to the sale. Joseph's "mark" under his signature on this document confirms that he was physically present in Berkeley County on the day of this transaction.

---

61 McCleskey, Nathaniel Turk, "Across the first divide: Frontiers of settlement and culture in *Augusta County, Virginia, 1738-1770*," College of William and Mary, Scholar Works p. 336

Joseph and Elizabeth had their second son, John, in 1780, and their second daughter, Mary, in 1782. They now had four children under the age of four. Casper Jr.'s mother Mary was now fifty-four years old and not able to perform the heavy physical labor around the farm she could do when she was younger. She started making plans to move to Redstone Settlement in Pennsylvania where she would be closer to her brothers Thomas, Maunus, and Adam.

She likely talked to all four of her children still living at home about making this move. Seventeen-year-old Casper, Jr. likely told her that he preferred to stay in Berkeley County with Joseph. Nineteen year old Catherine was in a serious relationship with future husband, John Starn, so she decided to stay in Berkeley County. In 1785, Mary made the move to Redstone Settlement, which had just changed its name to Brownsville. She was accompanied by her two youngest daughters, Mary Christina and Charlotte. Once there, she rented a house where she and her daughters lived. Casper, Jr. and Catherine remained with Joseph and his family on the Hedgesville farm.

On July 18, 1786, a year after her mother and two younger sisters moved to Brownsville, Catherine married John Starn in Berkeley County. Catherine and John moved to Hampshire County, Virginia (present-day West Virginia) where they lived the rest of their lives.

On July 24, 1789, Casper Böner posthumously received the deed from the Virginia Land Office for the 334-acre parcel of land on which Casper, Jr. and Joseph's family had been living. Casper Jr.'s mother, Mary, and his oldest brother John, the executor of Casper Sr.'s estate, took legal possession of the property.

Circa 1795, Casper Jr. married Sarah Morgan (some sources list her family name as Miller). He was twenty-eight, and she was twenty-one. It is believed the marriage took place in Berkeley County, perhaps at the Mt. Zion Church in Hedgesville. Because Joseph's family had grown to six children by this time, it is likely that Casper, Jr. built a separate log house on the Hedgesville farm for him and Sarah to live in.

Also in 1795, John Bonner subdivided the 334-acre farm that Casper Jr. and Joseph were living on and sold fifty acres to John Mercer. This was not the parcel that Casper Jr. and Joseph were living on, so the sale had no impact on them. They continued living on the larger, unsold parcel. It is believed that, during that same year, Mary Böner died at her home in Brownsville, Pennsylvania. She was sixty-seven years old.

In 1798, Casper Jr. and Sarah had their first child, a daughter named Hannah Nancy Bonner. She was called "Anna" or "Ann." That same year Joseph and Elizabeth had their ninth – and last – child, a daughter named Rutha.

A year later, in 1799, Casper Jr. and Sarah had their second child, a son named Reuben. In 1800, the Slaughter District, Town of Tuscarora, Berkeley County, Virginia tax list records both a Joseph Bonner and a Casper Bonner, Jr. living there.[62]

It is unknown what discussions took place among John, Joseph, and Casper Jr. over the next few years, but it is obvious that John intended to sell the remaining 284 acres to settle the estates of their parents. Whether John offered to sell the estate property to the two of them is unknown. If so, they declined the opportunity.

In 1806, John entered a contract with Jeremiah Evans of Berkeley County to sell 217 of the remaining 284 acres of the Hedgesville property. The sales price was $1,050, and the terms called for a down payment of $450, with three installment payments of $200 each payable in September 1807, September 1808, and September 1810. The deal allowed both Casper Jr. and Joseph to live on the land until Evans had paid for the property in full. Interest was charged on the $600 unpaid balance.

The initial signing of this contract with Jeremiah Evans seems to have motivated Casper Jr. to move his family to Monongalia County. The records are incomplete, but in 1806 or 1807, John Amos Bonner's son, John Jr. sold 125 acres of land near Colfax along the Tygart Valley River to his uncle, Casper Jr. The sales price was approximately $250. This tract was located approximately 3 miles southeast of present day Fairmont, West Virginia. It appears the land purchase was financed over a period of several years, with John Jr. holding the note.

---

62 Bridges, Steven A, "Virginians in 1800: Counties of West Virginia", 1987, p.13

Casper Jr. cleared enough of this land to have gardens and pastures. He built a log house for his family along with the necessary outbuildings to protect his animals. He used horses to plow his fields, and he grew several acres of corn and potatoes each year.

In 1810, his brother John Sr.'s health deteriorated rapidly, convincing him to write his last will and testament. John's will revealed that Jeremiah Evans was in arrears on his payments for the Berkeley County property. However, John stipulated in his will that when Evans did make his second installment payment of $200, $150 of that payment was to go to his son, John Jr. This was to pay off the loan that John Jr. had extended to his uncle, Casper Jr., to buy the 125-acre property.

In effect, this $150 from the sale of the Berkeley County property served as Casper Jr.'s share of his parents' estate. John Sr. willed that the funds were to be paid directly to John Jr. to retire the loan he had extended to Casper Jr. This arrangement also ensured that Casper Jr. would have an unencumbered title to the 125 acres he had purchased.

John died sometime between August 28 and October 10, 1810. Jeremiah Evans must have paid his second $200 installment payment on the Berkeley County property around September 1813, because in November 1813 John Jr. granted a free and clear deed to Casper Jr. for the 125 acre property he had sold him several years earlier.[63]

Casper Jr. and his wife Sarah had completed their family with eight children circa 1812. Their seven daughters were Hannah Nancy, Mary, Rebecca, Ara, Sarah, Eliza, and Emma. Their only son was Reuben.

During the summer of 1820, Casper Jr.'s health deteriorated and he prepared his last will and testament, a copy of which follows:

Last Will and Testament of Casper Bunner [Jr.]

Item. I give and bequeath to my son Reuben my plantation.

---

[63] Monongalia County Clerk's Office, Land Deed Grantee Index, John Miller to John Bunner, 123 acres, September 1797, pp. 153

Item. I will that my son Reuben take my plantation into care with the family my wife Sarah and my daughters (excepting Nancy Ann that are already come of age). Mary, Rebecca, Ara, Sarah, Eliza, and Emmy these my last named daughters are to be raised and learned to read out of my estate.

Item. My cattle, hogs, sheep I give to the use of my wife and children on the place for their use.

Item. My son Reuben shall maintain his mother comfortably with her industry so long as she continues my widow further I will my daughters assist their brother Reuben with their industry while they continue with him on the place.

Item. My mare, plough, gears, etc. I give to the use of my family on the place. My wife Sarah Bunner and my son Reuben I constitute and appoint my executrix and executor of this my last will and testament. In witness whereof I have hereunto set my hand and seal this seventh day of August in the year of our Lord one thousand eight hundred and twenty.

Casper Bunner (Seal)
His Mark

Signed, sealed, and delivered to be the last will of him the said Casper Bunner in the presence of us.

Moses Jeffries
Jordan Hall
Jacob Barnes

At a court held for Monongalia County September term 1820. This last will and testament of Casper Bunner deceased was produced in court and proven by the oaths of Moses Jeffries and Jordan Hall and witness thereto which is recorded.

The will was made on the 7th day of August 1820, and probated September 1820.[64]

Casper Jr. died in early September 1820 at the age of fifty-three. His place of burial is unknown, but it was probably on his farm. Sarah lived for forty-seven years after her husband's death. She died in 1867 at the age of ninety-three.

**Elizabeth Bonner Miller**

Elizabeth is believed to be the third child and first daughter of Casper and Mary Böner. She was born circa 1754 at the same location on the South Fork of the South Branch of the Potomac River (near present-day Moorefield, West Virginia) as her older brothers John and Joseph. Her life mirrored that of John and Joseph until 1774 when she was approximately twenty. The family was living along the upper Monongahela River at that time (present-day Rivesville, West Virginia). While living there, she met and married John Miller. John built a cabin on land owned by Elizbeth's father Casper Böner, where he and Elizabeth lived. In 1776 Elizabeth's parents and several younger siblings moved back to the Berkeley County farm they had moved from in 1772. Her father sold the 400-acre tract his family had been living on to John and Elizabeth.[65]

In 1790, John had his 400-acre property surveyed and recorded at the Monongalia County Clerk's office. In 1797, he sold 123 acres from this tract to his brother-in-law John Amos Bonner where he established a blacksmith shop.[66] John and Elizabeth continued living on this land until his death in 1820.[67] It is possible Elizabeth continued living there until her death circa 1825-1830. John and

---

64  Monongalia County Clerk Office, Morgantown, West Virginia, Will Book 1820, pp. 371-372

65  Lough, Glenn D., "Now and Long Ago – A History of the Marion County Area," Morgantown Printing and Binding Co., 1969, p. 245

66  Awhile Ago Times, Bunner Family edition, July 1976. This 10-page edition of a "historical newspaper of the Upper Monongahela Valley", edited and published by Glenn D. Lough of Fairmont, WV

67  Lough, Glenn D., "Now and Long Ago – A History of the Marion County Area," Morgantown Printing and Binding Co., 1969, p. 401

Elizabeth had several children, but their names and birth dates are currently unknown. Later in his life John was known as John Sr., which implies John and Elizabeth had at least one son.

## Margaret Bonner Harmeason
## (Harmison, Harminson, Harmanson)

It is believed Margaret was born circa 1755 on the South Fork of the South Branch of the Potomac River in the newly formed Hampshire County, Virginia. This was the same location where her older siblings John, Joseph, and Elizabeth had been born in what was originally Augusta County, Virginia. Margaret is believed to have been the fourth child and second daughter of Mary and Casper Böner. Her life mirrored that of her older siblings until early 1772, when it is believed she married a Harmison in Berkeley County, Virginia.[68] Shortly after she was married, her father Casper moved the rest of the family from their 334 acre farm in Berkeley County to a 400-acre tract he had purchased along the banks of the upper Monongahela River (present day Rivesville, West Virginia).

One possible candidate for Margaret's husband is Thomas Harmison, who lived in Berkeley County, Virginia. In 1766, he received a land grant of 247 acres. The tract was located on Ambrose's Run in Frederick County, Virginia (present-day Berkeley County, West Virginia). The tax list for Berkeley County (formed from Frederick County in 1772) shows Thomas Harmison owning 247 acres from 1782 to 1789.[69]

In the Berkeley County court records of 1772-73, Thomas Harmison and "Mary" his wife were plaintiffs in a lawsuit. It is unknown if this "Mary" was the former Margaret Bonner. In 1790, Thomas Harmison deeded his 247-acre tract of land to William Harmison. His wife did not cosign the deed, and whether William

---

68  Bunner, Alan N., "The Bunner Family in America" Alexandria, Virginia 7,300+ page document on CD, revision dated June 25, 2012, Chapter 47, pp. 1473-1474.

69  Bunner, Alan N., "The Bunner Family in America" Alexandria, Virginia 7,300+ page document on CD, revision dated June 25, 2012, Chapter 47, pp. 1473-1474.

was the son of Thomas was not stated. Thomas then disappeared from Berkeley County records. According to some descendants of Thomas Harmison, he was born about 1720, owned land in Berkeley County, Virginia, moved to Belmont County, Ohio, and died after 1790.[70]

A higher likelihood possibility for Margaret's spouse was James Harmison. In 1785 James Harmison was listed on the Berkeley County tax list with 70 acres, which increased to164 acres in 1786 and remained at this level through 1794. Then, from 1796 through 1809, he owned 800 acres. James Harmison died in Morgan County, Virginia (formed from Berkeley County, Virginia in 1820) in 1831, leaving numerous descendants. The name of James's wife has never been determined. It may have been Margaret Bonner. James Harrison was born circa 1753 and died circa 1831. [71]

Based solely on dates of birth and death, James Harmison would seem more likely to be the husband of Margaret than Thomas Harmison. Additional research will be required to determine which, if either, of these men was the husband of Margaret Bonner.

## Susanah Barbel Bonner Laramore (Larimore, Laremore)

Susanah Bonner is believed to have been the sixth child, and third daughter, of Casper and Mary Böner. She was born in 1758. Her baptismal record is included in the archives of the Evangelical Reformed Church of Frederick, Maryland. It reads, "Casper Bonner & Anna Maria, parents; Susanna Barbel Bonner, born 10 May 1758, Baptized." [72]

---

70  Bunner, Alan N., "The Bunner Family in America" Alexandria, Virginia 7,300+ page document on CD, revision dated June 25, 2012, Chapter 36, pp 1094-1097.

71  Bunner, Alan N., "The Bunner Family in America" Alexandria, Virginia 7,300+ page document on CD, revision dated June 25, 2012, Chapter 36, pp 1094-1097.

72  "Maryland Births and Christenings, 1650-1995", database, FamilySearch, Susanah Barbel Bonner, Frederick, MD, 1758, https://www.familysearch.org/search/collection/1674912

Susanah's life mirrored that of her older siblings until 1776. That year, her parents made the decision to return to their Berkeley County farm after living four years on the upper Monongahela River (present-day Rivesville, West Virginia). Her three older brothers had volunteered to fight in the war for America's independence and did not return to Berkeley County. Her older sister, Elizabeth, who had married John Miller two years earlier, remained behind in Monongalia County. Those siblings returning to Berkeley County with their parents were Susanah (18), Catherine (11), Casper Jr. (9), Mary Christina (6) and Charlotte (5).

A year later, in 1777, Susanah married James Laramore (or Larimore) in Berkeley County. James had immigrated from Ireland in 1760 and had settled in Hampshire County, Virginia (now West Virginia). James had received an assignment of a survey for 293 acres in Frederick County, Virginia in 1789. This land was located between Back Creek and Sleepy Creek Mountain. This may have been the location of the first home of Susanah and James.[73]

By 1795, James and Susanah were residents of Hampshire County, Virginia (present-day West Virginia). In February 1795 James was appointed surveyor of the road "from Rannells mill to the new Store." He and "the male laboring tithables in his district" were directed to clear and keep the road in good repair. James Laramore's name first appears in the tax assessment lists of the Lower District, Hampshire County in 1801. James and Susanna purchased a tract of 656 acres located near the present-day village of Neals Run, Hampshire County.[74]

A granddaughter of James, wrote this of her grandparents: "James Sr. was born in Ireland in 1740... He was a Presbyterian... with Scotch-Irish blood. He settled on the Little Capon Stream, on a

---

73 Bunner, Alan N., "The Bunner Family in America" Alexandria, Virginia 7,300+ page document on CD, revision dated June 25, 2012, Chapter 36, pp 1094-1097.

74 Wendel Brown and Descendants, Quarterlies, 1981-1987, Georgia E. Morgan and Jean Nepsund, Ewing Genealogical Services, West Covina, Calif. This series of quarterlies includes frequent chapters on the family and descendants of Casper Bunner, the immigrant, with excellent research data into the early generations.

plateau of rich limestone land, densely wooded. Grandfather called it Jersey Mountain. James Laramore was a weaver by trade." [75]

In 1817, James was bitten by a rattlesnake while climbing over a log. He died from the bite sometime between June 18 and August 18, 1817. He was approximately seventy-seven years old.[76]

The names of the children of Susanah and James was provided in a Hampshire County indenture dated August 16, 1822: "This indenture made this 16th day of August 1822... Eight undivided parts out of one tract of land containing 393 acres... Situate in the said County of Hampshire on the waters of Little Caphon adjoining the lands of William Miller, Phillip Devald & others; It being the real Estate of James Lairmore deceased and said Eight parts held in right of the Said parties above mentioned Children and Heirs of the said James Lairmore...

Robt Lairmore
Mary Lairmore
John Lairmore
Deborah (X) Lairmore
Samuel Lairmore
Catharine (X) Lairmore
Thomas McBride
Nancy (X) McBride
Joseph Hawkins
Sarah Hawkins
Thomas Lairmore
James (X) Lairmore
Naoma (X) Lairmore

(Recorded: 15 Nov 1823)

---

75 These Build Civilizations, William N. and Jo Ann Larimore, R.R. #1, Fowler, Illinois, 1979.

76 Bunner, Alan N., "The Bunner Family in America" Alexandria, Virginia 7,300+ page document on CD, revision dated June 25, 2012, Chapter 36, pp 1094-1097

From this list it can be concluded that James and Susannah had eleven children.[77]

Susanah was still living at their Hampshire County farm in 1821. She died in Hampshire County, Virginia, probably in 1825. She was fifty-seven years old. The administration of her estate was granted to her son Thomas on December 19,1825. [78] After Susannah's death, the family scattered. By 1850, the only sons remaining in Hampshire County were James Jr. and Samuel[79].

## Catherine Bonner Starn

Catherine is believed to have been the seventh child and fourth daughter of Casper and Mary Böner. She was born circa 1765 on the 27-acre farm owned by her father in Frederick County, Virginia (present day Berkeley County, West Virginia). At the age of three, in 1768, she moved with her family to their newly acquired 334-acre farm just three miles west of their 27-acre farm. She subsequently moved with the family to the upper Monongahela Valley in 1772 and returned with them in 1776 to their Berkeley County farm. Her father Casper died in 1779 when she was fourteen. Her mother Mary moved to Brownsville, Pennsylvania with her two younger sisters in 1785, but it appears twenty-year-old Catherine remained at the Berkeley County farm with her older brother Joseph and his family. Her younger brother, eighteen-year-old Casper Jr., also chose to remain in Berkeley County after his mother and younger sisters had moved.

---

77 Bunner, Alan N., "The Bunner Family in America" Alexandria, Virginia 7,300+ page document on CD, revision dated June 25, 2012, Chapter 36, pp 1094-1097

78 Wendel Brown and Descendants, Quarterlies, 1981-1987, Georgia E. Morgan and Jean Nepsund, Ewing Genealogical Services, West Covina, Calif. This series of quarterlies includes frequent chapters on the family and descendants of Casper Bunner, the immigrant, with excellent research data into the early generations.

79 Wendel Brown and Descendants, Quarterlies, 1981-1987, Georgia E. Morgan and Jean Nepsund, Ewing Genealogical Services, West Covina, Calif. This series of quarterlies includes frequent chapters on the family and descendants of Casper Bunner, the immigrant, with excellent research data into the early generations.

On July 18, 1786, a year after her mother and two younger sisters moved to Brownsville, Catherine married John Starn in Berkeley County. The minister in this marriage was Hugh Vance.[80] Catherine and John settled in Hampshire County, Virginia, where they raised six children.[81]

In 1791, John Starn began purchasing land for himself and his family. In two deeds recorded June 16, 1791, he purchased two parcels of land from Jacob Starn (his brother), one of 100 acres and the other of 85 acres. Both parcels were on Little Cacapon River, near Stewart's Run. This is likely where John and Catherine lived for many years.[82] It is also the probable location where Catherine's younger sister Charlotte met John's younger brother Joseph circa 1795-1796. Charlotte and Joseph married circa 1797.

In February 1802, John Starn, "from Hampshire County, Virginia," purchased 150 acres from William and Sarah Banbridge, part of a 200 acre tract of land granted to Richard Merrifield on the head of Little Creek and head branch of White Day Creek, in Monongalia County. This land was near where Catherine's oldest brother, John, owned two separate 400-acre tracts. John Starn also purchased a parcel of land in Monongalia County from Thomas Wilson, described as being on the waters of Little Creek or Morgan's Mill Run.[83] There are no records that John and Catherine Starn ever lived in Monongalia County.

Starn was granted 184 acres at North River, in Hampshire County, Virginia in 1812, followed by purchases of 58 acres in 1814 and 506 acres in 1816.[84]

---

80  Marriage Records of Berkeley County, Virginia, 1781-1854, G. L. Keesecker, 1970

81  Bunner, Alan N., "The Bunner Family in America" Alexandria, Virginia 7,300+ page document on CD, revision dated June 25, 2012, Chapter 47, pp 1361

82  Bunner, Alan N., "The Bunner Family in America" Alexandria, Virginia 7,300+ page document on CD, revision dated June 25, 2012, Chapter 47, pp 1361

83  Bunner, Alan N., "The Bunner Family in America" Alexandria, Virginia 7,300+ page document on CD, revision dated June 25, 2012, Chapter 47, pp 1361

84  Bunner, Alan N., "The Bunner Family in America" Alexandria, Virginia 7,300+ page document on CD, revision dated June 25, 2012, Chapter 47, pp 1361

Catherine died between 1825 and 1830. John died circa 1828.[85] A sale bill dated July 14, 1828, and a settlement dated May 28, 1832, is listed for a John Starnes in West Virginia Estate Settlements. [86]

## Mary Christina Bonner Gibson

It is believed that Mary Christina Bonner was born on the 334-acre family farm near Hedgesville in Frederick County, Virginia (present day Berkeley Count, West Virginia) circa 1769-1771. She was likely the ninth child and fifth daughter of Casper and Mary Böner. She was named after her mother Mary Christianna (or Christianna Mary) Brown Böner.

When she was two to three years old, she moved with her family from their Berkeley County farm to a wilderness property her father had purchased in the upper Monongahela Valley (present-day Rivesville, West Virginia). She returned with her family to their Berkeley County farm in 1776 after the outbreak of the Revolutionary War. Three years later, in 1779, her father Casper died. Mary Christina was nine years old.

In 1780, her older brother Joseph moved back to the family farm in Berkeley County after serving four years in in America's war for independence. Accompanying him were his wife Elizabeth, their one-year-old son Joseph Jr. and their newborn daughter Catherine.

Mary Christina continued living with her widowed mother, Joseph's family, and siblings Catherine, Casper Jr., and Charlotte on the family farm until about 1785. During that year, it is believed her mother made the decision to move to Brownsville, Pennsylvania to be closer to her brothers Thomas, Maunus, and Adam.

Fifteen-year-old Mary Christina and fourteen-year-old Charlotte moved to Brownsville with their mother. Five years later, the 1790 census lists two females over the age of sixteen living with Mary "Christianna Boner" in Luzerne Township of Fayette

---

85 Bunner, Alan N., "The Bunner Family in America" Alexandria, Virginia 7,300+ page document on CD, revision dated June 25, 2012, Chapter 47, pp 1361.

86 Research and family data from Louise B. Arnett, Rivesville, W. Va.

County, Pennsylvania.[87] Mary Christina, who would have been approximately twenty years old at that time, is assumed to be one of the two females living with her mother. The other is believed to have been her younger sister Charlotte, who would have been approximately nineteen at the time of the census. It is believed their mother Mary died circa 1795 in the home where she was living with Mary Christina and Charlotte.

Mary Christina married a man named John Gibson, having likely met him in Brownsville, Pennsylvania where she had been living with her mother and sister. One speculation, published in the *West Virginia Hillbilly* in 1978, is that Mary Christina Bunner married John Gibson, Jr., son of the John Gibson whose wife and children were captured by Indians in 1780. The story of the Gibson family tragedy is told in Withers' book *Border Warfare*.

> "The family of John Gibson were surprised at their sugar camp, on a branch of the (Tygart) Valley River, and made prisoners. Mrs. Gibson, being incapable of supporting the fatigue of walking so far and so fast, was tomahawked and scalped in the presence of her children."[88]

Some of the captured children were later released by the Indians and returned to the east of the Ohio River. It is said that John Gibson Jr., who is thought to have married Mary Bonner, lived at first in Berkeley County, Virginia, and later in Franklin Township, Fayette County, Pennsylvania.[89]

Mary Christina was living in Fayette County during the mid-1790's, so it is reasonable to believe she met John Gibson Jr. in Brownsville and that they were married there. A John and Mary

---

87 "Heads of Families at the First Census of the United States in the Year 1790 – Pennsylvania," Fayette County, Luzerne Township, https://www.census.gov/library/publications/1907/dec/heads-of-families.html

88 Withers, Alexander Scott, "The Chronicles of Border Warfare," Robert Clarke Company, Cincinnati, OH, 1895, p. 287

89 Bunner, Alan N., "The Bunner Family in America" Alexandria, Virginia 7,300+ page document on CD, revision dated June 25, 2012, Chapter 47, pp 1473

Gibson are said to be buried in Franklin Township, Fayette County, Pennsylvania.[90]

## Charlotte Bonner Starn

Charlotte is believed to have been born on the 334-acre family farm near Hedgesville in Frederick County, Virginia (present day Berkeley Count, West Virginia) circa 1770-1771 and is believed to have been the sixth daughter and youngest child of Casper and Mary Böner. Her life would have mirrored that of her sister Mary Christina through the mid-1790's.

The 1790 census lists two females over the age of sixteen living with Mary "Christianna Boner" in Luzerne Township of Fayette County, Pennsylvania.[91] Charlotte would have been approximately nineteen years old at that time and is assumed to be one of the two females living with her mother. The other would have been her sister Mary Christina.

Circa 1795, Charlotte's mother, Mary Böner, died at their rented home near Brownsville, Pennsylvania. Afterward, Charlotte and Mary Christina likely went their separate ways. It is believed that Mary Christina married John Gibson in Fayette County, Pennsylvania circa 1795-1796 and they remained in the Brownsville area for the rest of their lives.

It is believed Charlotte married Joseph Starn circa 1797. Joseph was the younger brother of John Starn, who had married Charlotte's older sister Catherine in 1786.[92] Joseph Starn had served in the Revolutionary War, drafted from Cumberland County,

---

90 West Virginia Hillbilly, 3 June 1978, 10 June 1978, articles on "The Bunner Family in Western Virginia," based on research by Scott Randolph Bunner

91 "Heads of Families at the First Census of the United States in the Year 1790 – Pennsylvania," Fayette County, Luzerne Township, https://www.census.gov/library/publications/1907/dec/heads-of-families.html

92 Bunner, Alan N., "The Bunner Family in America" Alexandria, Virginia 7,300+ page document on CD, revision dated June 25, 2012, Chapter 47, pp 1474-1475

Pennsylvania. Following the war he moved to Hampshire County, Virginia (present-day West Virginia). [93]

On June 16, 1791, Joseph bought one-third interest of his brother Jacob's two parcels of land consisting of 85 and 6 acres. These properties were located on Little "Caphon" River, near Romney. Their land was three mountain ridges west of the Bunner family farm near Hedgesville, Virginia.[94]

It is likely that Charlotte met Joseph while visiting her sister Margaret in Hampshire County sometime after the death of their mother in 1795. It is believed they married in 1797 and settled in Hampshire County, Virginia. In 1796 Joseph purchased 154 acres from John and Susannah Pancake. This is probably where Joseph and Charlotte lived after they were married. In 1810 Joseph expanded his total holdings to 340 acres.[95]

Joseph and Charlotte lived in Hampshire County until about 1814, when they moved to Adams County, Ohio.[96] They purchased land in Adams County on October 2, 1819, paying George and Mary Vinsonhaler $100 for 50 acres on the East Fork of Brush Creek. [97]

On July 28, 1834, Joseph applied for a Revolutionary War Pension. His application tells the following story:

> "...personally appeared in open court... of Adams County, Ohio, Joseph Sterns, aged 77 years... and stated that he [Joseph] was

---

93  Wendel Brown and Descendants, Quarterlies, 1981-1987, Georgia E. Morgan and Jean Nepsund, Ewing Genealogical Services, West Covina, Calif. This series of quarterlies includes frequent chapters on the family and descendants of Casper Bunner, the immigrant, with excellent research data into the early generations.

94  Bunner, Alan N., "The Bunner Family in America" Alexandria, Virginia 7,300+ page document on CD, revision dated June 25, 2012, Chapter 47, pp 1474-1475

95  Bunner, Alan N., "The Bunner Family in America" Alexandria, Virginia 7,300+ page document on CD, revision dated June 25, 2012, Chapter 47, pp 1474-1475

96  Wendel Brown and Descendants, Quarterlies, 1981-1987, Georgia E. Morgan and Jean Nepsund, Ewing Genealogical Services, West Covina, Calif. This series of quarterlies includes frequent chapters on the family and descendants of Casper Bunner, the immigrant, with excellent research data into the early generations.

97  Bunner, Alan N., "The Bunner Family in America" Alexandria, Virginia 7,300+ page document on CD, revision dated June 25, 2012, Chapter 47, pp 1474-1475

## THE SIBLINGS OF JOHN AMOS BONNER (BÖNER/BUNNER)

born in Cecil County, Maryland, March 2, 1757, that he has no record of his age, that he lived, when drafted into service [in July 1780], in New Cumberland County, Pennsylvania. In the year 1782 he moved back to Cecil County where he remained a short time and then moved to Adams County, Ohio, where he now lives. That in addition to the officers he served under, he knew General Washington, Stevenson, Lafayette, Wayne and Smallwood. Soon after he was drafted he joined the company of militia of Capt. William Huston and the Regiment commanded by Col. James Johnson. The company first marched to Carlisle, Pennsylvania, thence to Little York, thence to Lancaster on its way to join the American Army under Washington. When at Lancaster, he was recalled to defend the frontiers against the Indians and marched back to Carlisle. He remained in Cumberland County [for] his tour of six months." [98]

Joseph Starn died between 1834 and 1840 in Adams County, Ohio. Charlotte died between 1840 and 1850. According to family tradition, both are buried in a family cemetery on the original farm in Scott Township, Adams County. Many descendants in this branch of the family have since adopted Stern as the spelling of the family name. [99] [100]

All eight of the children of Joseph and Charlotte Starn were born in Hampshire County, Virginia. Their names and approximate birth dates are:

---

[98] Wendel Brown and Descendants, Quarterlies, 1981-1987, Georgia E. Morgan and Jean Nepsund, Ewing Genealogical Services, West Covina, Calif. This series of quarterlies includes frequent chapters on the family and descendants of Casper Bunner, the immigrant, with excellent research data into the early generations.

[99] Research and family data from Louise B. Arnett, Rivesville, W. Va

[100] Wendel Brown and Descendants, Quarterlies, 1981-1987, Georgia E. Morgan and Jean Nepsund, Ewing Genealogical Services, West Covina, Calif. This series of quarterlies includes frequent chapters on the family and descendants of Casper Bunner, the immigrant, with excellent research data into the early generations.

| | |
|---|---|
| Mary Ann | circa 1790-94 |
| Lucille | circa 1794-1800 |
| Joseph | circa 1798 |
| Charlotte ("Lottie") | circa 1800 |
| Elizabeth | circa 1801 |
| Catharine ("Katie") | circa 1800-10 |
| William | circa 1800-10 |
| Frederick | Oct. 14, 1810[101] |

---

101 Bunner, Alan N., "The Bunner Family in America" Alexandria, Virginia 7,300+ page document on CD, revision dated June 25, 2012, Chapter 47, pp 1474-1475

8.

# Reuben Adam Bunner – Oldest Son of John Amos Bunner
## *(circa 1778 – 1835)*

[Author's Note: Since there is no evidence that any Bunner during this generation could read or write, the spelling of family name was left to courthouse clerks who had to record those names in legal documents. Bunner was the spelling used as often as Bonner or Boner during this generation, so this is the default spelling I use in this chapter. I note in the text if a spelling other than Bunner is used in documents referenced in this chapter.]

There are two slightly different versions of the birth of Reuben Adam Bunner in family lore. One is that his parents, John Bunner and Martha Evans, married in late 1775 or early 1776 and that Reuben was born in late 1776 before or shortly after John left to fight in the Revolutionary War. Under this scenario, it is believed that Martha and newborn Reuben lived with Martha's parents in Monongalia County (present day Morgantown, West Virginia) while John served his one-year enlistment in the Pennsylvania 8th Regiment.

The second version is that John met Martha Evans during 1776, and the two may have been engaged when John enlisted in the Pennsylvania 8th Regiment at the beginning of the Revolutionary

War. Unfortunately, due to early Continental Army setbacks in the east, the Pennsylvania 8th was soon deployed to New Jersey as reinforcements. While deployed, John is believed to have fought in the Battle of Bound Brook (New Jersey) and the Battle of Saratoga (upstate New York). Afterward, John spent the winter of 1777-78 at Valley Forge.

In March 1778 his unit was ordered back to western Pennsylvania to defend the frontier from "back door" attacks by British and Indian forces. By the time John returned to western Pennsylvania, his one year enlistment had been completed. He married Martha Evans in early 1778 and enlisted in the local Westmoreland County militia based in Redstone Settlement (present-day Brownsville, Pennsylvania), where Reuben Adam Bunner was born in late 1778 or early 1779.

Assuming the first version, Martha Evans would have been fourteen or fifteen years old when she married John. Although the age of marriage in the 1700's, especially for women, was generally much younger than today, marriage at age fourteen was still rare. For this reason, I have assumed the second version, that John and Martha were married in early 1778, when John was twenty-eight and Martha was seventeen. Under this scenario, Reuben was born in late 1778 or early 1779 in Redstone Settlement. However, it is possible that the first version may be proven correct by future research.

Reuben Adam Bunner was named after his great-grandfather, Reuben Adam Böner. His great-grandfather was still alive in 1778 and living on his farm in Berks County, Pennsylvania. He was eighty-one years old when the great-grandson bearing his name was born.

There is no record that John's father Casper ever visited his father (Reuben) Adam after Casper married and settled on the Virginia frontier in 1748 or 1749. There are also no records that any of Casper's children ever visited their grandfather in Berks County. However, during their winter in Valley Forge, it is possible that both John and Joseph visited their grandfather at his home. The distance from Valley Forge to their grandfather's farm near Reading was only forty miles, and it is well documented that soldiers at Valley Forge were granted furloughs during the winter months to visit with family members within a reasonable travel distance. If John and

Joseph made this visit, it is certain to have brought great joy to their eighty year old grandfather.

Reuben's birth coincided almost exactly with his grandfather's death. Casper Böner died at his farm in Berkeley County in mid-February 1779. Because Reuben was a newborn, it is unlikely that either he or his mother made the 140 mile trip over the Allegheny Mountains to attend Casper's funeral. However, it is likely that John made this trip, as his mother had named him the executor of Casper's estate and there were issues with one parcel of land that Casper owned that required immediate attention.[1] John would be required to make this same trip one or two more times over the next eighteen months to sell a 365-acre parcel of land in Berkeley County to begin the process of settling his father's estate.

Reuben's earliest memories would have been from Redstone Settlement, Pennsylvania. His father was required to serve two months each year on active duty with his militia unit, and the rest of the year he was required to be on alert to provide immediate response to any attack by British or Indian forces on the western frontier. In the east, those serving in the local militias were called "Minutemen," because they responded "within one minute" to any attack in the local area.

The "Minuteman" moniker was never used along the western frontier, but those in the western militia units proved their mettle during the war by quashing every "back door" threat that arose. George Washington completely trusted the western militia. During his long winter with the Continental Army at Valley Forge he proclaimed, "If all else fails, I will retreat up the valley of Virginia, plant my flag on the Blue Ridge, rally around the Scotch-Irish of that region and make my last stand for liberty amongst a people who will never submit to British tyranny whilst there is a man left to draw a trigger."

During those times when John's marksmanship and fighting skills were not required by his militia unit, he developed the skills of a blacksmith and, probably by 1780, set us a blacksmith shop in Redstone Settlement where he specialized in making guns and

---

1 Joyner, Peggy (1987), "Abstract of Virginia's Northern Neck Warrants and Surveys, Volume 4, p. 80

bells.[2] Reuben often tagged along to watch his father work at his smithery. Sometimes in the evenings, he and his father would walk along the Monongahela River, where Reuben would throw rocks in the water and take great delight in the splash and the ripples that he caused.

During the five years that young Reuben lived with his parents in Redstone Settlement, it is believed that his brother Joseph was born in 1780 and that his twin sisters Mary and Rachel were born in late 1782 or early 1783.

Reuben lived in Redstone Settlement with his parents until the Treaty of Paris was signed in 1783. This treaty formally ended the Revolutionary War, granting America its independence as well as ownership of all British territories north and west of the Ohio River extending west to the Mississippi River. These vast lands would soon become known as the "Northwest Territory." This treaty also ended John's enlistment in, and commitment to, the Westmoreland County militia. All members of the victorious Continental Army and local militias were free to resume the lives they had voluntarily placed on hold after they heard the higher call of liberty and independence.

John moved his young family to his 400-acre tract near Prickett's Fort on the upper Monongahela River. This was the land he had initially claimed and partially cleared in 1772. Now he had to clear enough land for sufficient pasture and garden spaces to provide food for his family.

This was a daunting task, as John was dealing with a virgin forest that contained trees up to four feet in diameter and over one hundred feet tall. The root systems of the larger trees ran up to eight feet deep and eighty feet in diameter underground. This mountain frontier was often referred to as "the big shade" because the forests were so thick no sunlight ever hit the ground.[3] This timber had to be cut and removed, and the stumps and root systems dug out of the ground to create garden and pasture spaces. All of this work

---

2   Ellis, Franklin, "History of Fayette County, Pennsylvania," L.H. Everts and Company, Philadelphia, p. 658

3   Lough, Glenn D., "Now and Long Ago – A History of the Marion County Area," Morgantown Printing and Binding Co., 1969, p. 34

was done by hand with a sharp ax, a mattock and shovel, strong muscles, and unending quantities of drinking water to replace the sweat that freely dripped from the bodies of those wielding the axes and mattocks.

Clearing land was a community event, similar to house raising. Several of John's neighbors would have helped him with this task, and their wives would have prepared meals for the men and brought them to John's house so that Martha did not have to do all the work. When the land was finally cleared, John, like all of his neighbors who had cleared their land with the help of neighbors, realized the deep sense of obligation that all the men had to help each other to survive in the frontier. After getting his land cleared, John spent weeks and months through the course of his life helping to clear the land of new settlers who came after him.

Once the trees were down, they had to be removed from the land by hand with assistance from an ox, a mule, or a horse pulling the fallen timber with a log chain. The timber was rolled into vast piles in the most convenient hollow where it was burned.

**Jefferys, C.W., "Clearing Land"**
(Image courtesy cwjefferys.ca)

Reuben would have been too young to help his father clear the land, but he was old enough to help plant seeds in the garden. He quickly became proficient at performing the endless task of hoeing weeds out of the gardens through the spring and summer months. He then helped his parents harvest and store their crops in the fall.

By the time Reuben was seven, he was feeding the chickens and gathering the eggs each day for his family. By the time he was ten he had learned to shoot a rifle to catch squirrels, rabbits, turkeys, and deer for his family to eat. By the time he was twelve, he had learned how to use a mule or a horse to plow the gardens each spring. He also learned how to butcher a pig and salt its meat so that it did not spoil during the winter months when it served as the primary source of food for the family.

Like his parents and virtually all of his neighbors, Reuben never attended a school and never learned to read or write. While these skills were necessary to thrive in the newly emerging American society, they were not essential to survive. Survival skills were taught by the parents of each generation to their children, and by the time their children were twelve they had learned how to be self-sufficient. Frontier survival required a lot of toil, sweat, grit, and perseverance. Reading and writing skills did little to fell large trees, plow fields, milk cows, hoe corn, or shoot turkeys. Acquiring the skills of reading and writing were niceties. Acquiring the skills of farming and hunting were necessities.

Infrequent, random Indian attacks still occurred in the upper Monongahela Valley while Reuben was growing up. In 1785, when Reuben was seven years old, Thomas Stone, a neighbor, was murdered and scalped while walking alone in one of his fields. His body was found by Jacob Prickett, Sr. who, along with Nathaniel Springer, David Morgan, and Reuben's father John trailed the Indians for two days and nights to Middle Island Creek where the trail was lost during a rainstorm.[4]

It is likely that Reuben visited Prickett's Fort as a young boy, but there are no recorded instances that the local community ever used the fort as a place of refuge from Indian attacks between the time

---

4  Lough, Glenn D., "Now and Long Ago – A History of the Marion County Area," Morgantown Printing and Binding Co., 1969, p. 39

Reuben moved to the area with his family in 1783 and the time the fort was dismantled in 1799.

Jacob Prickett, on whose land the fort was located, also operated a trading post and a grist mill on his property. As a result, his settlement became somewhat of a community hub and Reuben, along with his younger brothers and sisters likely visited here many times while they were growing up.

Reuben Adam's uncle Reuben, John's brother, made the decision to move down the Ohio River to Kentucky in 1789. John's family turned out to say goodbye to Reuben, his wife Nancy Ann (Prickett) Bunner, and their five children as they embarked on the trip to their new life in Kentucky. They settled in Mason County, Kentucky for a few years. Then, sometime after 1794, they moved across the Ohio River into that part of the Northwest Territory that became Ohio in 1803.

This may have been the last time that anyone in John's family ever saw anyone in uncle Reuben's family. Uncle Reuben's legacy is still alive in the upper Monongahela Valley. The 400-acre tract of land he had originally claimed in 1773 (and which he sold in 1788 prior to moving to Kentucky) was located on land that soon became known as Bunners Ridge. Bunners Ridge has been the home of generations of Bunners ever since Reuben first settled there. (Bunners Ridge is easily found today by taking I-79 Exit 139 near Prickett's Fork State Park, five miles north of present day Fairmont, West Virginia. After the exit, Bunners Ridge is the road that runs to both the left and right.)

While John was still serving in the militia, he had purchased an additional 400-acre tract a short distance north of the 400-acre tract he had initially claimed in 1772.[5] The drains of this second parcel flowed into White Day Creek, which then flowed into the Monongahela River. It is unclear if John utilized this land for pasture space or for growing crops while Reuben was growing up. He may have rented it to provide a second source of income with the idea that when his sons were old enough, this would be their farm.

---

5  Bunner, Gale J., "Genealogy Descendents of Casper (Böner) Bunner And Mary Christianna Brown, Revised Edition, 1988, p. 15

Reuben gained several additional brothers and sisters after the family moved from Redstone Settlement to their Monongalia County farm in 1783. John Jr. was born circa 1785, Amos circa 1787, twins Rebecca and James circa 1790, and Enoch circa 1793. Reuben was the oldest of nine children, with his baby brother Enoch being fourteen or fifteen years younger.[6]

Reuben Bunner probably met Hannah Trader sometime during late 1794 or early 1795 when he was sixteen years old. They were married on July 23, 1795, in Monongalia County, Virginia when Reuben was sixteen or seventeen. Hannah Trader was the daughter of Tigal Trader. Tigal and his brother Arthur were among the first settlers in the upper Monongahela Valley, circa 1770.[7]

In April 1799, Reuben purchased 30 acres of land from Simeon Riggs in Monongalia County.[8] However, all indications are that Reuben and Hannah lived on the 400-acre tract on White Day Creek owned by Reuben's father's during the early years of their marriage. Reuben began using the farming and hunting skills learned from his father to provide for his own family.

Known children born to Reuben and Hannah over the ensuing twenty years are believed to have been Joseph (born circa 1796), Thomas (c. 1798), Alexander (c. 1802), Elizabeth (c. 1805), John (c. 1806), Amy (c. 1809), Rebecca (c. 1811), Hannah (c. 1812), Martha (c. 1815), [?] Gabriel (c. 1821), Samuel (c. 1823), and a daughter (c. 1825). According to 1810 census data, there were likely three additional sons born between 1800 and 1810. Their names may be discovered with additional research. All children of Reuben and Hannah were born in Monongalia County.[9]

---

6 Bunner, Alan N., "The Bunner Family in America" Alexandria, Virginia 7,300+ page document on CD, revision dated June 25, 2012, Chapter 9, p. 147

7 Lough, Glenn D., "Now and Long Ago – A History of the Marion County Area," Morgantown Printing and Binding Co., 1969, p. 269

8 Monongalia County Clerk's Office, Land Deed Grantee Index, Simeon Riggs to Reuben Bunner, 30 acres, April 1799, pp. 151,153

9 Bunner, Alan N., "The Bunner Family in America" Alexandria, Virginia 7,300+ page document on CD, revision dated June 25, 2012, Chapter 9, p. 147

## REUBEN ADAM BUNNER – OLDEST SON OF JOHN AMOS BUNNER

In 1797, two years after Reuben and Hannah were married, Reuben's father, John, purchased 123 acres of land along the Monongahela River from his brother-in-law John Miller.[10] He established a blacksmith shop on a small parcel of this land.[11] This purchase was part of the 400-acre tract that Reuben's grandfather, Casper, had originally purchased in 1772. Casper had subsequently sold that tract to John and Elizabeth Miller in 1776 before moving back to his farm in Berkeley County. (Elizabeth Bunner Miller was Casper's daughter, John's sister, and Reuben's aunt.)

On December 8, 1800, after John had established his blacksmith shop, he sold this 123 acre parcel to James West. On this same day John purchased 400 acres from James West located along the Tygart Valley River near the point where it merged with the West Fork River to form the Monongahela River.[12] It is unclear whether John retained a small parcel of land where his smithery was located, or whether he paid James West rent for that portion of the property taken up by the smithery. Whatever may have been the case, it appears that John continued to operate his blacksmith shop at this location (present-day Rivesville, West Virginia) until the time of his death.

The addition of this third 400-acre tract along the Tygart Valley River gave John ownership of 1,200 acres in the upper Monongahela Valley. In 1801, John was fifty-one years old and was probably thinking of the land he could bequeath to his six sons. His oldest son Reuben was now twenty-one with two sons of his own. John's second son, Joseph, was twenty. He had married Mary Knight the previous year and she was now pregnant with their first child.

---

10  Monongalia County Clerk's Office, Land Deed Grantee Index, John Miller to John Bunner, 123 acres, September 1797, p. 153

11  Awhile Ago Times, Bunner Family edition, July 1976. This 10-page edition of a "historical newspaper of the Upper Monongahela Valley", edited and published by Glenn D. Lough of Fairmont, WV

12  Monongalia County Clerk's Office, Land Deed Grantee Index, John Miller to John Bunner, 123 acres, September 1797, pp. 151, 153

Tragically, it appears that Joseph's young wife, Mary, died soon thereafter, perhaps during childbirth.[13] [14] Joseph married again on July 22, 1802, to Christena Hamilton, the daughter of Henry and Elizabeth (Fry) Hamilton of Monongalia County. Joseph was twenty-two and Christena was nineteen when they were married.[15]

In April 1801, Reuben's younger sister Rachel married James Morgan, called "Buffalo Jim Morgan", in Monongalia County. James was the son of Morgan Morgan and Drusilla Prickett, a grandson of David and Sarah (Stevens) Morgan and a great-grandson of Col. Morgan Morgan, generally attributed to be the first white settler in West Virginia.[16]

Rachel Bunner Morgan died in 1844. Capt. James Morgan married a second time to Sarah Means of Monongalia County. There were no children from this second marriage. James died in 1860 and Sarah died in 1861. Rachel, James and Sarah are all buried at Mount Zion Cemetery, Winfield District, Monongalia County.[17] Children of James and Rachel (Bunner) Morgan were Morgan (1802), John (1804), David (1806), Sarah (1808), Mary (1810), Rachel (1813, died 1816), James (1815), Drusilla (1817, died 1819), Salinda (1818), Stepen (1820), Alpheus (1823), Dority (son) (1825, died 1830).[18]

---

13 Wendel Brown and Descendants, Quarterlies, 1981-1987, Georgia E. Morgan and Jean Nepsund, Ewing Genealogical Services, West Covina, Calif. This series of quarterlies includes frequent chapters on the family and descendants of Casper Bunner, the immigrant, with excellent research data into the early generations.

14 Bunner, Alan N., "The Bunner Family in America" Alexandria, Virginia 7,300+ page document on CD, revision dated June 25, 2012, Chapter 8, p. 122

15 Bunner, Alan N., "The Bunner Family in America" Alexandria, Virginia 7,300+ page document on CD, revision dated June 25, 2012, Chapter 8, p. 122

16 Bunner, Alan N., "The Bunner Family in America" Alexandria, Virginia 7,300+ page document on CD, revision dated June 25, 2012, Chapter 15, p. 399

17 Bunner, Alan N., "The Bunner Family in America" Alexandria, Virginia 7,300+ page document on CD, revision dated June 25, 2012, Chapter 15, p. 399

18 Bunner, Alan N., "The Bunner Family in America" Alexandria, Virginia 7,300+ page document on CD, revision dated June 25, 2012, Chapter 15, p. 399

In 1802, Reuben and his wife Hannah welcomed their third son, Alexander, into the family.[19] It appears that after Reuben's brother Joseph married Christena, their father John arbitrarily subdivided his White Day Creek property so that Reuben and his family lived on one 90½ acre parcel and Joseph and his wife lived on an adjoining 90½ acre parcel. This left over 200 acres in this 400-acre tract not being allocated or utilized. It is assumed that the two 90½ acre parcels John had meted out to his sons were the best farmland on his White Day Creek property and that the rest of the tract was steep terrain unsuitable for farming.

Also in 1802, Reuben's sister Mary married Thomas Stacy in Monongalia County. His father was from Galway, Ireland and his mother was from Edinburgh, Scotland. Thomas and Mary moved to what is now Mahoning County, Ohio (then Trumbull County in 1806, where they were still living in 1850. They were among the earliest settlers in the Mahoning Valley. Thomas died in Mahoning County, Ohio in September 1852. Mary died in Poland Township, Trumbull County (now Mahoning County) in January 1867. Both are buried at Presbyterian Churchyard, Poland Township. Their children born in Monongalia County were Sarah (1803) and Matthew (1805). Children born in Ohio were Joseph (1807), Elizabeth (1809), Thomas (1811), John (1813), Seaton (1816), Charlotte (1818), William (1820), George Washington (1823), Mary Jane (1827), and possibly Catherine.[20]

In 1804, Reuben's younger brother, John Jr., married Sarah Carroll in Monongalia County. It appears they lived on land along the Tygart Valley River approximately six miles south of where John Jr. grew up, probably on the 400-acre tract John Sr. had purchased in 1800. Children of John Jr. and Sarah were James (1804), Enoch (1806), Sarah Jane (1807), Joseph (1810), Mary (1814), Elizabeth

---

19   Bunner, Alan N., "The Bunner Family in America" Alexandria, Virginia 7,300+ page document on CD, revision dated June 25, 2012, Chapter 9, p. 147

20   Bunner, Alan N., "The Bunner Family in America" Alexandria, Virginia 7,300+ page document on CD, revision dated June 25, 2012, Chapter 34, p. 1008

(circa 1816), George Washington (1818), and John Randolph (1819).[21]

In 1806, John Bunner, Sr. purchased an additional 200 acres of land along the Tygart Valley River from John Pettyjohn, possibly for the purpose of eventually bequeathing it to John Jr.[22] This increased John Sr.'s landholdings in the Monongahela River Valley to 1400 acres.

There are no known legal documents showing that John Sr. transferred ownership of this 200-acre property to John Jr., but John Jr. seems to have had ownership no later than 1807. John Jr. sold 125 acres of this 200 acre parcel to his uncle (John Sr.'s youngest brother), Casper Bunner, Jr. circa 1807-1808. The sales price was approximately $250. John Jr. extended a loan to his uncle with the expectation that it would be paid off over a period of a few years.

Besides having a knack for buying and selling land, both John Sr. and John Jr. were also known as inventors and innovators. John Sr. is believed to have been the first resident in the Monongahela Valley to use coal as an energy source. He used coal to fire a lime kiln he built on his farm and also used coal to heat metal in his blacksmith shop.[23]

John Jr.'s innovation was even more unique. After clearing his farm along the Tygart Valley River near present-day Colfax, he invented and built his famous river mill. This mill is described from a copy made of it, in Hildreth's "History of the Upper Ohio Valley." Bunner built two large flat-boats, "yoked them," placed the grinding stones in one boat, the "other necessaries" in the other boat, and set the wheel between the boats, on a slide, so it could be lowered and

---

21 Bunner, Alan N., "The Bunner Family in America" Alexandria, Virginia 7,300+ page document on CD, revision dated June 25, 2012, Chapter 11, p. 255

22 Monongalia County Clerk's Office, Land Deed Grantee Index, John Miller to John Bunner, 123 acres, September 1797, pp. 153

23 West Virginia Hillbilly, 3 June 1978, 10 June 1978, articles on "The Bunner Family in Western Virginia", based on research by Scott Randolph Bunner

raised. The boats were anchored in the river where the current was strongest, and there the grinding of the corn and wheat was done.[24]

In 1807, Reuben's younger brother James married Jenny Carroll, daughter of John Carroll, in Monongalia County. Jenny died young, possibly during childbirth. In September 1813, James married a second time to Susannah Ferrell in Monongalia County. In the 1820 and 1840 census, James was living in the Western Division of Monongalia County. In 1830, James was listed in the Eastern District, not far from Sarah Bunner, widow of Casper Jr. and close to where Joseph Bunner, brother of John Amos Bunner, had been living in 1820. In the 1850 census, James and Susannah were living in the Eastern District, Monongalia County. According to the 1870 census, Susanna was still alive and living at the farm of her son Ferrell Bunner in Sheridan Township, Calhoun County, West Virginia. [25]

James and Jenny (Carroll) Bunner had one child, a daughter, born circa 1805-1808. The children of James and Susannah (Ferrell) Bunner were Robert (circa 1814), Rachel? (circa 1820), Martha? (circa 1821), Elizabeth? (circa 1823), Hannah? (circa 1825), Amy (1828), Ara (circa 1829), Ferrell (circa 1834), Amos (circa 1837), and at least one other son and four other daughters (names unknown) born between 1815 and 1830. All children were born in Monongalia County.[26]

John Sr., as executor of the estate of his parents, Casper and Mary Bunner (Böner), had sold the family farm near Hedgesville in Berkeley County to Jeremiah Evans in 1806.[27] Casper Jr. had been living alongside his brother Joseph on this farm for over thirty years. The sales contract between John Sr. and Jeremiah Evans allowed the families of Joseph Bunner and Casper Bunner, Jr. to continue living

---

24 Bunner, Gale J., "Genealogy Descendents of Casper (Böner) Bunner And Mary Christianna Brown, Revised Edition, 1988, p.12

25 Bunner, Alan N., "The Bunner Family in America" Alexandria, Virginia 7,300+ page document on CD, revision dated June 25, 2012, Chapter 24, p. 814

26 Bunner, Alan N., "The Bunner Family in America" Alexandria, Virginia 7,300+ page document on CD, revision dated June 25, 2012, Chapter 24, p. 814

27 Berkeley County Clerk's Office, Martinsburg, WV, Deed Book 27, Page 542

on the farm until Evans had paid in full for the land, which was projected to be September 1810.

However, the signing of this contract in 1806 seems to have motivated Casper Jr. to move his family to the Monongahela Valley to be closer to his family. He purchased 125 acres along the Tygart Valley River from his nephew, John Jr. It appears that John Sr. orchestrated this sale by John Jr.

John Sr.'s brother, Joseph, had decided to continue living in Berkeley County until Evans had paid off the loan for the property. That occurred in 1815, and Joseph, his wife, and two youngest children moved from Berkeley County to Monongalia County soon afterward. They are believed to have rented a small farm near Casper Jr. and his family along the Tygart Valley River near Colfax in Monongalia County.

Also occurring In 1806, John Sr. and Martha legally transferred to their son Joseph the ownership of the 90½ acres along White Day Creek he and his family had been living on since 1802. This transaction is recorded as follows:

> "This indenture made in the year of our Lord One thousand eight hundred and six between John Bunner and Martha his wife of the county of Monongahela and Commonwealth of Virginia of the one part and Joseph Bunner, their son of the county and state aforesaid of the other part witnesseth that the said John Bunner and Martha his wife in consideration of the natural love and affection which they the said John Bunner and Martha his wife hath… Situate on the Monongahela River and White Day Creek being part of a larger tract of 400 acres by survey bearing date the twenty fourth of August, 1785 and bounded as follows… meeting up with Reuben Bunner's land…"[28]

In August 1809, Reuben's younger brother Amos married Sarah "Sally" Fink in Monongalia County. They lived on a 150-acre parcel of the 400-acre tract along the Tygart Valley River owned by John Bunner Sr. In the 1860 census, Amos and Sarah reported

---

28  Bunner, Alan N., "The Bunner Family in America" Alexandria, Virginia 7,300+ page document on CD, revision dated June 25, 2012, Chapter 8, p. 122

their ages as 72 and 68. Sarah died in March 1865 and Amos died seven weeks later in May 1865. They are buried at Bunner Cemetery, near Bunner Ridge Park, Winfield District. Children of Amos and Sarah were Martha (1810), Nancy Ann (1815), Mary Ellen (1817), Rebecca Ann (1818), Jacob ("Jake") (1819), Joseph (1820), Sarah (1824) Rachel (1827), Amos (1829), Elizabeth (1834), and James (1836, died young).[29]

Reuben's father, John Sr., died in 1810. In his will it states, "I give and bequeath to my son, Reuben Bunner, the land he now lives on (to him and his heirs), it being laid off to him some time past, being about ninety and a half acres more or less". This was the land along White Day Creek that Reuben and his family had been living on since his marriage in 1795.[30]

John Sr.'s will also detailed the land bequeathed (or already legally transferred) to his other sons.

- Joseph - 90½ acres on White Day Creek, adjoining brother Reuben, on which he lived
- John Jr. – 100 acres along Tygart Valley River on which he lived
- Amos – 150 acres along Tygart Valley River on which he lived
- James – 150 acres along Tygart Valley River on which he lived
- Enoch – 267 acres of John Sr.'s 400-acre tract originally claimed in 1772[31]

John Sr. also left to his widow Martha "one third of the land I now live on." John had been living on the 400-acre tract that he had originally claimed in 1772. His will states, "I give and bequeath to

---

29   Bunner, Alan N., "The Bunner Family in America" Alexandria, Virginia 7,300+ page document on CD, revision dated June 25, 2012, Chapter 20, p. 624

30   Monongalia County Clerk Office, Morgantown, West Virginia, Will Book 1, page 336

31   Monongalia County Clerk Office, Morgantown, West Virginia, Will Book 1, page 336

my son Enoch Bunner to him and his heirs the plantation I now live."³² This is the same tract of which he left "one third" to Martha. As a result, Enoch's inheritance was approximately 267 acres, and Martha's was approximately 133 acres.

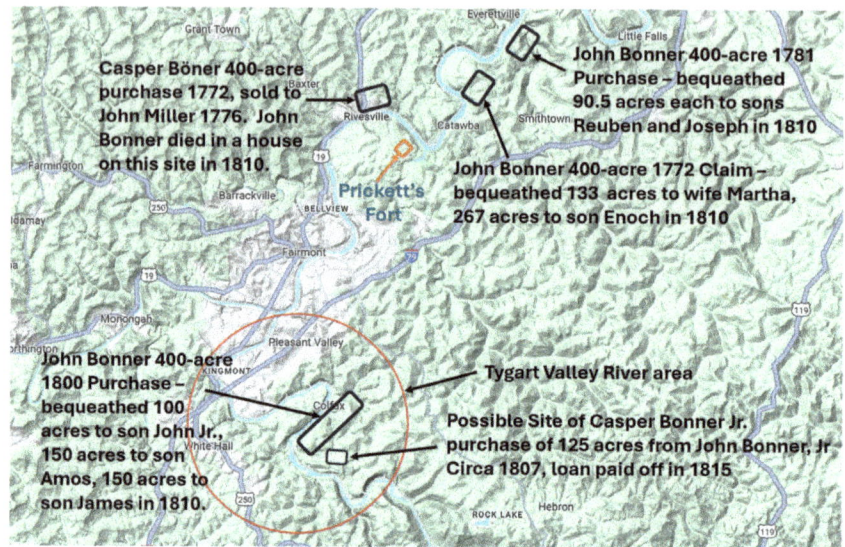

John Amos Bunner landholdings bequeathed to wife and sons – 1810

John's will also specified that when Jeremiah Evans made his second $200 installment payment for the Berkeley County land he was purchasing from John Sr., that $150 of this payment was to be given to his son John Jr. This was to pay off the loan John Jr. had extended to his uncle Casper (John's youngest brother) so Casper could purchase 125 acres of land from him. As a result, the note held by John Jr. was paid off in 1813, and Casper Jr. owned the 125 acres free and clear.³³

---

32  Monongalia County Clerk Office, Morgantown, West Virginia, Will Book 1, page 336

33  Monongalia County Clerk Office, Morgantown, West Virginia, Will Book 1, page 336

Reuben, as the oldest son, was named Executor of his father's estate. John's Estate Appraisal and Inventory was submitted to the Monongalia County Court on October 8, 1810, appraised on November 4, 1810, and recorded in March 1811.[34]

The 1810 census records the following breakdown in Reuben's household: One male 26-44 (Reuben); one female 26-44 (Hannah); one white male 16-25 (Joseph); two white males 10-15 (Thomas, Alexander); four white males under 10 (John and three others ); and two white females under 10 (Elizabeth, Amy). This census records that Reuben and Hannah had a total of nine children in 1810.[35]

On April 12, 1813, Reuben Bunner and his brother Amos essentially traded the properties that were bequeathed to them by their father. Reuben's original property was situated along White Day Creek, and Amos's original property was situated along the Tygart Valley River approximately seven miles south of White Day Creek.[36]

During September 1815, Reuben purchased fifty of the one hundred fifty acres that his father had bequeathed to Reuben's brother James. After the land exchange between Reuben and Amos in 1813, the properties owned by James and Reuben were adjoined. This purchase increased Reuben's landholdings along the Tygart River Valley to two hundred acres and decreased the acreage owned by James to one hundred acres.[37]

In 1818, Martha Evans Bunner, Rueben's mother, died in Monongalia County.

Her Estate Appraisal and Inventory was submitted to the Monongalia County Court on September 12, 1818, and recorded in October 1822.[38] It reads as follows:

---

34 Monongalia County Clerk Office, Morgantown, West Virginia, John Bunner Estate Appraisal and Inventory October 8, 1810

35 1810 U.S. Census, Monongalia County, Virginia

36 Monongalia County Clerk's Office, Land Deed Grantee Index, John Miller to John Bunner, 123 acres, September 1797, pp. 151, 153

37 Monongalia County Clerk's Office, Land Deed Grantee Index, John Miller to John Bunner, 123 acres, September 1797, pp. 151, 153

38 Monongalia County Clerk Office, Morgantown, West Virginia, Martha Bunner Estate Appraisal and Inventory submitted to the Monongalia County

Pursuant to an order of the Court in the County of Monongalia the subscribers met Reuben Bunner, Executor of John Bunner (deceased) and made the following Settlement with him on so much of the Estate of John Bunner (deceased) that was left with his widow during her life and has come to the hands of said Reuben Bunner since her death.

To wit,

Credit by voucher produced to James Morgan for paying

| | |
|---|---|
| The said Reuben Bunner, Executor to the amount of Sale of Said Estate | $110.29 |
| Credit by voucher produced to James Morgan for paying Doctor and Burial Expenses | $43.75 |
| Counsel Fee and Crier of Sale | $5.50 |
| Clerk Fees | $3.50 |
| Judgment paid Samuel Harefield (?) obtained on acct. of James Ferrel, Heir | $19.18 |
| Receipt of James Morgan one of the heirs per $19.18 on his part and the same sum as being Executor for John Gruble (?) an heir | $38.36 |

Given under our hand the fourth day of September 1820

William O. Haymond (?)
Joshua Hiekman (?)

At a Court held for Monongalia County October term 1822. This Settlement was produced in Court, Examined and ordered to be recorded.[39]

---

Court September 12, 1818, recorded in October 1822

39  Monongalia County Clerk Office, Morgantown, West Virginia, Martha Bunner Estate Appraisal and Inventory submitted to the Monongalia County Court September 12, 1818, recorded in October 1822

## REUBEN ADAM BUNNER – OLDEST SON OF JOHN AMOS BUNNER

Lester Everest (?)

| Name | Property | $ |
|---|---|---|
| Nancy Hoult | One log chain | $1.25 |
| Nancy Hoult | Log sled yoke and Doubletrees | $1.50 |
| Nancy Hoult | 4 axes | $3.00 |
| Nancy Hoult | 1 grindstone | $0.75 |
| Nancy Hoult | One shovel, plow, and clevis | $0.62 |
| Nancy Hoult | One shackle | $1.00 |
| Nancy Hoult | One bell | $0.12 |
| Nancy Hoult | Shoemakers tools | $1.37 |
| Nancy Hoult | 6 shoes | $1.50 |
| Nancy Hoult | Lott of Hank (?) | $2.00 |
| Nancy Hoult | 2 pot trammels and poker | $1.20 |
| Nancy Hoult | Mowing scythe | $1.50 |
| Nancy Hoult | Side saddle and bridle | $1.00 |
| Nancy Hoult | One man's saddle | $0.50 |
| Nancy Hoult | 2 pots, 2 ovens, and a skillet | $3.00 |

On October 18, 1818, Reuben's youngest brother, Enoch, married Margaret Bullet, daughter of Judge Bullet, in Monongalia County.[40] It is believed that they lived on the property Enoch inherited from his father. This was part of the original 400-acre tract that John Bunner had claimed in 1772.

---

40  Bunner, Alan N., "The Bunner Family in America" Alexandria, Virginia 7,300+ page document on CD, revision dated June 25, 2012, Chapter 31, p. 917

In November 1818 Reuben sold 200 acres to David Morgan in Monongalia County located on waters of Prickett's Creek and White Day Creek.[41] John's original 1772 land claim, which is where he and Martha lived until his death in 1810, drained to both creeks. As Reuben no longer personally owned land that drained to Prickett's Creek or White Day Creek in 1818, it is assumed this must have been the land that John Bunner left to his wife Martha in his will. If this assumption is correct, it could mean that Martha's inheritance from John was 200 acres, not 133 acres.

It could also mean that Reuben's youngest brother Enoch may have included some of the land he inherited along with the land his mother inherited to arrive at 200 acres. This could be the case because in July 1820 Enoch sold 183 acres (not the approximate 267 acres he is believed to have inherited) of the land bequeathed to him by his father, thereby liquidating the land he owned in Monongalia County.[42] In either case, this land sale likely means that Martha died prior to August 24, 1818, as it is doubtful Reuben would have sold this land while his mother was still alive.

The 1820 census shows the following breakdown in Reuben and Hannah's family: One free white male over 45 (Reuben); one free white female over 45 (Hannah); four free white males 15-25 (Joseph, Thomas, Alexander, John); one free white female 16-25 (Elizabeth); two free white males 16-18 (names unknown); two free white males 10-15 (names unknown); three white females under 10 (other sources list four daughters - Amy, Rebecca, Hannah, and Martha.); and one female slave under 14. There were four total persons in household engaged in agriculture.[43] Those listed as engaged in agriculture were likely Reuben and his three oldest sons, Joseph, Thomas, and Alexander.

Of significance in this census is that Reuben and Hannah had taken in a young female slave under age fourteen. Because of the

---

41 Monongalia County Clerk's Office, Land Deed Grantee Index, John Miller to John Bunner, 123 acres, September 1797, pp. 151, 153

42 Monongalia County Clerk's Office, Land Deed Grantee Index, John Miller to John Bunner, 123 acres, September 1797, pp. 151, 153

43 1820 U.S. Census, Eastern Division, Monongalia County, Virginia

passage of ten years and the age listed for this young slave girl, she is not the same slave girl named Nancy that Reuben's father, John, had bequeathed to his wife Martha at the time of his death in 1810.

On April 24, 1820, the United States Congress passed a law entitled "An Act making further provision for the sale of the Public Lands." [44] The law went into effect on July 1, 1820. The purpose of this Act was to make public lands more available and more affordable to encourage more settlers in Ohio, the Indiana Territory, and the Missouri Territory. The minimum price for lands in these territories was reduced from $2.00 per acre to $1.25 per acre, and the minimum tract size was reduced from 160 acres to 80 acres.

Because Reuben began selling his Monongahela Valley properties in 1821, it appears that he seriously began contemplating a move to Indiana soon after Congress passed this law. On September 29, 1821, he sold 32 acres to Jacob Knight on waters of Tygart Valley River.[45] This was likely the 30-acre property Reuben had purchased in 1799 and had added to with a three acre purchase from Morgan Morgan in 1814.

On March 2, 1822, Reuben sold 50 acres to John Johnson on the east side of Monongahela River.[46] This parcel may have been a remnant of land owned by the John Bunner estate after the lands John had bequeathed had all been accounted for. John potentially owned as many as 1400 acres in Monongalia County at the time of his death. The land bequeathed in his will, including the 125 acres sold by John Jr. to Casper Bunner Jr., amounted only to approximately 1150 acres.

In 1823, Reuben's wife Hannah gave birth to Samuel Bunner. It is believed she gave birth to a daughter circa 1825, but her name is currently unknown. This daughter was likely the last of the children

---

44 https://www.govinfo.gov/app/details/STATUTE-3/STATUTE-3-Pg566/summary

45 Monongalia County Clerk's Office, Land Deed Grantee Index, John Miller to John Bunner, 123 acres, September 1797, pp. 151, 153

46 Monongalia County Clerk's Office, Land Deed Grantee Index, John Miller to John Bunner, 123 acres, September 1797, pp. 151, 153

of Reuben and Hannah. By this time, they had at least twelve children, and possibly as many as fifteen.[47]

Also in 1823, Reuben and Hannah's third son, Alexander, married Lydia Little in Monongalia County.[48] It is uncertain where Alexander and Lydia resided during the first few years of their marriage, but it is known that Alexander purchased land from his father-in-law, Thomas Little Sr., on August 10, 1826.

The 1830 census shows the following breakdown for Reuben's family: One free white male 50-59 (Reuben); one free white female 50-59 (Hannah); one free white male 20-29 (Joseph); three white females 15-19 (of Amy, Rebecca, Hannah, and Martha, one must have died); and one female slave 10-23.[49] This census did not include Gabriel (born circa 1821), Samuel (c. 1823), and a daughter (c. 1825) listed in other sources. The 1840 census, taken after Reuben died in 1835, states that Hannah was the female head of the household and was living in Indiana with a young son and a young daughter, both under age fifteen. As a result, it must be assumed that the 1830 census was incomplete.

The 1830 census shows one son aged 20-29 still living in the household. This is assumed to be their oldest son Joseph, who moved to Indiana the following year with the family. There are no records to show that he ever married, and it is recorded that he died in Indiana in 1840. His will left property and money to relatives, but no wife or children are mentioned.

It is also known that Reuben and Hannah's son Alexander married Lydia Little in 1823 and no longer lived with them. It is also believed that sons Thomas and John had married by 1830 and no longer lived with their parents.

Reuben and Hannah still owned the slave girl in 1830 that was included in the 1820 census. She was likely about age twenty by then. It is unknown what actions Reuben and Hannah took regarding her

---

[47] Bunner, Alan N., "The Bunner Family in America" Alexandria, Virginia 7,300+ page document on CD, revision dated June 25, 2012, Chapter 9, p. 147

[48] Bunner, Alan N., "The Bunner Family in America" Alexandria, Virginia 7,300+ page document on CD, revision dated June 25, 2012, Chapter 9, p. 202

[49] 1830 U.S. Census, Eastern District, Monongalia County, Virginia

welfare when they moved to Indiana in 1831. Slavery was prohibited in Indiana, and there are no records that this slave girl accompanied them. Before they moved, Reuben and Hannah could have sold her, or could have granted her freedom.

By early 1830, it is certain that Reuben had thoroughly discussed his now fully crystallized plans to move to Indiana with some of his children and his siblings. There was no doubt that Reuben and Hannah's younger children (Rebecca, Hannah, Gabriel and Samuel) would move with them. His daughters Elizabeth, Amy, and Martha all had wedding plans in 1830 or 1831 and intended to remain in Monongalia County with their new husbands. Two of his older sons, Joseph and John were definitely interested in moving to Indiana with the family. Alexander, who had been married for seven years and had two young daughters, was interested but had reservations.

Interestingly, Reuben's youngest brother Enoch and his wife Margaret wanted to move to Indiana with Reuben's family. By this time, Enoch and Margaret had three children ranging in ages from three to ten, and Margaret had just learned she was pregnant with their fourth child.[50]

Enoch Bunner had already developed a local reputation as "a great hand with horses," either at working or racing them. He once entered a one-horse-wagon-race through the woods with "Sheepy" Wilson, after Wilson had chosen the course. Wilson had planned a turning place too small to accommodate Bunner's wagon, which was larger than Wilson's. On reaching the turning place, Bunner, seeing how he'd been tricked, did not try to turn, but rehitched his horse to the rear of the wagon, and came to the finish-line "back-side-to," winning the race. The story became a local legend about how Enoch Bunner had "out-foxed" "Sheepy" Wilson. [51]

In late 1830 or early 1831, Reuben, Enoch, and Reuben's oldest son Joseph made the final decision to move to Indiana. Reuben's

---

50  Bunner, Alan N., "The Bunner Family in America" Alexandria, Virginia 7,300+ page document on CD, revision dated June 25, 2012, Chapter 31, p.197

51  Bunner, Gale J., "Genealogy Descendents of Casper (Böner) Bunner And Mary Christianna Brown, Revised Edition, 1988, p.12

son Alexander and his pregnant wife Lydia finally decided to move to Indiana with the rest of the family. Reuben's son John and his wife made the decision to move, but opted to make the move a year or two later. On April 18, 1831, Reuben sold 128 acres of Monongalia County land to William Brown.[52] Three days later, on April 21, Alexander sold sixty-one acres he had purchased from his father-in-law, Thomas Little, in 1826 back to his father-in-law. Both Reuben and Alexander were now free to leave and had enough money from the sale of their Virginia properties to purchase land in Indiana. By early May 1831 the families of Reuben, Alexander, and Enoch Bunner had loaded all their belongings into a Conestoga Wagon, said goodbye to family and friends, and begun their trip toward their new lives in Indiana.

This extended Bunner family planned to take the new National Road to Indiana. The National Road had been approved by Congress in 1806 during the Thomas Jefferson administration. The intent of Congress was to provide a transportation corridor connecting the eastern United States with the Northwest and Missouri Territories. The original plan was for the road to run from Cumberland, Maryland to St. Louis on the Mississippi River. By 1831, it had been completed from Cumberland to Columbus, Ohio and was partially completed from Columbus to Indianapolis, Indiana.

The road was only the second in the United States to be surfaced with the macadam process pioneered by Scotsman John Loudon McAdam. This road-building technique eliminated the horrendous mud problems when it rained on these early American roads.

---

52  Monongalia County Clerk's Office, Land Deed Grantee Index, John Miller to John Bunner, 123 acres, September 1797, pp. 151, 153

**Construction of the National Road used new macadam techniques to ensure the road would remain smooth and even under the weight of covered wagons.**
(National Park Service – public domain)

As a result of the construction of this road, the new industry of manufacturing covered wagons had rapidly emerged to satisfy the huge demand for those wanting to move west. A new service, that of stagecoach travel, also emerged for those who needed or wanted to travel down the 620 mile length of the National Road in a few days rather than a few weeks.

Fully loaded wagons with a team of four to six horses could travel ten to twelve miles each day on the National Road. The road that paralleled the Monongahela River from the upper valley where Reuben and Enoch lived to Brownsville, Pennsylvania was still not well-suited for wagon travel. This sixty mile trip took several days. At Brownsville they got on the National Road with their wagons and headed west. Four days later they reached Wheeling, Virginia, where they had to pay a toll of 37½ ¢ to take the ferry across the Ohio River.

As they travelled more deeply into Ohio the land became much less mountainous and travel times improved a bit. Seven days after crossing the Ohio River they reached Zanesville, Ohio where they paid a 31½ ¢ toll to take the "Y" bridge across the Muskingum River.

**Conestoga Wagon Traveling on National Road.
Licensed from B & O Railroad Museum.**

Six days later, the Bunners arrived in Columbus, the new capital city of Ohio. It was a bustling village of approximately 3,500 people the day they passed through. After crossing the recently constructed stone bridges over the Little Darby and Big Darby Creeks and the Scioto River, the completed portion of the National Road ended. The road west of Columbus was still under construction and was much harder to traverse. Daily travel progress was significantly reduced. The distance from Columbus to Henry County, Indiana was approximately 135 miles but daily distance covered was reduced to 6-8 mile per day. Approximately 25 days after leaving Columbus, the Bunners reached their destination of Henry County, Indiana.

The trip from Monongalia County, Virginia to Henry County, Indiana had required 40-45 travel days. Assuming some non-travel days to rest the family, rest the horses, and make the inevitable repairs on the wagon, the trip likely took two months. If they left Monongalia County in early May 1831 as believed, they would have likely arrived in Henry County in early July.

Reuben applied for ownership of 240 acres at Luray, Prairie Township, on July 30, 1831. The location of his tract was one mile south of the Delaware County line, east of State Road #3.[53] In June 1832, Reuben's son Joseph applied for ownership of land adjacent to him.[54]

A copy of a certificate from the Indiana Land Office, dated August 5, 1834, documenting a sale of land to Reuben Bunner, has survived. It is for an 80-acre parcel defined as "the west half of the southeast quarter of Section Thirty-Five in Township Nineteen North of Range Ten East in the District of Lands." The document serves as a receipt that Reuben Bunner had "paid in full" for this parcel. Because of the three year lapse between these two transactions, it is assumed this eighty acre purchase was an additional parcel Reuben purchased that was not a part of his original 240-acre purchase.

---

53 Bunner, Alan N., "The Bunner Family in America" Alexandria, Virginia 7,300+ page document on CD, revision dated June 25, 2012, Chapter 9, p. 147

54 Bunner, Alan N., "The Bunner Family in America" Alexandria, Virginia 7,300+ page document on CD, revision dated June 25, 2012, Chapter 9, p. 147

Certificate confirming Reuben Bunner had purchased and paid for 80 acres in Henry County, Indiana, dated August 5, 1834. Andrew Jackson was President at that time.

Reuben's brother Enoch and his family settled near Reuben's family in Henry County, Indiana. Their six known children were Alpheus (born circa 1820), Mary Jane (c. 1823), Elizabeth (c. 1827), Gustavus (c. 1831), Reuben (c. 1832), and Ellen (c. 1834). There are likely others. All of Enoch and Margaret's children, and several of their grandchildren, also lived in Henry County. The dates for the deaths of Enoch and Margaret Bunner are unknown, and their gravesites have never been located.[55]

There is no currently known record indicating that Alexander purchased any land in Indiana. He and his wife Lydia, as well as their two children, Elizabeth and Lavina Jane, may have lived with Reuben and Hannah. Within a few months after arriving in Indiana, Lydia gave birth to Franklin, their first son.[56]

---

55 Bunner, Alan N., "The Bunner Family in America" Alexandria, Virginia 7,300+ page document on CD, revision dated June 25, 2012, Chapter 31, p.197

56 1880 U.S. Federal Census, Franklin Boner, West Virginia, Barbour County, Cove, 069

Reuben died in September 1835 at the age of fifty-six or fifty-seven. He did not leave a will, but letters of administration were issued to his widow Hannah on 11 September 1835. Reuben was buried on his farm in Indiana.[57]

Although Reuben Bunner's cause of death is not known, historical records from the 1830's incriminate Cholera as a likely cause. There was a global pandemic of Cholera in the mid-1830's that caused the deaths of thousands of people in the United States.

Sometime between 1832 and 1838, Alexander and Lydia decided to leave Indiana and move back to Harrison County, Virginia, where they again settled near her parents. It is certain they were back in Virginia by 1838, because their daughter Eliza Jane was born that year, and her 1921 death certificate states she was born on Lost Run in Harrison County in 1838.

Hannah and Reuben's oldest son, Joseph, died in Henry County in 1840 at the approximate age of forty-four. In his will, dated 29 February 1840 and probated 6 April 1840 in Henry County, Joseph does not mention a wife or children, but does name his brother, John Bunner, who had moved to Indiana by then, as his executor. It is possible Joseph never married.[58]

In the 1840 census, Hannah Boner (Bunner) is listed as "head of house" living in Prairie Township, Henry County, Indiana. The two youngest children, one male 15-20 years old and one female 10-15 years old were living with her. Hannah was listed at 50-60 years old, living next to her son John Bunner.[59]

Hannah died sometime between 1840 and 1850. She was likely buried in the small family cemetery established on their property after Reuben's death.[60]

---

[57] Bunner, Alan N., "The Bunner Family in America" Alexandria, Virginia 7,300+ page document on CD, revision dated June 25, 2012, Chapter 9, p. 147

[58] Bunner, Alan N., "The Bunner Family in America" Alexandria, Virginia 7,300+ page document on CD, revision dated June 25, 2012, Chapter 9, p. 147

[59] Bunner, Alan N., "The Bunner Family in America" Alexandria, Virginia 7,300+ page document on CD, revision dated June 25, 2012, Chapter 9, p. 147

[60] Bunner, Alan N., "The Bunner Family in America" Alexandria, Virginia 7,300+ page document on CD, revision dated June 25, 2012, Chapter 9, p. 147

The small Bunner family Cemetery is on the list of "Lost cemeteries of Henry County Indiana". It is located on the "old Bunner property" in Prairie Township, Henry County Indiana. The Mendal Bunner family is reported to have a list of those family members buried there. As of 2010, the cemetery had been abandoned for many years and was completely overgrown. The grave markers that were left were all down and stacked in piles. The Cemetery is on private property, and two privately owned fields must be crossed to get to it. However the cemetery commission has permission to come and go anytime that crops are not in the fields.[61]

Family tradition is that Reuben Bunner was the first to be buried there and that the site is the final resting place for approximately twelve family members who lived in Henry County in the mid-1800's. It is unknown if Hannah was buried here, but it is likely. This cemetery is in section #35 in Prairie Township about half a mile west of the intersection of county roads 875 north and 175 east, in the woods.[62] In 2012, Greg Bunner learned that the old Bunner Cemetery was on land owned at that time by Greg and Irene Martz.

Reuben and Hannah left many descendants in both Indiana and Virginia (present-day West Virginia). Many of their descendants live in Henry County, Indiana today. Most of the Bunners living in Wood County, West Virginia are descendants of Reuben and Hannah.

---

61  Greg Bunner conversation with Mike Birch, familiar with the Cemetery Commission in Indiana, 2010

62  Greg Bunner conversation with Irene Martz, 2012. Greg and Irene Martz owned the property on which the old Bunner family cemetery is located in 2012.

9.

# Alexander Bunner
## (circa 1802 – 1874)

[Author's Note: For the duration of this book, I spell the family name as Bunner, as it became the predominant spelling found in records and legal documents between 1830 and 1870. The names Bonar, Boner and Bonner are still found in some documents because that is how the local county clerks recorded it. As most of the Bunners during this time were uneducated and illiterate, they had no idea how the name should be spelled. They simply placed an X as their mark when they were required to sign documents. The clerks in Monongalia County, Virginia had begun using Bunner as the standard spelling by 1820-1830. Alexander settled in Harrison and Marion counties after he married, where the clerks initially spelled the name Bonar. Boner is the name found in all federal censuses for Alexander and Lydia as well as the name inscribed on their tombstones. By the end of the Civil War, literacy had begun to slowly creep into the Bunner family tradition and legacy. Soon thereafter, Bunner became the standard spelling of the last name of the far-flung descendants of Casper and Mary Böner]

Alexander Bunner was born in Monongalia County, Virgina circa 1802, the third child, and third son, of Reuben Adam Bunner and Hannah Trader Bunner. Thomas Jefferson had been President of the United States for one year when Alexander was born. He grew up on a 400-acre tract of land on White Day Creek that was owned by his grandfather, John Amos Bunner. John had purchased this land while he was still serving in the Westmoreland County militia during the Revolutionary War in 1781. This land had originally been owned by pioneer John Jolliffe, who was killed during a Revolutionary War battle in 1777.

In 1802, the same year that Alexander was born, his grandfather set off 90½ acres of this 400-acre tract for Alexander's father Reuben to live on, and 90½ acres for Reuben's younger brother Joseph to live on. This unofficial demarcation remained until John's death in 1810, when he bequeathed these two 90½ acre parcels to his sons Reuben and Joseph.[1]

Alexander grew up learning the same farming and hunting skills that had now been passed down through five generations of Bunners who had lived their lives on the American frontier. He worked alongside his father Reuben and his older brothers Joseph and Thomas to clear land, chop firewood, work in the gardens, mow hay, and tend the livestock. By the age of seven or eight, his father was teaching him how to shoot a rifle so he could help supplement the family meals with squirrels, rabbits, turkeys, bears, and deer. He never attended school and never learned to read or write.

As a young boy, Alexander lived less than a mile from his grandfather and grandmother, so he likely visited them frequently. Sadly, when he was eight years old, his grandfather's health rapidly declined and he died during late summer 2010. Alexander was probably too young to understand it, but his grandfather's will bequeathed ownership of the 90½ acres he and his family had been living on to his father Reuben.

On April 12, 1813, Alexander's father Reuben Bunner and his uncle, Amos Bunner, traded the properties their father had bequeathed to them in 1810. Reuben's original 90½ acre property was situated along White Day Creek, and Amos's original 150-acre

---

1 Monongalia County Clerk Office, Morgantown, West Virginia, Will Book 1, page 336

property was situated along the Tygart Valley River (near present-day Colfax, West Virginia).[2]

Although the move was only seven miles, it was a new world for eleven year old Alexander. Also living on this same stretch of land along the Tygart Valley River were his Uncle James and his family as well as his Uncle John (Jr.) and his family. James had been bequeathed 150 acres by his father, and John Jr. had been bequeathed 100 acres. The property Reuben had traded for and the properties owned by James and John Jr. all adjoined. They were part of the 400-acre parcel Alexander's grandfather, John, had purchased in 1800.

Also, a little further upstream, Alexander's great-uncle, Casper Bunner, Jr. had purchased a 125 acre parcel from his nephew (Alexander's uncle), John Bunner Jr. In addition to the 100 acres bequeathed to John Jr. by his father, John Jr. owned an additional 200-acre tract less than a mile upstream along the Tygart River. Circa 1807, at his father's urging, John Jr. had subdivided this tract so he could sell 125 acres to his uncle.[3]

Casper Jr. had moved his family there from Berkeley County in 1807 or 1808. He had previously lived for over thirty-five years on the Berkeley County farm originally purchased in 1768 by his father, Casper Sr. Casper Jr.'s brother Joseph (also Alexander's great uncle) had lived on this same Berkeley County farm alongside him during those years.

Twenty-six years after the death of his father, Casper Sr., and ten years after the death of his mother, Mary, Alexander's grandfather, John, wanted to sell the old family farm near Hedgesville in Berkeley County. This was because he had been named Executor of their estate and he wanted to finally get it settled.[4] After John signed a contract to sell the old family farm in Berkeley County, Casper Jr. made the move to Monongalia County to be closer to his family. Casper Jr. had seven daughters and only one son, whose name was

---

2 Monongalia County Clerk's Office, Land Deed Grantee Index, April 12, 1813, p. 151, 153

3 Monongalia County Clerk's Office, Land Deed Grantee Index, November 1813, p. 153

4 Berkeley County Clerk's Office, Martinsburg, WV, Deed Book 27, Page 542

Reuben. Reuben was four years older than Alexander, closer in age to Alexander's two older brothers Joseph and Thomas. They often went swimming together in the Tygart River to clean and refresh themselves after working in the fields on hot summer days.

John died in1810 before the sale of his parents old farm in Berkeley County was completed. In his will he left directions on how the sale was to be completed and how the proceeds were to be divided among family members.[5] The contract of sale for the Berkeley County property stipulated that the buyer could not occupy the property until it was completely paid for. In the meantime, John's brother Joseph continued living there.

Just two years after Alexander's grandfather died, trade provocations with Great Britain, impressment by Great Britain of sailors on American ships at sea, and British alliances with Native Americans who were resisting the expansion of the American frontier into the Indiana territory caused President James Madison to persuade Congress to declare war on Great Britain. This commenced the War of 1812, which lasted for two years, during which the British invaded Washington, D.C.

While occupying the Capitol, the British burned the White House and several other federal buildings housing government records and archives. Archives from the Revolutionary War, including soldier payroll records and Continental Army muster rolls, were destroyed. Also lost were many congressional records from the first twenty-five years of American history. Portions of the 1790 Census were also destroyed. Fortunately, clerks at the State Department grabbed the original copies of the Declaration of Independence and the Constitution as they fled the burning buildings.

In 1814, the British also bombarded Fort McHenry for two days during the Battle of Baltimore. The scene inspired Francis Scott Key to write the poem *"The Defence of Fort M'Henry,"* which later became the lyrics to *"The Star Spangled Banner."*

None of Alexander's immediate relatives are known to have fought in this war. The war ended in a draw, with the final terms of peace agreed to with the signing of the Treaty of Ghent in December

---

5   Monongalia County Clerk Office, Morgantown, West Virginia, Will Book 1, page 336

1814. Aside from Andrew Jackson becoming a folk-hero among the Appalachian Mountain frontiersmen after his victory over the British at the Battle of New Orleans, the impact of the war on those living along the Monongahela and Tygart rivers at the time it was being fought was minimal.

However, the long-term outcome of the War of 1812 proved to be very consequential for the Bunner family. That impact did not fully materialize until 1831 when many members of the Reuben Bunner and Enoch Bunner families decided to move to Indiana. However, this is getting ahead of the story of Alexander and Lydia Bunner. Events leading up to the War of 1812 and actions taken after the war led directly to the opening of the Indiana territory for settlement by American pioneers.

Chief Tecumseh had long defended the right of the Native Americans to retain their lands in the Northwest Territories. No matter how brave and courageous Tecumseh's forces may have been, they were never a match for the military might of the American armies. In 1794, as a young warrior, Tecumseh had fought in and lost the Battle of Fallen Timbers to the vastly superior military forces of General "Mad Anthony" Wayne.

After that defeat, Tecumseh laid low for sixteen years while slowly and methodically building alliances with various Indian tribes throughout the south and west. In 1808, Tecumseh and his younger brother Tenskwatawa established Prophetstown, a village in present-day Indiana, that grew into a large, multi-tribal community. Tecumseh's efforts caused sufficient alarm that, in 1811, President Madison ordered American forces led by General William Henry Harrison to attack the Indian stronghold at Prophetstown. Harrison defeated the forces led by Tenskwatawa at the Battle of Tippecanoe and destroyed Prophetstown.

In 1812, after the loss at Tippecanoe, the ever persistent Tecumseh sought and gained an alliance with Great Britain. The British, who had already implemented crippling trade restrictions against the United States, added to their provocations by providing financing and weaponry to Tecumseh. This allowed him to sustain his armed warfare against the Americans in the Indiana Territory.

After the start of the War of 1812, Tecumseh assisted the British in capturing Detroit. However, after the American Navy defeated the British at the Battle of Lake Erie in 1813, Detroit was recaptured by the Americans. After winning the Battle of Lake Erie, Commander Oliver Perry famously sent the message "We have met the enemy, and they are ours" to his commanding officer, Major General William Henry Harrison.

After the defeat at Detroit, Tecumseh's forces retreated into Canada. American forces pursued and defeated him at the Battle of Thames. Tecumseh was mortally wounded during that battle.

In 1814, as part of the Treaty of Ghent, the British agreed to cease all assistance to the Native Americans in the Indiana Territory. With the death of Tecumseh and the loss of financial assistance from Great Britain, the Native American tribes living in Indiana realized they had no other option but to retreat west of the Mississippi River. After thirty years of warfare between the Native Americans and the white settlers, this finally opened the Indiana Territory for white settlement.

In 1815 the buyer of the Berkeley County farm where Alexander's great uncle Joseph Bunner had been living finally paid off his loan and took ownership of the property.[6] At that time Joseph moved to the Tygart Valley River area with his wife, two youngest daughters, and two young grandchildren. He rented a small farm near where Casper Jr. was living with his family. Joseph was sixty-three at the time and was no longer able to perform the heavy labor necessary to efficiently manage the farm he was renting. Joseph was likely assisted by his brother, Casper Jr. and Casper Jr.'s son Reuben. It is also possible that Alexander may have sometimes walked the short distance to Joseph's farm to help him hoe his corn and feed his pigs and sheep.

In 1816, Indiana was admitted into the Union as the 19th state. Four years later, on April 24, 1820, during the first term of President James Monroe, the United States Congress passed a law entitled "An Act making further provision for the sale of the Public Lands." The law went into effect on July 1, 1820. The purpose of this Act was

---

6  Berkeley County Clerk's Office, Martinsburg, WV, Deed Book 27, Page 542

to make public lands more available and more affordable to encourage more settlers in Ohio, the Indiana Territory, and the Missouri Territory.

With the passage of this law, Alexander's father Reuben began dreaming about moving to Indiana. He often talked to his older children about making the move as a complete family. At about this same time, Alexander met Lydia Little, who lived with her family a few miles upstream on Lost Creek, a tributary of the Tygart Valley River. Lydia was born to Rachel Nixon and George Sparks December 26, 1801, so her birth name was Lydia Sparks. According to the "History of Marion County", a book produced by Marion County Historic Society,

> "'George disappeared never to be found again'. One snowy winter night [circa 1807], George Sparks stepped outside of the family's log house before going to bed. When he did not return in a reasonable period of time, the family went out looking for him. Tracks were found in the snow. The tracks went a short distance leading away from the cabin and then abruptly stopped. No human or animal tracks were found nearby. George had vanished.
>
> A year or two after George's disappearance, Rachel married Thomas Little in Harrison County, Virginia. Oral family tradition states that "Thomas Little observed Rachael Sparks plight with at least four orphaned children. He decided to help her with the kids." Rachael Sparks married Thomas Little July 18, 1808 in Harrison County, VA. Several children were born after their marriage."[7]

Following the marriage, Lydia took on the last name of her stepfather, Little.

Thomas Little was a Revolutionary War Veteran. His service record as a private in the Pennsylvania Legion entitled him to 200

---
7 Taylor County Historical Society, "History of Taylor County," "Little Family" article, Wood County Library, Parkersburg WV

acres of land in lieu of pay. This was the land he was living on in 1820.[8]

Alexander Bunner married Lydia Little in 1822-1823.[9] It is believed they were married in Harrison County, Virginia, which adjoined Monongalia County just a few miles south of where Alexandar was living with his family. It is uncertain where they lived during the first few years after their marriage, but it is believed they settled near Lydia's parents in Harrison County.

Alexander and Lydia's first child Elizabeth was born in 1825.[10] A year later, on August 10, 1826, Alexander purchased 61 acres of land from Lydia's stepfather Thomas Little Sr.[11] The property was a part of a one hundred ninety acre tract then owned by Thomas Little Sr. It was located on land that drained into the Tygart Valley River in Harrison County, Virginia. This may have been along Lost Creek, a tributary of Tygart Valley River. The last five miles of Lost Creek before it flows into the Tygart Valley River are extremely mountainous and unsuitable for farming. As a result, it is likely they settled further upstream where the land was flatter and more suitable for farming. This would place them 1-5 miles north of present-day Pruntytown, West Virginia. Alexander's deed records that his property adjoined property owned by Jesse Nixon.[12]

Over the next several years, the lives of Alexander and Lydia Bunner are somewhat clouded by three mysteries. One mystery involves the 1830 census. Alexander was a property owner in 1830 and likely had two daughters (Elizabeth and Lavina Jane). Under these circumstances, he should have been listed as a "Head of

---

8   Bunner, Alan N., "The Bunner Family in America" Alexandria, Virginia 7,300+ page document on CD, revision dated June 25, 2012, Chapter 9, p. 202

9   Bunner, Alan N., "The Bunner Family in America" Alexandria, Virginia 7,300+ page document on CD, revision dated June 25, 2012, Chapter 9, p. 202

10   Bunner, Alan N., "The Bunner Family in America" Alexandria, Virginia 7,300+ page document on CD, revision dated June 25, 2012, Chapter 9, p. 202

11   West Virginia State Archives, Charleston, WV, Thomas Little to Alexander Bonar deed, Harrison County, VA, August 10, 1826

12   West Virginia State Archives, Charleston, WV, Thomas Little to Alexander Bonar deed, Harrison County, VA, August 10, 1826

Household." However, Alexander and Lydia cannot be found in this census.

The second mystery has to do with children believed to have been born to Alexander and Lydia in the early 1830's. Some family records indicate that circa 1833, Alexander and Lydia welcomed a son named Hiram into the family. Hiram cannot be accounted for in the 1840 census, and his name is not listed in the 1850 census. It is surmised that if Hiram was born circa 1833, he died before the 1840 census.

The third mystery has to do with their move to Indiana in 1831 and their move back to Harrison County, Viriginia by 1838. It is known that on April 21, 1831, Alexander sold the sixty-one acres he had purchased from his father-in-law in 1826 back to his father-in-law.[13] This was three days after his father, Reuben, sold his last parcel of land in Virginia in preparation for the family's move to Henry County, Indiana. There has long been a question as to whether Alexander and Lydia made this move with the larger Bunner family. From data entered into the 1880 Federal census, it appears the answer is yes. In that census, Alexander and Lydia's oldest son, Franklin, states that his age was fifty and his birthplace was Indiana.[14]

The Bunner family arrived in Henry County, Indiana in July 1831, and it is believed Franklin was born soon afterward. As he would have been born in the second half of 1831, this would make him forty-nine years old, going on fifty, at the time of the 1880 census.

The real mystery is why Alexander and Lydia decided to return to Virginia. Their son Thomas was born in 1832, probably in Indiana. If they had a son named Hiram, his birth date has been commonly fixed as 1833, and it is surmised that he died prior to 1840. Perhaps he was born in Indiana and his death was the catalyst that caused them to return. Perhaps the death of Alexander's father, Reuben,

---

13   West Virginia State Archives, Charleston, WV, Alexander Bonar to Thomas Little deed, Harrison County, VA, April 21, 1831

14   1880 U.S. Federal Census, Franklin Boner, West Virginia, Barbour County, Cove District, 069

triggered their return. Perhaps the arrival of Alexander's younger brother John and his family to Indiana in 1837 led to overcrowding in the family house or to family squabbles, causing the decision to return.

Whatever the case, Alexander and Lydia decided to make the six week journey on the National Road back to Harrison County, Virginia. The earliest date for this move would have been 1833. The latest would have been 1838. They were accompanied by their daughters Elizabeth and Lavina Jane and their son Franklin. They were also likely accompanied by their son Thomas. It is possible they were also accompanied by their youngest daughter Hannah and their youngest son Hiram.

In 1835, Alexander's father, Reuben, died in Indiana.[15] A year later, in 1836, a daughter, Hannah, was born to Alexander and Lydia. Two years later, in 1838, their fourth daughter, Eliza Jane, was born.[16] Eliza Jane's 1921 death certificate states she was born on Lost Run in Harrison County in 1838, so this provides a confirmation that the family was living in Virginia at that time.[17] Lost Run is a creek that is today contained completely within the geographic confines of Taylor County, West Virginia. However, before Taylor County was formed in 1844, Lost Run was in Harrison County. The creek is approximately fifteen miles long and runs north from near Pruntytown, West Virigina until it empties into the Tygart Valley River about two miles south of present-day Colfax, West Virginia.

The 1840 census records that the total number of persons living in Alexander and Lydia's household was eight. These would likely have been Alexander (age 38), Lydia (38), Elizabeth (15), Lavina Jane (11), Franklin (9), Thomas (8), Hannah (4), and Eliza Jane (2). Alexander's occupation is listed as 'farmer.' This census records their

---

15  Bunner, Alan N., "The Bunner Family in America" Alexandria, Virginia 7,300+ page document on CD, revision dated June 25, 2012, Chapter 9, p. 147

16  Bunner, Alan N., "The Bunner Family in America" Alexandria, Virginia 7,300+ page document on CD, revision dated June 25, 2012, Chapter 9, p. 202

17  West Virginia State Archives, Charleston, WV, Eliza J. Boner Death Record, 1921

residence as simply Harrison County, Virginia.[18] When comparing this 1840 census record with the 1840 census of Lydia's parents, it appears that they lived close by, perhaps about three houses or farms away.

In early 1840, Alexander's oldest brother, Joseph, died in Henry County, Indiana at the approximate age of forty-four. It is believed he never married nor had children. He bequeathed $50 to Alexander in his will.[19]

Lydia's mother Rachel Nixon Little died on August 3, 1840, at age seventy-six. Rachel was buried in a small cemetery near Poplar Island (a small island in the Tygart Valley River) in Marion County, Virginia. Her marker read, "Here lies the body of Rachel wife of Thomas Little died Aug. 3rd, 1840, aged 76 years."[20]

In 1840 or 1841, Lydia gave birth to a son, Lafayette. In 1845, Alexander and Lydia completed their family with the birth of their son George.[21]

In 1842, Marion County, Virginia was formed from Monongalia and Harrison counties. Middletown was named the County Seat of Marion County. In 1843, Middletown's name was changed to Fairmont.

In 1844, Taylor County, Virginia was formed from parts of Barbour, Harrison, and Marion counties. Williamsport was named the County Seat. Soon thereafter, Williamsport changed its name to Pruntytown after John Prunty, one of first settlers in the county. These rapid political boundary changes occurred in the area where Alexander and Lydia were living at the time. Aside from the 1850 census, which records that Alexander and Lydia were living with

---

18  1840 U.S. Federal Census, Alexander Boner, West Virginia, Harrison County

19  Bunner, Alan N., "The Bunner Family in America" Alexandria, Virginia 7,300+ page document on CD, revision dated June 25, 2012, Chapter 9, p. 147

20  Bunner, Alan N., "The Bunner Family in America" Alexandria, Virginia 7,300+ page document on CD, revision dated June 25, 2012, Chapter 9, p. 202

21  Bunner, Alan N., "The Bunner Family in America" Alexandria, Virginia 7,300+ page document on CD, revision dated June 25, 2012, Chapter 9, p. 202

their family in the Eastern District of Marion County,[22] all known locations where Alexander and Lydia lived prior to 1849 and after 1850 were located in present-day Taylor County, West Virginia.

The 1850 census records the following members of the Alexander and Lydia Bunner (spelled Boner on the census) household, along with their ages: Alexander (48), Lydia (48), Elizabeth (25), Thomas (18), Hannah (14), Eliza Jane (12), Lafayette (10), and George (4). Alexander is listed as a farmer, and Thomas is listed as a laborer. Lavina is not included, but she was twenty-one at the time and had likely already married. Nineteen-year-old Franklin is not included, but he is found elsewhere in the 1850 census as a "laborer on the farm of James and Livorna Boice in Marion County."

Alexander is listed as a farmer. Whoever assisted Alexander and Lydia in filling out the census forms recorded that neither Alexander nor Lydia could read or write. They also recorded that their daughter, Elizabeth, could not read or write.[23] The census states the family was living in the Eastern District of Marion County in 1850. This district was the same in which Lydia's parents were living according to this same census.

It seems unlikely that Alexandar and Lydia, or Lydia's parents, would move from Taylor County to Marion County just for the census, and then move back to Taylor County. It would make more sense to conclude that the person filling out the census forms may have been confused by the rapid succession of county changes in the 1840's. What had been Harrison County in 1840 became Marion County in 1842 and then became Taylor County in 1844. The census takers possibly entered Marion County on the census forms when they should have entered Taylor County. Whatever the case, there is uncertainty about the reliability of the addresses recorded for Alexander and Lydia Bunner in the 1850 census.

In 1851, Lydia's stepfather Thomas Little died. He was buried next to his wife Rachel near Poplar Island in Marion County,

---

22   1850 U.S. Federal Census, Alexander Boner, West Virginia, Marion County, Eastern District

23   1850 U.S. Federal Census, Alexander Boner, West Virginia, Marion County, Eastern District

Virginia. His gravestone read "Here lies the boddy of Thomas Little husband of R. Little, died Sept. 27th, 1851, in the 86th year of his age". His stone also documents his service in the American Revolutionary War. The final resting place of Thomas and Rachel Little is known today as "Little's Cemetery."[24]

1852 was a year of massive infrastructure development for Taylor, Marion, and Harrison counties. The railroad junction in Grafton had been completed and railroad lines from Grafton to Wheeling and Grafton to Parkersburg were nearing completion. A suspension bridge for pedestrian and horse traffic was completed across the Monongahela River between Fairmont and Palatine (present-day East Fairmont). The new Fairmont to Beverly turnpike (which roughly followed present-day Route 250) was completed. And the world's longest steel railroad bridge crossing the Monongahela River south of Fairmont was completed. This bridge spanned 650 feet and rose 35 feet above the normal water level. This railroad bridge allowed the Baltimore and Ohio Railroad to provide service between Baltimore and Wheeling. It also allowed for the development of the rich coal fields west of Fairmont near the towns of Farmington and Monongah.

On April 5, 1852, a hundred-year flood ravaged communities long the Monongahela, West Fork, and Tygart Valley Rivers in the three-county area. Heavy rains the day before caused the Monongahela and West Fork Rivers to rise at rate of 5 feet per hour until Tuesday afternoon, when the water reached 43 feet above its normal level. The greatest damage was sustained on the West Fork, where over 40 houses and buildings were swept away and floated down the Monongahela River past Fairmont.[25]

The Tygart Valley River and its tributary, Lost Creek, near which Alexander and Lydia were living at the time, also flooded. The flood caused some damage along Lost Creek, but nothing as severe as that inflicted along the West Fork River approximately twenty miles to the west. The flood damaged the new railroad line

---

24  Greg Bunner, "Alexander Bunner Master," 2010

25  Dunnington, George (1880). History and Progress of the County of Marion, West Virginia. Fairmont, WV: George A. Dunnington. pp. 87–92.

running along the Tygart Valley River from Grafton to Fairmont. This new railroad line had been under construction for several years and was nearing completion when the flood struck. Fortunately, the new railroad bridge near Fairmont was not damaged by the flood.[26]

**Baltimore & Ohio Railroad Bridge over Monongahela River at Fairmont, WV – 1852**
(Library of Congress – public domain)

Within three months after the flood, the Baltimore and Ohio Railroad crews had repaired the damage and opened the new lines through Taylor County. These two new railroad lines connected Grafton to the towns of Parkersburg and Wheeling on the Ohio River to the west, and to large cities like Baltimore and Philadelphia to the east. The railroad opened Marion and Taylor counties for more commercial and industrial development than could have been imagined only a decade earlier.

However, few of the economic benefits from new railroads and turnpikes accrued to Alexander and Lydia. They rarely produced a surplus of agricultural goods on their farm that could be sold

---

26 Dunnington, George (1880). History and Progress of the County of Marion, West Virginia. Fairmont, WV: George A. Dunnington. pp. 87–92.

for cash, and because they lacked cash, they could purchase few of the goods delivered to the area by the new railroad. They lived the simple, but often difficult, life of self-sufficiency. Their labor and the land they farmed produced everything they needed to survive.

During the last few years of the 1850's, the debates over slavery and state's rights became extremely heated and divisive. Fathers disagreed with sons, brothers disagreed with brothers, and mothers, wives, and sisters became as vocal and as agitated as the men. When Abraham Lincoln emerged as a "dark horse" to become the Republican candidate for President in 1860, the chest-thumping, the rhetoric, and the bravado exhibited by both sides grew to levels unseen since the Revolutionary War. The issue of slavery was bringing America to a breaking point. Northerners wanted it abolished. Southerners wanted it continued.

Those who lived in the mountainous regions of western Virginia were caught in the middle. It is estimated that during this time, one in every three adults in Harrison, Marion, and Taylor counties in Virginia were for slavery and state's rights. Two in three were against slavery and for a strong federal government. In Barbour County, bordering Taylor and Harrison counties to the south, the sentiment was flipped, with two thirds of the population favoring slavery and state's rights. Something had to give. The American fabric could no longer be woven with both pro-slavery and anti-slavery threads. Compromise and accommodation were no longer possible.

The 1860 Census records Alexander and Lydia at yet another address that did not require a move on their part. This new address was Taylor County Post Office in Pruntytown, Virginia. As the farmable land along Lost Creek was closer to Pruntytown than any other town, it is reasonable to conclude that this new address was assigned to Alexander and Lydia's old location on Lost Creek. Alexander is recorded as 57 years old and Lydia as 60. There is an obvious entry error on this census, as all censuses in previous decades showed Alexander and Lydia being the same age, or with Lydia being one year older than Alexander. Alexander is listed as a farmer, and he placed a value of $100 on his personal estate. The only child recorded as still living with Alexander and Lydia was fifteen-year-old George. The occupation listed for George was farm laborer. Alexander and Lydia's twenty-year-old son Lafayette is neither recorded as living with his parents in the 1860 census nor can he be found in the broader census.[27]

In 1860, Abraham Lincoln was elected President of the United States. Between his election in November and his inauguration in March, seven southern states seceded from the Union. Lincoln took office on March 4, 1861, and on April 12, 1861, Confederate forces captured Fort Sumter in the Charleston, South Carolina harbor. Five days later, on April 17, 1861, Virginia seceded from the Union. Alexander and Lydia, as well as all other citizens of Virginia, were no longer living in the United States of America. Instead, they were now citizens of the Confederate States of America. The Civil War, the most destructive and devastating war in American history, had begun.

Suddenly, decisions had to be made regarding loyalties. Within Virginia, long-standing political tensions between the lowland residents of eastern Virginia and the mountain residents of western Virginia already existed at the beginning of the war. Basic differences over such things as taxation and infrastructure development had provoked heated debate in the Virginia legislature for many years. The secession of Virginia and the outbreak of the war only exacerbated these issues.

Because Grafton was the main junction for the railroad in western Virginia, its military significance was apparent to both sides. Both General Robert E. Lee, the newly appointed commander of the Confederate forces, and General George McClelland, commander of the Union forces in the west, understood the strategic imperative of controlling the town. In early May 1861, both generals began operations to secure that control. Grafton was only ten miles from where Alexander and Lydia lived. Not only had the war started, but its opening salvo was coming to their backyard.

Grafton was highly populated with Union sympathizers who had followed the railroad into the town from the industrial northeast. Southern troops led by Colonel George Porterfield arrived in Grafton first and occupied the town. The Union sympathizers

---

27  1860 U.S. Federal Census, Alexander Boner, West Virginia, Taylor County, Pruntytown, VA

gave Porterfield's soldiers such a difficult time in Grafton that the Confederates moved their recruiting operations eight miles west to Pruntytown. Even though Union troops had not yet arrived, both sides aggressively recruited and trained soldiers from the local area. Taylor County soon became a powder keg needing only a spark to set it off.

On May 22, two Union soldiers, Daniel Wilson and Thornsbury Bailey Brown went from Grafton to a rally in Pruntytown to recruit forces for the Union army. On their return that evening, the two men were ordered to halt by three Confederate soldiers who were doing picket duty at the Fetterman Bridge where the Northwestern Turnpike (present-day Route 50) crossed Tygart Valley River on the west side of Grafton. Brown answered their demands with pistol fire, injuring one of the Confederates in the ear. The injured confederate fired at Brown, killing him almost instantly. Thus, Thornsbury Bailey Brown became the first casualty of the Civil War. There would be over 600,000 more American citizens killed over the next four years.[28]

The next day, Colonel Porterfield learned that Union troops were massing in Wheeling with orders to proceed to Grafton to occupy the town and protect the critical railroad junction. Porterfield dispatched men to torch wooden trestles on the railroad west of Fairmont to slow the progress of the Union troops. On May 25, Confederate soldiers burned two railroad bridges on the Baltimore and Ohio Railroad near Farmington, a small town seven miles west of Fairmont. General George McClelland, from his command in Cincinnati, Ohio ordered Colonel Benjamin Franklin Kelley to advance from Wheeling to Grafton. When they arrived at Farmington, Colonel Kelley's soldiers hastily repaired the bridge trusses that had been burned and continued on to Grafton.

Colonel Porterfield, the Confederate commander, learned that Union reinforcements would soon arrive in Grafton. He realized he was in an untenable position and retreated with his soldiers up

---

28  Jon-Erik Gilot, "To Secure Western Virginia for the Union: The First Campaign," American Battlefield Trust, https://www.battlefields.org/learn/articles/secure-western-virginia-union-first-campaign

the Tygart River Valley to Phillipi, about fifteen miles to the south of Grafton.

Alexander and Lydia's son, Lafayette, was twenty years old when the war started. It is certain that he was approached by both Union and Confederate recruiters in April and early May 1861when they were aggressively recruiting in Taylor County. After extensive research by several members of the Bunner family during the twentieth and twenty-first century, there is no evidence that Lafayette served as a soldier for either side.

Instead, there is evidence that Lafayette worked as a teamster during the war,[29] delivering food and supplies to the Union forces stationed in Virginia (West Virginia after June 20, 1863). Teamsters wore the Union uniform and performed many of their duties near combat zones but were designated as noncombatants. The full implication of being a noncombatant would not become obvious for another fifty years when Congress deemed that teamsters who served during the Civil War were not eligible for Civil War pensions, military tombstones, or burial in national cemeteries.

None of those issues were in the minds of soldiers, civilians, or recruits during those tumultuous and ominous days in Taylor County, Virginia during the last week of May 1861. An opportunity arose for Lafayette to earn some quick cash, and he likely accepted what he may have believed was a short-term, one-time job. In all likelihood, he became a Union teamster on May 31, 1861. His assignment was to drive a team of horses pulling a covered wagon filled with Union army supplies to Philippi.

On May 30, the Union reinforcements from Wheeling arrived at Grafton by train. Additional Union reinforcements from Parkersburg, led by General Thomas Morris, arrived by train on June 1. The decision was quickly made by the Union commanders to pursue the Confederate troops in Phillipi. 3,000 Union troops began the march, accompanied by approximately twenty supply wagons. One of those wagons was manned by Lafayette Bunner. Heavy rains and muddy roads impeded the march of the Union soldiers toward Phillipi, but they persevered through the night.

---

29 Bunner, Alan N., "The Bunner Family in America" Alexandria, Virginia 7,300+ page document on CD, revision dated June 25, 2012, Chapter 9, p. 295

Battle of Philippi, June 3, 1861 –
Photo of Mural in West Virginia State Capital
(Photograph by Michael Bunner)

On the morning of June 3, 1861, the Union forces gained the element of surprise by arriving at Philippi before sunrise after marching through the night in heavy rains. The Union troops crossed the covered bridge over the Tygart Valley River at 4:00 A.M. and as soon as they were positioned, gunfire from unknown sources awakened the Confederate soldiers. What ensued is recorded in history as the first land battle of the Civil War. No deaths were recorded by either side, but approximately thirty confederate soldiers and four union soldiers were wounded. The battle lasted less than thirty minutes, and the rout of the Confederate troops was so complete that this battle was known thereafter as the "Races at Philippi." The Confederate troop retreated to Huttonsville, Virginia, approximately forty miles to the south.

After the Battle of Philippi, General McClellan stationed sufficient Union troops in Grafton and Clarksburg to maintain control of the railroads in western Virginia. A substantial number of Union troops remained in the Grafton-Clarksburg area for the duration of the war. The victory at Philippi and a subsequent Union victory over Confederate forces at Rich Mountain, twenty five miles south of Philippi, brought sufficient acclaim to General McClellan that President Lincoln elevated him to Commander of the Union Army of the Potomac one month later.

The victory at Philippi also bolstered the morale of the Second Wheeling Convention, which was comprised of Virginian citizens loyal to the Union seeking to nullify Virginia's secession. On June 19, 1861, the convention adopted an ordinance to reorganize Virginia as a loyal state, and on June 20, 1861, Francis H. Pierpont, a resident of Fairmont, was selected as the governor of the Restored Government of Virginia. Governor Pierpont called the legislature of the new government into session on July 1, 1861.

President Lincoln and Congress swiftly recognized the Restored Government of Virginia as the legitimate government of the entire Commonwealth of Virginia. In August 1861, the Restored Government of Virginia voted to approve the creation of a new state, West Virginia. According to Article IV, Section III of the U.S. Constitution, no new state can be formed from the territory of an existing state without the latter's consent. As Congress recognized the Reformed Government of Virginia as legitimate and the government of the seceded state of Virginia as illegitimate, the vote to carve the state of West Virginia out of the state of Virginia was deemed to be constitutional.

The residents of Taylor County were known to have held predominantly Union sympathies during the war, and it is believed that Alexandar and Lydia were Union sympathizers, but on any given day they could have been Confederate sympathizers.

An example of how the Bunner families living in Marion, Taylor, and Harrison county areas held starkly different loyalties can be seen in the stories of three different Thomas Bunners in 1863. All three of these Thomas Bunners were probably great-grandsons of John Amos Bunner and his younger brothers Joseph and Casper Jr. Thomas S. Bunner is recorded as having served in the Union Army in the 9th Regiment, Company D of the West Virginia Infantry. He entered the army as a private and left as a sergeant.[30]

---

30 U.S., Civil War Soldiers, 1861-1865, National Park Service, Civil War Soldiers and Sailors System,

Thomas A. Bunner is listed in U.S., Civil War Draft Registrations Records, 1863-1865 as a "Class l" potential recruit for the Union Army. On October 1, 1863, he is listed as a thirty year old farmer who is married. His address was 2nd Magisterial District, Taylor County, West Virginia (this Thomas Bunner was almost certainly the son of Alexander and Lydia Bunner).[31]

A third Thomas Bunner (no middle initial given) is listed as a Confederate sympathizing prisoner of war held for a time by the Union army. His address is listed simply as Marion County. He was arrested on August 1, 1863, as a "horse thief" involved in a ring to steal horses from local farms for Confederate soldiers. He was held in a military jail in Marion County until October 17, 1863, when he was released under orders by the U.S. Secretary of War, Edwin M. Stanton.[32]

Though Taylor County and neighboring Barbour and Randolph counties were home to the first few land skirmishes of the Civil War, the only conflicts that erupted in Taylor county over the next four years were a few neighbor-to-neighbor skirmishes such as barn and haystack burning. There were no more armed conflicts on Taylor County soil for the duration of the war.

However, neighboring Marion County was not so fortunate. Early on April 29, 1863, approximately 2,500 Confederate cavalry men under the command of General William ("Grumble") Jones attacked the town of Fairmont from the north. There were 300 Union militia soldiers available to protect the town, but they were easily overwhelmed by the much larger Confederate force.

---

http://www.itd.nps.gov/cwss/</a>&gt; 2007, Ancestry.com Operations Inc.,2007, Provo, UT, USA

31  U.S., Civil War Draft Registrations Records, 1863-1865, Ancestry.com, Records of the Provost Marshal General's Bureau (Civil War), Record Group 110. The National Archives in Washington D.C., Ancestry.com Operations, Inc., 2010, Lehi, UT, USA, https://catalog.archives.gov/id/4213514

32  National Archives at Washington DC; Washington, DC. USA; War Department Collection of Confederate Records; NARA film publication #:: M598; Record Group: War Department Collection of Confederate Records; Record Group Number: 109

The confederates had four main goals: destroy the suspension bridge crossing the Monongahela, destroy the railroad bridge crossing the Monongahela, kill Francis Pierpont (Governor of the Restored Government of Virginia), and create an opening in the Union defensive line between the North and the South that General Robert E. Lee could possibly use to advance troops into Pennsylvania to attack Harrisburg.

They succeeded at only one of their goals – that of destroying the railroad bridge over the Monongahela River. This crippled, for a time, the transport of soldiers and supplies between the western front in Ohio and Indiana and the eastern front in Virginia. As the massive stone piers that supported the railroad bridge over the river were not damaged, the Baltimore and Ohio construction crews were able to rebuild the bridge in a matter of weeks. The continuous presence of additional Union troops in the area for the duration of the war kept the peace in Taylor and Marion counties.[33]

On April 20, 1863, Congress voted to create the new state of West Virginia. President Lincoln signed the bill, which became effective two months after his signature was affixed. On June 20, 1863, West Virginia officially became the 35th state in the Union. It became the only state to secede from the Confederate States of America.

After the Civil War, the existence of the railroad contributed to the growth of Grafton and Taylor County. The Industrial Revolution was already underway and the natural resources of West Virginia were essential for the industrialization of America. Rich coal seams near Fairmont, which had been mined during the civil war to provide heat for homes in the east, were expanded to satisfy the new energy demands of industry. The railroads through Grafton and Fairmont were expanded to satisfy this rising demand.

Through these tumultuous times, the daily lives of Alexander and Lydia remained much as they had been before the war. Both were now in their sixties and unable to perform some of the labor chores that were necessary to maintain a farm. They relied heavily

---

33  Dora Kay Grubb, "The Battle of Fairmont," Apr 24, 2019, https://www.wvnews.com/fairmontnews/lifestyles/the-battle-of-fairmont/article_f86890a4-ff04-5598-a7e4-e5f0ec262086.html

on the help of their youngest son George, who still lived at home, to do a lot of the heavy labor required to maintain their farm.

In 1865, after the end of the war, Lafayette married Mary Shingleton. Mary had been born and had grown up in Taylor County. Lafayette and Mary took up residence near her parents in western Taylor County, approximately ten miles from where Alexander and Lydia lived. Sometime between 1865 and 1870, Alexander and Lydia moved from their Lost Creek farm to the Booths Creek District of Taylor County to be closer to their daughters Elizabeth and Lavina and their sons Franklin and Lafayette.

In the 1870 census, Alexander and Lydia are recorded as living in the Booths Creek District of Taylor County. Alexander's stated occupation is farmer and Lydia is listed as a housekeeper. They were living near the families of their two daughters Elizabeth Bunner Shingleton and Lavina J. Bunner Boice.[34] (Bunner was spelled Boner in this census).

Also in the 1870 census, Franklin Bunner, his wife, Nicey Jane, and their eight children are recorded as living in Booth's Creek District, Pruntytown, Taylor County, West Virginia. Just a few months later, Nicey Jane died, likely during childbirth. On 27 October 1873, Frank married Catherine Nestor, who was born in Barbour County, Virginia in1844-45. The 1880 census records Frank and Catherine as living in Cove District, Barbour County, West Virginia. Catherine died circa 1889. Frank died on January 28, 1895, in Barbour County, West Virginia.[35]

On August 19, 1874, Alexander Bunner died. There is no death record for him on file in the Taylor County Courthouse. He is buried in the Janes Memorial Church Cemetery in Taylor County (close to the Marion County-Taylor County line) on present-day Route 250. His last name is spelled Boner on his gravestone.[36]

---

34 1870 U.S. Federal Census, Alexander Boner, West Virginia, Taylor County, Booths Creek District

35 1870 U.S Federal Census, Franklin Boner, Booths Creek, Pruntytown, Taylor, West Virginia, USA

36 Bunner, Alan N., "The Bunner Family in America" Alexandria, Virginia 7,300+ page document on CD, revision dated June 25, 2012, Chapter 9, p. 202

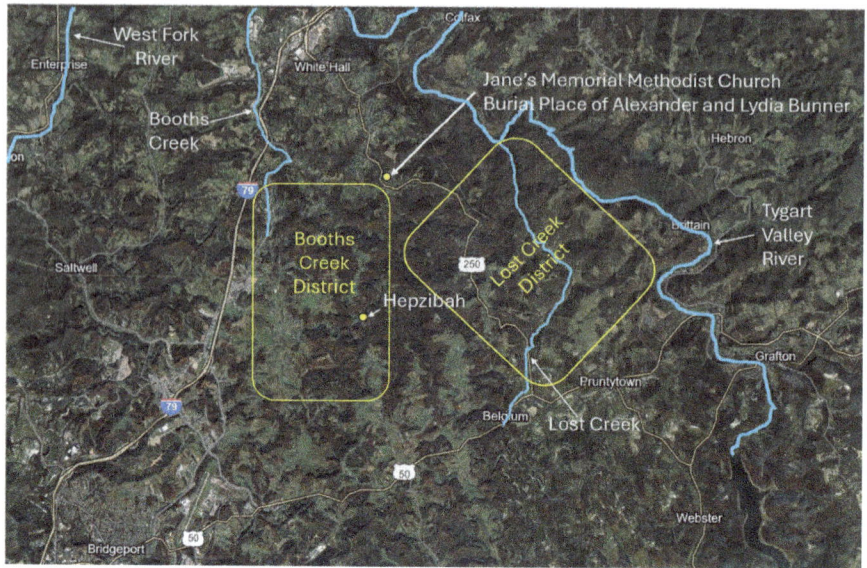

**Alexander and Lydia Bunner lived in the Lost Creek District from approximately 1838 until approximately 1868. Thereafter, they lived in the Booths Creek District near their daughters**

(Map by Michael Bunner overlaid on 2025 Google Earth image)

On September 8, 1874, a document purporting to be the Last Will and Testament of Alexander Bunner was presented to the Taylor County Court by Mortiman S. Corbin, the court appointed Executor. Because the document was not in the handwriting of Alexander Bunner (he could not read or write) and had not been witnessed or subscribed by two witnesses, the court decided it could not be admitted as Alexander Bunner's last will.[37]

As a result, the court appointed Mortiman Corbin as administrator of the Alexander Bunner estate and instructed him to obtain three appraisals to present to the court. The court order reads as follows: "On motion of said Corbin who made oath is appointed administrator of said Alexander Bunner (spelled Boner in this document) deceased and said Corbin now here before me in my

---

37  Will Of Alexander Boner Court Record. WV State Archives Charleston WV

office with James E. Riley interred into and acknowledged a bond in the penalty of 400 dollars conditioned according to law which bond is ordered to be recorded and on motion of said Corbin as administrator ordered that James E. Riley, Andrew Hertzog, and William [?] appraise the personal estate of said deceased which may be produced and shown them by said administrator."[38]

In the 1880 census, Lydia Bunner (spelled Boner in the census) is recorded to be living with her daughter Lavina Bunner Boice in Booth Creek District, Taylor County. Lydia was 77 years old. At the time the census was recorded, two categories of health problems were noted for Lydia. One box was checked in front of the question, "Is the person on the day the numerators [census takers] visit sick or temporarily disabled so as to lie unable to attend to ordinary business or duties? If so, what is the sickness or disability?" In response to the second question, the census taker recorded the name of the sickness. However the entry is difficult to read. It is believed to say, "weak in brain."[39]

The other box that is checked records that Lydia was "Maimed, Crippled, Bedridden, or otherwise disabled."

On August 13, 1882, Lydia Bunner died at the age of eighty or eighty-one. There is no death record on file for her in the Taylor County Courthouse. Lydia is buried next to Alexander at Jane's Memorial Church Cemetery in Taylor County. Her last name is spelled Boner on her gravestone.[40]

---

38   Will Of Alexander Boner Court Record. WV State Archives Charleston WV

39   1880 U.S Federal Census, Lydia Boner, Booths Creek, Taylor, West Virginia, USA, 083, Living in household of son-in-law James Boice and daughter Lavina Boice.

40   Bunner, Alan N., "The Bunner Family in America" Alexandria, Virginia 7,300+ page document on CD, revision dated June 25, 2012, Chapter 9, p. 202

*10.*

# Lafayette Bunner

[Author's Note: From Lafayette Bunner onward, the family name has been spelled Bunner in all family records, archives, and documents.]

Lafayette Bunner was born in Harrison County, Virginia in 1840 or 1841. He was the seventh child of Alexander and Lydia Bunner. In 1842, the area where he lived became Marion County. Two years later, in 1844, it became Taylor County. After its birth, Taylor County became Lafayette's home for the rest of his life. Lafayette became a farmer, like the five generations of Bunners in America who preceded him. He never learned to read or write.

In 1844, the total population of Taylor County was approximately 5,000. Williamsport, the largest town, had a population of approximately 150. (In 1845, Williamsport changed its name to Pruntytown, after early settler and Virginia delegate John Prunty.) The county was rural, and virtually all residents carved out a subsistence living by farming and hunting. The Northwest Turnpike (present-day U.S. Route 50) had been constructed in the late 1830's to accommodate horse and mule drawn wagons travelling east and west across the Virginia mountains. This road connected Winchester, Virginia with the Ohio River town of Parkersburg, Virginia. In 1852, when Lafayette was twelve, the Fairmont to Beverly Turnpike (present-day U.S. Route 250) was completed through Taylor County. This new road provided easier north-south travel across the never-ending mountains and valleys in this largely untamed region. Pruntytown was located at the crossroads of the Northwestern Turnpike and the Fairmont to Beverly Turnpike.

When Lafayette was approximately five or six years old, the Baltimore and Ohio Railroad began constructing a network of rail lines and stations across western Virginia. A major junction was being constructed in a narrow valley along the Tygart Valley River in southeastern Taylor County. That hub caused a new town to be built around it that was given the name of Grafton. Some claim the city was named for John Grafton, a civil engineer of the Baltimore and Ohio Railroad. Most claim that railroad construction crews referred to the town as "Graftin" because it was the point at which a number of branch railroad lines met and were "grafted to" the railroad's mainline. These rail lines were all operational by the end of 1852.

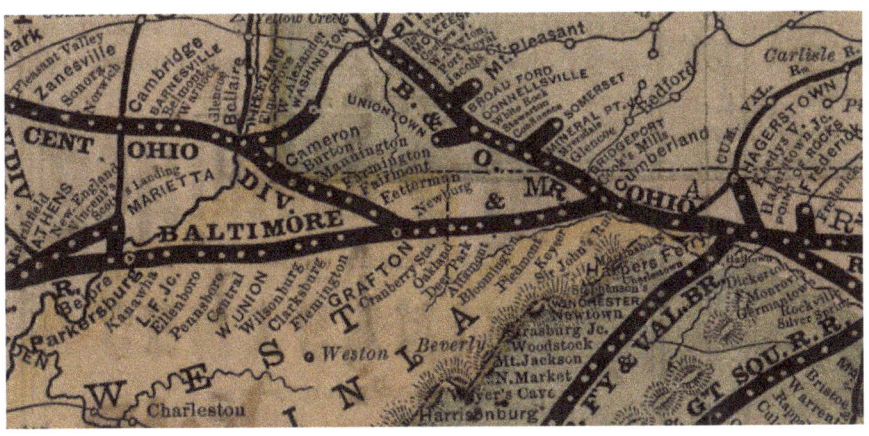

**Early Baltimore and Ohio Railroad Map across western Virginia. Grafton was the major hub.**

Grafton was incorporated in 1856 when Lafayette was sixteen. By then, approximately 600 people, most of them railroad employees, called Grafton home. Almost overnight, Grafton had become the largest town in Taylor County. Lafayette would often make the eight mile trip from his parents farm north of Pruntytown into

Grafton to purchase farm necessities such as salt, farming tools, and ammunition for hunting rifles.

By 1858, an ominous split was occurring among the citizenry of the United States. The argument was framed as a debate over states' rights, but that served only as a respectable cover for the real issue, which was the strain and the stain of slavery on the American psyche. An uneasy tension had existed since the Constitution had been ratified by the original thirteen states in 1789. The southern states permitted slavery, and felt it was necessary for the economic development of their mostly agrarian regions. The northern states were more industrialized and less agrarian. While many in the north engaged in farming, it was mostly subsistence farming to provide only the food necessary for the farmer's family to survive. Most who lived in the north believed slavery to be dehumanizing and sinful. Most who lived in the south pointed to the biblical verse that said slaves should honor their masters as proof that God was pro-slavery.

Those who lived in the mountains of western Virginia were torn. The mountainous terrain was not conducive to plantation farming, and most of these mountain residents were subsistence farmers. Many of those who had settled in western Virginia, especially those of German descent, were opposed to slavery on moral and spiritual grounds. On the other hand, they were citizens of Virginia, and the eastern two-thirds of the state were lowlands that were conducive to large plantations that grew tobacco and other crops for profit. Those profits were taxed, and although those living in the west felt a disproportionate share of tax revenues were spent in the lowlands to the detriment of those living in the mountains, some of those taxes did find their way to the western part of the state where they were spent on roads and bridges.

As the 1860 national election approached, Abraham Lincoln, who had served only one term in Congress as a Whig and had failed to be reelected, emerged as the presidential nominee for the newly formed Republican Party. His platform did not oppose slavery in the southern states, but did oppose slavery in all new territories that would eventually become states. Lincoln's opponents were John Breckinridge of the Southern Democratic Party, John Bell of the Constitutional Union Party, and Stepen Douglas of the Democratic

Party. Lincoln won by gaining 59% of the electoral votes with only 40% of the popular votes. Breckinridge carried nine of the eleven states that would soon comprise the Confederate States of America. Interestingly, Bell carried Tennessee and Virginia, the other two states that would soon join the Confederacy. Douglas won only the state of Missouri's electoral votes.

Lincoln's election in November 1860 caused seven Southern states to secede from the Union before his inauguration in March. Within six weeks after Lincoln became President, Fort Sumter had been attacked by Confederate forces, commencing the American Civil War. Within days of the Fort Sumter attack, four additional states, including Virginia, seceded. Officers and enlisted soldiers in the Union Army had to decide where their loyalties lay. Most chose the side of their home states.

Two notable officers who switched allegiances were Robert E. Lee and Thomas "Stonewall" Jackson. One of President Lincoln's first actions after his inauguration was to promote Lee to full Colonel in the Union army and offer him command to the army to protect Washington, D.C. after Virginia seceded. Rather than accept this new command, Lee resigned from the Union army the day after Virginia seceded and assumed his new role as General-in-Chief of the Confederate States Army.

"Stonewall" Jackson was serving as a major in the Union army when the war began. He had grown up near Clarksburg in Harrison County, Virginia approximately twenty miles from where Lafayette lived with his family. When Virginia seceded, Jackson resigned from the Union army and joined the Confederate army as a Colonel. Within a few months he was promoted to Brigadier General, and then Major General.

Many citizens in western Virginia made the same decision as Robert E. Lee and Stonewall Jackson – to cast their loyalties with their home state. However, they were not the majority. Many western Virginians who were members of the Virginia assembly remained loyal to the Union and on May 13, 1861, they quickly assembled as a group in Wheeling to plot a way to establish an alternate Virginia government that would position itself as the legitimate government of Virginia.

One of Robert E. Lee's first priorities was to gain control of the Baltimore and Ohio Railroad in western Virgina. On May 4, 1861, he dispatched several hundred soldiers under the command of Col. George Porterfield to the main railroad junction in Grafton. When Porterfield arrived in Grafton, he found a small contingent of Union soldiers were already there, but he had several hundred soldiers under his command so was able to easily occupy the town. He quickly discovered that the townspeople, mostly railroad employees who had moved there from the northeast to help construct and maintain the railroad, were Union sympathizers. Due primarily to the harassment of the townspeople and his inability to recruit confederate soldiers among Union supporters, Porterfield moved his recruiting operations eight miles west to Pruntytown. There, his team was able to recruit several new soldiers, most of whom Lafayette would have known or known of. They may have talked to Lafayette and tried to recruit him

Late in the evening of May 22, 1861, two Union soldiers who had left Grafton for Pruntytown to recruit soldiers for the Union were returning to Grafton. At the Fetterman Bridge where the Northwest Turnpike crossed the Tygart Valley River about one mile west of Grafton, they were confronted by three Confederate soldiers standing picket. One of the Union soldiers, Thornsbury Bailey Brown, responded by drawing his pistol and firing a shot. The shot injured one of the Confederate soldiers in the ear. The injured Confederate soldier responded by shooting Brown, killing him instantly. Thornsbury Bailey Brown unfortunately entered history books as the first soldier killed by hostile forces in the Civil War.[1] [2]Over 600,000 more soldiers would die before the Civil War came to an end four years later.

The next day, Colonel Porterfield gained intelligence that a large Union force was being assembled in Wheeling and would soon be dispatched to Grafton by train. On the night of May 25, 1861, Porterfield dispatched a contingent under the command of Colonel

---

1 Gilot, John-Erik, "To Secure Western Virginia for the Union: The First Campaign"

2 Cohen, Stan, "The Civil War in West Virginia," Pictorial Histories Publishing Co., Charleston, WV, 1976, p.22

William J. Willey to burn bridges on the Baltimore & Ohio Railroad line between Wheeling and Grafton. The intent was to sufficiently delay the arrival of the Union troops from Wheeling until after Porterfield had received his promised reinforcements.

Willey's soldiers succeeded at burning the trusses of two railroad bridges near Farmington, a few miles west of Fairmont. These actions by Colonel Willey were emblematic of the way the Civil War would divide families, communities, and the nation. Colonel Willey's brother was Waitman T. Willey, a staunch Union loyalist who was also a member of the Wheeling Convention that would soon develop a plan to carve the state of West Virginia out of Virginia. Two months after his Confederate brother burned the railroad bridges in Farmington, Waitman Willey began serving in the United States Senate representing the Restored Government of Virginia. In 1863, after the State of West Virginia was admitted to the Union, he became one of West Virginia's first two senators.[3]

Rather than prevent an invasion by Union forces, William Willey's bridge burnings precipitated the first campaign of the Civil War. When the Union troops travelling from Wheeling to Grafton encountered the two burned bridges at Farmington that were impeding their way, their commander, Colonel Benjamin Kelley, assembled a team of soldiers to repair the bridges. While the repairs were being performed, Kelley telegraphed his commander, General George McClellan, commanding officer of the Ohio Volunteers in Cincinnati, about the incident. McClellan ordered an additional Union battalion stationed in Parkersburg to Grafton to reinforce Colonel Kelley's forces. The Parkersburg unit was under the command of General Thomas Morris.[4]

On May 26 or May 27, Colonel Porterfield learned that the Confederate reinforcements he was expecting in Grafton had been delayed. Realizing he was in a tenuous position, he lead his troops on a retreat southward to the Confederate friendly town of Philippi,

---

[3] Gilot, John-Erik, "To Secure Western Virginia for the Union: The First Campaign"

[4] MI Digital, "First in War, First in Blood: Benjamin Franklin Kelley, West Virginia's first military commander" November 14, 2023

a distance of about fifteen miles. He planned to remain there until his promised reinforcements arrived.

By May 29, the burned bridges near Farmington had been repaired and the train carrying Kelley's troops continued toward Grafton. Kelley's unit arrived in Grafton on May 30 where they learned that Porterfield had retreated to Philippi. Kelley developed a plan to pursue and capture Porterfield's forces. Success would require a significant number of horse-drawn wagons to carry food, ammunition, armaments, and medical supplies necessary to execute his plan.[5]

Although no historical archives exist to support this contention, this is likely the point in time when twenty-year-old Lafayette Bunner, who lived on his father's farm just a few miles away, became involved in the Civil War. The Union soldiers who had held several recruiting events in Grafton and Pruntytown over the previous few weeks were likely aware of Lafayette and his skills. They may have learned about his ability to work with teams of horses to plow the fields on his father's farm. They may have also learned he had a wagon that could be used for carrying food and ammunition.

When Colonel Kelley was seeking advice from his staff regarding the fastest way to assemble a wagon train with skilled teamsters to support the troop movement to Philippi, Lafayette's name was likely among several mentioned. After listening to his staff, Colonel Kelley gave them orders to go out among the local farmers to recruit and assemble a wagon train, with drivers, that could accompany his troops on their march to Philippi.

The prevailing pay rate for teamsters at that time was $30/month.[6] The spring plowing had already been completed, and all the seeds were in the ground. Aside from some hoeing, all that would be needed over the next month for the crops to start growing was rain and sunshine. The local farmers were in a lull regarding the time spent each day to maintain their farms and crops. This could be an opportunity for many of the local farmers to earn some extra cash, which was always in short supply.

---

5 MI Digital, "First in War, First in Blood: Benjamin Franklin Kelley, West Virginia's first military commander" November 14, 2023

6 Hess, Earl, "Civil War Logistics," LSU Press, 2017, pp.137-138

Lafayette probably talked over this one-time opportunity with his father, Alexander, and they decided to do it. Any help that Alexander may need during Lafayette's absence could be provided by George, Alexander's youngest son, who was now sixteen. The most likely date that Lafayette agreed to accept this job as a teamster for the Union army was May 31, 1861.

On June 1, 1861, the Union forces led by General Morris arrived from Parkersburg. He and Colonel Kelley immediately reviewed Kelley's plan to pursue and capture the Confederate forces in Philippi and reached agreement on their strategy and tactics.[7] Word went out to the teamsters they had hired to arrive in Grafton within a few hours to have their wagons loaded. By early afternoon, approximately twenty teamsters arrived with their wagons. By late afternoon these wagons were loaded and the orders were given to the troops and the teamsters to move out. They followed the Northwest Turnpike (present day U.S. Route 50) west for eight miles and were approaching Pruntytown as the sun fell below the rolling mountain horizon. The troops stopped for the night near Pruntytown.

The soldiers unloaded their tents and food from the wagons and set up camp. Lafayette unhitched his horses and led them to a nearby field to allow them to graze. He then led them to a small stream running through the field where they quenched their thirst. Afterward, he took them back to his wagon where he gave them some of the oats he had stored in a container on his wagon.

The plan was to allow the soldiers to sleep later than normal the next morning. The previous day had been long and grueling. Only the commanding officers knew that the plan was for the troops to move out of their encampment the following afternoon and then to march through the night to Philippi. The intent was to surprise the Confederate soldiers by arriving and being in position for battle before sunrise the following morning.

By late morning on June 2, the soldiers had eaten breakfast, folded their tents, and loaded them on the wagons. A few of them played cards or whittled. Some congregated in small groups to trade stories. A few found a grassy spot and laid down to relax or sleep.

---

7  MI Digital, "First in War, First in Blood: Benjamin Franklin Kelley, West Virginia's first military commander" November 14, 2023

Lafayette had his wagon packed and the load secured. As soon as the orders came to move out, he would hitch his horses and start the fifteen mile journey down the Fairmont to Beverly Turnpike to Philippi.

By mid-afternoon, heavy rains started falling and they were unrelenting. As the rains and the subsequent mud would slow progress, the decision was made to depart earlier than planned for Philippi. Even with the rain, the gravel surface on the road was able to support the weight of the wagons without sinking into the mud under the gravel. The same with the field artillery. However, the rain kept falling and the ground under the gravel base continued to get softer and mushier. About halfway to Philippi, the wheels on the field artillery, which were much narrower than the wheels on the wagons carrying their supplies, began penetrating the gravel and sinking in the underlying mud. Each time a field artillery unit got caught in the mud, it took a team of soldiers and makeshift crowbars and fulcrums made of logs cut from the nearby forests to pry them loose.

Progress was slow, but it was not stopped. By 3:00 A.M. on the morning of June 3, the troops, their field artillery, and the teamsters wagons were approximately two miles north of Philippi. The bad news was that the rain was still pouring. The good news was that the Confederate soldiers were asleep in their tents, secure in the belief that no military unit would be travelling in such miserable weather.[8]

The Union soldiers broke into two units, one to cross the covered bridge in Philippi and take positions to the north of the sleeping Confederate troops. The other was to circle around the town and take up a position to the south to stop a retreat. This would entrap the Confederates so they would have to surrender and be taken as prisoners of war. The field artillery were ordered to take up positions on hills above the river where they could observe the progress of the battle. The signal for the disbursed Union troops to

---

8  MI Digital, "First in War, First in Blood: Benjamin Franklin Kelley, West Virginia's first military commander" November 14, 2023

start the battle would be a shot from the field artillery positioned on the hill above the town.⁹ ¹⁰

The unit designated to cross the covered bridge and take up positions in the town north of the Confederate troops marched double-time the last mile to ensure they were in position before sunrise. Lafayette and the other teamsters were ordered to follow the troops crossing the bridge and then to position themselves well behind the battle lines out of harm's way.

Most of the soldiers crossing the bridge were in their positions and most of the teamsters had crossed the bridge with their wagons when a shot rang out. One storyline is that a Confederate sympathizing woman living near the bridge woke up and looked outside. Seeing Union troops marching by, she immediately got a gun and shot in the direction of the last group of Union soldiers getting ready to cross the bridge but didn't hit anyone. A second storyline is that one of the Union soldiers who had already taken his position in front of the covered bridge had a twitchy trigger-finger and inadvertently fired his rifle into a nearby forest.¹¹ ¹²

It doesn't matter which, if either of these narratives is correct. What is certain is that a shot rang out, but it did not come from the field artillery positioned on the hill above the town that was to signal the beginning of the battle. That early shot did two things. First, it woke up the Confederate troops sleeping a few hundred yards downstream. Second, it caused the Union soldiers to think it was the signal to start the battle. The group that was to circle the city and take up a position to the south in order to trap the Confederate soldiers were still at least a mile from taking up their planned position.

---

9   MI Digital, "First in War, First in Blood: Benjamin Franklin Kelley, West Virginia's first military commander" November 14, 2023

10   Gilot, John-Erik, "To Secure Western Virginia for the Union: The First Campaign"

11   MI Digital, "First in War, First in Blood: Benjamin Franklin Kelley, West Virginia's first military commander" November 14, 2023

12   Gilot, John-Erik, "To Secure Western Virginia for the Union: The First Campaign"

What happened during the next thirty minutes is recorded in history books as the first land battle in the Civil War. Eyewitnesses called it the "Races at Philippi." Lafayette Bunner was in a position to watch all of this unfold. Because the Union forces were not in the position to trap the Confederates as they retreated to the south, they all ran for their lives and there was no one to stop them. They crossed the Tygart Valley River, got on the Fairmont to Beverly Turnpike, and did not stop until they reached Huttonsville forty five miles to the south. [13] [14]

During the thirty minutes of chaos, several shots were fired. Nobody was killed, but the Confederates reported thirty wounded and the Union reported four wounded. One of the four wounded Union soldiers was Colonel Kelley, the field commander. He took a bullet in the chest near one of his shoulders, from which it took him three months to recover. [15]

There is a family tradition that Lafayette was injured at the Battle of Philippi. The most common variant of this story is that the covered bridge was blown up while Lafayette was driving a wagon across it.[16] This story must be dismissed as a legend, as the bridge was not damaged during the battle. Knowing that only four Union soldiers were wounded during the battle and that the teamsters would have lined up their wagons well beyond the line of fire suggests that Lafayette sustained no injuries. Lafayette and his fellow teamsters would have returned safely to Grafton within two or three days after the battle took place.

Word spread quickly throughout the North and South about this Union victory. The victory at Philippi bolstered the courage and ensured the safety of the Second Wheeling Convention, which

---

13   MI Digital, "First in War, First in Blood: Benjamin Franklin Kelley, West Virginia's first military commander" November 14, 2023

14   Cohen, Stan, "The Civil War in West Virginia," Pictorial Histories Publishing Co., Charleston, WV, 1976, p.23

15   MI Digital, "First in War, First in Blood: Benjamin Franklin Kelley, West Virginia's first military commander" November 14, 2023

16   Bunner, Alan N., "The Bunner Family in America" Alexandria, Virginia 7,300+ page document on CD, revision dated June 25, 2012, Chapter 9, p. 295

would be meeting on June 19, 1861. The pro-Union delegates at that convention adopted an ordinance to reorganize Virginia as a loyal state, and on June 20, 1861, Francis H. Pierpont, a resident of Fairmont, was selected as the governor of the Restored Government of Virginia. Afterward, the path to statehood for the mountainous western counties of Virginia quickly took shape.

After the Battle at Philippi, no archives have been discovered that shed any light on the whereabouts of Lafayette Bunner for the duration of the Civil War. Extensive efforts by many Bunner family researchers have ruled out the possibility that he ever served as a soldier in either the Union or the Confederate armies. His name is not included in Civil War Draft Registrations Records, 1863-1865. This was a comprehensive list of all men between the ages of twenty and thirty five who were subject to be drafted for military duty. This list included the names of all men in that age category who were not already involved in the war as a soldier or a noncombatant.

Since research has led to the near certainty that Lafayette did not serve as a soldier for either side, and his name is not listed in the Civil War Draft Registration Records, by process of elimination he had to have served as a noncombatant. The most common noncombatant role during the Civil War was that of a teamster.

The National Archives in Washington, D.C., reports that it is possession of many records about noncombatant civilians connected with the Union Army during the American Civil War. They admit these records are currently underutilized because there is no comprehensive index, no "one" place to look. Current research requires endless hours leafing page-by-page through obscure, voluminous records. Using this technique to find information about the noncombatant activities of Lafayette Bunner during the Civil War would be like finding the proverbial needle in a haystack. Digitization is slowly improving the current situation, but it may take a Bunner family researcher one or two generations in the future to search these records after digitization is completed. In the meantime, we can learn something about what is was like being a Union teamster during the Civil War by looking at the surviving records of other military wagon drivers.[17]

---

17  Kluskens, Claire, National Archives and Records Administration, claire. kluskens@nara.gov, "CIVIL WAR UNION NONCOMBATANT PERSONNEL:

The name "teamster" originated because they transported goods in wagons pulled by teams of horses or mules. Military units obtained their teamsters one of two ways. They could be infantry soldiers selected by their commanding officer to perform teamster duties, or they could be civilians hired by a unit commander. Civilian teamsters were often difficult to obtain but hiring them lessened the need to take infantrymen from their units.

Civilian teamsters commanded salaries as high as $30 per month, and turnover was high. Infantrymen were paid their standard salary of $13 a month for driving teams. A commanding officer had to decide whether it was more important to have all the infantry possible for a battle (in which case he would hire civilian teamsters) or whether it was better for him to save as much money as possible (in which case he would assign some infantrymen in his unit to serve as teamsters). Infantrymen serving as teamsters got three government provided meals each day. Civilian teamsters received one free army meal per day plus forage for their horses or mules.[18]

**Photo of Union Teamster – 1862**
(Library of Congress, public domain)

---

TEAMSTERS, LAUNDRESSES, NURSES, SUTLERS, AND MORE,"(February 1, 2021 Edition)

18   Hess, Earl, "Civil War Logistics," LSU Press, 2017, pp.136-145

When military commanders were forced to operate distant from the railroads, which were the primary source of supplies for their troops, the need for wagons and teamsters increased. Most wagons carried food and tents for the troops and forage for the animals pulling the wagons. Separate wagons were necessary to carry ordnance supplies, such as infantry and artillery ammunition. Other separate wagons carried medical tents and supplies.[19]

Because wagon trains carrying military supplies were slow moving and defenseless, they were extremely vulnerable to enemy action. Every army commander had to plan troop movements with the wagon trains in mind. He had to ensure they stayed close enough to the troops to effectively supply the moving infantry, artillery, and cavalry units. He also had to keep them far enough away from combat action to minimize the possibility of having his supplies destroyed by a quick enemy strike. [20]

The more troops being moved, the larger the wagon train. The larger the wagon train, the slower the movement of the troops. If the commander decided to minimize the number of wagons carrying supplies so he could move his troops more quickly, he ran the risk of running out of ammunition if a large battle suddenly developed. The rule of thumb used by Union commanders during the Civil war was that seven wagons and drivers were required for each 1,000 soldiers. More would be needed if the troops were located far from the railroad lines which provided the supplies of food and ammunition.[21]

3,000 Union soldiers made the twenty-three mile march from Grafton to Philippi. Using the rule of thumb of seven wagons per thousand soldiers, twenty one wagons and teamsters would have accompanied these troops. A month later, at the Battle of Rich Mountain near the town of Beverly in Randolph County, a total of 5,000 Union troops under the command of General George McClellan would have required a minimum of 35 wagons, and since the fight was approximately sixty miles from Grafton, the nearest

---

19  Hess, Earl, "Civil War Logistics," LSU Press, 2017, pp.136-145

20  Hess, Earl, "Civil War Logistics," LSU Press, 2017, pp.136-145

21  Hess, Earl, "Civil War Logistics," LSU Press, 2017, pp.136-145

railroad supply point, they may have required several more to ensure adequate provisions for the troops. There is a high probability that Lafayette Bunner was one of thirty-five to forty-five teamsters that supported General McCllelans troops during their victorious fight at Rich Mountain in July 1861.

It is also likely that Lafayette served as a teamster in support of General William Rosencrans at the Battle of Carnifex Ferry on September 10, 1861. Rosencrans had fought with General McClellan at the Battle of Rich Mountain in July. After that battle Lincoln had made McClellan the Union Commander of the Potomac, and McClellan had made Rosencrans commander of Union forces in western Virginia, with headquarters in Clarksburg. Soon thereafter, the Confederates launched an effort to reclaim the Kanawha Valley to prevent West Virginia's separation from Virginia. At Kessler's Cross Lanes (near present-day Charleston), Confederate Brig. Gen. John B. Floyd defeated a small Union force, after which he retreated to the rim of the Gauley River Canyon, establishing an entrenched encampment with about 2,000 men. His encampment overlooked Carnifex Ferry, one of the few places along the rugged river canyon that could be crossed with troops.

In response, Rosencrans led 7,000 Union troops (which included the two future presidents of Rutherford B. Hayes and William McKinley) from Clarksburg to Summersville in early September.[22] As Grafton and Clarksburg were the closest railroad supply points to Summersville, it is likely that teamsters from this region were hired to accompany Rosencrans and his troops during their one hundred mile march. There were few north-south roads in this part of western Virginia at that time, and those that existed were rough, rocky, steep, and winding. A minimum of fifty teamsters would have been required for this movement, and because of the distance and ruggedness of the terrain, as many as one hundred may have been required.

---

22  Battle of Carnifex Ferry, https://www.battlefields.org/learn/civil-war/battles/carnifex-ferry

Teamsters accompanying Union troops to Carnifex Ferry, Virgina -
September 1861
(Alamy stock photo)

Rosencrans fought with the Confederate forces under General John Ford on the bluff overlooking Carnifex Ferry all day on September 10. Realizing that his 2,000 man unit could not withstand a prolonged battle with the vastly larger Union force, Floyd retreated down the mountain under the cover of darkness and escaped across the ferry. This victory allowed the Union forces to recover and maintain control of the Kanawha Valley for the duration of the war and solidified the plans of the Reformed Government of Virginia and its new governor, Francis Pierpont, to create the new state of West Virginia.[23]

In recognition of his win and his wound at the Battle of Philippi, Colonel Kelley received his brigadier general's star and command of the District of Grafton. The area encompassed the B&O Railroad from Cumberland, Maryland to Wheeling and the Northwest

---

23  Battle of Carnifex Ferry, https://www.battlefields.org/learn/civil-war/battles/carnifex-ferry

Virginia Railroad from Grafton to Parkersburg. General Kelley's mission was to protect 400 miles of strategic B&O rails and more than 24,000 square miles of rugged mountainous territory, a third of it populated by Confederate sympathizers. Soon after Kelley's recovery and promotion to General, General Rosencrans was transferred to Mississippi, and General Kelley assumed many of his responsibilities.[24]

When not leading his troops in battle, General Kelley split his time between his headquarters in Grafton and Cumberland, the two main hubs of the Baltimore and Ohio Railroad system within the Appalachian Mountains. In addition to guarding the railroad, he was now responsible for Union military operations in the northern two thirds of what is now the state of West Virginia. He had to combat not only Confederate troops that entered into his territory, but also the Confederate sympathizers who lived in this territory who were persistently trying to destroy railroad, turnpike, and telegraph infrastructure across this rugged and sparsely populated territory. Favorite targets of the Confederate saboteurs included railroad tracks and bridges, locomotives, railroad freight cars filled with military supplies, turnpike bridges, and telegraph lines in remote areas. There were also frequent thefts of cows and horses from those loyal to the Union for the use of Confederate troops and sympathizers.

It is believed that General Kelley had approximately 20,000 Union troops to carry out his mission in western Virginia. They were spread from Cumberland in the east all the way to Parkersburg in the west, a distance of nearly 200 miles. There were hundreds of railroad and turnpike bridges that, if any one of them was destroyed, would severely cripple the flow of military troops and supplies to the east and west. All could not be guarded with troops, so General Kelley assigned troops to guard those bridges that would take the longest time to repair or replace if they were damaged by saboteurs.

As a result of such a widespread dispersal of his troops, General Kelley would require the services of a significant number of teamsters to keep them supplied with food and ammunition. These

---

24  MI Digital, "First in War, First in Blood: Benjamin Franklin Kelley, West Virginia's first military commander" November 14, 2023

teamsters would most likely be based in Parkersburg, Wheeling, Clarksburg, Grafton, and Cumberland, as these were the primary supply points along the Baltimore and Ohio railroad lines during the Civil War. The role of these teamsters would be to pick up supplies at their local railroad terminal each morning and deliver them to locations where the soldiers were stationed. When the wagon was empty, they would return to the railroad station to have their wagons loaded for the next series of deliveries. When they were not supporting a combat mission, these daily "milk runs" would require the rest of their time. The soldiers had to be fed even when they were not fighting.

General Kelley had established relationships with a number of teamsters, including Lafayette Bunner, during his initial foray at Philippi and, although he was in Wheeling recuperating from his wound, had likely recommended them to General McClellan for the Battle of Rich Mountain. This initial group of teamsters lived near Grafton and had proven themselves to be reliable employees and loyal to the Union cause. They became his "go to" waggoners for delivery of food, ammunition, uniforms, tents, and medical supplies from the rail supply depot in Grafton to those troops stationed within a thirty or forty mile radius of Grafton. This type of logistical system was established at each of the other supply depots along the Baltimore and Ohio lines.

Being a Union teamster became full time work for Lafayette. Several historians have concluded that teamsters could travel as much as twenty five miles per day, but that the average distance teamsters traveled each day was fifteen miles. Assuming this was a full time job for Lafayette and that he worked six days per week, he and his team would have travelled over 18,000 miles during his Civil War service. He probably never traveled more than one hundred miles from Grafton.

The war ended with a Union victory on April 9, 1865. Five days later, on April 14, President Lincoln was shot by devastated Confederate sympathizer John Wilkes Booth while attending a performance at Ford's Theater in Washington, D.C. Lincoln died the next morning. His leadership had been critical for the passage of the 13th Amendment to the Constitution, which abolished slavery, on

January 31, 1865. His posthumous leadership ensured the passage of the 14th Amendment in June 1866 and the 15th Amendment in February 1869. The 14th Amendment granted citizenship and equal protection under the law, and the 15th prohibited denying the right to vote based on race.

President Lincoln had ended the scourge of slavery and had saved the American Union. The cost, in addition to money spent, was nearly 700,000 American lives, including Lincoln's. One in every fifty Americans alive in 1861 died as a result of the Civil War.

West Virginia was now a state, and one third of its citizens were devastated by the Union victory. All were devastated by the loss of fathers, husbands, brothers, sons, relatives, and friends. The healing process – for the nation, for the residents of the new state, for families, and for individuals - was going to take a long time.

Lafayette had to shift his focus and his daily routine from being a teamster to starting a family and being a farmer. On August 10, 1865, Lafayette Bunner married Mary Elizabeth Shingleton in Taylor County, West Virginia. Lafayette is recorded as twenty-two years old and Mary was nineteen in the marriage certificate.[25] However, Lafayette was at least twenty-four, and most likely twenty-five at the time of his marriage.

Mary Shingleton was born in 1845, the daughter of William and Melinda Shingleton. She was raised in Meadland, Virginia, a tiny farming community about four miles west of Pruntytown. Mary received some schooling, as she learned to read and write. She would live her entire life within three miles of where she grew up. Census records show Mary's mother and father were both born in Pennsylvania and moving to the Meadville area prior to 1840. They lived within five miles of where Lafayette's parents, Alexander and Lydia Bunner, lived and probably knew them and their children as they were growing up.[26]

---

25  Taylor County Clerk Office, Lafayette Bunner and Mary E. Shingleton Marriage Certificate, August 10, 1865

26  Bunner, Alan N., "The Bunner Family in America" Alexandria, Virginia 7,300+ page document on CD, revision dated June 25, 2012, Chapter 9, p. 295

In late 1865 or early 1866, Lafayette and Mary's first child, James William, was born. In late 1866 a second child, a daughter, was born dead. In the West Virginia State Archives, only the name Bunner is recorded on the death certificate for this child. On March 15, 1868, a third child, Ella, was born. Their fourth child, George Anderson, was born on December 6, 1869.[27]

In the 1870 census, Lafayette and family are recorded as living in Booths Creek District, Taylor County, West Virginia. Lafayette is listed as a 26 year old farmer and Mary is 23. Lafayette and Mary were living next to Andrew Shingleton Jr., Mary's brother and Drusella Mason. Other neighbors of Lafayette and Mary were George and Andrew Hertzog, and Francis M. Shingleton, Mary's other brother. The value of Lafayette's personal estate is listed as $300. Children of Lafayette and Mary included in this census were William (age 6), Ella (2), and George Anderson (8 months).[28] Lafayette and Mary's fifth child Virginia (Jennie) was born in 1871 or 1872.[29]

On February 20, 1872, Lafayette Bunner purchased property in Taylor County West Virginia from James E. Riley and his wife. The purchase was for seven acres located along Hustead Run near Hepzibah WV in Booths Creek District. Lafayette paid $105.00 for this property.[30] Hustead Run (present-day Hustead Branch) runs from the south to the north within Taylor County. It begins south of Meadland, runs north through Hepzibah, and flows into Booths Creek near Boothsville.

The exact location of Lafayette's seven acre farm has not been determined but is believed to be within one of the circles shown in the following picture.

---

27  Bunner, Alan N., "The Bunner Family in America" Alexandria, Virginia 7,300+ page document on CD, revision dated June 25, 2012, Chapter 9, p. 295

28  1870 U.S Federal Census, Lafayette Bunner, Booths Creek, Pruntytown, Taylor, West Virginia, USA

29  Bunner, Alan N., "The Bunner Family in America" Alexandria, Virginia 7,300+ page document on CD, revision dated June 25, 2012, Chapter 9, p. 295

30  Copy of 1886 Property Deed for Lafayette Bunner- copy obtained from West Virginia State Archives Library micro-film records for Taylor County; Charleston, West Virginia

**Likely locations of Lafayette Bunner
Taylor County, West Virginia homestead**
(Map by Michael Bunner overlaid on 2025 Google Earth image)

In 1873, when Lafayette was approximately 33 years old, Mary gave birth to Alexander Bruce Bunner. He was their sixth child and their third son. He was named after Lafayette's ailing father, Alexander, but would go through life being called Bruce.

In August of 1874, Lafayette's father, Alexander, died at the age of 71.[31] As Alexander and his wife Lydia had moved from the Lost Creek District to the Booths Creek District of Taylor County in the late 1860's to live beside their daughters (Lafayette's sisters) Elizabeth and Lavina,[32] they would have been living within 1-4 miles of Lafayette and his family at the time of Alexander's death.

In 1875 or 1876, their daughter Malinda (Vina) was born, followed by son Charles Homer on August 28, 1877. Thomas, their ninth child and fifth son, was born on December 2, 1879.[33]

---

31  Bunner, Alan N., "The Bunner Family in America" Alexandria, Virginia 7,300+ page document on CD, revision dated June 25, 2012, Chapter 9, p. 202

32  1870 U.S Federal Census, Lafayette Bunner, Booths Creek, Pruntytown, Taylor, West Virginia, USA

33  Bunner, Alan N., "The Bunner Family in America" Alexandria, Virginia 7,300+ page document on CD, revision dated June 25, 2012, Chapter 9, p. 295

The 1880 Booths Creek District, Taylor County West Virginia Census is the only census that shows a majority of Lafayette's children living with him and Mary. It is also the only census that lists Alexander Bruce living at home with his parents. Lafayette is recorded to be 38 years old and listed his occupation as a laborer rather than a farmer. This is the only record indicating that Lafayette may have worked somewhere – at least for a time - other than his farm. He is still recorded as not being able to read or write. Mary is shown at 35 years old, and she is recorded as being able to read and write. The children listed on this census are James W. (15), Ella M. (12), George A. (10), Virginia A. (8), Alexander B. (6), Malinda L. (4), Charles H. (2), and Thomas (6 months).[34]

In 1882, Lafayette's mother Lydia Bunner, died at 81 years of age[35]. Lydia had been living with the family of her daughter, Lavina, during the last few years of her life. The 1880 census recorded that Lydia was a bedridden invalid who was probably suffering from dementia.[36] At the time of his mother's death, Lafayette was about 42 years old.

September 4, 1886, Lafayette purchased another parcel of land from James E. Riley and his wife. These were the same persons he bought his first parcel of land from fourteen years earlier. This new tract of land consisted of 5 acres, and it was located along Carder Run in Taylor County, West Virginia.[37] This new land purchase was located in the Lost Creek District near where Lafayette had grown up. It was approximately ten miles east of the farm he and his family lived on along Husted Run in the Booths Creek District of Taylor County. It is unclear why Lafayette made the decision to purchase

---

34   1880 U.S Federal Census, Lafayette Bunner, Booths Creek, Pruntytown, Taylor, West Virginia, USA

35   Bunner, Alan N., "The Bunner Family in America" Alexandria, Virginia 7,300+ page document on CD, revision dated June 25, 2012, Chapter 9, p. 202

36   1880 U.S Federal Census, Lydia Bunner, Booths Creek, Pruntytown, Taylor, West Virginia, USA

37   Copy of 1872 Property Deed for Lafayette Bunner- copy obtained from West Virginia State Archives Library micro-film records for Taylor County; Charleston, West Virginia

this second parcel of land as it was too far away for him or his sons to tend to crops or livestock on a daily basis.

Maude, the tenth child of Lafayette and Mary, was born in 1881 followed by the eleventh and final child Eddie April 13, 1886. Of their ten children who were alive at the time of Eddie's birth, six were sons and four were daughters.[38] Between 1872 and 1888 Mary took the time to teach all but her two youngest children how to read and write.

By early 1888, Mary began having a persistent dry cough that she could not get rid of. She then became so low of energy that she was unable to perform the hundreds of chores required of a farmer's wife and a mother. By late 1888 she had to stay in bed most of the time as she did not have the energy and the stamina to do anything but lay down. Then, she started coughing blood. Around Christmas of 1888, the doctor who had been coming to their house to tend to her told Lafayette that Mary had Consumption, and that there was nothing he could do for her.

On the morning of February 22, 1889, Mary Shingleton Bunner took her last labored breath on earth and entered heaven. She was forty-four years old when she died.[39] In addition to her grieving husband, Lafayette, she left behind ten children. At the time of Mary's death, her children were James (age 23), Ella M. (21), George (18), Virginia (16), Alexander Bruce (15), Malinda (13), Charles (12), Thomas (9), Maude (8), and Eddie (3).

Consumption (now called tuberculosis) was the number one cause of death of persons under the age of fifty during the nineteenth and early twentieth centuries. Consumption in those days was a death sentence to almost all that contracted it. The name Consumption was given to this illness because it seemed to consume people from within. Coughing up blood was a common late stage symptom, and the person would gradually waste away before they died. It was not only lethal, but it was also contagious. It is a

---

38   Bunner, Alan N., "The Bunner Family in America" Alexandria, Virginia 7,300+ page document on CD, revision dated June 25, 2012, Chapter 9, p. 295

39   Ancestry.com, West Virginia, U.S., Deaths Index, 1853-1973, Ancestry.com Operations, Inc., Provo, Utah, 2011

miracle that Lafayette and his children did not contract this disease from Mary before she died.

This contagious disease caused an untreatable global epidemic for decades. It was not until the early 1900's that medical research determined that tuberculosis was caused by bacteria, and not until the 1950's that effective preventive measures and treatments were developed.

Mary's death record on file at the Taylor County Court House states she died in Hepzibah, West Virginia on February 22, 1889. James Davis of Boothsville, West Virginia was recorded as her undertaker. That record also states that she was buried in Hepzibah on February 23, 1889.[40] As it is believed that Lafayette and Mary were members of the Hepzibah Baptist Church, it is reasonable to assume that this is where she was buried. However, it cannot be proven.

In January of 1912, the Hepzibah Baptist Church, originally built in 1882, burned to the ground. The church had been rebuilt by the end of September 1912, but the records that existed prior to the fire, including church membership and burial records, were permanently lost. Any documents proving that Lafayette, Mary and family attended this church are no longer available. However, the close location of the church to where Lafayette and his family lived and the fact that Lafayette's brother Frank and Mary's brother Francis were among the founders of the church provides strong circumstantial evidence that Lafayette, Mary, and their children were members of this church.

Between 2008 and 2010, Greg Bunner, a great-great-great grandson of Mary and Lafayette Bunner, spent many hours looking at every tombstone and grave marker in the Hepzibah Baptist Church cemetery. He was unable to locate Mary's grave. Because the Hepzibah Baptist Church maintains the only cemetery in Hepzibah, Greg concluded that Mary's grave is located in this cemetery, but it is unmarked.

The 1890 census was destroyed by a fire on January 10, 1921, in the U.S. Department of Commerce building in Washington, D.C. As

---

40 Death Record of Mary Shingleton Bunner, Taylor County Courthouse death records; Grafton, West Virginia

a result, there is uncertainty as to where Lafayette and his younger children were living at that time. However, it is believed they still lived on the farm on Hustead Branch near Hepzibah. Lafayette was now raising his family on his own. His older children helped with the farm chores, preparing the meals, and the hundreds of small tasks that had to be performed on a daily basis to sustain the farm and the family.

In late 1890, Lafayette's older children began moving out and in some cases, moving away. His eldest son, James William, moved to Wood County, West Virginia near Parkersburg where he was married in 1891. In 1893 or 1894, twenty-year-old Alexander Bruce, who was called "Bruce," also moved to Wood County where it is believed he lived with his older brother for several years. Bruce was married in Wood County in 1899. [41] [42]

In 1898 or 1899, Bruce's younger brother, Charles "Homer" Bunner, also moved to Wood County where, on May 13, 1902, he married Hulda Jane Riley. They lived in the Parkersburg area until approximately 1918 when they moved with their family to East Liverpool Ohio where they lived the rest of their lives.[43]

According to the 1900 census, George Bunner married Zora Provance in 1892 and she died in 1895, probably from childbirth. He had then married Emma Rutherford in 1898 and was working as a fire clay miner in Marion County. Virginia ("Jennie") Bunner married Virgil Hillberry in 1893 and in 1900 was living in Grafton with their four small children. Malinda Bunner was married and living in Harrison County. Thomas Bunner was still single and working as a coal miner in Marion County. He was living in a boarding house near where he worked.[44]

---

41 Bunner, Alan N., "The Bunner Family in America" Alexandria, Virginia 7,300+ page document on CD, revision dated June 25, 2012, Chapter 9, p. 295

42 1880 U.S Federal Census, Lafayette Bunner, Booths Creek, Pruntytown, Taylor, West Virginia, USA, James Bunner, Alexander Bruce Bunner, and Thomas Bunner, Wood County, West Virginia

43 1880 U.S Federal Census, James Bunner, Alexander Bruce Bunner, and Thomas Bunner, Wood County, West Virginia, USA

44 1900 U.S Federal Census, all information in referenced paragraph obtained from federal census records provided in ancestry.com.

## LAFAYETTE BUNNER

The decade between 1890 and 1900 required extraordinary levels of patience, perseverance, grit, determination, and divine support for Lafayette to serve as both a father and a mother to his five youngest children. He sent his two youngest children, Maude and Eddie, to school, where they fulfilled their mother's wish to learn to read and write. These two may qualify as the first among the six generations of Bunners in America that attended school. In the U.S. censuses taken in the early 1900's, all ten of Lafayette and Mary's children recorded that they could read, and all recorded that they could write except for Bruce, who uniquely claimed the ability to read but not to write.

The 1900 Booths Creek District, Taylor County, West Virginia census lists Lafayette Bunner as head of house with children Ella (30) Maude (19), and Eddie (15) living at home. Lafayette is listed as a fifty-nine year old widowed farmer. His birth date was listed as March 1841. He was recorded as still being unable to read or write. However, his three children still living at home are recorded as being able to read and write. All three were recorded as having attended school, and Eddie was recorded as still attending school.[45]

This census recorded that Lafayette owned his farm outright. Neighbors to Lafayette included the Wilson's, Humphrey's, McGee's, Smith's, Shingleton's, Riley's, and Elder's. The 1900 census record would be the last showing Lafayette living at his farm on Hustead Run near Hepzibah, West Virginia[46].

On July 31, 1908, Lafayette sold his seven acre homestead on Husted Run, where he had lived for thirty-six years, to Matilda Smallwood. He also sold the five acres he owned on Carder Run in eastern Taylor County on the same day to the same person.[47] It may have been that by this date, all his children, including his youngest Eddie, were adults and married or capable of supporting themselves. By this time, Lafayette was in his late sixties and likely

---

45 1900 U.S Federal Census, Lafayette Bunner, Booths Creek, Pruntytown, Taylor, West Virginia, USA

46 1900 U.S Federal Census, Lafayette Bunner, Booths Creek, Pruntytown, Taylor, West Virginia, USA

47 Taylor County Clerk's Office, Deed Book 47, p. 184

unable to do the heavy physical labor necessary to tend gardens and livestock. With no children to help him, and no children to provide for, he may have looked at the funds from the sale of his property as his retirement fund.

From the 1910 census, we learn that Lafayette was living in the Fetterman District, Taylor County, Grafton, West Virginia. This was the western part of town near the Tygart Valley River. Lafayette was listed as head of household at age 68. Only his youngest son Eddie, age 22, was living with him. The two were renting a house at 815 Jones Street in Grafton. Eddie was recorded as a laborer for the Baltimore and Ohio Railroad, and able to read and write. Lafayette recorded "own income" on the occupation line of the census form. He also checked the box that said he was "not out of work." He was still unable to read or write.[48]

Lafayette outlived two of his children. In 1911 his daughter Jennie (Virginia) Hillberry died in Grafton at the age of forty. Her cause of death is unknown. She left behind her husband Virgil and four teenage children. Then in 1914, his oldest son, James, died suddenly at his home in Wood County at the age of forty-eight. He left behind his pregnant thirty-seven year old wife Hannah and six children between the ages of nineteen and two. It is unclear if Lafayette or any of James's brothers and sisters from Taylor, Marion, or Harrison counties attended his funeral.

According to Eddie Bunner's World War 1 draft registration card dated September 12, 1918, he was no longer living with his father on that date. Eddie was living at 364 West Main Street in Grafton. He lists his father, Lafayette, as his nearest relative and records his address as R.F.D. Grafton, West Virginia.[49]

In the 1920 census, Lafayette was living with his sister Liza (Eliza) J. Bunner Barker back in the Booths Creek District of Taylor County. Lafayette was recorded as 79 years old and his sister Liza listed as 81. A few of Liza's middle aged children were living with

---

48   1910 U.S Federal Census, Lafayette Bunner, Fetterman District, Taylor, West Virginia, USA

49   Ancestry.com, U.S., World War I Draft Registration Cards, 1917-1918, Registration State: West Virginia; Registration County: Taylor County, Eddie Bunner

them. The record shows Liza and Lafayette having no income, apparently living off the farm and whatever income Liza's children were able to provide.[50]

On April 29, 1921, Eliza J. Bunner Barker, the sister Lafayette was living with in 1920, died of neuritis.[51] Her death record states she was born at "Lost Run." When she was born in 1838, Lost Run was located in Harrison County, Virginia. At the time of her death, Lost Run was located in Taylor County, West Virginia. It is uncertain if Lafayette remained living with his nephews and nieces after Eliza died or if he moved back to Grafton to live with his son Eddie.

By 1924, at the age of approximately eighty-four, Lafayette's health started to decline. On March 6, 1925, he was admitted as an "inmate" to the Taylor County Infirmary, also known as the Taylor County "Poor Farm." His admission was ordered by J.M. Price, a county official responsible for the welfare of old, infirmed, and impoverished residents of Taylor County.[52]

In the early 1900's, County Infirmaries were county run institutions where paupers, mainly elderly and disabled people, were supported at public expense. Poor Farms were common in the United States beginning in the mid-1800's. They declined in use after the Social Security Act took effect in 1935 and had disappeared completely by 1950. Most Poor Farms were working farms that produced some of the produce, grain and livestock consumed by the residents. To the extent they were able, the residents of the facility were expected to tend the gardens and livestock, and also to provide housekeeping and care for residents unable to do any of this work. Rules for the residents were strict and accommodations were stark.

On April 15, 1925, less than one month after being admitted to the Taylor County Poor Farm, Lafayette checked out. However, he returned within a few weeks. Lafayette Bunner spent the last year

---

50  1920 U.S Federal Census, Lafayette Bunner, Booths Creek District, Taylor, West Virginia, USA

51  Eliza J. Boner Barker death record. West Virginia State Archives; Charleston, West Virginia

52  Taylor County Infirmary Register. West Virginia State Archives micro-film; Charleston, West Virginia.

of his life in residence at the Taylor County Poor Farm as his health continued to deteriorate.

Between November 1925 and February 1, 1926, his health declined rapidly until he was at the point of death. On February 9, 1926, at the Taylor County Poor Farm, Lafayette Bunner died at twelve o'clock noon. He was approximately eighty-six years old. His death certificate lists his cause of death as old age and kidney complications.[53]

Lafayette's funeral was held at Bartlett Funeral Parlor (present-day Bartlett Funeral Home) in Grafton, West Virginia on February 10, 1926, the day after he died. Lafayette was buried at Smith Cemetery in Pruntytown, West Virginia. According to records provided by the funeral home, the bill for Lafayette's funeral and burial was $145.00.[54] It is unknown who paid this funeral bill. Lafayette's son Eddie applied for a military headstone, but the request was denied. This was probably because only combat soldiers qualified for government funded headstones. Congress had deemed Civil War teamsters to be noncombatants, making them ineligible for military pensions or headstones. The funeral home may have placed a small marker on Lafayette's grave at the time of burial but, if so, it was not permanent and disappeared with time. Within a year or two after his death, Lafayette's body lay in an unmarked grave in a cemetery that gradually became overgrown. Over a period of many years, the collective family memory of Lafayette's final resting place was lost.

---

53  Lafayette Bunner death record. West Virginia State Archives; Charleston, West Virginia.

54  Bartlett Funeral Home, Grafton, West Virginia, archived records

# LAFAYETTE BUNNER

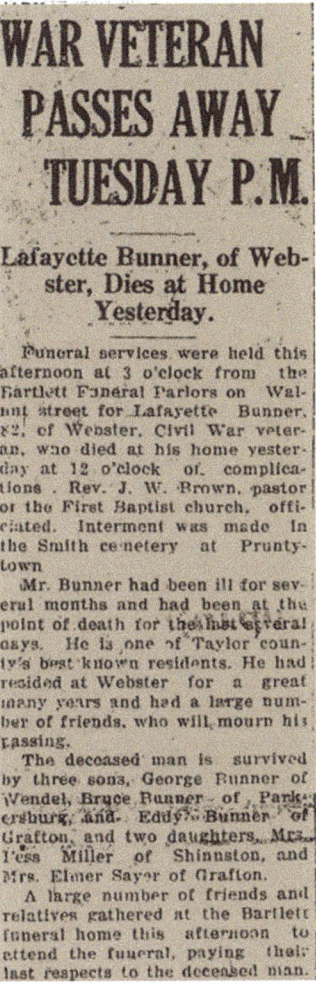

**Lafayette Bunner Obituary - Grafton Sentinel
Wednesday February 10, 1926**

In 2008 and 2009, while doing family research, Lafayette's great-great-great grandson, Greg Bunner tried unsuccessfully to locate the long-forgotten gravesite of Lafayette Bunner. His luck changed when he visited the West Virginia State Archives Library in Charleston, WV in 2009. Here, while investigating Lafayette's Civil War background, a 1934 map of Smith Cemetery in Pruntytown was discovered. This map, which showed the gravesites of Union Civil War veterans who were buried in the cemetery, was also able to locate the gravesite of Lafayette Bunner.

In 2009, Greg revisited Smith Cemetery in Pruntytown and, by taking precise measurements as shown on the map, was able to pinpoint the site of Lafayette's grave. On Memorial Day 2018, Greg took his uncle Michael Bunner to visit Lafayette's gravesite. After the visit, they made the decision to purchase a small granite ground level grave marker to place on his grave. Greg commissioned the marker to be engraved by a company in Parkersburg and returned in July 2018 to permanently place the marker on Lafayette's grave. Descendants can now easily locate Lafayette's gravesite after eighty-three years of being forgotten and ninety-two years of being unmarked.

**Lafayette Bunner Grave Marker Placed by 3X great grandson Greg Bunner - July 2018**

*11.*

# Alexander Bruce Bunner
## *(1873 – 1938)*

Alexander Bruce Bunner was the sixth child and third son of Lafayette and Mary Shingleton Bunner. He was born at the home of his parents on Husted Run near the small town of Hepzibah in Taylor County, West Virginia. Several records exist saying he was born in 1873, several say 1874, and one record – his marriage license – says 1875. The earliest record of Bruce is the 1880 census, which records his birth in 1873. The last record – the date recorded on his tombstone - also says 1873. No birth record has ever been found, so a birth date of 1873 is assumed.

Alexander Bruce was named after his grandfather, Alexander, who lived nearby at the time Bruce was born. His grandfather died in August 1874 at the age of seventy-one or seventy-two, meaning Bruce would have no memories of him. Bruce's grandmother, Lydia, also lived nearby so he would have visited her as a child and would have formed memories of her. Unfortunately, Lydia's health declined significantly in the late 1870's and by the time of the 1880 census she was bedridden with dementia. She died in 1882 at the age of eighty-one. Bruce was nine years old.

Bruce grew up near the small town of Hepzibah on Hustead Run in the Booths Creek District of Taylor County, West Virginia. This community is located on present-day State Route 3 approximately two miles north of U.S. Route 50 between Bridgeport, West Virginia and Pruntytown, West Virginia.

It is unclear if Bruce attended school as a child. However, according to the 1880 census, when Bruce was six, his older brothers and sisters were attending school. Bruce's mother, Mary, could read and write, and it appears she was intent on making certain that all her children were also able to do so. She may have taught them herself. In all censuses conducted after 1900, all her children indicated they could read and write – except Bruce. Bruce indicated on the 1900 census that he could neither read nor write. He still signed his name by affixing an "X" for his mark. However, in the 1910 census he indicated he could read but not write. In both the 1920 and 1930 censuses he indicated that he could read and write.

Bruce learned the skills of subsistence farming from his father on the family's seven-acre farm. His father also taught him how to shoot a gun and how to hunt in the forests along Husted Run.

By the time Bruce was seven, he had two new brothers and two new sisters. Six years later, in 1886, Lafayette and Mary had their eleventh child, Bruce's baby brother Eddie. Bruce was thirteen.[1]

When Bruce was fourteen, his mother became ill. The doctor who came to their house diagnosed her illness as Consumption (known today as tuberculosis). It is unknown what the doctor told Lafayette or what Lafayette told his children, but during the 1880's Consumption was considered a terminal disease. Doctor's didn't understand how it was contracted or how it was spread. They had no effective treatment for it. Approximately 10% of those who contracted Consumption survived and eventually recovered, but the other 90% slowly deteriorated with ever more severe symptoms. Death came to most within a year or two of contracting the disease.

It is now known that the disease is caused by bacteria and is spread to others who have personal contact or are in close proximity to those who have the disease. It is believed that Mary remained at home, and often in bed, as her disease progressed. It is miraculous

---

1  Bunner, Alan N., "The Bunner Family in America" Alexandria, Virginia 7,300+ page document on CD, revision dated June 25, 2012, Chapter 9, p. 295

that neither Lafayette nor any of his children contracted the disease from Mary.

On February 22, 1889, Bruce's mother died of Consumption.[2] She was forty-four. She left behind her forty-nine year old husband, Lafayette, and her ten living children ranging in age from twenty-three down to three. Lafayette's oldest daughter, Ella, had already assumed most of the housekeeping responsibilities during her mother's illness and continued to do so after her mother's death. James was twenty-three and within a few months after his mother's death he moved out and began working as a laborer on a neighbor's farm. Bruce and his older brother George continued helping their father with the daily farmwork. The younger children continued attending school during the day.

There was an 1890 census, but that data was lost due to a fire in Washington, D.C. at the Department of Commerce in 1921. What is known from other sources is that during the 1890's seven of Lafayette's children reached adulthood and left home.

James moved to Wood County, West Virginia in 1891 where he soon married Hannah Hardin, who had moved with her mother, Martha, and stepfather, Jacob, from the Hepzibah area to Parkersburg at about the same time as James had made that move.

Martha Gardner Hardin was a widow raising her daughter Hannah in Taylor County when she met Jacob Riffee, an older widower raising several children who lived nearby. They married in 1890[3] and Jacob adopted Martha's daughter, Hannah. It appears that Jacob and Martha were friends with James Bunner while they all were still living in Taylor County.

In 1891 Jacob and Martha moved their family to Wood County, West Virginia. Jacob had previously purchased property in the small town of Walker near the Baltimore and Ohio railroad stop, and this is where they settled. The proximity of the railroad stop to the land Jacob and his new family lived on suggests that the family

---

2 Death Record of Mary Shingleton Bunner. Taylor County Courthouse death records; Grafton West Virginia

3 Ritchie County, WV, Marriage Register Feb. 25, 1890, John Riffee (age 65) to Martha Hardin (age 49), p. 71

made the move from Taylor County to Wood County on the B&O Railroad from Grafton to Walker.

James Bunner may have accompanied Jacob and Martha on this move. If he did not, he moved from Taylor County to Wood County within a few weeks after James and Martha had moved there. From all indications, the force that drove James to make this move was his infatuation with Jacob and Martha's daughter, Hannah.

Hannah was only fourteen at the time, but she and James told her parents that they wanted to get married. Hannah's parents consented, and Jacob had to sign legal documents allowing the marriage. A short article in the Parkersburg Daily Sentinel on November 10, 1891, had the headline, "A Young Bride". The article states John [Jacob] Riffee secured a marriage license at the Wood County Clerk's office that morning for J.W. Bunner and Hannah Hardin.[4] James married Hannah in the Walker home of Hannah's mother and step-father on November 15, 1891.[5]

James was twenty-five when he married Hannah. He and his young wife took up residence near the small town of Dallison along the Northwestern Turnpike (present-day U.S. Route 50) about ten miles east of Parkersburg. There are no records that they purchased property in Wood County between 1891 and 1894, so they probably rented.

Regarding Bruce's father and siblings back in Taylor County during the 1890's, his older brother George married Zora Provance in Taylor County in 1892. They had a son, Walter, in 1893, but Zora died in 1895, possibly from complications of childbirth. George married Emma Rutherford in Taylor County in 1898 and moved to Marion County, West Virginia where he got a job as a fire-clay miner.[6]

Bruce's older sister Virginia ("Jennie") married Virgil Hillberry in 1893 and moved to Grafton where she had four children by 1899. It is unknown what Bruces younger sister Malinda was doing in

---

4 Parkersburg Daily Sentinel, November 10, 1891, "A Young Bride"

5 Wood Count Clerk's Office, Marriage License, James Bunner and Hannah Hardin, 1890, p. 137

6 Ancestry.com

1900, but she was not living at home. It is known that she married Sylvester Miller in 1907 and that they lived in the Clay District of Harrison County.[7]

Bruce's younger brother, Thomas, moved to Marion County circa 1898 and got a job as a coal miner. He married Mae Parker in 1902, and they had nine children over the next several years.[8]

Sometime between 1894 and 1899, Bruce's younger brother Charles "Homer" Bunner also moved to Wood County. It is unknown if he accompanied Bruce on the trip from Taylor County to Wood County in 1894 (when Bruce was twenty-one and Homer was seventeen), or if Homer waited a few years before moving. According to the 1900 Taylor County census, Homer was not living at home with his father in 1900, and the assumption is he moved to Wood County prior to that census.[9]

According to the 1900 census, the only children remaining at home in Taylor County with Lafayette were his oldest daughter Ella, (age 30), his youngest daughter Maud (19), and his youngest son Eddie (15).[10] It is known that Ella married Porter Morris in 1902 and they lived near Lafayette in Taylor County. Maud married Elmer Sayres in 1902 and moved to Grafton, where she lived the rest of her life.[11]

Back in Wood County, on June 8, 1893, James Bunner's father-in-law, Jacob, purchased his second parcel of property in Wood County. This was a ten-acre farm which included a house. It was eight miles from the property he already owned and lived on in Walker, West Virginia. The farm he purchased was located on top of a hill located about one mile south of the Northwestern Turnpike (U.S. Route 50) near Dallison, West Virginia.[12] It later became

---

7 Ancestry.com

8 Ancestry.com

9 Ancestry.com

10 1900 U.S Federal Census, Lafayette Bunner, Booths Creek, Pruntytown, Taylor, West Virginia, USA

11 Ancestry.com

12 Wood County Clerk's Office, Deed Book 77, p. 459

apparent that he purchased this farm in order to sell it to his stepdaughter Hannah and her husband James.

On May 26, 1894, Jacob Riffee sold this ten-acre farm with a house to James and Hannah Bunner.[13] Two months later, on July 31, 1894, Hannah gave birth to their first child, Mary Ellen Bunner, in this house.[14] The availability of extra rooms in this house may have been a factor in James inviting Bruce to move to Wood County. If he could tolerate the noise of the crying new baby, Bruce was welcome to live with his brother and sister-in-law in their new house.

As James now owned ten acres of farmland, Bruce could earn his keep by working in the fields, the only skill he had learned while he was growing up in Taylor County. Although Parkersburg was rapidly industrializing during the 1890's and factory jobs were available, the town was ten miles west of Dallison on the Northwestern Turnpike. Travel was still primarily by horse, and when it rained during the late 1890's and early 1900's, the Northwestern Turnpike turned into a muddy, impassable quagmire. It would have been impractical to live near Dallison and commute by horse each day to work at a factory job in Parkersburg. All evidence points to Bruce living with his brother James and sister-in-law Hannah near Dallison between 1894 and 1899.

Sometime between 1894 and 1900, Bruce's younger brother Homer moved from Taylor County to Wood County. He probably lived for a time at the home of James and Hannah Bunner on the hill above Dallison along with Bruce. Homer and Bruce probably served as farmhands for James, tending the gardens and livestock in return for room and board.

On March 20, 1897, James and Hannah had their second daughter, Cordelia Louisa. Their house had started to become crowded.

There are no archives that shed light on the whereabouts and activities of Bruce Bunner from the time he arrived in Wood County until he married Maggie Townsend in 1899. It is unknown how Bruce and Maggie met. One clue may come from the 1900

---

13  Wood County Clerk's Office, Deed Book 77, p. 459

14  Ancestry.com

Walker District, Wood County, West Virginia census. It reveals that Peter A. Townsend, Maggie's father, lived within two or three farms of James and Hannah Bunner near Dallison.[15] If Bruce lived in such close proximity to Maggie beginning in 1894, there would have been ample opportunity for them to meet over the next five years before they were married.

Bruce Bunner and Maggie Townsend were married on April 13, 1899, in Wood County, West Virginia.[16] Bruce was twenty-six and Maggie was nineteen. They were married by Reverend Daniel Smith, a local Methodist minister, at the house of Maggie's father. Reverend Smith had also married James and Hannah Bunner eight years earlier.

Maggie Leota Townsend was born to Peter ("Pete") Townsend and Mary ("Mollie") Givens Townsend on May 26, 1880, near Ravenswood in Jackson County, West Virginia. According to the 1900 Federal Census records, Peter's parents were from New Jersey and Mary's parents from Pennsylvania. The 1900 census recorded that Peter could read but not write, and Mary could read and write. Peter was recorded as a general farmer. There is no death record for Peter on file at the Wood County Courthouse. However it is known that he died in Belpre, Ohio on November 24, 1924.[17]

Pete's father was John Townsend who was born in 1797 in Burlington, New Jersey. His mother was Ann Marie Williams Townsend. She was born in New Jersey in 1809. John and Ann had moved to Jackson County, Virginia (present-day West Virginia) after 1841. Pete was born in Jackson County on December 5, 1847.

Mary Givens, Peter's wife, was the daughter of John Givens and Hannah Wilson Givens, both born in Pennsylvania. At the time of Mary Givens birth on March 29, 1850, John and Hannah Givens resided in Belmont County, Ohio.

---

15  1900 U.S. Federal Census, Walker District, Wood County, West Virginia

16  Wood County Clerk's Office, Marriage Records, Bruce Bunner and Maggie Townsend

17  Ancestry.com

**Pete and Mollie Townsend Family circa 1902**
Boy standing on left thought to be Walter. Adults on second row left to right are Peter, "Mollie", Maggie, and Mazie. Boy with bow-tie thought to be John, girl standing in rear thought to be Anna Bell. Maggie may be holding infant son Robert Harrison Bunner

Mary "Mollie" Givens Townsend died September 26, 1927. Her death certificate states the cause of death as "Insanity".[18] Her obituary states "Complications due to her advanced years."[19] It seems that Mary was afflicted with what is today known as Alzheimer's disease, the same disease her daughter Maggie would suffer from prior to own death in 1958.

Both Peter and Mary Townsend are buried in the Core Cemetery, located on Core Road which runs along the eastern edge

---

18  Wood County Clerk's Office, Death Certificate, Mary Townsend, Sept. 26, 1927

19  Parkersburg News, Mary Townsend Obituary, Sept. 27, 1927

of Parkersburg. Peter and Maggie have a modern granite headstone thought to have been installed sometime after 1980, likely by members of the Townsend family. The tombstone includes the names of their three daughters who preceded them in death.

Following the marriage of Bruce Bunner and Maggie Townsend in 1899, they rented a log cabin located near the end of what was known in the early 1900's as Alton Hollow Road. Their first child, Robert Harrison Bunner, was born there on June 6, 1900.[20] (This road became known as Dawson's Run in the 1970's. After the new four-lane U.S. Route 50 was built during the 1970-1972 period, several Dawson families who had been displaced by the new highway built houses along this road.)

Alton Hollow Road was a dirt road that ran north from U.S. Route 50 in Dallison. It was a dead end road that was less than a mile long. There was only one house on this road prior to 1970, an old log cabin that had several additions built on through the years. This is where Bruce and Maggie Bunner lived after they were married and where their son Robert was born. The old house, including the original cabin, caught fire due to an electrical malfunction circa 1982 and burned to the ground. A house trailer, which still remains, was set at this site within a few months after the fire.

The 1900 census records that Bruce was twenty-seven years old and Maggie was twenty. They were living in the cabin they were renting on Alton Hollow Road. This census recorded that Bruce could neither read nor write, but that Maggie was able to read and write. Bruce and Maggie lived within two farms of Maggie's maternal grandmother, Hannah Wilson Givens. Bruce is listed as a general farmer.

By early 1901, Bruce and Maggie moved with their new son to a rental house and farm located along the Northwestern Turnpike on the east side of Dallison. According to a 1979 interview with Mable Bunner (daughter-in-law to Bruce and Maggie), this farm was owned by the Congleton family and was near the intersection of Progress Ridge Road and U.S. Route 50 (Northwestern Turnpike).

---

20 Ancestry.com

Old Wood County courthouse records revealed that this farm was owned by D.D. Congleton. It was a house on approximately thirty acres of land located on the south side of U.S. Route 50. It was almost straight down the hill from the George Bunner farm where Bruce had lived before he married Maggie. The house was located approximately ½ mile east of Dallison and approximately ¼ mile west of Progress Ridge Road.

It is believed that Bruce's brother, Homer, had continued living with his older brother James near Dallison after Bruce and Maggie had married. On May 13, 1902, Homer married Hulda Riley in Wood County. After Homer's marriage, he and his new wife remained in Wood County, but their address is unknown. The 1910 census records that Homer was working as a laborer in the tie-hoist industry and that he and his family were living in a rented house near the Baltimore and Ohio railroad in the Clay District of Wood County. He and Hulda had three children by 1910.[21]

Bruce and Maggie were still living on the D.D. Congleton farm at the time of the 1910 census. On January 6, 1903, Bruce and Maggie's second child, John Andrew, was born at this location. No birth record for John was ever recorded. Many years later, John's birthplace was referred to as the "old Conklin place", or "Congleton place" by his wife, Mable Bunner.

There is a family tradition that, in addition to farming, Bruce made quite a bit of money on the side as a "horse trader," acquiring and selling things in whatever fashion he could. An elderly man claiming to have known Bruce Bunner once told Darrell Bunner, a resident of Dallison and a great-grandson of Bruce Bunner, that Bruce was notoriously good at "horse trading." He believed that because of Bruce's ability to earn a profit on most of his deals, he had a somewhat negative image among others in the community, especially those he had traded with. An objective observer would probably conclude that Bruce Bunner was a good businessman, and those who traded with him were not.

On January 28, 1907, a third son Franklin (Frank) was born to Bruce and Maggie. His birth is recorded at the Wood County

---

21  1910 U.S. Federal Census, Homer Bunner, Clay District, Wood County, West Virginia

courthouse. However only the last name "Bunner" is written on the birth record. The physician who completed the birth record was Dr. D.F. Ireland, a doctor who practiced in Dallison at the time.[22] Although the first name Frank is not recorded on the birth record, the date of birth leaves no doubt that this was the birth record of Frank Bunner.

In 1908, back in Taylor County, Bruce's father Lafayette sold the two parcels of property he owned for many years and that Bruce had grown up on.[23] All of Lafayette's children had grown and moved on with their own lives. Lafayette rented a house in Grafton where he lived with his youngest son, Eddie, who had taken a job in Grafton as a laborer for the Baltimore and Ohio Railroad.[24]

On August 3, 1909, William "Howard" Bunner, Bruce and Maggie's fourth son, was born on the D.D. Congleton farm near Dallison. The 1910 Census records that Bruce and Maggie's children living at home were Robert (age 9), John (7), Frank (3), and Howard (0).[25] Agnes and Kermit are not listed. Although the chronological order is unknown, Agnes and Kermit were born no earlier than June 1910 and no later than December 1918. They could have both been born before their sister Mary Ethel was born in 1915, or one could have been born before Ethel and one after Ethel. There is no birth record at the Wood County courthouse for either of the two.

The nineteen "teens" would be a tough time for Bruce and Maggie Bunner. In 1911, Bruce's older sister Virginia ("Jennie") died in Grafton at the age of forty. Her cause of death is unknown. She left behind her husband Virgil and four teenaged children, two sons and two daughters.[26] It is unknown if Bruce made the train trip to Grafton to attend Jennie's funeral.

---

22  Wood County Clerk's Office, Birth Records, 1907, "Bunner"
23  Taylor County Clerk's Office, Deed Book 47, p. 184
24  1910 U.S Federal Census, Lafayette Bunner, Fetterman District, Taylor, West Virginia
25  1910 U.S. Federal Census, Walker District, Wood County, West Virginia
26  Ancestry.com

In 1914, James William Bunner, the older brother who seems to have influenced Bruce to move from Taylor County to Wood County, and who was most likely the family member Bruce was closest to, died suddenly at his home high on the hill over Dallison.[27] No death record for James has been located, so his cause of death is unknown. James was forty-nine years old at the time of his death. He left behind his pregnant wife Hannah, and six children all living at home. James was buried at the Pleasant Valley Church Cemetery (Skidmore).

Bruce, Maggie, Robert, John, Frank, and Howard Bunner attended the funeral service and the burial of James Bunner. It is also reasonably certain that Homer Bunner and his family attended the funeral service and burial. There is no evidence that James's aging father, Lafayette, or any of James's siblings from Taylor, Marion, and Harrison counties attended the service.

Circa 1915, Bruce's brother Homer moved his family from Wood County, West Virginia to Columbiana, Ohio (near Youngstown) where he was hired as a laborer in a pottery factory. He and his wife Hulde had four children at the time they moved.[28] There is no record that Bruce had any contact with Homer or his family after they moved to this northern Ohio location.

Sometime between 1910 and 1917, Bruce and Maggie moved the family from the D.D. Congleton farm where they had been living since 1901 to the D.R. Congleton farm located approximately one mile to the east. This new farm was more remote, being almost a mile south of U.S. Route 50 and accessible only by a crude dirt road branching off Progress Ridge Road. This dirt road doubled as a creek after a heavy rain. The farm was surrounded on all sides by forests. Bruce and Maggie's nearest neighbor was more than ½ mile away.

---

27  Date of death on tombstone of James Bunner
28  1920 U.S. Census, District 105, East Liverpool Ward 1, Columbiana, Ohio

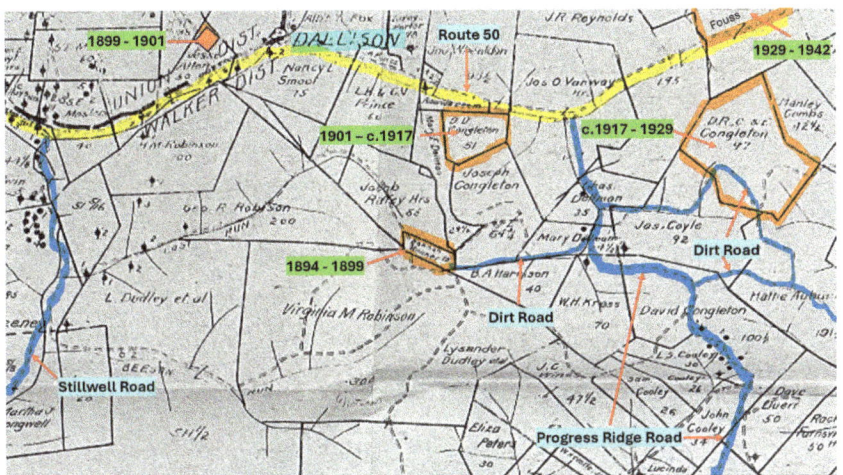

**Bruce Bunner rented homes near Dallison,
West Virginia area, 1894 – 1938**
(rental properties in orange, map shows 1925
Walker District, Wood County, WV farms)

It is believed that sometime in 1912 Maggie gave birth to her and Bruce's first daughter, Agnes. In 1914, World War I broke out in Europe and soon engulfed Russia, northern Africa, the Middle East, and Asia. The United States adopted a policy of neutrality and, although the carnage in the war zones was horrific, the war only peripherally impacted life in America through 1916.

In 1915, a daughter named Mary Ethel became the sixth child born to Bruce and Maggie. The Bunner family continued their daily farm routines almost oblivious to the devastating events taking place daily in other parts of the world. It is believed that in late 1917 or early 1918, they welcomed their seventh child and fifth son, Kermit, into the family

Although the United States had succeeded in maintaining neutrality during the first three years of the war, that all changed in early 1917. With the German resumption of unrestricted submarine warfare on American ships, President Woodrow Wilson asked Congress to declare war on Germany. Congress passed the war resolution on April 6, 1917, and the United States entered World War I.

As a result of America's entry into the war, all able bodied men in the United States between the ages of 21 and 31 were required to register for the selective service draft. As the war continued, the window expanded on the ages of men required to register. The "Third Registration" approved by Congress on September 12, 1918, required all men between the ages of 18 and 45 to register.

As Bruce was age forty-four, he was required to register. His oldest son Robert, who had just turned 18, was also required to register. John was only 15, so he was still too young.

Bruce's World War I draft card provides one of the only physical descriptions that exist of him. It depicts Bruce as being tall, of medium build, with blue eyes and brown hair. His mailing address was Route 1, Eaton, West Virginia, confirming that he and his family were living on the D.R. Congleton farm at the time he registered for the draft. The address for the D.D. Congleton farm, where Bruce and his family had lived from 1901 until sometime after 1910, was Walker, West Virginia. Bruce's registration date for the draft was September 1918.

Fortunately for those potential draftees in this "Third Registration," the war effectively ended eight weeks later. On the 11th hour of the 11th day of the 11th month of 1918, the Armistice with Germany went into effect. The end of World War I was formalized with the signing of the Treaty of Versailles on June 28, 1919.

As a result of this treaty, Bruce Bunner and his oldest son Robert were never called to serve. Afterward, November 11 was celebrated as Armistice Day in America until 1954, when Congress officially changed its name to Veteran's Day to honor all military veterans.

It is estimated that 20 million persons were killed during World War I. However, as the war was winding down in 1918, another scourge was emerging that would kill an estimated 50 to 100 million people worldwide. This scourge would soon hit the Bruce and Maggie Bunner family and result in the death of three of their seven children.

Frank, Kermit and Agnes Bunner all had short lives. If not for the oral family history, three small granite stones at Skidmore Cemetery purchased during the 1940's by John and Mabel Bunner, and a sentence in Maggie Bunner's 1958 obituary stating she was preceded in death by two sons and one daughter, there would be no evidence that Agnes and Kermit ever existed.

The lives of Frank, Kermit, and Agnes Bunner were cut short by the global Spanish flu pandemic of 1918-1919. According to Mabel Bunner, Frank, Kermit and Agnes all died from this lethal strain of influenza within several weeks of each other during 1918.[29] Frank would have been about eleven years old, Agnes may have been about six, and Kermit was likely still an infant. All three are buried in adjacent graves at Pleasant Valley Church Cemetery (Skidmore). The three small stones are engraved with their names but show no dates. These stones not only mark the lives of Frank, Agnes and Kermit Bunner, but also silently mark the Bunner family connection with the influenza epidemic of 1918-1919.

**Frank, Agnes, and Kermit Bunner died during the Spanish Flu Epidemic of 1918 – 1919**
(photographs by Greg Bunner)

During this same period of time, Maggie had two sisters die as well. Her twenty-nine year old sister Minerva Maude Townsend and her twenty-five year old sister Anna Bell Townsend Riser died during the influenza epidemic in 1918 and 1919.[30] According to Anna Bell's obituary, her husband, Thomas Riser, had died six months before her death. The timing of his death also suggests that he succumbed to the Spanish flu.

---

29  Mable Bunner interview with Mike Bunner, 1979

30  Ancestry.com

Back in Taylor County, Bruce's youngest brother Eddie had married Emma Thorn in Grafton on April 24, 1917. Emma was a young widow with two children. She had married James Musgrove circa 1906, and James had died in 1911. She married Eddie Bunner in April 1917 and died one year later on July 30, 1918.[31] Her death certificate states tuberculosis as the cause of death, but it could have also been the Spanish flu, which killed over 675,000 Americans in 1918 and which had symptoms similar to tuberculosis.

In 1919 Bruce and Maggie's eighth child, Dale Herbert, was born. In 1921, their final child, Carl Eugene, was born. When Carl was born, Bruce was approximately forty-eight years old and Maggie was forty-one.

The 1920 Walker District, Wood County, West Virginia Census records all of Bruce and Maggie's living children still living at home on the D.R. Congleton farm. Neighbors in 1920 were J.P. and Susan Boyce on one side and John T. Frost on the other.[32]

(John Frost is believed to be the man Mabel Bunner was referring to in her 1979 interview when describing a property that adjoined the property she and her husband John were renting during the 1930's. Mable referred to this adjoining property, as the "Old Frost Place".[33] This seems to confirm that the house Bruce and Maggie lived in at the time of the 1920 census was the same house John and Mable Bunner lived in when they returned from Zanesville, Ohio during the Great Depression in 1933.)

This 1920 Census record is the first record showing Bruce being able to read and write. It is unknown if Maggie helped Bruce improve his reading and writing skills after they were married, as in the 1900 census Bruce is recorded as being illiterate, unable to read or write.

All three of Bruce and Maggie's children over age six (Robert, John and Howard) were listed as able to read and write. Robert is listed as never having attended school, but John and Howard are listed as having attended school. In 1979, Mable Bunner stated that

---

31  Ancestry.com
32  1920 U.S. Federal Census, Walker District, Wood County, West Virginia
33  Mable Bunner interview with Mike Bunner, 1979

John completed sixth grade, which was the maximum extent of schooling for most children in the early 1900's. [34]

Back in Taylor County, the 1920 census revealed that Bruce's father Lafayette had moved from Grafton, where he had lived with his youngest son Eddie since 1908, back to the Hepzibah area. This move probably occurred in 1917 at the time Eddie had married Emma Thorn. Lafayette was living on a farm with his older sister Eliza and some of her children. Lafayette was seventy-nine and Eliza was eighty-one.[35]

On April 29, 1921, Eliza J. Bunner Barker, the sister Lafayette was living with in 1920, died of neuritis.[36] It is unclear if Lafayette continued to live with Eliza's children, but it is possible that he did. He was now eighty one years old and all of his family had moved away except Eddie. Eddie had married his second wife, Mary Elizabeth Neal, on April 20, 1920, and had purchased a small farm on the western side of Grafton.[37] It is possible that after Eliza died in 1921, Lafayette may have moved back to live with his son Eddie and his new wife.

Lafayette's health and finances had declined sufficiently by 1925 that he was assigned by the Taylor County agency responsible for the welfare of old, infirmed, and impoverished residents of Taylor County to the County Infirmary.[38] This was more commonly known as the "County Poor Farm." Lafayette had resided at the Poor Farm for ten months when he died on February 9, 1926, at the age of eighty-six.[39] His funeral and burial were held the following day [40],

---

34 1920 U.S. Federal Census, Walker District, Wood County, West Virginia

35 1920 U.S Federal Census, Lafayette Bunner, Booths Creek District, Taylor, West Virginia, USA

36 Eliza J. Boner Barker death record. West Virginia State Archives; Charleston, West Virginia

37 Ancestry.com

38 Taylor County Infirmary Register. West Virginia State Archives microfilm;Charleston West Virginia.

39 Lafayette Bunner death record. West Virginia State Archives; Charleston West Virginia-website.

40 Lafayette Obituary, Grafton Sentinel Feb. 10, 1926- copy obtained from West Virginia State Archives Library micro-film records of Taylor County; Charleston,

so it is doubtful that Bruce attended the funeral. It is even doubtful that Bruce learned of his father's death until several days after it happened.

In October 1929, the U.S. stock market collapsed. Although financial tycoons on Wall Street were jumping off buildings in New York City in despair, the impact was not immediately felt by most Americans. It would take another three to four years before the full impact of the stock market collapse would be felt by the average U.S. citizen.

The 1930 Walker District, Wood County, West Virginia Census would be the last census to include Bruce. This census record revealed that Bruce and Maggie had moved from the D.R. Congleton farm, where they had lived for approximately ten years, to what was commonly known as the "Fouse place" but which Mable Bunner called "the Prunty Place." [The original German settlers spelled their name 'Fauss,' but the spelling was changed to 'Fouse' by subsequent generations.] It was a house on approximately 200 acres located on the north side of the Northwestern Turnpike, officially known as U.S. Route 50 after 1930.[41] It was approximately one mile north – through the woods – of the D.R. Congleton farm where Bruce and Maggie had been living.

Locals called this new area where Bruce and Maggie now lived "Pleasant Valley". According to the 1930 census, new neighbors of Bruce and Maggie in Pleasant Valley were the Reese, Allman and Dunlap families. (This house in Pleasant Valley was the same house John and Mabel Bunner would live in from 1942 until 1946.) The 1930 census recorded that Bruce and Maggie's four youngest children, Howard, Ethel, Dale and Carl, were still living at home. Robert and John were gone.

---

West Virginia.

41  1930 U.S. Federal Census, Walker District, Wood County, West Virginia

**Siblings Mazie Townsend Buck, Walter Townsend,
Maggie Townsend Bunner circa 1925**

Robert had married Minnie Buck in 1925 [42] and moved to Parkersburg where he got a job as a laborer at the new American Viscose manufacturing company located along the Little Kanawha River in South Parkersburg. He was employed as a "spinner" in the rayon manufacturing process. He and Minnie rented a house on Ward Street on the Parkersburg "south side". This house was near the American Viscose factory which allowed Robert to walk to work.[43]

John Bunner and Mable Reynolds were engaged in 1922 just before her family moved from the Walker-Eaton area of Wood County to Zanesville, Ohio where Mable's father had accepted a job working for a dairy. John stayed behind in Wood County and worked for the State Road improving and upgrading U.S. Route 50 through the county. This road essentially followed the old Northwestern Turnpike but would be straighter, wider, and paved. When the project John was working on was completed circa November 1922, he travelled to Zanesville, Ohio where he and Mable were married

---

42  Wood Count Clerk's Office, Marriage Records, 1880-1925
43  1930 U.S. Federal Census, Tygart District, Wood County, West Virginia

on January 5, 1923. In 1924, John got a full time job as a "tile glazier" working for the A.E. Tile Company in Zanesville. By the time of the 1930 U.S. census, John and Mable had three children, Ellen, Ruth, and Don.[44]

The gradual decline in the strength of the U.S. economy in the early 1930's was slow, steady, and insidious. Banks were failing, companies and stores were closing, and the first generation of Americans ever to earn their living doing something other than farming was about to be forced to dust off their farming skills in order to survive.

By 1932, the economy had moved beyond a recession into the realm of a full-fledged depression. A quarter of all American workers were unemployed and hundreds of thousands had lost their homes due to foreclosure. In America's mid-western farm states, a debilitating drought forced tens of thousands of farmers to abandon their farms, setting off a great migration to California. Hunger was endemic and long food lines proliferated as people waited for hours for a one day supply of food. The homeless set up encampments in virtually every major U.S. city. Private charitable organizations ran out of funds to provide for such basic necessities as food, clothing, and medicine.

In this environment it is little wonder that Franklin Roosevelt won the 1932 election over incumbent Herbert Hoover. Roosevelt prevailed by selling hope and promising that government would prove to be the savior. But after Roosevelt was elected, the economy continued deteriorating.

In early 1933, at about the same time as Roosevelt was inaugurated as President, John Bunner lost his job at the A.E. Tile Company. With so many in the local community now unemployed, there were no other viable opportunities for employment in Zanesville. By the summer of 1933, John and Mable were back in Wood County, West Virginia where they rented the D.R. Congleton farm where John had lived with his family before leaving for Zanesville in 1922. This was approximately one mile from where Bruce, Maggie, and their

---

44   1930 U.S. Federal Census, District 53, Zanesville, Muskingum County, Ohio

younger children were living. This is where John, Mable, and their five children would endure the Great Depression.

**Bruce and Maggie Bunner at Parkersburg City Park – September 5, 1938**

At 5:00 A.M. on December 18, 1938, Alexander Bruce Bunner died suddenly from a heart attack at his home in Pleasant Valley. The cause of death was arterial sclerosis. He was sixty-four years old.[45] Bruce was the first Bunner known to have this heart disease, which plagued several of Bruce's male descendants for the next three generations.

---

45  Wood Count Clerk's Office, Death Certificate, Alexander Bruce Bunner, 1938

At the time Bruce died, sons Dale and Carl were still living at home with Bruce and Maggie.

Don Bunner, son of John and Mable Bunner and grandson of Bruce and Maggie, was the only person still alive in 2010 who could remember the events surrounding Bruce's death. Don was eight years old when Bruce died. His memories, as told to Greg Bunner, follow:

> "I remember we heard Carl [Johns youngest brother, age seventeen at the time] yelling, "John, John, John" before we could ever see him when he was coming up the hill to the house to tell us Bruce had died.
>
> I remember going to the funeral. The Pleasant Valley church was packed. It seemed like people came from all over. I remember singing songs in the church at the funeral. When going up the hill to the cemetery, the hearse got stuck in the mud and some guys had to help push it up the hill.
>
> I remember seeing Bruce as a kid. He looked a lot like Glenn and Robert [Don's younger brothers]. Robert especially looked like Grandpa Bunner."

Leavitt Funeral Home of Parkersburg handled the burial arrangements. The funeral service for Bruce was held on December 20, 1938, two days after his death and five days before Christmas. It was held at the Pleasant Valley Baptist Church, less than a mile from where Bruce lived. Reverend Moats officiated the service.[46]

Following Bruce Bunner's death, Maggie remained living with her sons Dale (age 19) and Carl (age 17) at the house where Bruce died. In 2010, Don Bunner, who got on and off his school bus in front of his grandmother's house each day recalled:

> "I remember visiting Grandma Bunner on my way to school. Grandpa Bunner had already died. I would stop and milk her two

---

46 Parkersburg News, Dec. 19, 1938, Bruce Bunner Obituary

cows on my way to school when I was attending Pleasant Hill School. Sometimes I would stop and visit on my way home as well".

During this time in both Europe and Asia, World War II was raging. Nazi Germany and its ally Italy had conquered most of mainland Europe. Japan had conquered huge swaths of Asia, including the Philippines Islands, Indonesia, Singapore, Hong Kong, Burma, Guam, and parts of China. As in World War I, the United States had tried to stay out of the war by remaining neutral.

Everything changed on December 7, 1941, when Japan attacked the American Pacific fleet based in Pearl Harbor, Hawaii. The United States declared war on Japan and Germany the following day. Virtually overnight, the American war effort began.

Maggie's two sons who were living at home enlisted. Dale enlisted in the Army on August 8, 1942, where he served in the 494th Bomb Group in the U.S. Army Air Corps. The 494th Bombardment Group, or "Kelly's Cobras", was the last B-24 Liberator bombardment group to be dispatched from the United States during the World War II. The group entered combat with a series of attacks on Japanese held islands in the Palau group (approximately 500 miles southeast of the Philippines), and the first of a long series of attacks on the Philippines, including the islands of Luzon, Corregidor, and Mindanao.

On June 24, 1945, the group moved to Okinawa. Its aircraft began to arrive on July 1, and on July 5 forty-eight aircraft from the 494th became the first Liberator bombers to attack the Japanese home islands from Okinawa. Their targets were Japanese airfields, starting with Omura Airfield and facilities around the Nagasaki area. During the last two months of the war the group attacked targets on the Japanese islands and in Japanese occupied China. The group was in the air making bombing runs when the first atomic bomb was detonated over Hiroshima on August 6, 1945. After the end of the war the 494th was used to transport personnel and supplies into Tokyo and to liberate Allied prisoners of war being held in

Japan.[47] Dale was honorably discharged from the Army Air Corps on February 15, 1946.

Carl enlisted in the Army on October 20, 1942, and served as a bombardier in the 529th Bombardment Squadron in the Army Air Corps for the duration of the war. After training as a heavy bomber unit in B-24's at Davis Monthan Air Base in Arizona, the unit moved to the Southwest Pacific Theater, entering combat in May 1943, flying combat missions from Australia while attached to the Royal Australian Air Force. In 1945 it moved forward to the Philippines, then to Okinawa. Following V-J Day, the squadron returned to the Philippines and was inactivated there in February 1946.[48] Carl was honorably discharged from the Army Air Corps on October 4, 1945, six weeks after Japan surrendered to end the war.

In 1942, with both Dale and Carl fighting in the war, Maggie was suddenly living alone. She was sixty-two, and although her grandsons Don, Robert, and Glenn stopped by frequently to do chores for her on their way to and from school, she knew she was incapable of fending for herself on the farm. She had neither the time, the energy, nor the stamina to do the farm work that had previously been done by Dale and Carl.

Maggie's oldest son Robert offered to have her live with him and his family on Ward Street in South Parkersburg. Maggie made that move in September or October 1942.

After Maggie had moved out of the Fouse house, John and Mabel Bunner moved from the D.R. Congleton farm into the Fouse house with four of their five children (Their daughter Ellen had married Burl Hewitt earlier in 1942). With the outbreak of the war, John had been hired by the O. Ames Company in South Parkersburg to make bomb casings for the war effort. He rode to and from work every day with Lester Dunlap who lived one farm down the road from the Fouse house.

---

47 http://www.historyofwar.org/air/units/USAAF/494th_Bombardment_Group.html#google_vignette

48 https://en.wikipedia.org/wiki/529th_Bombardment_Squadron

Living on U.S. Route 50 saved John a lot of time every day walking up and down the hill to the D.R. Congleton farm. It also made it easier to work the ten and eleven hour days O. Ames was requiring of all its employees to meet their aggressive manufacturing quota for bomb casings. Since John now lived closer to Lester Dunlap, Lester's travel time each day was also reduced.

While Dale was on a thirty day leave from the war, he married Edith Hescht on August 15, 1944.[49] After the war, Dale and Edith moved to a rental house at 3313 Kanawha Street in South Parkersburg. He got a job working as a millwright at the American Viscose factory where his older brother Robert was working.

After the war, on October 25, 1946, Carl married Anna Gantz.[50] They purchased a farm on State Route 31 with a mailing address of Waverly, West Virginia. Carl got a job working as an operator at the American Cyanamid chemical plant in Willow Island, West Virginia, about ten miles from where he lived.

Sometime in the late 1940's, while still living with her son Robert, Maggie started showing early signs of dementia. In late 1949 or early 1950, Carl and Anna agreed to take her in at their house on Route 31.[51] Over the next six years, Carl and Anna had five children – all boys. During this period, Maggie's condition continued to deteriorate. Her mind became very weak, and her body became frail. She began wandering off and not being able to find her way home. In 1956, Carl and Anna had their sixth child, a daughter named Karen. With the two-fold challenge of raising six children, including a newborn, while serving as a full-time caregiver to Maggie, Carl's wife Anna reached her human limits.

---

49  Wood Count Clerk's Office, Marriage Records, 1944, Dale Bunner and Edith Hescht

50  Wood Count Clerk's Office, Marriage Records, 1946, Carl Bunner and Anna Gantz

51  U.S. Federal Census, Union District, Wood County, West Virginia

**Maggie Bunner circa 1950**

John and Mable wanted to help, but their house was full. John and Mable's son Glenn, his wife Dorothy, and their young children Babara and Larry were living with them. Also, their son Robert's two little boys, Mike and Darrell were living with them. There was no physical space available for them to also accommodate Maggie.

This changed in the spring of 1957. Robert had married Rosie Carpenter in 1955. John and Mable purchased the old house in Dallison owned by widow Hattie Henderson after she died in 1955. The house was in great disrepair, but John and Mable spent over a year fixing it up to make it livable again. In early 1957 Robert and Rosie moved into this house, and Mike and Darrell moved in with them. This freed up the space in John and Mable's house for them to take in Maggie.

Maggie moved to John and Mable's house in the spring of 1957. Her memory was completely gone, and she rarely uttered a coherent sentence. With John still working at O. Ames, it fell completely on Mable to be Maggie's caretaker.

John and Mabel gave Maggie their downstairs bedroom. They slept upstairs where Mike and Darrell had slept for the previous four years. There are several memories that family members have of this time that Maggie was living with John and Mable. Some of these memories include:

- Maggie would collect pencils and pens from around the house and hide them in her bedroom.

- Maggie once filled the baby bottle of Larry Bunner (her great-grandson) with bleach and gave it to him to drink. Fortunately, Mable saw what she had done and took the bottle from Larry before he could drink it.

- She frequently announced she was going to go visit her son Robert, whom she believed lived "just on the other side of the hill." John would try to reason with her by telling her that Bob lived ten miles away, and, failing at persuasion, would ultimately take her by the hand and lead her back into the house.

- When she was not being watched, Maggie would often wander off, requiring John or Mable to go looking for her. It got so bad that John would lock her in her bedroom when he and Mable had to go outside to work in their garden for a while. They still frequently checked on her to ensure she was all right.

- She often would talk to dolls as if they were her children. She would call them by her children's names and then engage in discussions with them that only she could understand. She would also cover the dolls with newspapers before she would go to bed each evening so they wouldn't get cold during the night.

On March 21, 1958, Maggie died while sitting in the rocking chair in the living room of John and Mable's house. She was seventy-eight years old.

According to Mable, who was sitting in the room with her when she died, Maggie's last actions and words were to raise her right hand to her forehead and say, "I have a bad headache." That was quite a lucid statement from a woman who had been unable to utter a lucid statement for several years.

She was dead on arrival at Camden Clark Hospital in Parkersburg and was given a death time of 6:30 pm. Her cause of death was recorded as natural causes. [52] Because of her last words, Mable always believed she actually died of a brain hemorrhage.

Maggie's funeral was held on March 24, 1958. She was buried at Pleasant Valley Church cemetery (Skidmore) beside her husband Bruce.

## The Children of Bruce and Maggie Bunner

### Robert Harrison Bunner

Robert ("Bob") Bunner worked at the American Viscose rayon factory in South Parkersburg for most of his working life. He and his wife Minnie Buck Bunner lived in a rental house on Ward Street in South Parkersburg from 1928 until about 1954 when they purchased a small farm on State Route 31 (near his brother Carl) with a mailing address of Waverly, West Virginia. He became a gentleman farmer in his spare time, raising, among other things, chickens and ducks. Bob and Minnie had three daughters: Betty (1925 – 2014), Helen (1927 – 2007), and Minnie (1931 – 2008). Bob died on June 19, 1970, at the age of seventy. He is buried at Arlington Cemetery (Evergreen North) in Parkersburg, West Virginia. Minnie died in 1997 and is buried beside him.

**John Andrew Bunner** will be discussed in the next chapter of this book.

---

52  Wood County Clerk's Office, Death Certificate, Maggie Bunner, Mar. 21, 1958

## William Howard Bunner

Howard Bunner and Margaret Modesitt were married in 1936. Howard started working for the American Viscose company in South Parkersburg that same year. Howard and Margaret lived on Juniper Steet near the American Viscose factory. The 1940 census records that Howard and Margaret were living on Rayon Drive in South Parkersburg, and that Howard was working as a "bleacher" for American Viscose. They had a daughter Betsy who was born in 1937 and a son James born in 1938. According to the Glenn Bunner interview in 2010, Howard and his family were living on the "Allman place" on the western side of Pleasant Hill along U.S. Route 50 in 1946.[53] This was two farms east of where John and Mable were living at the time. The 1950 census shows Howard living in Roanoke, Virginia (the hometown of his wife). He was working for the Virginia State Road department as a "tar pourer." He and Margaret still had only two children.

Howard and Margaret moved to Columbus, Ohio circa 1956 where they lived until Howard's death on February 3, 1979, at the Ohio State University Medical Center.[54] Cause of death is unknown. Margaret moved back to Roanoke where she married George Howard Savage, Sr. on March 8, 1980. Margaret died on December 1, 2000.

## Frank Bunner

Frank was born near Dallison, West Virginia on January 28, 1907. He started attending school in 1913. In 1918 he contracted the Spanish flu and died at the age of eleven. He is buried at the Pleasant Valley Church Cemetery (Skidmore).

## Kermit Bunner

Kermit was born near Dallison, West Virginia. His birth date is unknown. In this chapter, his birth was assumed to be in late 1917

---

53 Glenn Bunner interview with Greg Bunner, 2010
54 Ancestry.com, Ohio, U.S., Death Records, 1908-1932, 1938-2022

or early 1918. However, it could have been as early as October 1910 and as late as December 1918. His short life was lived between the 1910 and 1920 census. He contracted the Spanish flu in 1918 and died. His age at death could have been as old as eight, or as young as a newborn. He is buried at the Pleasant Valley Church Cemetery (Skidmore).

**Agnes Bunner**

Agnes was born near Dallison, West Virginia. Her birth date is unknown. In this chapter, her birth was assumed to be in 1912. However, it could have been as early as October 1910 and as late as December 1918. Her short life was lived between the 1910 and 1920 census. She contracted the Spanish flu in 1918 and died. Her age at death could have been as old as eight, or as young as a newborn. She is buried at the Pleasant Valley Church Cemetery (Skidmore).

**Mary Ethel**

Ethel was born in 1915 and survived the 1918-1919 Spanish influenza pandemic that killed three of her siblings. She married Barney Clyde Modesitt in 1936. Barney's World War II draft card states he was working for the American Viscose company in South Parkersburg and that he and Ethel were living on Camden Avenue in South Parkersburg in 1942. It is unknown if Barney served in the military during the war. Barney and Ethyl were living in Cleveland, Ohio in 1957. John Bunner's January 1965 obituary states that Ethyl was living in Florida at that time. Ethel and Barney divorced in Cleveland on June 8, 1967, after thirty-one years of marriage. Barney died in Phoenix, Arizona on April 8, 1988. Ethel's place and date of death is unknown. There are no known children from this marriage.

**Dale Herbert Bunner**

Dale was a World War II veteran. He married Edith Hescht in 1944. After the war he got a job for a few years as a millwright at the American Viscose plant in South Parkersburg. While working there, he and Edith lived in a rental house on Kanawha Street in South Parkersburg. Around 1950 he got a job at the American Cyanamid factory in Willow Island, West Virginia. He lived at 2107 42nd street in Parkersburg for a few years. In the late 1950's he was living in a brick house he purchased on State Route 2 about a mile south of the Route 31 intersection.

He died on October 17, 1963, at age 44 from cancer. He is buried at the Willow Island Cemetery next to the plant where he worked. Children of Dale and Edith were Judith Ann (1949 – 2021), and Buddie Dale (b.1952) who was living in Vienna, West Virginia in 2022. Dale and Edith's first child, Gary Lee, died in infancy in 1947. After Dale's death, Edith remarried and had the last name of Stout. Edith died on July 27, 1976, and is buried beside Dale in Willow Island. The name "Stout" is also engraved on the tombstone over her name.

**Carl Eugene Bunner**

Carl lived on a 30 acre farm on Route 31 with a mailing address of Waverly, West Virginia. Carl was a World War II veteran and worked at American Cyanamid in Willow Island, West Virginia, the same place as his brother Dale. His wife was Anna Gantz. Carl died on July 14, 1975, at age fifty-four of a heart attack. He is buried at Riverview Cemetery in Williamstown, West Virginia. Children of Carl and Anna include Kenneth E. (born 1949), Roger Steven (1950), David (1951), Tom (1952), Denny (1953 – 1968), and Karen (1956). Carl's youngest son Denny was killed after being hit by a truck while crossing a road near his home in 1968.

*12.*

# John Andrew Bunner
## *(1903 – 1965)*

[Author's Note: John had two brothers and a sister who died during the Spanish flu epidemic in 1918. No birth records, death records, or family records exist for two of them - Kermit and Agnes Bunner. They are known of only through family oral history, grave markers bearing their names in the Pleasant Valley (Skidmore) Cemetery in Wood County, West Virginia, and a statement in their mother's 1958 obituary that she was preceded in death by two sons and one daughter. What is known is that Agnes and Kermit were born no earlier than June 1910 and no later than October 1918. For the sole purpose of depicting them as real people who once possessed the gift of life, I have arbitrarily given Agnes a birthdate of 1912 and Kermit a birthdate of 1918 in this narrative.]

John Andrew Bunner was born on January 6, 1903, on the D.D. Congleton farm his parents were renting on the Northwestern Turnpike on the eastern end of Dallison in Wood County, West Virginia.[1] He was the second child, and second son, of Alexander Bruce Bunner and Maggie Leota Townsend Bunner. John started learning farming skills from his parents at a young age, but at age six his parents enrolled him in the Pleasant Hill Elementary School. As they lived along the Northwestern Turnpike (present-day U.S.

---

1  Mable Bunner interview, 1979

Route 50), he was able to catch the "kid hack," a horse-drawn early version of the school bus, that transported him the two miles to and from school every day.

For unknown reasons, Bruce and Maggie never enrolled John's older brother, Bob, in school. Maggie taught Bob to read and write. John's younger brother Frank was only two years old and when John started going to school. As a result, John was the only member of his family to ride the "kid hack" to school each day until he entered his fifth grade year. Then Frank began riding with him.

John had to be at school by 8:00 A.M. each morning and was dismissed at 4:00 P.M. each day. The school year started in late September after the crops had been harvested. It ended in late April so the students could help their parents plow their fields and plant seeds as soon as the risk of frost had passed.[2]

Pleasant Hill was a one-room school where one teacher taught six different grades through the course of the day. John learned to read and write, and by second grade was learning basic arithmetic. He had to memorize a lot of things, such as the multiplication and division tables, the exact spelling of words, the names of states and continents, poems, and short Bible verses. John would practice his memorization assignments in his head while his teacher was teaching students in other grades during the school day.[3]

John's teacher used hornbooks and battledores to teach him how to read. Hornbooks were wooden paddles with the alphabet and a short text, often with a short Christian prayer such as "Our Father who art in heaven." Battledores were handout pamphlets with the alphabet and simple text, such as lists of one-syllable words or easy reading passages. After first grade, John improved his reading skills using McGuffey Readers. During his fifth and sixth grade years, books that John and his fellow students read out loud in school included "The Wizard of Oz" and "The Call of the Wild."[4]

---

2  Mable Bunner interviews with Mike Bunner 1965-69

3  Mable Bunner interviews with Mike Bunner 1965-69

4  Mable Bunner interviews with Mike Bunner 1965-69

In 1910, when John was in second grade, his brother Howard was born.[5] There were now four boys in the family and no girls. That changed in 1912 when his sister Agnes was born.

In April 1915, when John was twelve years old, he finished his sixth grade year. His formal education was completed. To receive further education would require that his parents pay for him to stay in a boarding house close to Parkersburg High School and that they pay the school a substantial tuition fee. This problem of distance and money is why most children living in rural areas of Wood County received only sixth grade educations in the early 1900's.[6]

In the summer of 1915, John's focus turned from school to helping his father and older brother, Bob, tend the family's gardens, fields, and livestock. The family had two milk cows and two work mules, so one large field was set aside for growing hay so the cows and mules would have food through the winter months. John became proficient at mowing this field with a mowing scythe and then using a mule to pull a hay rake to create haystacks.

The smaller gardens near the house were used for growing tomatoes, cucumbers, green beans, peas, lettuce, carrots, onions, and radishes. In addition to the large hayfield, there were two other large fields in the flat area between the Northwestern Turnpike and the creek which hugged the base of the mountain ridge behind their house. One of these fields was used for growing potatoes, the other for growing corn. Corn and potatoes were the primary staples that fed the family during the winter months. John's mother Maggie did most of the work in the smaller gardens. Bob and John were responsible for the potato and corn fields.

Both the potato and corn fields required work every day to keep the wild animals, the weeds, and the insects from destroying these crops. After the corn was planted, the fields had to be continuously monitored for deer that would come into the garden and eat the tender shoots of new corn. When the deer arrived, which they did almost every day, a family member had to immediately run out into the field to drive them away. John learned that after the corn plants

---

5  1910 U.S. Federal Census, Walker District, Wood County, West Virginia
6  Mable Bunner interview, 1979

had about ten leaves showing, the deer were no longer interested in eating them. Most years, corn would reach this size by the end of June. It was always a great relief to John when this day was reached each year because it meant the deer would no longer destroy their corn crop by eating the new plants.

Because of the size of the corn and potato fields, hoeing was required every day. It generally took four or five days to completely hoe one of the fields. As soon as one end of the field was reached, weeds were starting to grow again at the other end so the endless cycle was repeated.

As soon as the potatoes started sprouting by late May, potato beetles would begin eating the potato plants. If the beetles weren't removed from the plants, the plants would die and the potato crop would fail. The beetles were a continuous problem from late May until the potatoes were harvested in the fall. John spent many days each summer plucking beetles from the potato plants and putting them in mason jars. When the jars were full, he emptied the beetles onto the ground and quickly crushed them with large flat rocks so they couldn't fly back to the garden.

Harvest time in the fall required all family members to pitch in. The potatoes had to be dug, placed in a basket, and carried to the potato bin in the cellar house, a small stone building built into a steep earthen bank near the house. The cellar house was covered with two feet of dirt on top and surrounded by the earthen bank on three sides. Entrance was through a wooden door in the front. The potatoes could remain stored in the cellar house until spring without rotting.

Sweet potatoes were stored by digging a hole in the ground, burying them under several inches of dirt, and then covering the area with hay to mark the spot and to reduce the mud when it rained. They would be dug out of the hole in small family meal size quantities throughout the winter. When the corn was harvested, some was canned, some was ground into cornmeal for dry storage, and some was stored in an outdoor bin to supplement the hay the mules and cows ate through the winter.

Maggie had a large supply of quart and half-gallon mason jars that she used for canning food for the winter. In Septembers and

October each year, she spent virtually every day canning vegetables and fruit from their gardens so the family would have enough food to eat through the winter months. By the end of canning season, she would have approximately 800 jars of canned food in storage.

When all the harvesting and canning activities were completed each fall, the final activity to prepare for winter was to butcher one or two of the pigs. This was generally done in late November or early December to take advantage of the colder weather for natural preservation of the meat. On butchering day, John's father, Bruce, would shoot the pig with his rifle. John and Bob would then assist Bruce in dragging the pig out to an open field where they would use a rope and pulley to hoist the pig up by its hind legs on a tripod. The pig's throat was then cut to drain the blood. Using saws, cleavers, and knives, the pig was cut into small pieces that included pork chops, spareribs, bacon, and ham. Sausage was made from some of the pigs meat, and lard was made from its fat. The meat was sprinkled with salt to preserve it and then wrapped in butcher paper. Then it was placed in a cool, dry, dark outdoor storage building for the winter. The family would eat from this meat supply through the winter. By spring all the meat would be consumed.

Tending to the animals, bringing in water from the well, and chopping firewood were generally the only farming activities during the winter months. Each morning John would feed the chickens, and younger brothers Frank and Howard would gather the eggs. Bob would milk the cows. They took turns feeding the cows and the mules.

Bruce, Bob, and John were responsible for cutting down the trees during the spring and summer to make firewood. They used their mules to drag the cut trees back to the house. The small limbs would be cut off and stacked in a pile to be used as kindling. The trunk and the large limbs would be "seasoned" through the summer to dry the wood so the logs would be easier to burn in the winter. In the fall and early winter these trees were sawed into logs short enough to fit into their pot-bellied stove in the living room and the cooking stove in the kitchen. John and Bob then split these logs in half using iron wedges and a sledgehammer. These daily activities built not only calloused hands but also physical strength and stamina.

A larger pot-bellied stove was in the living room to keep the rest of the house warm during the winter. The stovepipe from this stove ran up through the living room ceiling. The heat did not circulate well into the bedrooms, so a large number of blankets and quilts were used to stay warm at night.

In September 1915, John's second sister, Mary Ethel, was born.[7] A few weeks later, Frank began his third grade year at school. John had completed his schooling and Howard was only five years old, The following year, in September 1916, Frank and Howard were both going to school while Bruce, Bob, and John took care of all the farm chores.

During this time John also began taking off from the farm a few hours each week to play baseball with other boys his age. There were sufficient other teenage boys living in the Dallison area that were also interested in playing baseball that they formed a team. During the summers of 1915, 1916, 1917, and 1918 John's team played other teams from Wood County. Over these four summers, he played first base, shortstop, and third base.[8]

John enjoyed playing baseball and was a good fielder and hitter. He dreamed of one day playing for the Cincinnati Red Legs. He accumulated a collection of baseball gloves from that era that he still had in the 1960's. On several occasions in 1959 and 1960, John got out two of his old baseball gloves and took his eight-year-old grandson Mike out in his yard to teach him how to catch and throw a baseball. In 1961, he taught Mike's younger brother, Darrell, how to do the same.[9]

Sometime between 1910 and 1917, Bruce and Maggie made the decision to move their family from the D.D. Congleton farm on the Northwestern Turnpike near Dallison to a more secluded farm approximately one mile to the east.[10] [11] This farm was owned by

---

7  1920 U.S. Federal Census, Walker District, Wood County, West Virginia

8  Mable Bunner interviews with Mike Bunner 1965-69

9  Memories of Mike Bunner

10  1920 U.S. Federal Census, Walker District, Wood County, West Virginia address is the D.R. Congleton Farm

11  Bruce Bunner World War I Draft Card, obtained in Sept 1918, shows Eaton Route 1, the address of the D.R. Congleton farm

D.R. Congleton, a relative of D.D. Congleton on whose farm Bruce and Maggie had been living since 1901. The D.R. Congleton farm was accessible only by a rough dirt road that branched off Progress Ridge Road. It was located approximately one mile south of the Northwest Turnpike over forest covered hills. The address of the new farm was Route 1, Eaton, West Virginia.

Just before the end of the school year in April 1917, the United States entered World War I by declaring war on Germany. All men between the ages of 21 and 31 were required to register with the Selective Service for the military draft. As Bruce was over 31 and Bob and John were under 21, this didn't impact the family, but it did impact many of the young men in Wood County. Some were drafted and went off to fight the war in Europe.

In early 1918, Maggie gave birth to a new brother, Kermit. He was Bruce and Maggie's seventh child.

Just before the end of the school year in April 1918, news began circulating about a strain of influenza that was more severe and lethal than the normal types of flu that people were accustomed to dealing with during the winters. Although this deadly strain of influenza did not originate in Spain, it was dubbed the "Spanish flu" because Spain was so transparent about communicating the severity of the symptoms and the number of deaths caused by this disease. There were many reported cases in the United States and a number of deaths, but health authorities believed this was simply a more virulent strain than normal seasonal flu. During the summer, the number of cases diminished and the "Spanish flu" was thought to have run its course.

During the late spring and summer of 1918, Bruce and Maggie's family engaged in normal daily farm activities. John still played baseball one or two times each week. The Parkersburg News was reporting that the Germans had begun a major offensive against the allied forces in Europe, and they seemed to be succeeding. On June 5, 1918, Congress called for a "Second Registration" for the military draft for all men in the United States who had turned age 21 since the first registration date of June 5, 1917. At this point, John and his family were more concerned about the progress of the war than the spread of the flu.

## JOHN ANDREW BUNNER

On September 12, 1918, Congress modified the Selective Service Act passed in 1917 to call for a "Third Registration" requiring all men between the ages of 18 and 45 to register. As Bruce was age forty-four, he was required to register, as was his oldest son Robert, who had just turned 18. John was only 15, so this mandate did not apply to him.

Within two weeks Bruce went to Parkersburg to register for the draft.[12] At about this same time, the school year started again with Frank entering fifth grade and Howard entering second grade.

Unbeknownst to anyone, the Spanish flu virus had mutated and rapidly spread among the allied military forces fighting in Europe. A military ship leaving Plymouth in England for Boston in August 1918 brought this new, very deadly strain of the virus to the United States. American soldiers who were being rotated out of combat service in Europe showed no symptoms of the flu when they boarded the ship. However, when these soldiers disembarked in Boston, a few had developed symptoms and were taken to infirmaries. Unfortunately virtually all of those who showed no symptoms were infected. As they and other soldiers returned to American ports and then to their home states over the next few weeks, they carried this deadly virus with them. As these soldiers returned home to points all across the United States, the virus began spreading like wildfire.

It is believed that within two weeks after returning to school in late September, Frank Bunner was exposed to the virus and contracted the Spanish flu. He became contagious and by the time he showed symptoms, his five year old sister Agnes and his nine month old brother Kermit had contracted the disease from him.

In early October 1918 it became obvious that an epidemic was rapidly spreading in the United States. Seeing how contagious and how lethal this strain of flu was, health authorities recommended that those with the disease be quarantined in rooms by themselves to minimize the spread. They advised people to avoid public meetings and other places where groups or crowds congregated. They suggested wearing masks.

---

12  Bruce Bunner World War I Draft Card, obtained in Sept 1918

Unfortunately, none of these actions helped those who had already contracted the disease. They developed fevers of 104°F, had persistent, deep, phlegm-filled coughs, severe headaches and other body pains. They had no energy and no appetite.

It is unknown what, if any, precautions Bruce and Maggie took to protect their four children who did not yet exhibit symptoms of the flu. It is doubtful that Maggie took many precautions for herself as she took care of Frank, Agnes, and Kermit. She gave them aspirin and placed cold, damp washcloths on their foreheads to try to counteract the high fevers. She ensured they were drinking plenty of water. She spoke comforting words to each of them. She prayed.

But Maggie knew from the public pronouncement of health authorities that there were no medicines or treatments to alleviate the symptoms of this disease. Not all who contracted the disease died, but many did. She may have even told Bruce to take the four healthy children to live in the barn or in one of the fields that had recently been harvested. In case she became infected and died, the children would at least have one parent.

During the full month of October 1918, 165,000 Americans died of the Spanish flu. Over the nine month period from October 1918 through June 1919, 675,000 Americans died. Three of them were Bruce and Maggie's children. According to Mable Bunner, Frank, Agnes, and Kermit Bunner all died within a few days or weeks of each other in late 1918. They did not have funerals.[13]

With the widespread panic across America that was induced by this epidemic, it is doubtful that any funeral home would have taken the bodies to prepare them for burial. With the United States suddenly in a full quarantine it is doubtful that caskets could be ordered and delivered. With so many unexpected deaths, the demand for caskets significantly exceeded the supply.

Taking these issues into account, the most likely scenario for the events following the deaths of his children is that Bruce built a rough wooden casket for each of them. John and Bob probably helped him to place their bodies inside. Bruce, Bob, and John likely took shovels and mattocks up the hill to the Pleasant Valley Cemetery and, over a

---

13  Mable Bunner interview, 1979

period of a few days to a few weeks, dug three graves. There they buried Frank, Agnes, and Kermit. Their graves were near that of Bruce's brother, James Bunner, who had died four years earlier in 1914.

There were no markers to show where the three children were buried. This must have tormented John's soul for the next twenty-five years because one of the first things he did after the Great Depression, when he had a little cash in his pocket for the first time in many years, was to buy grave markers for Frank, Agnes, and Kermit.[14]

The gloom and the grief brought on by their losses hung heavily over the Bunner household. It was exacerbated by the news from Maggie's family that her twenty-five year old brother-in-law, Thomas Riser, had succumbed to the Spanish flu at about the same time as Frank, Agnes, and Kermit. Three months later, Maggie's twenty-nine year old sister, Minerva Maude, died of the flu. Three month after that, in July 1919, Maggie's younger sister Anna Bell Riser, who had become a widow six months earlier when her husband, Thomas, died of the flu, also died from the disease.[15]

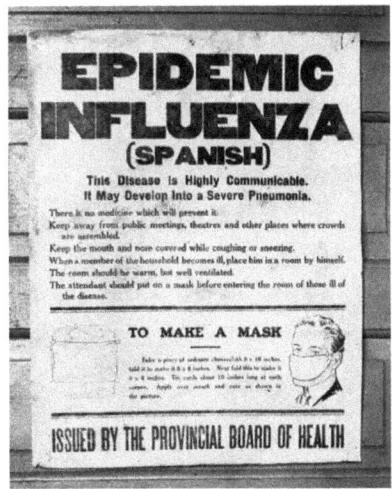

These Public Service Announcements by the various state Provincial Boards of Health were posted in virtually all public areas in the United States during late 1918 and 1919.

---

14  Mable Bunner interview, 1979
15  Anna Bell Riser obituary, Parkersburg News, July 23, 1919

At the same time as Maggie was having to bury three children, she realized she was pregnant again. This promise of new life helped to provide a little joy for a family that was overwhelmed with sorrow.

One can only marvel at the strength of character and the faith that Maggie and Bruce possessed to eventually recover from this horrendous tragedy. Sixteen-year-old John had to come to grips with the fragility and the shortness of life, and the recognition that events controlled him more than he had the ability to control events. John carried the pains from 1918 for the rest of his life, but he never talked about it.

One must also marvel at Providential fate. Maggie and Bruce were exposed to a deadly virus while caring for their dying children, and yet there is no evidence that either ever contracted the Spanish flu. John and Bob were young men when the epidemic hit. They were also exposed to the virus but if they did contract the disease, they survived. Perhaps the physical strength and good health they developed while performing the physically demanding, never-ending chores around their farm gave additional strength to their immune systems. That leaves eight year old Howard and three year old Ethel. Both had older and younger siblings die from the Spanish flu, yet the disease passed over them. Was it that they were born with immune systems uniquely prepared to ward off of the Spanish flu, was it Divine Providence, or perhaps a combination of the two?

During the time the Bunners were burying three members of their family, the allied forces in Europe had successfully repelled the German spring offensive in Europe. Germany agreed to an armistice. Peace was at hand. World War I ended just two months after Bruce had registered for the draft. Although this was a momentous event, Bruce and Maggie hardly paid attention to it because of the personal tragedies they were enduring at the time.

Their survival as a family mandated that Bruce, Maggie, Bob, John, and Howard continue to work on their farm every day to ensure they had food to eat. They each quietly dealt with their own grief as they did their work. There was no time for withdrawal to deal with their grief.

John's brother Dale was born on June 5, 1919,[16] while the Spanish flu epidemic still persisted. However, by the spring of 1920, the epidemic had run its course and by the end of 1920 life in America had returned to the kind of normalcy that had existed before the epidemic.

In mid-December 1920, John attended a community or church Christmas party somewhere on Progress Ridge Road. While there, he met Mable Reynolds. Mable was the daughter of William Reynolds, who had been one of the founders of Cooley Chapel Methodist Church on Progress Ridge in the late 1800's. Bill Reynolds owned a farm on Walker Creek and was well known in the area as a lay-preacher who would often ride his horse on Sunday mornings to deliver sermons at other small churches and home churches in the area. By the end of the party John had asked Mable for a date, and Mable had accepted. John was seventeen, and Mable was fifteen.[17]

At the time John and Mable met, Mable had reenrolled at Walker School, which in 1917 had begun offering what today would be considered junior high school or pre-high school classes. Mable had completed the standard sixth grade program at Walker School in the spring of 1914. She had been a good student who obtained good grades. She enjoyed school and enjoyed learning. When Walker School started offering seventh and eighth grade classes during the autumn of 1917, she told her parents she would like to enroll. They not only approved but encouraged her to see it through.

---

16  1920 U.S. Federal Census, Walker District, Wood County, West Virginia
17  Mable Bunner interview, 1979

**Girlhood home of Mable Reynolds Bunner on Walker Creek, Wood County, West Virginia.**
(Picture take circa 1980. Old house was razed circa 2000)

Mable completed her seventh grade year in the spring of 1918. However, due to the Spanish flu epidemic, classes were not offered during the 1918-1919 school year. Classes were offered during the 1919-1920 school year, but Mable's parents were still concerned about the flu epidemic and persuaded her to wait until the 1920-1921 school year to finish eighth grade. She was in the middle of her eighth grade year at Walker School when she met John.[18]

It is unknown what John and Mable did on their first date, but Mable revealed in a 1979 interview that after John had walked her home he asked her for a second date. Mable accepted, and then John asked if he could give her a kiss at the end of their second date. Mable told him that she would think about it. At the end of their second date, Mable allowed him to give her a very brief kiss.[19]

---

18  Mable Bunner interview, 1979

19  Mable Bunner interview, 1979

During this time, John's mother Maggie was pregnant again, and on May 14, 1921[20], she gave birth to her son Carl. Carl was John's baby brother, and the last child born to Bruce and Maggie.

In the spring of 1921, John was eighteen and itching to do something besides farm work. He learned that the West Virginia State Road Commission was beginning a major upgrade of the Northwestern Turnpike though Wood County. He applied for a job and was hired as a member of the construction crew. His duties included spreading gravel and pouring tar. The work was full-time, and he was paid $.20/hour. During this same time, Mable finished the eighth grade at Walker School. John and Mable continued their courtship by seeing each other frequently.[21]

Just a few weeks later, John's work with the State Road and his courtship of Mable were temporarily suspended when he suffered a serious injury. In her 1979 interview, Mable Bunner stated that John was involved in a road construction accident during the summer of 1921. In a 2010 interview, John's son Don Bunner said he had been told when he was a little boy that John was riding a horse along Route 50 in a construction zone when an ice-cream truck attempted to pass him. The truck brushed against the horse and John's leg, and the door handle on the truck penetrated into John's leg, pulling him off the horse and breaking his leg just above the ankle.[22] [23]

John was taken to the hospital in Parkersburg where the doctors determined the break had shattered and fragmented a 1-2 inch portion of his lower leg bone so badly that it could not be reset. John was given the choice of amputating his foot and leg below the break or removing approximately two inches of his shattered leg bone so the bone could be reset and healed. The second option would mean that John would go through life with one leg being two inches shorter than the other leg. He was advised the second option had a high risk of failure and that if it did fail, amputation would be necessary.

---

20  Wood Count Clerk's Office, Birth Certificates, Carl Bunner, 1921
21  Mable Bunner interview, 1979
22  Mable Bunner interview, 1979
23  Don Bunner interview, October 2010

John chose the second option. The risky bone setting procedure worked. His broken leg healed quickly, but he would have to walk with a limp for the rest of his life.

By October 1921 John was again walking and performing strenuous farm chores. He was so happy to still have his leg and foot that he became determined to learn to walk anywhere he wanted to go with a limp, to do everything he could do before the injury, to always be thankful, and to never complain about it.

In late October 1921, John went back to work doing the same heavy labor tasks he was doing before his injury - spreading gravel and pouring tar. His crew worked until early December, when the winter weather began hampering the road construction efforts.

John and Mable continued their courtship through the winter months. In February 1922 Mable told him that her father had accepted a job working for a dairy in Zanesville, Ohio and that he planned to move the family to Zanesville as soon as he could sell his farm on Walker Creek.[24] This was devastating news to John, as by then he had fallen in love with Mable. He started developing a plan.

**John Bunner and Mable Reynolds – circa 1922**

Spring arrived, and John started working full time again with the State Road. The section of the Northwestern Turnpike he was working on was a three mile stretch that ran from Pleasant Hill to Montgomery Hill. The road was being straightened, widened, and paved. The road from Pleasant Hill to Dallison was fairly straight so all that had to be done was to widen and pave it.

---

24  Mable Bunner interview, 1979

The biggest problem was in Dallison where the existing road ran through the town where several houses had been built that would have to be torn down to widen the road. Also, the bridge in Dallison was not wide enough for the new road specifications, so it would also have to be demolished and replaced. In addition, the existing road through Dallison had a large bend that was suitable for horse and buggy traffic but not for higher speed automobiles. The decision was made to blast through a hill in Dallison to bypass the town and allow for a major straightening of the road as it approached Montgomery Hill. The State Road estimated this construction project would be completed by November 1922.

With this information, John finalized his plan. He would ask Mable to marry him before she moved to Ohio with her family. He would continue working with the State Road until they finished the project he was working on. This would allow him to save enough money to cover initial living expenses after he and Mable were married. After the road project was completed he would move to Zanesville where he would marry Mable and get a factory job.

In April 1922, John proposed to Mable and outlined his plan. She accepted. John was nineteen, and Mable was sixteen.[25]

By June, Mable's father had sold his property and rented a house in Zanesville for the family to move to. In late June 1922, John went to the B & O Railroad platform in Eaton, West Virginia to say goodbye to Mable. The entire Reynolds family, along with a number of suitcases and trunks, was there waiting for the train to take them to their new lives in Ohio. The train arrived, the suitcases were loaded, and John gave Mable one long goodbye kiss before the train departed.[26]

John's job ended in October 1922 when the highway construction project was completed. He said goodbye to his family and travelled to Zanesville. He and Mable were married on January 5, 1923, one day before John's twentieth birthday. They rented a house on Linden Avenue where they lived for three years.[27]

---

25  Mable Bunner interview, 1979

26  Mable Bunner interview, 1979

27  Mable Bunner interview, 1979

It is unclear why John and Mable were back in Wood County, West Virginia in July 1923, but while there Mable gave birth to their first child, Rosella Leona. Tragically, Rosella died one day after birth. Her death certificate stated cause of death as "shock from delivery" and records that she was buried in the Pleasant Valley Cemetery (Skidmore) later in the afternoon on the day that she died. John's father Bruce signed the death certificate as a witness.[28]

A few days later John and Mable returned to their Zanesville home to recover from their loss. John submitted his application at several manufacturing companies in Zanesville, but there were no immediate openings. While he waited, he took several short-term and part-time jobs to cover rent and other living expenses.

In 1924, John was hired as a "tile glazier" by the A.E. Tile Company in Zanesville. On July 10, 1925, a daughter Ellen Lenora Bunner was born. In 1927, with the next child on the way, John and Mable rented and moved to a larger house on Taylor Street. Here Ruth Elizabeth Bunner was born on August 28, 1927, Donald Rex Bunner was born on January 25, 1930, and Robert Lee Bunner was born on October 10, 1931.[29]

In October 1929, the stock market collapsed. Financial tycoons on Wall Street had already been wiped out, but the impact of the stock market crash on the rest of the U.S. economy was slower and more insidious. By 1932, businesses were closing all over and many men were losing their jobs, their houses, and their life savings. Americans were losing hope. Franklin D. Roosevelt was elected President in November 1932 by promising hope.

During Roosevelts inauguration speech in March 1933, he famously said "the only thing to fear is fear itself." That same month, John was advised by A. E. Tile Company that, due to ever dwindling sales, his job was being eliminated. All A.E. Tile employees were advised that the Zanesville plant would be shut down and all production moved back to England, where the parent company was

---

28  Wood County Clerk's Office, Death Certificate, Rosella Bunner, 1923
29  Mable Bunner interview, 1979

located. With the entire American economy now in a full depression, John could not find any kind of work in Zanesville.[30]

**A.E. Tile Company – Zanesville, Ohio.
John Bunner worked here from 1924 until 1933**
(Picture is from an old postcard circa 1920)

John and Mable decided to move back to West Virginia, where they could survive by working together as a family on a small farm. Sometime prior to 1930, John's parents had moved from the D.R. Congleton farm to a nearby farm known as the "Fouse place" along U.S. Route 50.[31] [The original family from Germany spelled the last name 'Fauss,' but the spelling had been changed to 'Fouse' by subsequent generations.] John and Mable inquired if the D.R. Congleton farm was available to rent. They were relieved to learn that it was.

Three months later, in July 1933, John and Mable, along with their four children, were living on the D.R. Congleton farm. Shortly thereafter, on September 7, 1933, their last child, Glenn Andrew Bunner, was born. The next four years, the worst of the Great Depression, were also the toughest years financially of John and Mable's lives. There

---

30  Mable Bunner interview, 1979
31  1930 U.S. Federal Census, Walker District, Wood County, West Virginia

was little income. John and Mabel worked from sunup to sundown every day of the week in order to grow and prepare enough food to survive. Their five young children and their ages at this time were Ellen (8), Ruth (6), Don (4), Robert (2), and newborn Glenn. The children were too young to do much productive farmwork. Mable had to spend most of her time tending to the children and preparing meals. It fell on John to do all the farm work.[32]

In the fall of 1933, Ellen and Ruth began attending school at Pleasant Hill. Two major improvements had been made over the twenty years since John last attended this school. The first was that Pleasant Hill was now a two-room schoolhouse. The second was that a school bus, and not a horse drawn wagon, picked up children along Route 50 and transported them to the Pleasant Hill School. During the 1920's, John's father Bruce had widened a shortcut path through the woods from the Congleton farm to U.S. Route 50. A horse drawn wagon could barely traverse this rough road, and it was totally impassable for cars. However, it made for an easy one mile walk from the house to the Route 50 school bus stop. After getting on the bus, it was a quick five minute ride to the school.[33]

Don started to school in the fall of 1936. As the oldest boy, he was also being taught how to perform important farm chores to help his parents. He was assigned responsibility for several chores that had to be completed each morning before he left for school. These included chopping enough firewood to last until the next morning, feeding the chickens, gathering the eggs, milking the cows, cleaning leaves and other debris from the outdoor spring that was the source of the family's water, and carrying five gallons of water from the spring to the kitchen for his mother to use during the day.[34]

After dinner each evening during the school year, Ellen, Ruth, and Don would gather in the living room to do their homework. A kerosene lamp was lit so they could see what they were doing. When the homework was done, everyone took turns going to the outhouse for one last bathroom trip after which everyone went to bed. Don,

---

32  Mable Bunner interview, 1979

33  Don Bunner interview, October 2010

34  Don Bunner interview, October 2010

Bob, and Glenn all slept in the same large bed. Ellen and Ruth slept in another large bed in the same room.[35]

There was a large pot-bellied wood stove in the living room that kept it warm on winter nights. The stovepipe rose through the living room ceiling and continued upward thought the upstairs bedroom where the children slept. It then extended through the roof. The heat emanating from the stovepipe added some heat to the bedroom but Don Bunner, in a 2010 interview, said the key to staying warm during the night was to utilize multiple blankets and quilts that his mother had made.[36]

Soon after the school year ended in the spring, Don would help his mom pull weeds out of the small gardens near the house where cucumbers and other vegetables were grown. He also helped his dad hoe the corn and potato fields and helped to remove the persistent potato beetles from the potato plants. Bob and Glenn were given the job of crushing the potato beetles with rocks.

Also in his 2010 interview, Don recalled that most Sundays his mother would get all his siblings out of bed and have them wash and get dressed to go to church. Some Sundays they went to Cooley Chapel, the church their grandfather, William Reynolds, had helped found in the late 1800's. Other Sundays they would go to the Pleasant Valley Church, which was an easier walk because the hills weren't as steep. Don noted that Cooley Chapel was a Methodist church and Pleasant Valley was a Baptist church, but as a young boy he never saw any difference between the two. Don remembered that his father, John, would go to church with the family on Easter and Christmas, but for the rest of the year it was just Mable and the children.[37]

---

35  Don Bunner interview, October 2010

36  Don Bunner interview, October 2010

37  Don Bunner interview, October 2010

**D.R. Congleton Farm where John and Mable Bunner family
lived during the Great Depression**
(drawings by Greg Bunner, based upon descriptions
provided by Don and Glenn Bunner)

By 1937 and 1938, Bob and Glenn were old enough to assume responsibility for most of the jobs Don had been doing. Don graduated to harnessing the two mules to do work too hard for a human. Don used the mules to plow the gardens in the spring, pull the hay mowing machine, pull the mechanical rake to build haystacks, and pull trees that he had cut in the forest back to the house where they would be sawed and split for firewood. Don became adept at using an axe and spent several hours every week cutting and splitting logs small enough to fit inside the kitchen stove. His firewood chopping duties quadrupled during the winter months because of the need to have sufficient firewood to keep the house warm.[38]

---

38  Don Bunner interview, October 2010

**Mable Bunner (left) and friend Justine Allen circa 1939**
(Justine delivered Glenn Bunner on the Congleton farm in 1933)

During the years of the Great Depression, the Fourth of July was always a highly anticipated summer holiday for the Bunner family. They had a hand cranked ice cream maker. A company in Parkersburg that had refrigerated trucks would travel the rural roads of Wood County selling blocks of ice during the summer. John would buy a block of ice and he and the boys would put it in a gunny sack and then use a sledgehammer to break it up into pieces small enough to fit in the ice cream maker.[39]

Mable had an ice cream recipe that everyone liked. She, Ellen, and Ruth would mix the ingredients and pour it into the metal canister of the ice cream maker. John would put the canister in place and attach the crank. He would pack the crushed ice and salt around the canister. Don, Bob, and Glenn then took turns cranking the handle as the canister rotated in the salted ice. In fifteen or

---

39  Don Bunner interview, October 2010

twenty minutes, the ice cream was ready and everyone would have a large bowl filled to the brim. Most Fourth of July's, at least three canisters of ice cream were made and everybody had their fill. [40]

After eating all their ice cream, the Bunners, as well as many other families living on Progress Ridge, would climb Boston Hill to watch the fireworks that were being set off in Parkersburg ten miles to the west. Boston Hill was the highest point on Progress Ridge and provided an excellent view of the distant fireworks. After the fireworks, everyone walked home in the dark using kerosene lanterns for light, thankful for this one day respite from the drudgery of farm work.[41]

John and Mable Bunner children on Congleton farm circa 1940. Left front – Robert, Right front – Don, on mule – Glenn, Left rear – Ellen, Right rear – Ruth, mule's name was Jack.
(colorization by Mike Bunner)

---

40  Don Bunner interview, October 2010
41  Don Bunner interview, October 2010

In 1938, John got a job in the Worker's Progress Administration (W.P.A.), working various public works projects in Wood County. The W.P.A. was often mocked as a welfare program which stood for "We Piddle Around," but during her 1979 interview, Mabel said that John worked on a crew that performed legitimate and necessary road and bridge repairs. With John working at the W.P.A. every day, Mable and the five children worked the farm all day during the summer months, with John pitching in as soon as he got home in the evening. With John's weekly paycheck from the W.P.A., John and Mable began the long process of pulling themselves out of the poverty they had endured during the Great Depression.[42]

In December 1938, John's father, Bruce, died of a heart attack at the house he was renting from the Fouse family. He was sixty-four years old. After Bruce's death, Maggie continued living at the Fouse place along with her nineteen year old son Dale and her seventeen year old son Carl. As their bus stop was on the road in front of her house, Don, Robert, and Glenn would sometimes stop to visit their Grandma on their way home from school. Don would often stop on his way to school in the morning to milk his Grandma's two cows.[43]

In early 1942, John and Mable's oldest daughter, sixteen-year-old Ellen, married twenty-one year-old Burl Hewitt, who was operating an auto repair garage in Dallison. Burl had been born in Braxton County, West Virginia and had been physically abused at a young age by his stepfather.[44] As a result, he had come to live with relatives on Progress Ridge in Wood County. After their marriage, Burl and Ellen lived in the house on the second floor above his garage.[45]

When America was forced into World War II with the Japanese attack on Pearl Harbor in December 1941, the war effort called for the factories at home to be retooled to produce items necessary to fight the war. O. Ames, a shovel manufacturing plant in South Parkersburg, was retooled to make bomb casings. John, who was too old to fight the war (he was 41 at the time, with five children

---

42  Mable Bunner interview, 1979

43  Don Bunner interview, October 2010

44  Juanita Hewitt Smith written answer to Mike Bunner questions, March 2025

45  Mable Bunner interview, 1979

at home, and a permanent limp from the old leg injury suffered in 1921), was hired full time at the O. Ames plant on Camden Avenue in South Parkersburg. He began working 50-60 hour workweeks and helped to make tens of thousands of bomb casings between 1942 and 1945.[46]

After the United States declared war on Japan and Germany in 1941, John's younger brothers Dale and Carl enlisted in the U.S. Army Air Corps. They both served as B-24 crew members fighting against Japan in the Pacific theatre for the duration of the war. Maggie was sixty-two and suddenly living alone. She was unable to keep the farm running on her own, so the decision was made for her to move in with her oldest son Bob, who was living in South Parkersburg.[47]

Because of the long hours and the need to commute to and from Parkersburg every day, John and Mabel immediately stepped in to rent the house and farm where Maggie had been living. For the rest of her life, Mable Bunner referred to this farm as the "Prunty place" even though it was owned by the Fouse family. They moved there in 1942 after Ellen had married Burl. At the time, Ruth was 14, Don was 12, Robert was 10, and Glenn was 8.[48]

In 2010, Don Bunner remembered this move.

> "Yea I remember moving from the Congleton farm to the Prunty place. Well see, during World War II, Carl and Dale, which were dads brothers, went into the service. Grandpa Bunner [Bruce] had already died so that left Grandma Bunner there in that house all by herself. She decided to move to town so we decided to move to that house where Grandpa and Grandma Bunner had lived for years."
>
> We used mule sleds to move everything from the Congleton farm down to the Prunty Place. I was twelve at the time and drove one of the mule sleds. After unloading the first sled, I went back to the

---

46  Mable Bunner interview, 1979

47  Mable Bunner interview, 1979

48  Mable Bunner interview, 1979

Congleton farm and brought a second load. Finally, we brought down the cows and the chickens."

Mable and the children worked the farm full time, but, because of his long work hours at O. Ames, John was not able to help except on weekends. However, for the first time since John and Mable were married, they were able to consistently save money. Their dream was to buy their own farm so they could stop paying rent.

In 1942, Don continued his education beyond sixth grade by enrolling in seventh grade at the new one-room school at Pleasant Valley, less than one mile west of where he lived on U.S. Route 50. Bob and Glenn were still attending elementary school at Pleasant Hill, about one mile to the east of where they lived. The school bus stop was right in front of their house.

Soon after America's entry into World War II, Ellen's husband Burl began working for the Atlas Powder Ordnance Plant in Ravenna, Ohio. They manufactured gunpowder. On October 12, 1942, Burl was drafted into U.S. Army and attended training at Camp Perry, Ohio and then was assigned to the Red River Army Munitions Depot in Texarkana, Texas. Ellen traveled to Texarkana with Burl and remained with him until his deployment to the Pacific theatre in December 1943.

Burl saw combat in Guam in 1944. Ellen returned to Parkersburg during Burl's deployment, where she lived at 509 Ward Street. She gave birth to her first child, Sandra Kay Hewitt, in Parkersburg on August 13, 1944. This was three days after America's victory over the Japanese on Guam. Burl was on Guam feverishly helping to establish an airfield for the U.S, Army Air Corps on the day Sandra was born. Burl was honorably discharged from the Army after the Japanese surrendered in August 1945 to end the war. He returned home to Ellen and his new daughter in Parkersburg.

In 1944, Don entered 9th grade at Parkersburg High School. He rode a school bus that took a serpentine route through eastern Wood County to pick up students living in rural areas. Because of this, Don was on the bus for 1½ hours each morning before arriving to school. It took the same amount of time to return home in the evening.

In late 1944, seventeen-year-old Ruth, who had slept in her own bed but in the same bedroom with her brothers for fifteen years, wanted more privacy. As there were no more rooms in the four room house they were renting, Ruth's grandparents, Bill and Ida Reynolds, invited her to move to Zanesville with them as they had purchased a big house with plenty of room. Ruth moved in with them and initially helped them with housework. Within a few weeks, she got a job at a nearby glass manufacturing company. There she met fellow employee Paul Withers who had just returned from a three-year tour of duty with the U.S. Navy in the Pacific theatre during World War II. They began dating, and by late 1945 they were engaged.

In April 1945, President Franklin Roosevelt, who was just beginning his fourth term as President, died. His Vice-President, Harry S. Truman, became President. A month later, in May 1945, Germany surrendered to the allied forces, ending the war in Europe. In August 1945, after Truman had authorized the use of the newly developed atomic bomb on the Japanese cities of Hiroshima and Nagasaki, the Japanese surrendered. World War II was over.

In the summer of 1945, Ellen's husband Burl returned home to West Virginia. One day Burl was watching Don and Bob saw firewood at their house with a handsaw and came up with the idea of using a car engine linked to a fan belt turning a circular saw blade to cut the logs. Don and Robert assisted Burl in building this contraption and then took lessons from Burl on how to perform maintenance on the car engine that powered it.

The contraption worked great. According to Don, the motorized saw blade cut firewood at least fifty times faster than sawing by hand. In retrospect, Don admits that this was an extremely dangerous machine that was constantly throwing sawdust in in their eyes, but that he and Bob never lost any fingers, hands, or arms. It freed Don and Bob from a sweaty, tiring, lengthy daily job. It taught both of them a lifelong lesson that doing work with power tools was infinitely preferable to doing the same work by hand. It also taught them how to repair, rebuild, and maintain automobile engines.

Burl, who had reopened his auto repair garage in Dallison after returning from the war, was always available to give Don and Bob advice if they encountered a mechanical problem they couldn't solve. Glenn started spending a lot of time watching Burl do work in his garage. He learned enough that his first job after quitting school was that of an auto mechanic.

In October 1945, John's brother, Carl, who had served as a B-24 bombardier in the Pacific theatre for the previous three years, was discharged from the Army Air Corps and returned home to Wood County, West Virginia. In February 1946, John's brother Dale, who had also served on a B-24 crew in the Pacific, was discharged and returned home.

Paul, Burl, Dale, and Carl had each done their part to save the world from tyranny. They never bragged about what they had done. In fact, they rarely ever talked about it. All they wanted to do was get a job and raise a family.

In 1946, with the war over and American factories going back to peacetime production, John was asked to stay on full time at O. Ames to make shovels and other garden tools. With the assurance of a post-war job, John and Mabel took their savings and made a down payment on the purchase of a house on approximately three acres in Dallison, on U.S. Route 50. The sales price was $1,000. They paid $300 down and agreed to make payments of $20 per month until the $700 loan was paid off. The loan was repaid and they had a free and clear title to their property by 1950.

Don, Robert, and Glenn all made the move with their parents to Dallison. Don was sixteen, Bob was fourteen, and Glenn was twelve. Don was in tenth grade at Parkersburg High School, Bob was in eighth grade at Pleasant Valley School, and Glenn was in sixth grade at Pleasant Valley School.

In a 2010 interview, Don Bunner remembered this two mile move in 1946 from the "Prunty place" to the first – and only - house to be owned by John and Mable in Dallison:

"Burl Hewitt had a car and his cousin, Riley Hewitt, had a truck. It took several trips, but they moved everything for us in one day.

Dad sold the cows and the mules before the move since we didn't have room for them in Dallison.

We did bring all the chickens with us. There was an old building at the top of the hill that dad converted into a chicken coup.

The greatest thing about the move to Dallison is that we had natural gas for heating and cooking. I have never chopped one stick of firewood in my life since that day we made the move."[49]

**Dallison home of John and Mable Bunner – 1946**
(Drawing by Greg Bunner)

In January 1947, just a few weeks after John, Mable, and their three sons had completed the move to Dallison, Ruth and Paul traveled from Zanesville to South Parkersburg for their wedding.[50] This was done so more Bunners would be able to attend. After the wedding, they had a brief honeymoon and returned to Zanesville, where their first child, Phyllis Kay, was born in September 1947.

---

49  Don Bunner interview, October 2010

50  Wood County Clerk's Office, Marriage Licenses, Paul Withers and Ruth Bunner, January 1947

Don Bunner had enjoyed school at Pleasant Hill and Pleasant Valley, but he did not like high school. The boys who lived in Parkersburg treated country boys like Don as ignorant hicks and were constantly taunting them. In February 1947, in the middle of his tenth grade year, Don and two of his "country boy" friends decided to quit school, join the U.S. Army and see the world.[51]

Don went on active duty in Columbus, Ohio. One of the first things he did was get his military driver's license. He then took an aptitude test and was selected to go to school to learn to repair army motor vehicles. During his three year tour of duty he served in Guam and Washington state.[52]

Bob entered Parkersburg High School in 1946. He was not a motivated student and quit school in October 1947 on his sixteenth birthday. He got a job working at a sawmill owned by Denzill Blair in Dallison. This was the same person who established the Dallison general store next door to the sawmill. In the early 1950's this was known as "Blair's Store." [53]

Bob got his driver's license shortly after his sixteenth birthday, but didn't yet have a car to drive. He continued to live with his parents and walked to work at the sawmill each day.

Glenn was also not a motivated student and quit school after eighth grade in 1948. He obtained his driver's license and got a job working as an auto mechanic at Cliff Miller's garage in Murphytown.[54]

In 1950, Bob married Imogene Hendershot and they moved into a two bedroom apartment over Burl Hewitt's auto repair garage in Dallison. Don's three year tour in the Army was also completed in 1950. He returned home and was living with John and Mable. [55]

---

51  Don Bunner interview, October 2010
52  Don Bunner interview, October 2010
53  Robert Bunner as told to his son, Mike Bunner, 1965
54  Don Bunner interview, October 2010
55  Don Bunner interview, October 2010

**Left-Ruth and Phyllis Withers on steps, Gary, Larry, and Sandra Hewitt at Dallison house – 1948 Right – Ruth and Phyllis Withers at Dallison house after Paul left for Korea – 1951**

In 1951, Ruth's husband, Paul Withers, was recalled by the U.S. Navy to fight in the Korean War. While he was serving, Ruth and their daughter Phyllis moved from Zanesville to live with John and Mable in Dallison. They lived there at the same time as Don.[56]

After leaving the Army, Don got a job working at O. Ames, but not in the same department where John worked. He didn't share a ride with John because he was always working evening and night shifts whereas John was working only the day shift. After the war, many of the factory jobs in Parkersburg were contract specific. As soon as the contracts were fulfilled, the employees were laid off. Don had several contract jobs lasting two to three months at a time at both O. Ames and the nearby American Viscose factory. He never had the same job long enough to build up the seniority necessary to not be susceptible to lay-offs.[57]

By 1952, Don was being aggressively recruited by the Army to reenlist. Frustrated with the kinds of jobs he was getting in Parkersburg, he reupped and left West Virginia. Within a few months, he was on a three-year assignment in Germany. The Army would become his career.[58]

---

56  Don Bunner interview, October 2010

57  Don Bunner interview, October 2010

58  Don Bunner interview, October 2010

Toward the end of 1952, Paul Withers returned from his Navy tour in the Korean War. He, Ruth, and Phyllis were back in Zanesville by late 1952. Their son Danny was born in August 1953.[59]

When Don took his military physical to reenter the Army, he learned that he had diphtheria. At the same time, Mable was diagnosed with diphtheria. The root cause of the disease for both Don and Mable was the water well at the house in Dallison. The health department investigated and concluded that bacteria from the outdoor toilet on the hill above the house had migrated downhill into the water well. They recommended the existing well be permanently abandoned and that a new water well be drilled on the other side of the house that would be out of the gravity flow from the outhouse.[60]

In 1952, after getting a job at Storck's Bakery in Parkersburg, Bob had purchased a 1942 Chevy. In a 2010 interview, Glenn remembered giving his mother a driving lesson using Bob's 42 Chevy. He said she did great driving the car from her house in Dallison to Pleasant Valley and back, but when she pulled in the driveway at her house she was going too fast and hit the guy wire that anchored the guardrails along the road. This caused a small scratch on the front bumper. Mable got out of the car to assess the damage. Bob, who had been watching from the porch, had broken out in such hysterical laughter that Mable pronounced "I will never drive again." And she never did.[61]

In 1953, Glenn met Dorothy Buchanan, who was a bar waitress in Parkersburg. They were married in March 1954 just after Glenn received his draft notice from the Army. The Korean War had just stalemated and Glenn was led to believe he would be assigned to Korea to help keep the peace. He was assigned to sixteen weeks of training at Fort Knox, Kentucky. After training, Glenn was assigned to a battalion in Korea. Before he arrived, that battalion was deployed from Korea to Japan. It was in Sapporo, Japan that Glenn joined his unit. It was winter and Glenn worked every day

---

59  Don Bunner interview, October 2010
60  Don Bunner interview, October 2010
61  Glenn Bunner interview, October 2010

operating a large grader plowing snow to keep runways clear so the military planes could take off and land. In March 1955, Glenn was reassigned to Guam where he completed his two year active duty stint. He returned home to West Virginia in early 1956.[62]

In early 1953, John and Mable had an empty house for the first time in nearly thirty years. But not for long. Their son Robert and his wife Imogene filed for divorce less than three years after they were married. They had two little boys, Mike (age 2) and Darrell (newborn). After Bob and Imogene separated, she took the boys with her to Parkersburg where she got a job in housekeeping at St. Joseph's Hospital. She hired a babysitter to take care of Mike and Darrell during the day. After a few weeks of coming home and consistently finding that the boys had neither been fed nor had their diapers been changed during the day, Imogene realized she was unable to provide the care and support they needed. [63]

Imogene traveled to Dallison with Mike and Darrell and asked Mable and John if they would take the boys and raise them as their own. They said yes. Robert learned of this arrangement the next day when he stopped at John and Mable's house and found his two sons living there.[64] Though Robert visited his boys virtually every day from August 1953 until March 1957, Mike and Darrell lived with John and Mable. John and Mable were true to their word and raised the boys as if they were their own.

In 1954, John and Mable began a long planned upgrade and modernization of their Dallison house. They started by drilling a new water well which was tested and certified as bacteria free. They closed and sealed the old well and built a new kitchen over it. They enclosed and insulated the back porch and turned it into a bathroom with hot and cold running water, a bathtub, and a commode that flushed into a septic tank. A new "back porch" was added on in front of the kitchen.

Concrete sidewalks and steps were poured. The old wood siding on the house was removed and a new "forever" green and white

---

62  Glenn Bunner interview, October 2010

63  Imogene Schupp interview, 2011

64  Imogene Schupp interview, 2011

siding was installed. The old outdoor toilet on the hill above the house was torn down and the pit was filled in. The old tin roof on the house was replaced with a new tin roof. The house had a completely different look and feel. Modernity had come to Dallison. Life was good.[65]

Left – Mable, Mike, and Darrell Bunner during the 1954 house modernization project. Right – the house in 2017 sixty-three years after the modernization.

Also in 1955, John and Mable purchased a dilapidated house on an adjoining parcel of property. A widow named Hattie Henderson had lived there alone for several years and had been unable to maintain the house. She had died in early 1955. By then, John and Mable's son Robert had married Rosie Carpenter and they were living in a small apartment in Parkersburg. They were looking for a permanent place to live. The plan that was developed was for John and Mable to purchase the Henderson property and fix it up to make it livable again. Then Robert and Rosie would rent the house from John and Mable.

John and Mable spent over a year fixing up the old house after they purchased it. In March 1957 Robert, Rosie and their new son Johnny Leroy moved into this house. Mike and Darrell were also reunited with their father and moved into this house with them.

In 1956, a few months after being discharged from the Army, Glenn moved with his wife, Dorothy, and two-year-old daughter,

---

65 Mike Bunner's memories of Dallison house renovations in 1954

Barbara, into John and Mable's house. What was originally thought to be a temporary arrangement lasting two or three months turned into a five year residency.

Immediately after Mike and Darrell moved back with their dad and new stepmother, John and Mable took John's mother Maggie into their house to take care of her. Since 1942, Maggie had lived eight years with her son Robert, and then six years with her son Carl. Maggie had started showing signs of dementia in the late 1940's, and her condition had progressively deteriorated ever since. By 1956, her memory was completely gone and her body had become very fragile. Carl's wife Anna was raising five boys and had just given birth to her first daughter in 1956. All six children were under eight years old, and Anna could not raise six young children and also continue to serve as a full time caregiver for Maggie. That is why Maggie came to live with John and Mable.

John was still working full time at O. Ames so it fell on Mable to be Maggie's caregiver. In 1957, Glenn and Dorothy, who were still living with John and Mable, had a son named Larry. Maggie was enamored with the new baby and wanted to take care of him. Maggie had to be watched full time because she wanted to pick Larry up and carry him around, but she was physically unable to do so. One day when Larry was crying, Maggie went to the kitchen, filled a baby bottle with bleach, and gave it to Larry. Fortunately Mable walked in the house just as Maggie was giving the bottle to Larry and immediately interceded. After that, Larry was kept in the upstairs bedroom almost all the time to protect him from Maggie.

Maggie was a challenge and a burden, but John and Mable cared for her with love. Mable told her grandson Mike that God's plan was for parents to take care of their children when they were young, and for children to take care of their parents when they grew old.

Maggie died at John and Mables house on March 24, 1958.[66] She was buried at the Pleasant Valley Cemetery (Skidmore) beside her husband Bruce, who had died twenty years earlier.

During the summer of 1958, Robert and Glenn helped John build a new front porch on John's house. A tin roof was installed to

---

66  Wood County Clerk's Office, Death Certificate, Maggie Bunner, March 1958

match the rest of the roof on the house, and matching green siding was installed to blend in with the siding that had been installed on the rest of the house in 1954.

This front porch served as a family and community meeting place for the next sixty three years. Six generations of Bunner's and Reynolds's sat on that porch, engaging in conversations, building family bonds, watching mud daubers build their nests in the rafters, enjoying the warm breezes, and silently listening to the soothing sound of rain falling on the tin roof. The old house was razed in 2021 by Larry Bunner to make way for a new house and garage.

Also in 1958, John and Mable purchased their first television. In the valley where they lived, they were only able to receive one channel – WSAZ-TV in Huntington, West Virginia. It was part of the NBC network. In 1960, more modernity arrived in Dallison when phone lines were first installed across much of rural Wood County. John and Mable were among the first in Dallison to have a home phone.

In 1960, Robert and Rose built a new house next door to John and Mable in Dallison. When Robert's family moved into their new house, Glenn and Dorothy and their three children moved into the house Robert and Rose had just vacated. John and Mable had an empty house again.

Beginning in 1960, John and Mable started taking an extended sightseeing vacation each summer. One summer they traveled through Kentucky and parts of central Tennessee with Dallison neighbors Bill and Anna Richards. They visited Mammoth Cave National Park, the birthplace of Abraham Lincoln, and Lincoln's boyhood home. They also visited a place called Dogpatch, Kentucky, the mythical home of Sunday newspaper comic strip character Li'l Abner. The Li'l Abner character was a low-energy hillbilly who was long on physique and short on intelligence.

They brought home a newspaper with the headlines "John and Mable Bunner Visit Historic Dogpatch." Li'l Abner disappeared from the Sunday comics by mid-1977 and the tourist attraction in Kentucky known as Dogpatch disappeared with it.

Another summer John and Mable traveled with Carl and Anna Bunner along with Bill and Anna Richards to Harper's Ferry,

West Virginia and then on to Washington D.C. They toured the Capitol and the White House and visited the Lincoln Memorial, the Jefferson Memorial, and the Washington Monument. They accompanied Carl when he visited Arlington National Cemetery to pay his respects to buddies who had been killed in World War II. That same day they visited the Iwo Jima Memorial in Arlington.

The last summer vacation taken by John and Mable was to Virginia Beach and then the Smoky Mountains. They again traveled with neighbors Bill and Anna Richards. This was in the summer of 1964, and it was the first time either John or Mable had ever seen the ocean. While at Virginia Beach, they stayed for one or two nights with their son Don, his wife Jeanette, and their two-year-old daughter April Denise. Don was still in the Army and had just purchased his first house in Newport News.

**John and Mable Bunner at Virginia Beach – August 1964**
(colorization by Mike Bunner)

Afterward John and Mable visited the Great Smoky Mountain National Park. While there, they spent a day on the Cherokee Indian reservation in North Carolina. The souvenirs they purchased for their grandchildren on this trip were peace pipes handmade by Native Americans living on the Cherokee reservation.

Just five months after this vacation, in January 1965, John arrived home from work, ate dinner, read the newspaper, and watched the evening news on TV. He then watched a comedy show that caused him to laugh uncontrollably. According to Mable, he laughed so hard that tears came out his eyes.

About an hour later, John started complaining of chest pains. Mable told John she was going to run next door to their son Robert's house (Robert did not have a phone at the time), but John told her he didn't want her to leave him their alone. Mable called neighbor Bobby Harris to ask if he could drive John to the hospital. When Bobby arrived John was laying in the floor and unable to walk. Bobby ran next door to ask Robert to help. In the meantime John's condition worsened and Mable called for an ambulance. The ambulance arrived about twenty minutes later and the medical attendant quickly determined that John was dead. His cause of death was a heart attack, the same as his father Bruce twenty-five years earlier.[67]

John's funeral was delayed for over a week to allow Don to travel from Antarctica back to West Virginia. Don had been on a four-month assignment with the Army doing scientific research at the South Pole. John's funeral was held at the Leavitt Funeral Home in Parkersburg, followed by his burial in the Pleasant Valley Cemetery (Skidmore).

After John's death, Mable continued being the best daughter, sister, mother, grandmother, great-grandmother, and great-great grandmother that she knew how to be. She continued living at her house in Dallison and subsisted on her monthly Social Security check for the next thirty-one years.

In 1969 Mable's mother Ida Mae Reynolds died at age eighty-six.[68] This left her ninety-nine year old father, William Reynolds, living alone in Zanesville, Ohio. After her mother's funeral, Mable brought her father back to Dallison to live with her. On February

---

67  Wood County Clerk's Office, Death Certificate, John Bunner, January 1965

68  Ida Mae Reynolds obituary, The Times Recorder, Zanesville, Ohio, Jul 12, 1969

22, 1970, Bill Reynolds celebrated his 100th birthday while living with Mable. He was still as physically fit and as mentally sharp as many persons half his age. However, in late January 1971, her father's physical condition started to deteriorate rapidly and Mable and her three sisters decided to return him to live with Lela Burkett, the sister living in Zanesville, as they believed the end was near. On February 12, 1971, William Reynolds died just ten days shy of his 101st birthday. He was buried beside his wife Ida Mae in Memorial Park Cemetery in Zanesville, Ohio.[69]

**William J. Reynolds – 100th Birthday – February 22, 1970**
(photograph by G.E. Brown, Parkersburg News and Sentinel)

In the 1970's and 1980's, Mabel took several sightseeing tours with her friends and ladies groups. Destinations included Niagara Falls, the Adirondack Mountains, Williamsburg, and an autumn foliage tour through Vermont. Her neighbors Walter and Ruby Epler picked her up for church services at Cooley Chapel Methodist Church almost every Sunday. She planned and attended annual

---

69  William J. Reynolds obituary, The Times Recorder, Zanesville, Ohio, Feb 14, 1971

Bunner – Reynolds reunions into the early 1990's. She volunteered as a Republican poll worker for every primary and general election between 1956 and 1980. During many of those elections she had the responsibility for transporting the raw ballots from her Ogden precinct to the Wood County Courthouse.

Mable was diagnosed with colon cancer in the mid – 1970's, but surgery removed the cancer from her body. She had one heart attack circa 1990, but her grandson Larry quickly got her to the hospital where the doctors were able to stabilize her condition and save her life.

In the mid-1980's Mable accompanied her grandson, Darrell, and his family for a weeklong visit to her grandson Mike near the Adirondack Mountains in upstate New York. Also in the mid 1980's, she accompanied Darrell and his family on a vacation trip to Florida.

Mable continued growing vegetable gardens into her mid-eighties. She maintained her perennial and annual flower gardens until she died. Her grandson Larry often told the story of the time he pulled into her driveway when she was eighty-nine years old and saw her laying on her side on the ground in one of her flower beds. Fearing the worst, he ran over to check on her and found her pulling weeds out from around her flowers. She told him she could no longer stoop or squat to pull weeds, but she was able to lay down and pull them. They both had a good laugh about Larry's first reaction when he saw her laying there. Though Mable's body started deteriorating in her late eighties, her mind remained crisp, strong and sharp.

Mabel and three of her sisters, Opal, Hazel, and Lela, inherited a remarkable set of genes. All lived to their nineties. Opal lived to be 100, just like her father. Each of her sisters would visit Mable at least once every two years until she died. When they visited they almost always stayed for one week so they could catch up on all family activities since they had last had a chance to spend time together.

(Left) Mable (l), Opal, Hazel and Lela (r) Reynolds circa 1915. (Right) Front left – Opal, front right – Mable, rear left – Bea, rear center – Lela, rear right – Hazel, circa 1985

Mable Bunner 90th (and last) birthday – December 13, 1995

On February 9, 1996, Mable talked to her grandson Mike on the phone for over thirty minutes. They caught each other up on current family affairs, talked about politics and the upcoming presidential primaries, and talked about tentative travel plans. She told Mike a joke she heard on television that she thought was funny and they both had a good laugh. Then, she told Mike that she had passed by her bedroom mirror earlier that day and was shocked at how old she looked. Mike dismissed her comment by reminding her that her father lived to be 100 years old, so she still had at least a decade to go. They said goodnight and hung up the phone.

The next evening, Saturday, February 10, 1996, Greg Bunner, Mabel's great-grandson brought his newborn daughter, Rachael, to Mable's house to meet her. Greg's wife Melissa also came, as did Greg's father Darrell and Darrell's granddaughter Tawny (Mable's great-great granddaughter). They had a wonderful visit, and Mable took delight in her great-great granddaughters. Pictures were taken and smiles abounded. After Greg and his family walked outside to their car to go home, Mable opened her door and shouted, "Come back next week and I'll cook dinner for you." Greg called back "OK, we will!"

**Mable's great-great granddaughters Tawny (left) and Rachael Bunner (being held), Mable, and great-grandson Greg Bunner. This was the last picture ever taken of Mable (Feb 10, 1996)**

Thirty six hours later, on Monday morning, Mable recognized that she was having symptoms of a heart attack. She called the Emergency Response team and then called her grandson Larry who lived nearby. Larry arrived within two minutes and found Mable sitting on the floor breathing heavily. He took her hand and told her everything was going to be all right. She told him that she was dying. Larry sat down with her, put his arms around her, and told her the ambulance would arrive soon. She went limp in his arms. When the ambulance arrived a few minutes later, she was pronounced dead. She died on February 12, 1996, exactly twenty-five years to the day after her father, William Jeremiah Reynolds, had died.[70]

Mable's funeral was held at the Leavitt Funeral Home in Parkersburg. She was buried beside of her husband John in the Pleasant Valley Cemetery. She had outlived him by thirty-one years.

The impact she had on the lives that she touched will last forever.

## Children of John and Mable Bunner

### Ellen Bunner Hewitt

Burl and Ellen were married in early 1942. Burl served in the U.S. Army in the Pacific theatre during World War II. Their daughter Sandra was born in 1944 in Parkersburg, West Virginia while Burl was fighting in Guam. After returning from the war he operated an auto repair garage in Dallison, West Virginia. Twin sons Larry and Gary were born in Parkersburg in 1947.[71] In 1954 the family moved to Grafton, West Virginia, where son John was born. Burl's health was not good after returning from the war and during 1955 he entered the VA hospital in Clarksburg, West Virginia where it was determined that his stomach had ruptured and had attached itself to his backbone. Surgery was performed to repair the damage. He was fully recovered by mid-1956, when the family moved

---

70  Mable Bunner obituary, Parkersburg Sentinel, February 13, 1996
71  Don Bunner interview, October 2010

to Buckhannon, West Virginia. Soon after settling in Buckhannon, daughter Juanita was born. Burl established "Hewitt's Body Shop," where he worked for many years.

In 1968, Burl started working as a Tipple Operator for a coal mine near Buckhannon. He never worked underground and when offered an underground tour of the mine he worked for, he nailed his lunch bucket to the wall, telling his boss that he had never been inside a mine and he wasn't going inside one now.

Burl was a CB radio enthusiast and was instrumental in establishing the Radio Emergency Associated Citizens Team (REACT) in Upshur County. He was also the financial secretary for the United Mine Workers of America Local 8106.

Ellen contracted hepatitis in the early 1980's. Upon learning that her disease was most likely terminal, Burl bought a camper and he and Ellen traveled extensively for the next 2-3 years. Ellen succumbed to her disease on August 21, 1984.

Burl's health remained good until his mid 80's when he started having circulation problems in his legs. By the time of his death, both legs had been amputated and Burl was living in an assisted care home. He died on September 21, 2016, at the age of 96. His mother had lived to 100, and his grandmother had lived to 101.[72]

## Ruth Bunner Withers

Ruth attended Parkersburg High School in 1943 and 1944. Paul served in the U.S. Navy in the Pacific theatre from February 1943 until the Japanese surrendered in August 1945. In late 1944, at the age of 17, Ruth moved to Zanesville, Ohio to live with her grandparents, William and Ida Reynolds. She got a job at Mosaic Tile Company where she met Paul after he returned home from World War II.

Ruth and Paul started dating and were engaged later that year. In early 1947 they were married in Parkersburg, West Virginia where most of Ruth's relatives lived. They returned to Zanesville where daughter Phyllis was born later that year. In 1950, Paul was recalled

---

72 Information provided by Juanita Hewitt Smith, daughter of Burl and Ellen Hewitt

back into the U.S. Navy to fight in the Korean War. Ruth and three year-old Phyllis went to live with Ruth's parents at their home in Dallison, West Virginia. Paul was discharged from his second Navy tour in late 1952. He, Ruth and Phyllis returned to Zanesville, where their son Danny was born in 1953.[73]

Paul became manager of a steel recycling company in Zanesville. In the late 1960's he and Ruth built a new house at 1279 Ellen Drive in Zanesville, where they were living when Ruth died of heart complications on November 13, 1982. Ruth was 55 at the time of her death. Paul remained in Zanesville where he died on September 25, 2000, at the age of 75.

Phyllis and Danny were both living in the Phoenix, Arizona area in 2024.

**Donald Rex Bunner**

Don served in the U.S. Army from 1947 to 1950, and then from 1952 to 1969. During his career he served at bases all over the world, including Germany, Guam, Viet Nam, and Antarctica. During his first few years in the Army he was responsible for maintaining motor vehicles, but in the late 1950's he was selected to attend school to become a helicopter mechanic. For the rest of his career, he served as a helicopter crew chief at multiple global locations.

Don married Jeanette Shope in North Carolina in 1961. Soon after their marriage, he left for a one year assignment in Viet Nam. While serving there, daughter April Denise was born in North Carolina. Upon his return from Viet Nam, Don was assigned to Fort Eustis in Newport News, Virginia. There Don and Jeanette bought a house at 171 Edsel Drive. Don spent the last few years of his Army service on a team doing scientific research in Antarctica. From 1964 until he retired from the Army in 1969 he spent four months every year in Antarctica with his team.

During one of those assignments, Don accompanied two helicopters which landed on a large glacier to set up scientific equipment. When the team began its return from the glacier, one

---

73  Information provided by Phyllis and Danny, children of Paul and Ruth Bunner Withers, Don Bunner

of the helicopters had mechanical problems and was not able to fly. Since there was insufficient room in the remaining helicopter to accommodate the full team, Don volunteered to remain on the glacier with the inoperable helicopter. Two days later, the operable helicopter returned with the necessary spare parts. Don repaired the faulty helicopter on the glacier, and both helicopters returned back to their base. Soon thereafter, the Army assigned the name 'Bunner Glacier' to the glacier that Don had stayed on by himself for two days. Bunner Glacier can still be found on maps of Antarctica.

Ronald Keith Bunner was born to Don and Jeanette on June 3, 1966. Don retired from the Army in 1969 and worked for the next twenty-five years as a heating and air-conditioning system repair mechanic for Sears. Their daughter April was tragically killed in a car accident on February 28, 1982, on an icy road near Charlottesville, Virginia as she was travelling back to college. Jeanette died of cancer on September 21, 2001, at the age of sixty. Ronnie graduated from the University of Mississippi and became a senior executive in the D.R. Horton Company and was living in Mt. Pleasant, South Carolina as of 2025.

Don lived at his home in Newport News until late 2024 when, after a series of falls, he moved to a senior retirement home near his son Ronnie in Mt. Pleasant, South Carolina.[74]

**Robert Lee Bunner** - will be discussed in the following chapter

**Glenn Andrew Bunner**

Glenn quit school after eighth grade. He had already proven himself as an adept auto mechanic and easily landed a job at the age of seventeen. He was still working as a mechanic in 1953 when he was drafted by the U.S. Army. He had been dating Dorothy Buchanan for several months and they married soon after he received his draft notice. A month after they were married, Glenn left for active duty. He attended heavy equipment operation and repair

---

74  Don Bunner interview, October 2010

training for sixteen weeks at Fort Knox, Kentucky, after which he received orders to join a squadron which had seen action during the Korean War. A ceasefire had recently been negotiated, so Glenn's squadron would now be to working to keep the peace.

Before arriving in Korea, Glenn's squadron was transferred to Chitose Air Base on the island of Hokkaido, Japan. Glenn spent the winter putting his training as a heavy equipment operator to use. He operated a grader to plow the two hundred inches of snow that fell that winter from the runways so military planes could take off and land. After that winter at Chitose Air Base, Glenn's squadron was reassigned to Guam, where he spent the rest of his time on active duty.

Glenn was discharged from the Army in 1955 and reunited with his wife and daughter Barbara, who had been born while he was on active duty in Asia. During the period 1956 – 1960, Glenn and his family lived with his parents at their house in Dallison. Glenn had jobs operating tractors and backhoes. His first son Larry was born in 1957, and second son Jerry was born in 1958.

In 1960, Glenn and his family moved into a nearby house owned by his parents in Dallison. In 1961, daughter Carolyn was born. In 1965, Glenn purchased an abandoned 65 acre farm on Progress Ridge Road and spent over a year fixing up the old house to make it livable again. He moved there with his family in 1966. He worked at Premier Photo, later known as Best Photo in Coolville, Ohio from 1965 until the late 1970's when the business closed down.

Glenn and Dorothy divorced in the late 1970's. Dorothy died of cancer in April 1988 at the age of 56. Glenn followed a work cycle as a heavy equipment operator during nine months of the year and then as an auto or heavy equipment mechanic during the winter months. He had several lady friends through the years but never remarried. Around 1990, he moved in with his mother Mable at her house in Dallison and was living there when she died in February 1996. Mable left the house to Glenn in her will. Glenn developed throat cancer in 2007 and received radiation and chemotherapy treatment from the VA Hospital in Clarksburg, West Virginia. They were able to slow the growth of the cancer, but not to eradicate it. Glenn died on May 29, 2013, and was buried at the Pleasant Valley Cemetery (Skidmore).[75]

---

75 Information provided by Mable Bunner, Don Bunner, Greg Bunner, and Mike Bunner

*13.*

# Robert Lee Bunner
## *(1931 – 1981)*

Robert Lee Bunner was born in Zanesville, Ohio on October 10, 1931. He was the fourth child, and second son, of John and Mable Bunner. When Bob was born, the Great Depression was underway. When he was eighteen months old, the Depression cost John, his father, the job he had held for nine years at A.E. Tile Company in Zanesville. Unable to find another job, John made the decision to move back to West Virginia where he and Mable had been born and had grown up. There they rented the same D.R. Congleton farm in rural Wood County that John had lived on with his family from approximately 1917 until John left to move to Zanesville in October 1922.[1]

This farm held sad memories for John because it was where his brother Frank, his sister Agnes, and his brother Kermit had died as children during the Spanish flu epidemic of 1918-1919.[2] However, when John had made inquiries regarding farms in Wood County that were available for rent in early 1933, this farm was available. John signed the rental agreement with the Congleton family and by July 1933, he and Mable had completed the move of their family from Zanesville back to West Virginia.

---

1 Mable Bunner interview, 1979

2 Mable Bunner interview, 1979

**John and Mable Bunner Children – Summer 1933 –
Congleton Farm, Wood County, WV
Left front – Don, left rear – Ellen, in highchair – Robert, right - Ruth**

Two months later, Mable gave birth to Bob's little brother, Glenn. At this time, all five of John and Mable's children were under the age of eight - too young to help with the farm work that was necessary to provide for the family. John purchased two milk cows, two pigs, a mule, a rooster, and fifteen hens. During that first year, John did virtually all the outdoor farm work. Mable assisted him with whatever time she could find after taking care of five children and making three meals a day for everyone.

In the fall of 1933, older sisters Ellen and Ruth began going to Pleasant Hill school each day. As the move to the Congleton farm was too late in the summer to plant and harvest crops, neighbors from nearby farms shared some of their corn and potato harvest with John and Mable. John stored the potatoes in the root cellar and Mabel canned approximately one hundred quarts of corn. Existing apple trees on the farm provided several bushels of apples from which Mable canned applesauce and apple butter. As cold weather set in, John spent more time hunting each day and caught enough squirrels, rabbits, deer, and wild turkeys to keep the family fed through the winter.

The following spring, John used his mule to plow the gardens for growing corn and potatoes. Because of a broken leg injury he had suffered at the age of eighteen, John walked behind the mule with a noticeable limp because one leg was two inches shorter than the other.[3] However, the disability caused by this injury paled when compared to the enormity of the task he had of providing for his family. He bore down and did all the work that was necessary to put food on the table. He never complained about the difficulty or unfairness of the life that had been handed to him.

John and Mable taught Ellen, Ruth, and Don how to plant corn and potatoes. Mable took responsibility for the smaller gardens near the house where she grew tomatoes, green beans, peas, cucumbers, onions, carrots, lettuce, and radishes. She taught Ellen, Ruth, and Don to pull weeds out of the garden by their roots, and how to pour water from a sprinkling can onto the growing plants during periods of infrequent rain.

John also started taking four-year-old Don with him as he performed his morning chores of feeding the animals, milking the cows, gathering the eggs, chopping a day's supply of firewood, and carrying water from the spring in the backyard to the kitchen for Mable to use during the day. The following year, in 1935, John assigned Don the task of completing some of these chores.[4] Bob and Glenn were still too young to be reliable help.

In September 1936, Don started to school, leaving only five-year-old Bob and three-year-old Glenn at home during the day. Bob started assuming some of the chores Don had previously been responsible for such as gathering eggs and carrying water from the

---

3  Mable Bunner interview, 1979

4  Don Bunner interview, 2010

spring to the kitchen each morning.[5] He wasn't chopping firewood yet, but he carried firewood chopped by his dad into the kitchen for his mom to use in the cooking stove.

That fall, Bob helped his family harvest the crops by pulling the ripe ears of corn off the stalk and putting them in a bushel basket. The family needed about 160 bushels of corn each year to get through the winter. Mable would can about 20 bushels each year and grind about 20 bushels into corn meal. The rest was used as a food source to supplement the hay they fed the cows and the mule during the winter.

Bob and Don had the task of picking potatoes out of the ground after John overturned each hill with his potato fork. When the basket was full, John would carry it to the root cellar where he would dump it into the potato bin for winter storage. They harvested about eighty bushels of potatoes each year. This would be enough to feed them through the winter with enough left over to serve as seed potatoes to plant the following spring.

By the time these crops were harvested the apples on the trees growing on the farm would be ripe. Bob and Don would climb up in the trees to pick apples to throw down to their parents standing on the ground. They needed to pick five bushels of apples in order for Mable to can one hundred quarts of applesauce.[6]

In the spring of 1937, when he was five, Bob had become a productive laborer on the family farm. He helped plant the seeds in the garden and learned how to hoe weeds without damaging the new corn and potato sprouts growing out of the ground. He plucked jars full of potato beetles from the plants and then crushed them with a large flat rock. His dad took Don and Bob hunting with him. After John shot the squirrels or rabbits, Don and Bob would run and retrieve them. When John would shoot a deer, Don and Bob would help drag it back to the house where they would immediately gut and skin it and carve it into pieces small enough to cook on the kitchen stove. Wild game had to be eaten the same day it was caught as there were no refrigerators to preserve the meat. Deer

---

5  Don Bunner interview, 2010

6  Don Bunner interview, 2010

meat was shared with neighbors, who would return the favor when they would catch a deer.

On July 4$^{th}$, the family would take a day off from farm chores to celebrate Independence Day. They made ice cream in their hand cranked ice cream maker and sometimes had watermelon. As the sun started setting, they would make their way up the steep road to Boston Hill, so called because it was on land owned by Ted Boston. It was about one mile from their farm. Boston Hill was the highest point along Progress Ridge Road and provided a good view of the fireworks being set off at the Parkersburg City Park ten miles to the west.[7]

During the fall of 1937 and the spring of 1938 Bob had taken over the farm chores Don had previously been responsible for, and Don took responsibility for harnessing the mules (they now had two) and using them to plow the corn and potato fields, mow the hayfields, rake the hay into haystacks, and pull trees back to the house that John and Don had sawed down for firewood. Bob was taught how to use a handsaw and an ax, and he and Don spent at least one hour every day chopping the next day's supply of firewood for the family.

In the fall of 1938, Bob started to school at Pleasant Hill Elementary School. Ruth was in fifth grade and Don was in third grade. The three walked together down the path through the woods from their house to the school bus stop on Route 50. The bus stop was directly across the road from where their Grandpa and Grandma Bunner lived on a 200-acre farm known as the "Fouse place." [The original German settlers spelled the name 'Fauss,' but subsequent generations changed the spelling to 'Fouse.'] Once the school bus picked them up, it was only a five minute ride to the school.[8]

---

7   Don Bunner interview, 2010

8   Don Bunner interview, 2010

**Bunners in front yard of Bruce and Maggie Bunner's house at "Fouse place" circa 1937**
Left to right – front: Justine Allen son, Don Bunner, Robert Bunner. Middle: Ruth Bunner, Ellen Bunner, Justine Allen daughter. Rear standing – Glenn Bunner. Standing to right – Mable Bunner

That fall, Ellen was in seventh grade and enrolled in the new one-room Pleasant Valley School at the intersection of U.S. Route 50 and Progress Ridge Road. It was a ¾ mile walk for Ellen. Also in the fall of 1938, John got a job working for the Worker's Progress Administration (W.P.A.) His crew worked every day doing maintenance work on roads and bridges in Wood County. It was the first time in five years that John had a job and a steady income. It was the beginning of the end of the backbreaking poverty the family had lived through during the previous five years.[9]

On December 19, 1938, Bob's Grandpa Bunner died of a heart attack at his home on the Fouse farm. Bob was seven years old. His Grandpa's funeral was held at Pleasant Valley Church on December 20, 1938. Bob went to the funeral and the burial at the Pleasant Valley Cemetery (Skidmore) with his family.

---

9  Mable Bunner interview, 1979

After Bruce's death, Ruth, Don, and Bob would sometimes visit with their Grandma Bunner at her house after getting off their school bus. They would start walking home on the path through the woods so they would always be home before dark.[10]

**Robert Bunner circa 1940 – Age 9**

At the end of the school year in 1939, John was still working every day with the WPA. One of the first things he purchased with some of his discretionary money was a battery powered radio. (This battery was the same 6-volt battery used in the late 1930's to start car engines.) They couldn't pick up many stations during the day, but each evening when some radio stations turned up their power to 50,000 watts, they could pick up stations broadcasting from Wheeling (WWVA), Pittsburgh (KDKA), Cleveland (WTAM), and Cincinnati (WLW). On Saturday nights, they could pick up the Grand Ole Opry being broadcast live on WSM-AM from Nashville, Tennessee. In 2010, Glenn remembered listening to Bill Monroe, Roy Acuff, and Cousin Minnie Pearl on the Grand Ole Opry on the Nashville station.[11]

---

10   Don Bunner interview, 2010

11   Don Bunner interview, 2010

During the summer of 1939, with John working full-time, it fell to Mable, Don, Bob, and Glenn to work the farm every day from planting time in the spring to harvest time in the fall. Ruth and Ellen did many of the household chores that their mom normally performed around the house. John pitched in to finish some chores when he got home in the evening, but he relied on his family to grow enough food for the winter. That was the summer that all of John and Mable's children truly learned the meaning of responsibility. They each had a job to do, and if they didn't do it well, it negatively impacted every other member of the family. They each developed a work ethic between 1939 and 1941 that they maintained for the rest of their lives.[12]

John would give his paychecks to Mable and let her manage the family's finances. Mable would walk to Route 50 at Pleasant Valley once a month where she would catch a Greyhound bus to Parkersburg. At that time, there was one bus running from Washington, D.C. to Parkersburg that passed through Pleasant Valley each morning at about 9:00 A.M., and a bus running from Parkersburg to Washington D.C. that passed through Pleasant Valley each afternoon at about 3:00 P.M. Mable would do her monthly shopping in Parkersburg, buying grocery items like salt and sugar, clothing items like shoes and coats, and rolls of material for making shirts for the boys and dresses for the girls. Don and Bob knew exactly when the bus would arrive at Pleasant Valley so they would team the mules to a wagon and meet her there so she didn't have to carry everything home by herself.[13]

At this time, World War II was raging in Europe, Northern Africa, and Asia. President Roosevelt was attempting to navigate a path of neutrality to stay out of the war, but that all ended on December 7, 1941, with the Japanese bombing of Pearl Harbor. Everyone in the Bunner family gathered around their radio that Sunday evening to listen to the news. President Roosevelt came on and delivered the following message:

---

12  Don Bunner interview, 2010

13  Don Bunner interview, 2010

"Good evening, ladies and gentlemen, I am speaking to you tonight at a very serious moment in our history. The Cabinet is convening and the leaders in Congress are meeting with the President. The State Department and Army and Navy officials have been with the President all afternoon. In fact, the Japanese ambassador was talking to the president at the very time that Japan's airships were bombing our citizens in Hawaii and the Philippines and sinking one of our transports loaded with lumber on its way to Hawaii.

By tomorrow morning the members of Congress will have a full report and be ready for action.

In the meantime, we the people are already prepared for action. For months now the knowledge that something of this kind might happen has been hanging over our heads and yet it seemed impossible to believe, impossible to drop the everyday things of life and feel that there was only one thing which was important - preparation to meet an enemy no matter where he struck. That is all over now and there is no more uncertainty.

We know what we have to face and we know that we are ready to face it.

I should like to say just a word to the women in the country tonight. I have a boy at sea on a destroyer, for all I know he may be on his way to the Pacific. Two of my children are in coast cities on the Pacific. Many of you all over the country have boys in the services who will now be called upon to go into action. You have friends and families in what has suddenly become a danger zone. You cannot escape anxiety. You cannot escape a clutch of fear at your heart and yet I hope that the certainty of what we have to meet will make you rise above these fears.

We must go about our daily business more determined than ever to do the ordinary things as well as we can and when we find a way to do anything more in our communities to help others, to build morale, to give a feeling of security, we must do it. Whatever is asked of us I am sure we can accomplish it. We are the free and unconquerable people of the United States of America.

To the young people of the nation, I must speak a word tonight. You are going to have a great opportunity. There will be high moments in which your strength and your ability will be tested. I have faith in you. I feel as though I was standing upon a rock and that rock is my faith in my fellow citizens."

In 2010, Don and Glenn recalled listening to President Roosevelt on the radio that evening. Everyone was stunned. They remembered that their mother, Mable, started crying, something they had never seen her do before. John and Mable didn't know what the future held, but it was now beyond their ability to control that future. Remarkably, after that day, the citizens of the United States came together as they had never done before. Everybody - young or old, man or woman, rich or poor, black or white, Christian of Jew, Democrat or Republican – developed a common resolve. They were going to do everything within their power to defeat the German Nazi's and the Japanese imperialists. The fear and panic they felt on the evening of December 7 was quickly replaced by a national resolve that was stronger than tempered steel.[14]

Within just a few months, virtually all factories in the United States were retooled to manufacture products required for the war effort. O. Ames, a shovel and garden tool manufacturer in South Parkersburg was retooled to make bomb casings and armored plating. Most of the younger men in Wood County between the ages of 18 and 30 were being drafted into military service. This meant that women and older men had to provide the labor in the factories. By May 1942, John had been hired by O. Ames to work five days per week, eleven hours per day, to make bomb and machine gun shell casings. John was not going to be drafted, as he was forty-one years old, had four children at home, and was crippled due to his 1921

---

14  Don Bunner interview, 2010

injury which left him with one leg being two inches shorter than the other leg.[15]

Bob's brother-in-law Burl Hewitt, who had married his older sister Ellen in January 1942, had been hired to work at Atlas Powder Ordnance Plant in Ravenna, Ohio (near Akron). This company manufactured gunpowder. Burl had to close his auto repair shop in Dallison to accept this job, but in 1942 making gunpowder was much more important than repairing automobiles.[16]

Even with the war effort ramping up nationwide, the schools continued operating just as they did before the start of the war. In early 1942, Ruth was completing ninth grade at Parkersburg High School, Don was completing seventh grade at Pleasant Valley School, Bob was completing fifth grade at Pleasant Hill Elementary School, and Glenn was completing third grade at Pleasant Hill. Ruth had become the first Bunner to ever attend high school.

During the last six months of 1942 all the fighting age men in the family were drafted into military service. John's younger brother Dale enlisted in the Army Air Corps on August 8. On October 12, 1942, Burl Hewitt enlisted in the U.S. Army. On October 20, John's youngest brother Carl enlisted in the Army Air Corps. On February 4, 1943, a seventeen-year-old young man named Paul Withers in Zanesville, Ohio, enlisted in the Navy. Paul was unknown to the Bunners at that time, but he would join the Bunner family four years later when he married Bob's older sister Ruth. After training, all four of these young soldiers were assigned to the Pacific theatre to fight the war against Japan.

With John's younger brothers Dale and Carl off to war in the Pacific, John's sixty-two-year-old mother, Maggie, was suddenly living alone on the 200 acre farm she had been renting. As it was impossible for Maggie to continue working the farm by herself, John's older brother Robert persuaded Maggie to move in with his family at their home in south Parkersburg. Maggie made this move in September or October 1942.[17]

---

15   Mable Bunner interview, 1979

16   Information from Burl Hewitt WWII draft card, 1942

17   Mable Bunner interview, 1979

As soon as Maggie made the move to Parkersburg, John and Mable assumed the lease on the Fouse property and moved the family from the D.R. Congleton farm.[18] The move added significant conveniences to all members of John and Mable's family. For John, it saved approximately forty minutes of walking each day between the Congleton farmhouse and Progress Ridge Road, where Lester Dunlap, his coworker at O. Ames, picked him up and dropped him off. Since all four children still at home were attending school, it eliminated forty minutes each day for them to walk between the Route 50 bus stop and the Congleton farmhouse. The bus stop for all four children was now directly in front of their house. For Mable, who still had to take the Greyhound Bus to and from Parkersburg at least once per month to go grocery shopping, the bus could now be flagged down in front of her house.[19]

Because John was working eleven hour days and his commute required an additional hour each day, he was unable to work the farm except on weekends. Though still relatively young, Don, Bob, and Glenn, with some supervision from Mable, spent their summers planting and tending the gardens, taking care of the livestock (they had two milk cows, two pigs, two mules, and about two dozen chickens), mowing the lawn (they had two old fashioned push reel mowers that required considerable strength to maneuver over the lawn), and cutting, chopping, and splitting firewood.[20]

During the late fall, after all the crops were harvested and canned, Bob enjoyed going hunting. He would generally catch 7-8 squirrels and bring them back to the house where he would gut and skin them and cut them into smaller pieces for cooking. His mother would cook the squirrels and that would be the meat the family would eat for dinner that evening.

Bob would also go deer hunting around Thanksgiving, but he only caught one deer during the four years he lived on the Fouse place. In a 2010 interview, Don also recalled that he saw very few deer in Wood County during the 1940's. It may have been that the

---

18  Mable Bunner interview, 1979

19  Don Bunner interview, 2010

20  Don Bunner interview, 2010

deer were overhunted during the Great Depression when it may have sometimes been the only food available for a hungry family.[21]

On June 6, 1944, Allied Forces executed the greatest amphibious landing of military forces in the history of the world along the coast of France. Though the allies had the element of surprise on their side, D-Day still cost the lives of over 4,400 allied soldiers, including over 2,500 Americans. Though these sacrifices were heavy, they were not in vain. The invasion succeeded and allowed the allied forces to begin their relentless drive of the Nazi forces back toward Germany. The morale and the resolve of the American soldiers – and all the citizens back home working to support them – grew stronger. D-Day was the beginning of the end of Hitler's maniacal tyranny.

At about the time of D-Day, Ruth completed tenth grade at Parkersburg High School and decided that was enough school for her. During the summer of 1944, she no longer wanted to be sharing a bedroom with her three younger brothers. In his 2010 interview, Don stated that there were only two bedrooms in the Fouse house, one for his parents, and one for the kids. There was one big bed in the kids bedroom where Don, Bob, and Glenn slept. There was a smaller bed where Ruth slept.[22]

Though John and Mabel tried to keep the boys out of the room while Ruth was dressing and undressing, it was impossible to provide her with the level of privacy she wanted. Letters between Mabel and her parents, Bill and Ida Reynolds, in Zanesville, Ohio resolved this dilemma. Mable's parents owned a large house in Zanesville where Ruth could have her own bedroom. During the fall of 1944, Ruth moved to Zanesville, leaving Don, Bob, and Glenn living at home.[23]

During the first few months after moving to Zanesville, Ruth helped her grandmother with the housework. However, in early

---

21  Don Bunner interview, 2010

22  Don Bunner interview, 2010

23  Don Bunner interview, 2010

1945, she got a job at the nearby Mosaic Tile Company factory. She was working there when World War II ended.[24]

In the fall of 1944, Don entered ninth grade at Parkersburg High School. He rode a school bus that took a serpentine route through eastern Wood County to pick up students living in rural areas. Because of this, Don was on the bus for 1½ hours each morning before arriving to school. It took the same amount of time to return home in the evening.[25]

At the same time Robert entered seventh grade at Pleasant Valley School, and Glenn entered fifth grade at Pleasant Hill Elementary School. John continued getting up at five o'clock every morning. Lester Dunlap picked him up at six o'clock to drive to work at O. Ames. John and Lester both worked eleven hour days, and Lester would drive the two of them home every evening. John would arrive home every evening at 6:00 P.M.[26]

After D-Day, the news coming from the war front in Europe became ever more positive. By the end of September 1944, large parts of France, Belgium and the Netherlands had been liberated from Nazi control. The news coming from the Pacific front was also encouraging. Allied victories in Saipan, Guam, New Guinea, and Burma gave hope to all Americans that the Japanese forces would eventually be vanquished.

The good news on both fronts continued in early 1945. In Europe, the allies had crossed the Rhine River and successfully invaded the German homeland. In April, the Russian forces, who were allied with America and England, captured Berlin in the eastern part of Germany. In the Pacific, victories in the Philippines, Iwo Jima, and Okinawa, allowed American forces to start bombing the southern Japanese islands directly.

In April 1945, President Franklin Roosevelt died and was succeeded by Vice President Harry S. Truman. A month later, on May 8, 1945, Germany surrendered to the allied forces, ending the war

---

24 Information provided by Phyllis and Danny Withers, children of Ruth Bunner Withers

25 Don Bunner interview, 2010

26 Mable Bunner interview, 1979

in Europe. In August 1945, after President Truman had authorized the use of the newly developed atomic bomb on the Japanese cities of Hiroshima and Nagasaki, the Japanese surrendered. World War II was over.

After the news of the Japanese surrender reached America, euphoria and spontaneous celebrations broke out all over the United States. V-J Day brought a sense of relief and joy after years of military conflict and sacrifice.

In the summer of 1945, Ellen's husband Burl returned home to West Virginia. He spent a few days getting reacquainted with his wife and getting to know his daughter Sandra, who was now almost one year old. He promptly reopened his auto repair garage in Dallison. He reestablished his relationships with his brothers-in-law who had been too young to fight in the war. He helped Don and Bob build a mechanized saw to replace the handsaw and axe they had been using to cut firewood into small logs. He allowed fourteen-year-old Glenn to roam at will in his garage, where Glenn quickly showed an aptitude for diagnosing and fixing mechanical problems with cars.[27]

Bob's uncles Dale and Carl were discharged from the Army Air Corp several months later. Dale came home to his wife Edith. Carl married Anna Gantz soon after returning home. They both got jobs in chemical plants in the Parkersburg area and started families.

In early 1946, Paul Withers, who had served three years in the Navy, seeing action in the Pacific theatre, returned home to Zanesville, Ohio and got a job at Mosaic Tile Company. There he met Bob's sister Ruth, who had been working at the Mosaic Tile for several months. Ruth and Paul started dating and were engaged just a few months later.[28]

In September 1945, O. Ames began the transition from wartime to peacetime production. They asked John to stay on as a production worker making shovels and other farm tools. With the guarantee of an ongoing job, John and Mable used the money they had saved

---

27  Don Bunner interview, 2010

28  Information provided by Phyllis and Danny Withers, children of Ruth Bunner Withers

during the war for a down payment on a house on three acres in Dallison, two miles west of where they had lived during the war.[29]

Don, Bob, and Glenn made the move to Dallison with their parents during the summer of 1946. Bob was fourteen years old. This move brought about a fundamental shift in his young life. There was no longer the need to grow crops to survive. Because the new house had natural gas, there was no longer the need to spend an hour every day chopping firewood. The cows, mules, and pigs had been sold prior to the move to Dallison, so the time Bob had previously spent tending the animals was no longer necessary. The only animals they brought with them were their chickens, which were relatively easy to care for. Bob's life as a farm boy had come to an end.[30]

Don quit school in February 1947 during his eleventh grade year. He travelled to Columbus, Ohio with two of his friends from rural Wood County where all three enlisted in the Army. Their ambition was to see the world.[31]

Bob entered ninth grade at Parkersburg High School in the fall of 1946. The 1946 high school yearbook included a picture of him as a member of the Aeronautical Club. The description of this club included in the yearbook reads: "Did you say you need a good pilot? Call up one of the members of this club in about ten years and you'll probably get one of the best, for already they have learned something of plane structure, aerial navigation terms, and other aeronautical knowledge from their textbook, "Your Wings." [32]

---

29  Mable Bunner interview
30  Don Bunner interview, 2010
31  Don Bunner interview, 2010
32  Parkersburg High School 1946 Yearbook, Aeronautical Club

Aeronautics Club – Parkersburg High School – 1946 – Row one: Frank Acree, Denzil Bennet, Jack Ross, Carl Chadock, Jack Schneid, Ross Miller. Row two: Miss Helmick, Harold Rexroad, Gary Hines, John Dye, Fred Hinshelwood, David Cutlip, Robert Bunner, Carman Adams. Row three: Ronald Overton, Porter Louding, Gene Harris, Earl Smith, David Trout, James Woodyard, Robert Wile, Absent – Edward McAtee

School didn't interest Bob. As a result, he was only an average student. On October 10, 1947, he quit school on his sixteenth birthday. He had just begun his tenth grade year.

After quitting school, Bob got a job working at a sawmill in Dallison owned by Denzill Blair. He was able to walk to work. He earned $0.75/hour.[33]

During 1948 Bob got his driver's license but did not have enough money to buy a car. During 1948 and 1949 he continued working at the sawmill in Dallison. He also continued living with his parents and walking to and from work every day.

In February 1950, Don completed his three-year enlistment in the Army and returned home. He got a job working night shift at O. Ames, the same place his father worked. At this time, Don, Bob, and Glenn were all living with their parents in Dallison. Don had a 48 Chevy that he let Bob and Glenn drive.[34]

In May of 1950, Bob went to a church social at the Pleasant Valley Church where he met Imogene Hendershot who, like Bob, had quit school on her sixteenth birthday. Many years later Imogene confided that neither she nor Robert were at the church

---

33  Imogene Schupp interview, 2011

34  Don Bunner interview, 2010

that day for the "right" reason. They were both high school dropouts and their sole purpose for attending this social was to meet other kids their age.[35]

Imogene said that during the social she and Bob found a grassy spot away from the crowds where they sat, ate and flirted. When the social ended, Bob and Imogene got a ride to Bob's house in Dallison. Don's car was not available for Bob to drive Imogene home, so Bob walked with her from Dallison to the top of Montgomery Hill, a distance of approximately two miles. Before saying goodnight, Bob asked her for a date the next week, and she accepted. Imogene then walked to her home on Loomis Ridge Road and Bob walked back to his parents' house in Dallison.[36]

Bob and Imogene were soon dating steadily. In a 2011 interview, Imogene recalled that she and Bob would often go to the house of Imogene's cousin, where they would just hang out and listen to the radio. During the summer of 1950, Imogene worked for Helis and Lela Barnes on Montgomery Hill cleaning their house. Lela Barnes was from Sutton in Braxton County, West Virginia.[37]

On June 25, 1950, the Korean War started. All men between the ages of eighteen and twenty-six were required to register for the draft. Bob was 18½, so he had to register.

During the summer of 1950, the relationship between Bob and Imogene quickly became serious. In July, just two months after they met they were talking about marriage. The problem was that parental consent for marriage was required for all men under age twenty-one and all women under eighteen. Bob was eighteen and Imogene was seventeen. Imogene asked her parents to sign a consent for the marriage. As she had only been dating Bob two months, they refused.[38]

Imogene drew in Lela Barnes as her confidante and revealed how her parents had refused to consent to the marriage. Lela told

---

35  Imogene Schupp interview, 2011

36  Imogene Schupp interview, 2011

37  Imogene Schupp interview, 2011

38  Imogene Schupp interview, 2011

her that the County Clerk in Braxton County, where she was from, never asked for a birth certificate from couples applying for a marriage license. Imogene discussed this with Bob, and they both decided to pursue this option. They recruited Helis and Lela Barnes as their coconspirators.[39]

At that time Bob still didn't own a car, so Helis and Lela agreed to drive Bob and Imogene to Braxton County so they could get married. However, the process was more difficult than they had initially imagined. All Bob and Imogene accomplished on this trip was completing their blood tests. Two weeks later Helis and Lela drove them back to Sutton to get married. As a contingency, Imogene had completed a parental consent form and had forged the signatures of both of her parents.[40]

When Bob and Imogene applied for their marriage license at the County Clerk's office in Sutton, Bob gave his age as twenty-one, and Imogene gave her age as twenty. No birth certificates were requested to verify their ages, and the marriage license was issued. Imogene did not have to resort to the forged parental consent form that she had in her purse. Simply lying about their ages had been enough. Their marriage license was issued on September 15, 1950. They were married that same day in the parsonage of the Sutton Methodist Church by Reverend Shirley Cottrell.[41]

---

39  Imogene Schupp interview, 2011

40  Imogene Schupp interview, 2011

41  Imogene Schupp interview, 2011

Left - Robert and Imogene Bunner after marriage in 1950 (colorization by Mike Bunner). Right – Garage apartment they rented, upper two windows on right (picture taken circa 2010).

Neither Imogene's parents nor Bob's parents knew anything about this marriage before it happened. Both sets of parents were extremely upset when they learned about it but took no steps to have the marriage annulled. Imogene's mother did write a letter to Braxton County Courthouse to find out if it was true. The reply from the County Clerk's office confirmed they were married.[42]

After their marriage, Bob and Imogene rented a two bedroom apartment over Burl Hewitt's garage in Dallison. Bob continued working at the local sawmill and started thinking about looking for a better job in Parkersburg.[43]

Over the Thanksgiving holiday weekend in 1950, the greatest snowfall in the recorded history of Wood County, West Virginia paralyzed the area. Over a five day period, a total of 34 inches of snow fell. All roads, schools, and businesses were closed. Everyone was housebound for nearly ten days before the roads could be cleared. Sixty years later, Imogene told her son Mike that it was during this snowstorm of 1950 that he was conceived.[44]

---

42  Imogene Schupp interview, 2011

43  Imogene Schupp interview, 2011

44  Imogene Schupp during hospital visit by son Mike, May 2012

During that time, some men Bob's age were being drafted to fight in the Korean War. However, Bob never received a draft notice. Historical archives show that 50 million American men were registered for the draft during the Korean War. Of those, 1.5 million, or 3%, were drafted. Bob was among the 97% that were not drafted.

On August 30, 1951, Bob and Imogene had their first child, Robert Michael. They initially called him "Bobby," but when others began calling him "Little Bob," Bob made the decision to call him by his middle name. He became known as "Mike." Bob was adamant that he did not want his son to go through life being called "Little Bob."

Around the time of Mike's birth, his Uncle Paul Withers was called back to the Navy for a second active duty tour. While he was away, Bob's sister Ruth and her four-year-old daughter Phyliss moved from Zanesville to Dallison to live with Ruth's parents. During Christmas 1951, Ruth, Phyliss, Don, and Glenn were all living with John and Mable in Dallison.[45]

In 1952, Bob got a job working for Storck's Bakery in Parkersburg. He purchased a 42 Chevy so he could commute to work. In her 2011 interview, Imogene said that, after Bob got the job at the bakery, both she and Robert thought they had hit the jackpot. They believed they would now be able to afford all that they needed and a few things they wanted.[46]

Also in her 2011 interview, Imogene revealed that her marriage to Robert was not sound from the very beginning. She remembered how they would argue and scream at each other all the time. They would split apart then get back together over, and over, and over again. Sixty years later and with the wisdom that comes with old age, Imogene confessed that she and Robert were two young kids that jumped into marriage way too fast without really knowing each other well.[47]

In 1952, Don reenlisted in the Army and was sent to Germany to begin a three year tour of duty.[48] At about the same time as Don left,

---

45  Don Bunner interview, 2010
46  Imogene Schupp interview, 2011
47  Imogene Schupp interview, 2011
48  Don Bunner interview, 2010

Bob traded his 42 Chevy for a sleek and sporty 40 Ford Coupe. He owned this car until July of 1953 when he traded it for a 48 Chevy. The 40 Ford Coupe is the first car that his son Mike remembers riding in.

**Bob's car from mid-1952 to mid-1953 was a black 40 Ford Coupe**

While working at Storck's Bakery, Robert began to frequent the "Corner Café", a small restaurant across the street from the Bakery. One sweltering day in the summer of 1952, Robert was sitting in the Café waiting to order a sandwich. The waitress noticed he was looking extremely sad and gloomy. Trying to lighten up his countenance, the waitress asked, "Do you think it's going to snow?" Bob gave her a slight smile. She asked him what was wrong and he replied that he and his wife were having problems. The waitress was Rosie Carpenter.[49]

In August 1952, Imogene became pregnant with her and Robert's second child. During this time, the marriage between Robert and Imogene was disintegrating. After continually separating and then getting back together, they separated for the last time in the spring of 1953 and would never get back together again. They gave up their apartment over the garage in Dallison. Robert moved back in with

---

49  Rose Carpenter Bunner interview, 2010

his parents. Imogene approached her parents to see if she could move back with them. They refused, telling her that she now had a family and needed to work things out for herself. Imogene took Mike and moved in with her sister Ruth and her husband Clyde in Parkersburg.[50]

On May 26, 1953, Robert and Imogene's second son, Darrell Lee, was born. Ruth's husband, Clyde, took Imogene to the hospital when she went into labor. Robert came to the hospital after Darrell was born.[51]

Imogene took Darrell home from the hospital to Ruth and Clyde's house. Within a few weeks after Darrell was born, Imogene got a job working in housekeeping at St. Joseph's hospital. She moved with Mike and Darrell from her sister's house to a small apartment that she rented that was part of a private home on Madison Avenue in Parkersburg. A woman living in the same house agreed to take care of Mike and Darrell during the day while Imogene was working.[52] Unfortunately, when she came home each day she could tell that Mike and Darrell's diapers had not been changed all day and she was unsure they were even being fed.[53]

Some days she was reasonably certain Darrell had not been picked up from his bed all day. One day when she came home she learned that a good Samaritan had found Mike walking down sidewalk steps toward a busy street when he retrieved him, checked with neighbors to see who he belonged to, and eventually returned him to his mother's apartment. She talked to the woman who had agreed to watch the boys during the day, and she claimed she would do a better job in the future. A week later, when the childcare had not improved, Imogene concluded that she had to make a change.[54]

In August 1953, Imogene went to Dallison with Mike and Darrell and asked John and Mabel if they could keep the boys and raise them as their own. John and Mabel agreed to take the boys.

---

50 Imogene Schupp interview, 2011
51 Imogene Schupp interview, 2011
52 Imogene Schupp interview, 2011
53 Imogene Schupp during hospital visit by son Mike, May 2012
54 Imogene Schupp interview, 2011

Reliving this event sixty years later with her son Mike, Imogene confessed that she was unfit to be a mother at that time in her life.[55]

She also told Mike that his grandfather, John, became a saint in her eyes that evening. Imogene said she had been crying while she was with John and Mabel and after she left the house without Mike and Darrell she broke down and started sobbing on their front porch. John saw her, came out, sat down beside of her, and put his arm around her. He told her not to worry, that he and Mable would make sure her boys were well taken care of. He then told her that he was certain that, with time, she would work through all the problems she was facing. Imogene told Mike that throughout the rest of her life, she never met a kinder, more compassionate, and more caring person than John Bunner.[56]

During this time, Storck's Bakery had a tradition of giving a free cake to one employee every week. One week, Bob was the recipient. He took the cake home to his mother, but then he and John came up with an alternative plan for the cake. After dinner that evening, Mable got the cake out of the box to cut it in pieces to serve as desert. Before she could cut the cake, John winked at Bob and they simultaneously got up, picked Mable up and planted both of her feet in the cake. Everyone in the family hooted and laughed except for Mable, who felt a perfectly good cake had been ruined.[57]

By late 1953, Robert Bunner and Rosie Carpenter had begun to spend a lot of time together.[58] Imogene had also started seeing other men. According to Imogene's 2011 interview, even though she and Bob were seeing other people, the two of them would still spend time together.[59]

In late 1953, Imogene became pregnant again. At about the same time, she filed for a divorce from Robert. On March 10, 1954, Imogene and Robert were scheduled to appear in divorce court at the Wood County Courthouse. Although a divorce was granted, it

---

55 Imogene Schupp during hospital visit by son Mike, May 2012
56 Imogene Schupp during hospital visit by son Mike, May 2012
57 Rose Carpenter Bunner interview, 2010
58 Rose Carpenter Bunner interview, 2010
59 Imogene Schupp interview, 2011

could not be finalized because Imogene was not present. Sixty years later, Imogene said she missed the court date because she misunderstood her lawyer and believed she did not have to be present during the court proceedings.[60]

According to the divorce court record, with evidence presented by several witnesses appearing on behalf of the Defendant (Robert), the court found the Plaintiff (Imogene) guilty of adultery and the Defendant, Robert Lee Bunner, was entitled to divorce from the Plaintiff. Robert was given full custody of Mike and Darrell. The court record states actual physical custody and care was to be in the home of the paternal grandparents. Imogene was granted the right to see and be with Mike and Darrell at all reasonable times and places.[61]

In June of 1954, Imogene went into labor. However the baby was born premature and died. The death record for this baby names Robert Bunner as the father.[62] In her 2011 interview, Imogene said she wasn't sure whether Robert or the other man she had been seeing was the father. She was unaware that Robert's name was on the death certificate.[63] Imogene's mother, Anna Hendershot, was named as the informant on the death certificate.[64]

In January 1955, Rosie Carpenter became pregnant with her and Robert's first child. On September 20, 1955, Johnny Leroy Bunner was born.

---

60 Imogene Schupp interview, 2011

61 Wood County Clerk's Office, Divorces, 1955, Robert Lee and Imogene Hendershot Bunner

62 Wood County Clerk's Office, Death Certificate, Bunner Infant, 1954

63 Imogene Schupp interview, 2011

64 Wood County Clerk's Office, Death Certificate, Bunner Infant, 1954

Robert Bunner and Rosie Carpenter – circa 1954

In March of 1955, Robert and Imogene's divorce became final.[65] According to Rosie Carpenter Bunner, Robert thought he was legally divorced after the court hearing in March 1954. There was a legal fee that had to be paid before the divorce could be considered final. Robert paid this fee on March 10, 1955, and the divorce was finalized on that date.[66]

On September 25, 1956, Robert Bunner married Rosie Carpenter.[67] When renovations had been completed in the spring of 1957, Robert, Rosie, Mike, Darrell, and Johnny Leroy moved into the rental house belonging to John and Mabel. This was referred to by the Bunner family as "the little house." It had a living room, a kitchen, and two

---

65 Wood County Clerk's Office, Divorces, 1955, Robert Lee and Imogene Hendershot Bunner

66 Rose Carpenter Bunner interview, 2010

67 Wood County Clerk's Office, Marriage License, Robert Bunner and Rosie Carpenter, September 1956

bedrooms. Bob, Rosie, and Leroy moved from their small apartment in Parkersburg. Mike and Darrell moved from their nearby grandparent's house after residing there for nearly four years.

**The "little house" where Robert, Rosie, Mike, Darrell, and Leroy lived from 1957 to 1962. This was also the first home for Pam (b. 1960) and Tricia (b. 1961). Picture taken circa 1958.**

The "little house" did not have indoor plumbing, so there was no bathroom and no hot water. Bob's father John had built an outdoor toilet on the bank near the house. The outhouse was a "two-seater," with a small hole for the children and a large hole for the adults.

Also in 1957, Bob became the envy of Dallison when he purchased a new turquoise and white 1957 Chevy Belair. It was the first new car Bob had ever purchased and, in retrospect, was the only new car he ever purchased in his life. To celebrate his new car, Bob took the family, including his parents John and Mable, to Blackwater Falls State Park in eastern West Virginia. Soon afterward, he enrolled his oldest son Mike in first grade at Pleasant Valley Elementary School.

Left to right: Darrell, Mike, Leroy, and Rosie Bunner with new 57 Chevy

At that time, Robert was working at Storck's Bakery and Rosie was working as a waitress at Traveler's Restaurant in Parkersburg. Bob had his 57 Chevy and Rosie had a 52 Chevy. Rosie's brother Lloyd was hired to live with the family in "the little house" and work as a babysitter for Mike, Darrell, and Leroy while Rosie was working during the day.

One evening in early 1958, Rosie became distracted from her driving while turning a corner in Parkersburg and ran into a phone pole near the City Park. She wasn't hurt, but the car was assessed to be a total loss. Rather than replace the car, Rosie quit her job, her brother Lloyd returned to Ritchie County, and Rosie became a full-time housewife.

The first upgrade to the "little house" was made in 1958 when a water well was drilled, indoor plumbing with a hot water tank and septic tank was installed, and a full bathroom was added onto the house. The outdoor toilet was demolished and the pit was filled in.

In January 1960, Bob and Rosie's first daughter, Pamela Jayne, was born. The two bedroom "little house" would soon prove to be "too little."

**Robert Bunner circa 1960 (colorization by Mike Bunner)**

In 1960, Bob and Rosie decided to build a new house. They studied multiple designs and selected a house plan that had four bedrooms, a living room, dining room, kitchen, and full bath. It also had a full basement. They purchased one acre from John and Mable that lay between their house and the "little house." Construction started in late 1960 and was completed in late1961. While the new house was being built, a second daughter, Patricia Louise, was born on March 25, 1961.

The move to the new house was completed during the winter of 1961-1962, but the joy of living in the new house only lasted for a few months. The first heavy spring rain fell before grass had started growing on the hill behind the house. The drainage pipes that had been installed around and under the house became clogged with red clay mud that flowed like a stream off the hillside, forcing the muddy water runoff into the basement.

The new basement was flooded, and after the water was pumped out a six inch thick layer of red clay muck remained. It had to be shoveled out by hand and removed one bucket at a time. The clay had clogged and hardened in the drains that had been installed around the perimeter of the basement and under the basement floor, rendering them forever unusable. As a result, a sump pump to drain water from under the basement floor became a permanent necessity.

The red clay also permeated into the dry well where the septic tank effluent was to flow. This necessitated that the septic system be pumped at least once every six months for the next ten years until a new dry well was installed in another location in the early 1970's. On top of these problems, the steep bank behind the house turned out to be a thick layer of red clay laying on top of a sloping rock formation.

**Dallison Swimming Hole with New House in Background – Summer 1961**
Front left to right: Darrell and Barbara Bunner, back turned – Danny Withers, Rear, in water – Mike Bunner, standing on log ready to dive – Phyllis Withers

About a year after the house was built, the massive clay layer on the bank behind the house slipped downhill. The resultant pressure on the rear basement wall caused a one inch crack to open in the cement blocks along the entire length of the back wall.

**Robert and Rosie Bunner – New House under construction – October 1961**

Robert and Rosie did not have the money to fix any of these expensive problems, so they lived with them and came up with makeshift, partial fixes they could afford but which did not get to the root cause of their problems. It also became apparent very quickly that Bob and Rosie got in over their heads financially with their decision to build this new house. In 1962, the monthly mortgage payments on the new house consumed nearly 40% of Robert's take-home pay. Robert became a slave to his house payment. It was his highest priority payment every month, but most months he ran out of money before all his bills were paid. He started falling behind on these other bills, and bill collectors started using aggressive collection tactics.

The only way Bob could his head above water was to volunteer to work as much overtime as his employer would allow. Every few months he would get an overtime paycheck that was large enough to pay down most of his overdue bills, but then the debt would start expanding again. This was the endless treadmill that Bob and Rosie were on for most of the 1960's. They ultimately paid all their bills, but aside from their house payment, they would generally be thirty to ninety days late in paying them.

On November 12, 1962, Robert and Rosie's third daughter, Sherri Eileen, was born. Just after Sherri's first birthday, President John F. Kennedy was assassinated while riding in a motorcade in Dallas, Texas.

In December 1963, a previously unheard of musical group from England called "The Beatles" took America by storm and for the next year it seemed that every other song played on the radio was a Beatles tune. On April 29, 1964, during the height of Beatlemania, Rosie gave birth to her and Robert's fifth child, Russel Dewayne. Counting Mike and Darrell there were now seven children in the family.

Bob's father John died suddenly from a heart attack in January 1965. He was sixty-two years old. His funeral had to be delayed by over a week to allow Bob's brother Don the time to travel from Antarctica where he was on assignment with the U.S. Army.

During the 1960's Bob received two weeks of vacation each year from his employer. He always took one week in the summer and one week during deer season in November. His summer vacations generally consisted of going fishing for two or three days along the Ohio or Little Kanawha River. One day would be set aside for a picnic either at the Parkersburg City Park or North Bend State Park, which was located about twenty miles from Dallison. Rosie and Mable would share in food preparations for the picnic.

Bob's job never had set hours. He generally worked day shift, but sometimes his workday started at 5:00 A.M. and ended at 1:00 P.M. and other days it started at 10:00 A.M. and ended at 6:00 P.M. He always worked overtime any time he was given the opportunity, so some days he would work for sixteen hours. He always had to work on holidays, which was especially problematic on Christmas Day. He sometimes had to start working at 5:00 A.M. on Christmas morning and would not be home when the kids opened their presents. Two or three times during the 1960's, the kids would open their presents the night before so Bob could be there when they were opened. None of the kids liked this option because it made Christmas Day not seem like Christmas Day.

The time Bob spent with Mike and Darrell during the 1960's was focused primarily on baseball, hunting, and fishing. He spent a lot of time teaching them how to catch and throw a baseball. With Mike, he spent many hours throwing a baseball high in the air so Mike could learn to catch it. By the time Mike was ten, he could be counted on to catch any fly ball hit his way in left field. If his work schedule permitted it, Bob attended most of the Little League practice sessions and games in which Mike and Darrell played.

Fishing and hunting were therapeutic for Bob. These activities provided him a respite, if only for a few hours, from the debilitating financial burdens that he had to bear every day of his life during the 1960's.

By the late 1950's, Bob had become an avid West Virginia University Mountaineer football fan. Every Saturday afternoon during the fall football season he would turn on the radio to listen to the play-by-play calls by Jack Fleming, the "Voice of the Mountaineers." The rest of his Saturday schedule during football season had to fit around the WVU football game, as between 1:00 P.M. and 4:00 P.M. he was glued to the radio.

By 1966, the maintenance costs on Bob's 57 Chevy had become untenable. He purchased a 64 Mercury Comet, but as his seven children continued to grow, they soon could no longer all fit inside. This problem was exacerbated when Kevin Douglas was born on August 21, 1967. In 1968, Bob traded in the Comet for a 1965 Oldsmobile. It was a much larger car than the Comet and, at least for a while, all eight children could squeeze in. This was still a time when seat belts and infant car seats were not mandated.

In 1968, during Mike's senior year in high school, Bob was asked by Mike's guidance counselor to come to the high school to discuss college plans. Mike had received several scholarship offers that would pay up to 80% of all of his college expenses, but the other 20% would require obtaining a student loan. The counselor told Bob that he would need to cosign for Mike's student loan. On the drive home, Bob told Mike that he would cosign for any loans but was concerned that the banks may not extend him a loan because he was so far in debt.

Bob also expressed to Mike how proud he was of his school grades and of the fact that he was going to be the first Bunner to ever go to college. He also confided that he had no idea why Mike had done so well in school since both he and Mike's mother, Imogene, had hated school and had both dropped out on their sixteenth birthday.

In the summer 1969, Mike left home to start attending West Virginia University. After Bob's visit to Mike's guidance counselors, Mike had been awarded an all-expense paid Air Force R.O.T.C scholarship so Bob and Rosie did not have to cosign for any student loans.

Also in the fall of 1969, Rosie got the job as janitor of Pleasant Valley Elementary School. The income from this part-time job made a huge difference in the family's finances. For the first time in nearly ten years, they were able to pay their bills on time every month and still have a little money left to spend on things they wanted, not just things they needed.

In 1970, Darrell had a falling-out with Rosie and moved next door to his grandmother's house, where he lived during his senior year in high school. He graduated in June 1971, started working at Storck's Bakery in May 1972, and married Linda Riddle in June 1972.

In 1970 and 1971, Rosie's income continued to improve the family's financial situation. They now had two cars. They had a home telephone installed, a luxury the family had done without since the initial four-party line had been removed in 1962 in order to free up money to pay other bills.

During Mike's four years in college, his Christmas present to his dad each year was two tickets to a WVU football game the following year. In 1970 and 1971, Bob gave his second ticket to his brother-in-law, Lloyd Lauderman. Both years they arrived in Morgantown by 8:00 A.M. on game day where they would have breakfast, then go to a bar to have a beer or two, and then to a restaurant for lunch. After lunch they would have another beer or two and then walk to the stadium for the game. It was as if they were inventing game day "tailgating" before the tradition came into existence. After the game, Mike would meet them for a quick dinner before they drove back home.

During Mike's senior year in college, Lloyd had canceled at the last minute so Bob drove to Morgantown by himself where he met up with Mike for breakfast. He was concerned about wasting the second ticket. Mike told him not to worry, he would take care of it. After breakfast, Mike walked with Bob to the Women's Hall dormitory, which was near the football stadium. There Mike introduced him to his girlfriend and future wife, Linda Gray.

Linda was a very attractive young woman and after meeting her, Bob turned to Mike and teasingly said, "She is really nice considering she is so ugly!" Linda didn't quite know how to take Bob's comment, but Mike later translated his joking tease to her. Bob was telling Mike that he liked Linda and he thought she was very pretty. Bob's unique form of teasing and joking, while often misunderstood by more refined and sensitive persons, was an integral part of his character.

Later that morning and well before the game started, Mike walked by an entrance gate at the stadium holding Bob's unused ticket in the air over his head. In less than a minute he sold it for more than he had originally paid for it eight month earlier.

In 1973, Mike graduated from college, married Linda Marie Gray, and started pilot training with the U.S. Air Force in Del Rio, Texas. In 1975, Leroy graduated from high school and married Julie Horner.

During the early 1970's, Bob started expanding his summer vacation from one-day fishing outings and picnics to overnight and multi-day camping trips. He purchased a tent large enough to accommodate the five children still living at home. Along with it he purchased the requisite camping stove, lanterns, air mattresses, and sleeping bags. He took the family on camping trips to several locations in West Virginia and Ohio.

Perhaps the most memorable camping trip they took was to Ocean City, Maryland, where the family spent several days at a public campground. It was the first time that Bob, Rosie, and their five youngest children had ever seen the ocean.

One of the unplanned experiences during this trip was a side excursion into Washington, D.C. The thought was that Bob would drive by the Capitol, Washington Monument, and Lincoln Memorial so the family could say they had seen them and then get back on the road to Ocean City. Bob quickly became disoriented because of Washington's unique street pattern of rectangular grids overlaid by traffic circles with streets running from them that were at angles with the rectangular grid of streets. After Bob had given up on navigating his way through the city, he happened to drive past the White House. Everyone else in the car was excited at seeing it and wondered if the President was inside. Bob's response was that he "didn't give a damn" about who was in the White House, he just wanted to find Route 50 to get out of Washington as fast as he could and back on the road to Ocean City.

The Arab oil embargo of 1973 started an eight year period of inflation in the American economy where prices for everything increased by an average of 8% every year. This inflation was devastating to most Americans, as prices went up faster than their salaries. This inflation compounded for eight consecutive years before President Reagan and Federal Reserve Chairman Paul Volcker decided to induce a recession to kill it once and for all in the early 1980's.

However, for Bob and Rosie, this extended period of high inflation provided them with a net benefit. This was because their monthly mortgage payment was fixed in 1962, and while all other living expenses increased because of inflation, their mortgage payment remained the same. Due to inflation, Bob's pay increased 6-8% every year during this period. The bottom line was that in the mid 1960's nearly 40% of Bob's paycheck was used to pay his monthly mortgage. By the late 1970's, only 20% of his pay was necessary to pay his mortgage. Even with inflation in all other aspects of their life, Bob and Rosie found themselves in a much improved financial situation by the late 1970's. They had more discretionary spending money than at any time since their marriage.

# AN AMERICAN JOURNEY

**Bunner Family Picnic – Mount Wood Park – 1975**
Front left to right: Rusty, Sherri, Linda (Mike's wife), Jason, Mable. Back left to right: Doug, Tricia, Pam, Rosie, Greg, Linda (Darrell's wife). Standing left to right: Robert, Darrell. Missing: Leroy (Mike is taking the picture and also colorized the original black and white photo)

Bob continued hunting and fishing through the 1970's. He would often go with one or more of his sons who was still living in the area. One year his teenage daughter Tricia expressed a desire to go deer hunting with her dad and "the guys." Bob poo-poohed the idea. Undeterred, Tricia took a 12 gauge shotgun with "pumpkin ball" shells and went deer hunting on the hill behind her house. She saw a deer and shot it. Not knowing what to do next, she walked back down the hill to her grandmother's house and told her she had just killed a deer. Mabel accompanied Tricia back up the hill where she gutted the deer and then helped Tricia drag it back down to her house. There they skinned it and, using a tree limb as a pulley, they hoisted it up off the ground by its hind legs.

Later that afternoon, Bob and "the guys" returned from their hunt empty handed. Tricia then shamed them by taking them over to her grandmother's house and showing off her catch. "The guys" did pitch in and carve the deer meat into smaller pieces. Some was eaten that evening for dinner and the rest divvied out to "the guys" to take home for their families.

During the early-1970's, when his son Rusty was developing an interest in baseball, Bob increased his involvement with the Little League baseball program in Wood County. He was one of the founders of the Eastwood Baseball League, which was composed of teams from each of the eastern Wood County schools. Darrell was a coach in this league, and Rusty played in the league for four years. Years later, after Bob's death, his grandsons Jason and Greg played Little League baseball in the Eastwood Baseball League.

Bob also supported his daughters during the years they played in the softball league in Wood County. He was also involved in building a ball field on property owned by Bennie Cowan near Route 31 in Wood County.

After Mike graduated from West Virginia University, Bob continued the tradition of attending at least one WVU football game each year. He would go with Darrell as well as neighbors in Dallison. He followed the same routine of arriving early on game day in Morgantown, having breakfast, drinking beer, having lunch, and then going to the game.

Darrell recalled that at one game they attended, Bob took a pocketful of grapes into the stadium with him. Before the game started, he threw the grapes – one at a time - at a security officer standing down on the football field. Darrell feared that the entire group would be thrown out of the stadium, but fortunately Bob ran out of grapes without ever hitting the security officer with one of them. Rosie claimed in a 2010 interview that she was convinced that Bob had to buy a newspaper the day after each WVU football game he attended to find out who won.

**Robert and Rosie Bunner – circa 1978**

On July 3, 1981, Bob's brother Glenn let him borrow his camper trailer so Bob, Rosie, Rusty, and Doug could go camping for a week at North Bend State Park near Cairo, West Virginia. Leroy and his family joined them for part of their vacation. They spent the week fishing, hiking, and relaxing, and on the last day of their vacation they trapped a raccoon by placing a trash can over it. The raccoon had been hanging around the campsite all week to scavenge food from the campers.

On Thursday, July 9, Leroy and his family left the campsite to return home. On Friday, July 10, Bob, Rusty, and Doug prepared the camper trailer for the return trip home. Rosie made a big breakfast of bacon and eggs which everyone enjoyed. Bob hooked the camper to his truck and Doug got in with his dad to head back to Dallison. Rosie and Rusty followed behind the camper in Rosie's car.

Bob lit a cigarette and started smoking it. A few minutes later he started feeling nauseous and told Doug that one of his arms felt numb. He put out his cigarette in the ashtray. At the next spot that was wide enough to pull the camper off the road, he stopped, told Doug that he was going to go talk to his mom in her car, and got out. He never made it to Rosie's car. Instead, he fell to the ground and laid there motionless.

Rosie started yelling for help. A person who lived nearby heard her and came running to see what was wrong. Realizing the situation, he went back to his house and called an ambulance from nearby Harrisville. Within fifteen minutes the ambulance arrived and rushed to the St. Joseph's hospital in Parkersburg, thirty miles away. Bob was pronounced dead on arrival. The cause of death was a heart attack. He was forty nine years old.

Bob's funeral was held at the Leavitt Funeral Home in Parkersburg on July 13, 1981. He was buried in the Pleasant Valley Cemetery (Skidmore).

About a year after Bob's death, Rosie completed several training classes to earn her certification as an accounting bookkeeper. She supported herself as a bookkeeper until she retired in the early 2000's. After retirement she lived in a small rental home in Parkersburg with her son Rusty. In 2010, after her health had started to deteriorate, she moved to a Senior Living apartment in Parkersburg. On her 80$^{th}$ birthday in 2013, approximately one hundred family and friends, some of whom lived over six hundred miles away, gathered for a surprise birthday party in Parkersburg.

Rosie died on June 23, 2015, at the age of eighty-two. Her funeral was held at Leavitt Funeral Home. She was buried beside Robert at the Pleasant Valley Cemetery (Skidmore).

Bob's first wife Imogene was married two different times after their divorce. The first was to Dennis Schrader from about 1959 until 1963. They had a daughter named Denise. Imogene married Ralph Schupp circa 1964 and they had a daughter Maureen. Ralph drowned while swimming in the Ohio River near Pittsburgh circa 1969. Imogene returned to the Parkersburg area in 1970 where she reestablished communications with her sons Mike and Darrell. She joined a church and strove to live a Christian life. She never remarried and died on February 3, 2012. Her funeral was held at the

Leavitt Funeral Home in Parkersburg. She was buried at the Shiloah Cemetery in eastern Wood County, West Virginia.

## Children of Robert and Imogene Hendershot Bunner

### Robert Michael Bunner

Mike graduated from West Virginia University in 1973, with a degree in Chemical Engineering. He married Linda Gray in Sutton, West Virginia and soon afterward started pilot training with the U.S. Air Force at Laughlin AFB in Del Rio, Texas. After his Air Force tour, he worked for Air Products and Chemicals in Texas, New York, Japan, and Pennsylvania. He left Air Products in 1997 after purchasing Electro Chemical Engineering and Manufacturing Company in Emmaus, Pennsylvania. He served as President of Electro Chemical until he sold the business and retired in May 2022. He and Linda live near Kutztown, Pennsylvania. Their three children are son, Brady Michael, daughter Christina Marie, and daughter Laura Michelle.

Brady married Rebecca Shoemaker and has two children, daughter Maycen and son Noah. They live in Zionsville, Pennsylvania. Christy married Jeff Helzner and has two daughters, Sasha and Scarlett. They live in Brooklyn, New York. Laura married Nick Noreus and has two sons, Hendricks and John. They live in Wilmington, North Carolina.

### Darrell Lee Bunner

After high school, Darrell worked at the Vitro Agate Company and then Storck's Bakery in Parkersburg, West Virginia. He married Linda Riddle in 1972 and they had two sons, Jason and Gregory. Darrell and Linda divorced in 1991. After Storck's Bakery closed in 1998, Darrell worked for the Pleasant Valley Trading Company and as an auctioneer. He worked for the Wood County Board of Education as a custodian at Parkersburg High School from 2006 until his retirement in 2023. He married Cathy Hardman Harrison in 2017 and both are living in Dallison, West Virginia.

Jason married Michelle Crippen and they had a daughter, Tawny. Jason and Michelle divorced in 2009. Jason works for Blue Cross Blue Shield West Virginia. He married Stephanie Yost Rose in 2016. They reside in Vienna, West Virginia.

Greg married Melissa Siebel and they had two daughters, Rachael and Madison. He works for the Parkersburg Utility Board. Greg and Melissa live in Parkersburg, West Virginia.

## Children of Robert and Rosie Carpenter Bunner

### Johnny Leroy Bunner

After high school, Leroy held several jobs as an auto mechanic. He married Julie Ann Horner and they had one son, Brian. He founded and was owner of "Leroy's Auto Repair" shop near Parkersburg which he operated for several years before his untimely death due to a motorcycle accident on Route 50 near Dallison, West Virginia in September 1994. He was thirty-nine years old. He was buried near his father in the Pleasant Valley Cemetery (Skidmore). His son Brian lives in Parkersburg, West Virginia. His widow Julie remarried several years after Leroy's death.

**Leroy and Julie Bunner – circa 1990**

## Pamela Jayne Bunner

After high school Pam married Jeff Jackson and had two children, Jeff and Amy. Pam and Jeff divorced circa 1980. Pam never remarried. She worked for many years as a hearing aid specialist. She lives in Parkersburg, West Virginia.

## Patricia Louise Bunner

After high school Tricia married Stephan Ward and had two sons, Joshua Lee and Kyle Nicholas. She and Stephan divorced circa 1988. She married Matthew West in 1997 and they had a daughter, Megan. Tricia lives in Parkersburg.

## Sherri Eileen Bunner

After high school Sherri married Steve Barnes. They had two children, Adam and Savannah. Sherri died of a brain hemorrhage while visiting her sister Tricia in July 2009. She was buried in the Pleasant Valley Cemetery (Skidmore)

**Sherri Eileen Bunner Barnes circa 2000**

## Russell Dewayne Bunner

After high school, Rusty was briefly married to Anita Lynch during the 1980's. They had no children. He has worked for many years as a telemarketer and lives in Parkersburg, West Virginia.

## Kevin Douglas Bunner

After high school, Doug married Sharon Barker. He got his Commercial Driver's License and worked for over thirty years as a cement truck driver in the Parkersburg area. They had two daughters, Kylie and Tristan, each of whom graduated from West Virginia University.

Doug and Sharon loved the outdoors. Doug spent much of his spare time camping, hiking, fishing, hunting, motorcycling, and boating. Doug had an emergency appendectomy in February 2024 after which he was sent home to recover. Tragically, he died during his recovery due to a blood clot. He was fifty-six.

Sharon continues living at their home in Dallison, West Virginia. Her daughter Kylie gave birth to Doug and Sharon's first grandchild during the summer of 2024, just four months after Doug's passing.

**Left to right: Kylie, Sharon, Doug, Trista Bunner - 2013**

www.ingramcontent.com/pod-product-compliance
Lightning Source LLC
Chambersburg PA
CBHW050735010526
44107CB00010B/864